D1446360

Parenting From Afar and the Reconfiguration of Family Across Distance

Parenting From Afar and the Reconfiguration of Family Across Distance

EDITED BY

MARIA ROSARIO T. de GUZMAN

JILL BROWN

AND

CAROLYN POPE EDWARDS

OXFORD
UNIVERSITY PRESS

Oxford University Press is a department of the University of Oxford. It furthers the University's objective of excellence in research, scholarship, and education by publishing worldwide. Oxford is a registered trade mark of Oxford University Press in the UK and certain other countries.

Published in the United States of America by Oxford University Press
198 Madison Avenue, New York, NY 10016, United States of America.

CIP data is on file at the Library of Congress
ISBN 978-0-19-026507-6

9 8 7 6 5 4 3 2 1

Printed by Sheridan Books, Inc., United States of America

For our children, Janek, Naala, Sam, George, and Becca, who make us continually think and rethink parenting, love, and life. We dedicate this book to families around the world—intact and dispersed across distance—configured and constructed in myriad ways for the love and well-being of their members.

Themes of family life in various forms run throughout this book. Carolyn Pope Edwards has been family to us for close to 20 years. She has inspired, pushed, and cared for so many over her career. Her commitment to connecting her fierce intellect with her informed heart has encouraged us to ask the questions that help us discover and reconnect to the deepest parts of ourselves. This book is only possible because of it.

—MdG & JB

CONTENTS

FOREWORD

Three themes drive this important collection of studies on parenting at a distance. First, families parenting from afar and family across distance include a "vast diversity" of forms and circumstances around the world, and there are many such families. Second, cultural notions of family life and parenting in these diverse contexts make a big difference in the experiences and consequences of separations. Third, what is considered "normal" family life and parenting is changing; yet some practices, such as fosterage, grandparenting, and economic migration, for example, remain common and continue from past generations in many communities. The goals of the editors and authors are to broaden our ideas of parenting, broaden our definitions of parenting through understanding the ways our ecocultural niches influence family forms and family life, and use these findings to "create a place for more sound developmental science in policy affecting families and children around the world." These admirable goals are very relevant to the topic of parenting from afar, and they are goals that are just as important for the study of parenting and child development in general.

For example, the putative "standard family model"—that is, the normative presumption of a co-resident conjugal family in a single household—is not the majority, "standard," or default expectation around the world. This volume provides strong examples of the many kinds of families and households operating across distance that have to be included in that diverse set of family and parenting models. This book provides a rich variety of examples of nonconjugal households, nonmaternal or nonpaternal care, and kinds of families where children and parents are dispersed for many reasons. Most contemporary family research samples in Western research journals and in clinical practice are not representative of the family forms and family practices with regard to parenting to be found around the world. Our growing knowledge of the world diversity in family life and how and why such variations occur depends on qualitative, ethnographic, and mixed-method accounts of these variations, and this book shows the value of such work.

The circumstances that lead to parenting at a distance also are diverse and, unfortunately, increasingly common (e.g., forced migration, war, environmental dislocation, economic pressures, and others). The volume both establishes an analytic and descriptive category (parenting from afar, from a distance) and shows many variations within the category. The conventional social address categories for family residential situations (conjugal, single-mother, dual-earner married, extended, joint, and so forth) do not fit these circumstances very well or are incomplete descriptive categories. The close-in, on the ground observations and field studies of parenting and family life under conditions of separation in this book provide new evidence about parenting contexts and surely show the need for new, more useful categories for describing and analyzing parenting situations and household and family formations.

A simple example is the "one family, two households" (or better, "one family, multiple households") unit of analysis for the study, initially, of rural–urban migration in Africa and elsewhere (Weisner, 1997). The household and relationship category "living together apart (LTA)" is another contemporary example developed in the United States. Frequent separations followed by reunifications and cohabitation of a couple along with (either partner's) children can create an LTA family unit. Parents, children, and other family and household members share responsibilities, caretaking, and support while living apart from others. LTA households and families are very widespread in the United States and throughout the world—yet there is no category for them available in standard census or survey work (Cross-Barnet, Cherlin, & Burton, 2011).

Other useful categories describe family processes in addition to static residential or household classifications (Weisner, 2014). Youth and young adults often have to do "surfing," for example—moving from one place to another, from household to household, due to poverty, legal issues, child lending and fosterage, family disruptions, and other reasons, as do some children and parents described in this book. This is a not uncommon practice among children and parents today (Roy, Buckmiller, & McDowell, 2008). "Kinscription" is a useful descriptive term for relationship processes and negotiations (Roy & Burton, 2007). Kinscription describes the constant attempts by single mothers (or other caregivers and parents described in this volume) to recruit and involve biological fathers and other romantic/intimate partners and their kin to help their families and be involved in their and their children's lives. Kinscription processes are central to the lives of millions of mothers in the United States and elsewhere around the world, and there are a number of examples of kinscription at a distance throughout this book.

Framing parental relationships with children and other caregivers as *trajectories through time*, rather than fixed statuses, and recognizing that parenting can be "suspended" for periods of time, yet not abandoned since the potential for reengagement continues, also are constructs that fit with many of the reports from this book. New family and parenting terms and analytic categories hopefully will emerge from research on parenting from a distance and will contribute to stronger comparative, international, and cross-cultural research on family, parenting, and child development.

The findings from these studies also can challenge standard developmental theories. What do the many kinds of parenting from afar (and the alloparenting and caretaking at home by others that replaces and supplements parents' roles) suggest regarding classical attachment theory, for example? Attachment theory is among the most widely described, taught, and accepted developmental theories in Western psychology and clinical work today. Attachment research is an important field that includes universal developmental mechanisms (such as the attachment-sensitive period in children and the stress-buffering roles of privileged caretakers) with likely universal developmental outcomes (security, safety, buffering of stress, emotion regulation, learning favoring the attachment figures). Yet there is far more diversity and pluralism than is claimed in most developmental research on these topics. What does parenting at a distance suggest regarding ecologically and culturally valid ways to assess children's security, or parent's and other caregivers' sensitivity and attunement, given that so many children are living with parents far away and experience multiple caretaking, fostering, and other arrangements? Many children described in this volume seem to have a sufficient sense of social trust and attachment security from other caregivers, though certainly not all children do so. The experiences are complex.

Mesman et al. (2016) point out that "Attachment theory without contextual components is as difficult to conceive of as attachment theory without a universalistic perspective" (p. 808) and also remark that "the current cross-cultural database is almost absurdly small compared to the domain that should be covered" (p. 809). Yet both these concerns are not widely recognized and acted upon—or even admitted as a serious problem—within most of the attachment research field, and the implications are not often appreciated in literature reviews, theory, research design, and sampling frames (LeVine, 2014). Popular and journalist versions of "attachment parenting," attachment theory, and its clinical implications remain remarkably unaware of these legitimate concerns, much less the kinds of circumstances described in this book for parenting at a distance (for example, see "Yes, It's Your Parent's Fault," in the *New York Times* [Murphy, 2017]).

This volume shows the importance of research incorporating multiple caretaking, including parenting from afar in conjunction with other caregivers, for the study of attachment and also for other developmental processes (Leinaweaver, 2014). It shows the importance of considering cultural beliefs about security, trust, whom to orient toward for social learning and safety, and the many mechanisms in addition to attachment through which children acquire security. Responsive care is clearly important for children everywhere; indifference or outright rejection is not good for children regardless of the form it might take. Socially distributed care, including many of the situations described in this volume, can provide responsive care. These studies provide examples of the many functional ways caregivers can provide security and social trust other than through monomatric attachment to a single co-resident maternal caregiver.

There are many other developmental processes and theories in addition to attachment theory that would benefit from incorporating evidence such as presented in this volume. Learning responsibility and tasks in the family and household, emotion regulation, gender socialization and task expectations, self-construal and identity development, expectations for children's competence at different ages, cultural beliefs about developmental stages, and training for interdependence, among others, are all social and cognitive developmental processes influenced by the situations described in this volume.

Parenting From Afar and the Reconfiguration of Family Across Distance encourages thinking about a set of principles for future research programs worth considering for the next generation of scholarship on parenting and families on the move, who are separated, and who experience fluid relationships and family networks. These increasingly common circumstances require samples and designs that reflect the actual behavior, beliefs, and experiences of those studied. More sophisticated designs can take advantage of the ethnographic and qualitative, intimate evidence such as reported in this volume. Research methods and conceptual frameworks at least should not cover up the circumstances in these local social worlds. The authors in this collection provide terrific examples of situations where new units for analysis and designs can be increasingly used and hopefully made the default standard for research.

It is exciting, then, to consider the next steps in research programs that could follow from this volume. Theorizing on the topics of parenting and families at a distance will benefit from this work, and offer a broader range of concepts and situations for understanding distance parenting and its consequences. Local beliefs and meaning systems, ecocultural theories, and religious and family traditions are important, for example, and these all are shown to be important for parenting in many chapters. Research designs can now be expanded based on these findings. For example, sending and receiving communities should be part of the research design wherever possible. In fact, there are often more than just one sending and one receiving places that matters for the children, parents, and other caregivers. Many chapters show how parents, siblings, grandparents, and other caregivers near and far from the child have important roles in financial support, in providing direct as well as indirect care, and in children's imaginations and memory.

The value of adding improved, contextualized outcome measures and process measures also comes through in many of these studies. The chapters describe reasonably successful accommodations to dispersed parenting even in the face of hardship, inequality, and separation. Locally valid and meaningful ways to assess the consequences of parenting at a distance on all concerned should be developed and tested and then perhaps used in complement with other comparative assessments.

Let us imagine an ideal model research collaboration among scholars interested in parenting and child development more generally and parenting at a distance specifically. Let's call it the "Parenting from Afar Study." The team selects eight or so communities with different forms of parenting from afar from around the world. Ethnographic research done alongside local partners describes the situations and then proposes samples and research designs that reflect those parents' and children's circumstances. A suite of mixed methods are developed that incorporate normative developmental and family assessments, some regional measures appropriate for situations in, for example, India, East Africa, China, or other culture areas, as well as local measures sensitive to parent and child in each local place (Weisner, 2013). These measures move across levels of analysis (physiological, psychological, behavioral, social, cultural, structural, and historic). Samples will be large enough for statistical analysis, and each site has a nested ethnographic subsample within the larger sample for qualitative, intensive studies as well. Some sites may add an appropriate comparison sample of co-resident families as well. The children are selected at comparable ages and family sizes and then followed longitudinally along with their parents and caregivers in both sending and receiving locales. Cross-talk among quantitative and qualitative researchers about their findings, along with local researchers and community partners, improves the study and measures as the project moves along. Each site has a policy researcher and practitioner collaborating, developing, and piloting possible interventions.

Funders surely will recognize the importance of this work and provide continuity and stability of funding for this multiyear international study. Results are reviewed and disseminated by local and national organizations interested in this work, along with scientific publication and policy follow-on projects. Junior researchers and students from each nation participating in this research program gain invaluable apprenticeship skills and go on to contribute to their nation's research and policy capacity. These younger team members, along with the more senior members, form a convoy and cohort of collaborators who benefit and influence future studies of families and children on other topics related to parenting from afar.

Well, perhaps this idealized, gold standard project is not all achievable—but even a good portion of such a longitudinal comparative research program would be terrific! Of course, there already are many examples of research programs like this in the field of culture and human development; this can be done.

Future comparative work, even if only partially meeting this ideal, will help further the goal of the many fine authors in this volume to create better policy. It is likely that research programs for assessment of what might improve the lives and well-being of children, parents, and caregivers in conditions of distance parenting require initial close-in ethnographic knowledge, such as we find in this volume. These kinds of holistic, contextual, policy-related studies can reverse the policy paradox in which children, parents, and families that don't easily fit the "standard expected model"—though clearly likely to benefit from support—miss out on programs or are in institutions not well adapted for them (Yoshikawa, 2011). The next steps, then, are to construct a logic model for how and when to provide useful supports that add value to the successful accommodations that already exist for parenting from a distance, to test that model, and then to improve the difficult economic and sociopolitical situations that also go along with separation and change. This can improve the well-being of all children, parents, and communities, including those parenting from afar.

—Thomas S. Weisner

REFERENCES

Cross-Barnet, C., Cherlin, A., & Burton, L. (2011). Bound by children: Intermittent cohabitation and living together apart. *Family Relations, 60*, 633–647.

Leinaweaver, J. (2014). Informal kinship-based fostering around the world: Anthropological findings. *Child Development Perspectives, 8*(3), 131–136.

LeVine, R. A. (2014). Attachment theory as cultural ideology. In H. Otto and H. Keller (Eds.), *Different faces of attachment* (pp. 50–65). New York: Cambridge University Press.

Mesman, J., van IJzendoorn, M. H., & Sagi-Schwartz, A. (2016). Cross-cultural patterns of attachment: Universal and contextual dimensions. In J. Cassidy & P. Saver (Eds.), *Handbook of attachment* (pp. 790–815). New York: Guilford.

Murphy, K. (2017, January 7). Yes, it's your parents' fault. *The New York Times*. Retrieved from https://www.nytimes.com/2017/01/07/opinion/sunday/yes-its-your-parents-fault.html?_r=0.

Roy, K., Buckmiller, N., & McDowell, A. (2008). Together but not "together": Trajectories of relationship suspension for low-income unmarried parents. *Family Relations 57*, 197–209.

Roy, K., & Burton, L. (2007). Mothering through recruitment: Kinscription of nonresidential fathers and father figures in low-income families. *Family Relations 56*, 24–39.

Weisner, T. S. (1997). Support for children and the African family crisis. In T. S. Weisner, C. Bradley, & P. Kilbride (Eds.), *African families and the crisis of social change* (pp. 20–44). Westport, CT: Greenwood Press/Bergin & Garvey.

Weisner, T. S. (2013). Why qualitative and ethnographic methods are essential for understanding family life. In S. McHale, P. Amato, & A. Booth (Eds.), *Emerging methods in family research: Approaches to measuring families* (pp. 163–178). Dordrecht: Springer Verlag.

Yoshikawa, H. (2011). *Immigrants raising children*. New York: Russell Sage Foundation.

ACKNOWLEDGMENTS

This book, for the most part, was born out of our own childhoods and experiences with families in various forms in different parts of the world. As researchers, we have found ourselves conducting work on issues deeply connected to our own roles within our families. We also wanted to add to the existing literature that is helping to reshape the cultural narrative of the "normal family." The call for papers produced a fascinating spread of work and depth of expertise on a range of societies in different parts of the world. Almost all of the data in the book is based on original fieldwork and how families reconfigure themselves "in real time" and in the daily routines of their lives. We thank all the contributors to this volume. Their passion to address and improve the well-being of vulnerable families through their scholarship inspires us to continue with this work. We want to acknowledge all the participants in the studies presented in this book—each living the reality of family reconfiguration across distance, at times against the dominant notions of what family should look like in their communities.

We would like to thank our editors, Andrea Zekus, for her confidence in this project and guidance in the publishing process, and Courtney McCarroll, for carrying this endeavor over the finish line. Our students Aileen Garcia and Sarah Taylor provided invaluable support in editing and organizing materials to prepare for submission. Laura Padilla-Walker shared her support and experience in navigating the proposal submission process at the very onset of this undertaking.

To Ninel Constantino, visual artist and faculty at the University of the Philippines, College of Fine Arts—thank you for generously allowing us the use of your work for the book cover. We were so drawn by paintings in your *Road Trip* series. Each piece evoked a sense of distance and separation that was also expressed in many of the works in this volume. Maria and Ninel first met in 1976 at the JASMS preschool in Quezon City and were best friends throughout their childhood years. Collaborating on this project added another layer of reconnecting with family at a distance.

ACKNOWLEDGMENTS

ABOUT THE EDITORS

Maria Rosario T. de Guzman, PhD, is an Associate Professor and Extension Specialist in the Department of Child, Youth, and Family Studies at UNL. Her work focuses on the intersections among culture, migration, family life, and child and adolescent development, as well as on sociocultural factors relevant to children's prosocial socialization.

Jill Brown, PhD, is an Associate Professor of Psychology at Creighton University in Omaha, Nebraska. She received her BA and her PhD from the University of Nebraska-Lincoln. While her roots are in the Midwest, her work has taken her to other parts of the world. She was a Peace Corps volunteer in Namibia and she received a Fulbright Fellowship to study in Varanasi, India. She is the current President of the Society of Cross Cultural Research. Her current research focuses on kinship, adoption, and socially distributed child care and family life, and on cognition and thinking across cultures.

Carolyn Pope Edwards, EdD, is Willa Cather Professor Emeritus of Psychology and Child, Youth, and Family Studies at the University of Nebraska, Lincoln. Her interests center on social and moral development in cultural contexts, socialization processes within the family, and international early childhood education. She has conducted research and held research positions at universities in Italy, Norway, and Kenya.

CONTRIBUTORS

Joyce A. Arditti, PhD
Professor
Department of Human Development and Family Science
Virginia Polytechnic Institute and State University
Blacksburg, Virginia

Jesse Beatson, MSc, JD (Cand.)
Osgoode Hall Law School
York University
York, Ontario (Canada)

Jonathon J. Beckmeyer, PhD
Assistant Professor
School of Public Health
Indiana University
Bloomington, Indiana

Michelle Bemiller, PhD
Professor of Sociology
Walsh University
North Canton, Ohio

Yvonne Bohr, EdD
Associate Professor
Department of Psychology
York University, Toronto

Jill Brown, PhD
Associate Professor
Department of Psychology
Creighton University
Omaha, Nebraska

Stephen H. Chen, PhD
Assistant Professor
Department of Psychology
Wellesley College
Wellesley, Massachusetts

Kristen E. Cheney, PhD
Associate Professor
Children & Youth Studies
International Institute of Social Studies, Erasmus University Rotterdam
The Hague, Netherlands

Maria Rosario T. de Guzman, PhD
Associate Professor and Extension Specialist
Department of Child, Youth and Family Studies
University of Nebraska—Lincoln
Lincoln, Nebraska

Ruth Ellingsen, PhD
Postdoctoral Fellow
UCLA Semel Institute for Neuroscience and Human Behavior
Los Angeles, California

Aileen S. Garcia, MA
Doctoral Candidate
Department of Child, Youth and Family Studies
University of Nebraska—Lincoln
Lincoln, Nebraska

Shelene Gentz, PhD
Lecturer
Department of Psychology
University of Namibia
Windhoek, Namibia

Brita Gjerstad, PhD
Senior Researcher
International Research Institute of Stavanger
Stavanger, Norway

Edmund T. Hamann, PhD
Professor
Department of Teaching, Learning, & Teacher Education
University of Nebraska—Lincoln

Berit Ingersoll-Dayton, PhD
Professor
School of Social Work
University of Michigan
Ann Arbor, Michigan

Jeehun Kim, PhD
Associate Professor
Department of Social Studies Education
Inha University
Incheon, South Korea

Natasza Kosakowska-Berezecka, PhD
Assistant Professor
Division of Cross-Cultural Psychology and Psychology of Gender
Institute of Psychology
University of Gdansk
Gdansk, Poland

Kuba Kryś, PhD
Assistant Professor
Institute of Psychology
Polish Academy of Sciences
Warsaw, Poland

Anna Kwiatkowska, PhD
Professor
Institute of Psychology
Polish Academy of Sciences
Warsaw, Poland

Patricia Lester, MD
Jane and Marc Nathanson Family Professor of Psychiatry
UCLA Semel Institute for Neuroscience and Human Behavior
Los Angeles, California

Cindy H. Liu, PhD
Assistant Professor
Department of Psychiatry
Beth Israel Deaconess Medical Center
Harvard Medical School
Boston, Massachusetts

Yao Lu, PhD
Associate Professor
Department of Sociology
Columbia University
New York, New York

Ana A. Lucero-Liu, PhD
Independent Scholar (United States)

Mandi MacDonald, PhD
Lecturer in Social Work
School of Social Sciences, Education, and Social Work
Queens University
Belfast, Northern Ireland

Catherine Mogil, PsyD
Assistant Clinical Professor
UCLA Semel Institute for Neuroscience and Human Behavior
Los Angeles, California

Gunhild Odden, PhD
Director, Centre for Intercultural Communication
Associate Professor, VID Specialized University, Norway
Stavanger, Norway

Sumie Okazaki, PhD
Professor
Department of Applied Psychology
New York University
New York, New York

Carolyn Pope Edwards, EdD
Professor Emeritus
Departments of Psychology and Child, Youth, and Family Studies
University of Nebraska—Lincoln
Lincoln, Nebraska

Sureeporn Punpuing, PhD
Associate Professor
Institute for Population and Social Research
Mahidol University
Salaya, Thailand

Heather Rae-Espinoza, PhD
Professor
Department of Human Development
California State University
Long Beach, California

Mónica Ruiz-Casares, PhD
Associate Professor
Division of Social and Transcultural Psychiatry
McGill University and SHERPA-Institut Universitaire
Centre Integré Universitaire de Santé et de Services Sociaux du Centre-Ouest-de-l'île-de-Montréal
Montreal, Quebec, Canada

Oleksandr Ryndyk
Researcher
Centre for Intercultural Communication
VID Specialized University, Norway
Stavanger, Norway

Juan Sánchez García, PhD
Director, Research and Innovation Program for Educational Improvement
Instituto de Investigación, Innovación y de Estudios de Posgrado de la Educación
Monterrey, Mexico

Marcela Sotomayor-Peterson, PhD
Associate Professor
Escuela de Psicología y Ciencias de la Comunicación
Universidad de Sonora
Sonora, Mexico

Justyna Świdrak
Doctoral Candidate
Institute of Psychology
Polish Academy of Sciences
Warsaw, Poland

Kanchana Tangchonlatip, PhD
Assistant Professor
Institute for Population and Social Research
Mahidol University
Salaya, Thailand

Minerva D. Tuliao, MA
Doctoral Candidate
Department of Educational Administration
University of Nebraska—Lincoln
Lincoln, Nebraska

Gunn Vedøy, PhD
Senior Researcher
International Research Institute of Stavanger
Stavanger, Norway

Leslie K. Wang, PhD
Assistant Professor
Department of Sociology
University of Massachusetts
Boston, Massachusetts

Thomas S. Weisner, PhD
Professor Emeritus
Department of Psychiatry and Department of Anthropology
University of California
Los Angeles, California

Laura Yakas
Doctoral Student
School of Social Work and Department of Anthropology
University of Michigan
Ann Arbor, Michigan

Magdalena Żadkowska, PhD
Assistant Professor
Faculty of Social Sciences, Division of Sociology of Everyday Life
University of Gdansk
Gdansk, Poland

Víctor Zúñiga, PhD
Professor of Sociology
Doctorate Program in the Social Sciences
Tecnológico de Monterrey
Monterrey, Mexico

Introduction

MARIA ROSARIO T. de GUZMAN, JILL BROWN, AND CAROLYN POPE EDWARDS ■

Field notes, Outside of *Little Tykes* preschool in Lawin Gated Community, 8:15 AM, December 2013:

> I am sitting at the waiting area outside the preschool along with several *yayas* (nannies) and drivers whose *alagas* (charges) are inside. Most of the children have been dropped off for the 8 AM preschool session. One woman is running towards the preschool gate carrying a little girl about 3 years of age. Child's hair is wet and child is crying—clinging to the woman. Woman rings the bell and waits for personnel to let them in. "Be good, okay? It will be okay. Love you . . . " she tells the child while smoothing out the child's hair and wiping away her tears. "I love you, too," the child says back. "Give me a kiss," she asks and the child complies—giving her a tight hug and kiss as the gate opens and the preschool teacher lets the child in. After the child enters the school, the woman joins the other nannies. The other women then chide her, mostly commenting that it has been months into the school year and the little girl is still crying. The woman defends the child—saying she has a cold and did not sleep well. Had I not known this was Sheila, the child's nanny, I would have thought she was the mother.

This scenario comes from fieldwork we conducted in a preschool within an affluent gated community in Manila, Philippines. It is typical in these private preschools and elementary schools to have nannies sitting outside for the entire duration of the school session, waiting for their charges. The women sit and chat, waiting for the hours to tick away until dismissal time. As the field notes illustrate, many of these women are involved in the most intimate care of their charges—tending not only to their physical and basic needs but also to their socioemotional and cognitive well-being, support of schooling, and other aspects of their development. Most of these nannies are rural-to-urban migrants, having left their communities to take up work in Manila. Several of the women, Sheila included, have young children of their own with whom they have very limited direct contact, if any. Thus, they were employed to care for young children in wealthy families while their own children are reared by alternative caregivers or spouses left behind.

Anthropologists have provided a rich research literature on family life, documenting the quite extreme variations in emotional and interactional closeness of the husband–wife relationship with respect to sleeping, eating, work, and leisure. For example, John and Beatrice Whiting (1975*a*) studied the dimension of what they characterized as husband–wife "aloofness versus intimacy." They and other anthropologists have correlated this dimension of husband–wife closeness with male cross-sex identity, male involvement in warfare and group defense (extensive vs. unpredictable), marriage type (monogamous vs. polygynous), household structure (nuclear vs. extended, joint, or polygynous), preferred leisure and work partners (same-gender vs. mixed gender, paternal interaction with infants and young children (extensive vs. minimal), and other facets of culture, economy, and society (e.g., Chasdi, 1994; Harkness, Mavridis, Liu, & Super, 2015; Shwalb & Shwalb, 2015; Whiting & Edwards, 1988; Whiting & Whiting, 1975*b*).

Yet, in all of the common household and normative arrangements, sets of parents and children nevertheless tend to live their days and nights, if not dwelling under the same roof and sharing common social space in at least part of the same homestead or compound except during times while the father was away at war or engaged in other temporary demands related to livestock or subsistence agriculture. It seems that although definitions of family constellation and household structure have been found to vary by culture, in general, parental–child units in the past were usually found to dwell in close geographic proximity to one another. This expectation included the cases of one husband with multiple wives and sets of children, commonly found, for example, in sub-Saharan Africa; in the husband-wife-children units deeply embedded in complex multigenerational joint family compounds, commonly found in India, Pakistan, and other parts of the Mideast and Southeast Asia; and in the single mother-children-but no husband or partner units that have become highly frequent in all countries with complex and stratified industrial economies in North and South America and Western Europe.

Thus, what is striking in the contemporary world is that the very expectation for geographic unity of parents and children is in the process of a profound reworking to include a greater diversity in constellations of family life that exists around the world. Increased migration and mobility, as well as societal shifts, have challenged these traditional notions, yet much of mainstream research and prevailing societal views rely on past notions of the family as a cohesive unit in one domicile or set of contiguous domiciles (de Guzman, 2014; Smith, 1993).

The present volume is dedicated to examining the various circumstances surrounding nuclear and extended family life across physical distance, how families operate and maintain ties in the context of dispersal, and how the very notion of "family" is redefined in these various settings. Research on the topic of long-distance family life has flourished in recent years as scholars from various disciplines—anthropology, sociology, migration studies, feminist studies, and psychology—have paid closer attention to the experience, causes, and consequences of separation from the individual to the societal level. This volume brings together scholars representing these various perspectives and fields of study, utilizing diverse methodologies and approaches, and examining family separation in numerous geographical locations. We highlight the following themes in this book:

Theme 1: There is vast diversity in the contexts of families living across distance.

The idealized picture of "normal family life," sometimes referred to as the "Standard North American Family code" (Smith, 1993), is one that problematizes any picture of family life that does not include a two-parent household with children under the same roof. Physical distance among members of the nuclear family is assumed to be undertaken only out of pure necessity or as a response to crisis. The only solution, then, is nuclear family reunification and, in the meantime, the work of family life is defined as bridging the physical distance by mediated communication and remittances (Madianaou & Miller, 2011). Several chapters in this volume highlight this point. Michelle Bemiller (Chapter 12), in particular, addresses the very issue of how traditional notions of family life may contradict the changing reality for many families in her chapter on non-custodial mothers either voluntarily or nonvoluntarily living away from their children. Despite an increase in diverse family forms, diversity in the definition of motherhood is slow to be accepted. Emphasis is still placed on motherhood as a natural phenomenon, something that should not be questioned (Åhäll, 2012), and mainstream ideologies of motherhood support self-sacrifice and unconditional love. To challenge the notion of motherhood, which sits squarely at the center of the nuclear family model, challenges the core of Western beliefs about parenting. Edmund T. Hamann, Víctor Zúñiga, and Juan Sánchez García (Chapter 16) similarly address the issue of the "intact nuclear family" as the ideal when, in fact, circumstances may make this arrangement difficult, impractical, or even unsafe for binational (Mexican and American) children. Their study takes an in-depth longitudinal look at Mexican migrant parents' difficult decisions on family configuration and whether to live together as a family or to parent from afar. Parents in their study are faced with the daunting task of weighing complex factors such as educational opportunities for children, safety, and availability of reliable caregivers, in addition to the ideal of family unity.

Family separation and long-distance parenting occur in a multitude of circumstances, such as sociopolitical unrest and war (e.g., Swaroop & DeLoach, 2015) and personal crises, such as parental incarceration (e.g., Christian, 2005; Gabel, 1992), and at other times are undertaken as a normative cultural practice meant to extend kinship relationships, such as fosterage (e.g., Pillai, 2013). Separation can also occur due to shifts in the traditional caregiving context, as in cases of divorce or in pursuit of educational opportunities for children (Lee, 2010). How broader societal shifts and events impact on family life was evident in all chapters represented in this volume. For example, Ruth Ellingsen, Catherine Mogil, and Patricia Lester (Chapter 9) examine how parental separation as a result of military deployment challenges families to operate not just across distance but with much uncertainty about the safety of the parent who is away.

Although there is a growing body of research examining family life across distance, this work has not fully captured the diversity of circumstances under which separation is undertaken, how various family members are affected, and how families cope with distance. Much of the scholarly work examining this area has focused on transnational families living apart due to economic migration, with a focus on parents (typically from the Global South migrating North) and their children left behind. In this scenario, the adult breadwinner has moved abroad to earn a living for the family left behind. Indeed, in this so-called age of migration with more than 244 million international migrants, most of those who cross national borders do so in pursuit of economic opportunities (United Nations Population Fund, 2015). Supporting this claim, the International Labour Organization (2015) further reports that 73% of migrants who are of working age are laborers. It is difficult to ascertain the proportion of these migrants who experience long-distance family life; nonetheless, it is clear that millions of families undergo geographic dispersion due to economic migration.

Corresponding to the substantial number and continued surge in economic migration, a rich body of work has explored transnational family life and its impact on families, shedding light on important issues such as implications of immigration and labor policy on migrants' rights and well-being (e.g., Stenum, 2011), the disruption of traditional gender roles in light of physical distance and family reconfiguration (e.g., White, 2017), family coping and mediated communication to bridge physical distance (e.g., Cabanes & Acedera, 2012; Madianaou & Miller, 2011), and the impact of family separation on the physical and socioemotional well-being of family members (Graham & Jordan, 2011). Nonetheless, even among economic migrants, for example, there are diverse family forms, coping strategies, and experiences. Marcela Sotomayor-Peterson and Ana Lucero-Liu (Chapter 8) argue that, even in the context of economic migration from Mexico to the United States, there is diversity in family forms and experiences born out of various factors, including the migrant family's location. Families living within close proximity of the US–Mexico border experience family separation quite differently from those more typically represented in the literature on transnational families. The *fronteriza* (transborder) context becomes a "culture" unto itself, affording families access to unique resources (e.g., more frequent family reunifications) that consequently may lead to unique socioemotional outcomes for parents and children.

We cannot claim to have captured the full range of circumstances surrounding family separation; nonetheless, we have sought to represent strong examples and some of the range of this diversity in the current volume. Chapters highlight such varied pictures of family dispersal due not only to economic migration, but also due to adoption, military deployment, fosterage, divorce, and incarceration. In many cases, the families described are in some form of economic, sociopolitical, or personal crises. Yet in other circumstances, families are doing economically well and choose to separate for reasons beyond seeking safety or economic well-being. Moreover, separation can occur between parents and young children as well as elderly parents and adult children, married spouses from their families of origin, nuclear family from extended family, and more.

Theme 2: Remaking family life is a culturally embedded process. A second theme we highlight in this volume is how the broader socioecological background and "ecocultural niche" (e.g., distribution of tasks and responsibilities, cultural norms and practices around schooling and childcare, parental ethnotheories of child development) shape how families cope with separation, how family members renegotiate roles to bridge distance, and how the notion of family is defined and redefined in the various circumstances of separation. Cultural contexts shape children's daily lives, the settings that they can access, and the typical cast of characters involved in their upbringing. Similarly, the experience of separation and redefinition of family occurs within a cultural context. Just as culturally embedded beliefs and the broader cultural context are intricately intertwined with all aspects of the developmental and family landscape (e.g., see Keller, 2013 and the volume by Kagitçibasi, 2013), socioecological background plays a significant role in the separation process and all that it entails.

Few studies have specifically looked at culturally embedded responses to family separation or even cultural underpinnings of family dispersion. The lens through which families experience separation is shaped by culturally embedded beliefs about family and the roles and obligations that membership entails. We challenged contributors to reflect on this issue in the works they are presenting. Most chapters address the issue of cultural notions of family and socioecological aspects of family life; however, several chapters in this volume directly address how cultural context and cultural beliefs are intertwined with how individuals and families cope with and view separation. For example, in Chapter 2, Berit Ingersoll-Dayton, Sureeporn Punpuing, Kanchana Tangchonlatip, and Laura Yakas examine the experiences of elderly parents in Thailand whose adult children have migrated for work. In this scenario, elderly parents are left to care for young children while the parents work elsewhere. The authors highlight how cultural conceptions of parents' and grandparents' roles in the family, as well as traditional cultural beliefs (e.g., karma) and religion (i.e., Buddhism) contribute to grandparents' decisions to care for their grandchildren despite the hardships that this may entail. In Chapter 1, Heather Rae-Espinoza describes the landscape of a kin network in Ecuador where decisions regarding family separation and migration are embedded at each step in cultural rules of child rearing, as families look first for maternal kin to be caregivers before any decision to separate is made. In Chapter 3, Maria Rosario T. de Guzman, Minerva Tuliao, and Aileen Garcia illustrate how Filipina rural-to-urban migrants in the domestic care sector "build" family life not just across the distance but also in their new communities with their employers and their charges, as well as with other domestic workers in the vicinity. They argue that the structure and nature of the support systems reflect facets of the traditional Filipino family in such aspects as hierarchy and the establishment of strong ties through mutual obligation and support.

To some degree, the very notions of what constitutes family also appear to play a role in the decision to parent from a distance. In Chapter 14, Yvonne Bohr, Cindy H. Liu, Stephen H. Chen, and Leslie K. Wang describe the phenomenon of "satellite children"—the process of temporarily boarding infants and toddlers with extended family abroad. Here, notions of alloparental and distributed care play into parents' decisions about how to care for their children and, to some extent, may even underlie the parents' decisions to live apart from their children. In Chapter 15, Sumie Okazaki and Jeehun Kim describe cultural and social underpinnings of "*kirogi* parenting" or the practice of mothers' and children's migration from Korea to English-speaking countries for the purpose of furthering educational opportunities while the father is left behind to continue his paid employment. Both chapters discuss the sociocultural context in which separation occurs and recent trends in the prevalence of both *kirogi* and satellite parenting.

In cases where parents are the primary caregivers and they move away or are otherwise unavailable for direct care, the choice of alternative caregivers often reflects culturally embedded beliefs about who cares for the children. Research in several countries in Southeast Asia suggest that when fathers migrate, the care of children falls to the mothers, who are typically considered the main caregivers even when the family is intact (Hoang, Lam, Yeoh, & Graham, 2015). However, when mothers migrate, although fathers may participate more in childcare (Hoang et al., 2015), gendered notions of care leave unmarried aunts and maternal grandparents as the preferred caregivers over fathers (de Guzman, 2014; Parreñas, 2001). It is these gendered and cultural notions of care that Joyce Arditi and Jonathon Beckmeyer (Chapter 11) address as families reconfigure during and after incarceration. While research acknowledges a great deal of risk for children and families separated when a parent goes to jail, the authors stress that resiliency born from broad and flexible family boundaries, practices, and arrangements reflecting cultural strengths can serve as protective factors.

Theme 3: Stability and change in notions of family. A final theme of the volume returns to our earlier assertion that although what is considered normal family life is shifting in many ways, notions remain resistant to change to some degree. Globalization, increased mobility, and shifts in the caregiving context are indeed altering some of the ways in which family life is being carried out around the world. The typical cast of characters in the family and the roles that they play are changing—the roles of primary breadwinner, caregivers, and recipients of care are all in flux when mobility and separation permeate family life. Indeed, this shift is reflected in most chapters—with traditional caregivers, often the parents, physically absent in many of the scenarios posed in this volume and the families reconfiguring and adjusting to new realities that they face.

Nonetheless, beliefs about family life are deeply embedded, and their stability over time plays an important role in the experience of family separation. In Chapter 13, Jill Brown writes about child fosterage in Namibia and illustrates how the cultural practice of child migration and gifting of children creates new, often changing constellations of family, at times extending family and creating "fictive kin." In communities without institutionalized welfare systems, this practice secures social capital for the future. This practice of fosterage is generations old, and the inherent stability of family life in many communities in Africa is built on the very foundation of parenting from a distance. This stability, however, is tenuous, as described in (Chapter 6) by Kristin Cheney, who examines how the "orphan industrial complex" took root in Uganda in large part because of the socially distributed care system and families' relative comfort with parenting from afar. Cheney illustrates how cultural beliefs are exploited in our global age.

Whereas it is evident in many of the contributions that family separation is experienced through one's own cultural lens, this very lens can in fact be shaped by the migration experience and separation from one's natal home. The rich body of work on enculturation and acculturation (e.g., Kuo, 2014; Yoon et al., 2013) and social remittances (Ionela, 2013; Levitt, 1998) support this point, showing how behaviors, practices, and beliefs can shift in response to the norms of the receiving community. In Chapter 4, Natasza Kosakowska-Berezecka, Magdalena Żadkowska, Brita Gjerstad, Kuba Kryś, Anna Kwiatkowska, Gunhild Odden, Oleksandr Ryndyk, Justyna Świdrak, and Gunn Vedøy provide an excellent example of shifts in culturally embedded notions in the context of family life. They examine the extent to which culturally embedded gender roles in the family are in part static and in part dynamic, and they show how shifts in roles and expectations emerge when moving to a nation with gender norms that run counter to predominant beliefs in one's country of origin.

Throughout the volume, authors highlight the psychological complexity (at times daunting and at times seamless) of parenting from afar for parents and children. In Chapter 7, Mandi McDonald describes how adoptive parents mediate birth connections. The intricacies that require adoptive parents to develop family boundaries that are rigid enough to provide autonomy, security, and cohesion, yet permeable enough to retain a connection between the child and his or her birth parents are purposefully forged in the distance between these separated families. In Chapter 5, Yao Lu critically reviews the growing body of work on parent–child separation and extends the discussion regarding the complexity of underlying processes and their impact on children.

Definitions of family life are broadened by the many excellent cases presented in this volume. Although most chapters focus on family life when parents live away from their children, family across distance can also occur when children are living apart from all adults in the family, as we see in the discussion about child-headed households (CHHs) in Namibia by Monica Ruiz Casares, Shelene Gentz, and Jesse Beatson (Chapter 9). Sometimes emerging as a result of parental death or migration to urban areas, children live together in households with no resident adult. Although some children in CHHs have extended family, nonetheless, living on their own with only occasional or sometimes no contact with adult family members was in many cases the safest or most practical arrangement.

ORGANIZATION OF THE CURRENT VOLUME

The current volume brings together contributions by leading scholars from around the world who have examined long-distance family life in its many forms, contexts, and circumstances. The sections are organized around various circumstances in which family separation occurs. Section I provides examples of family separation in the context of economic migration. When laborers take on jobs abroad, the family unit faces numerous challenges that necessitate a renegotiation of traditional roles, a reconstruction of children's caregiving contexts, and the development of alternative strategies to maintain ties. In Chapter 1, Heather Rae-Espinoza describes parental economic migration from Ecuador and how the family shapes and reshapes in the process. She presents four cases that highlight the diversity in migratory trajectories among economic migrant families in one country and suggests the need to broaden our perspectives on family life and family reconfiguration across distance.

In Chapter 2, Berit Ingersol-Dayton and her team discuss the experiences of elderly parents in Thailand whose adult children have migrated for work. Although the typical picture of so-called left-behind members are children whose parents are living away, this chapter highlights how migration affects the broader family—particularly in a caregiving context where the intact extended family and obligations to provide care for elderly parents are cultural norms. In Chapter 3, de Guzman and colleagues discuss the experiences of rural-to-urban migrants in the Philippines who work in the domestic care sector. The chapter focuses on how migrants remake family not by bridging ties across distance but by building social support networks in their host communities (e.g., hierarchical). In Chapter 4, Natasza Kosakowska-Berezecka and her team examine gender roles among Polish economic migrants in Norway. Examining shifts and stability in gender norms when couples move to a more gender-egalitarian country, their work illustrates stability and change in culturally embedded beliefs. Finally, in Chapter 5, Yao Lu provides a thorough review and analysis of the large body of work on parental migration and discusses the complexities involved in understanding the impact on children's well-being. She argues for more nuanced examinations that take into account the child's characteristics, parents' migration status, and contextual factors in examining impact on child well-being and suggests future directions for research in the area. These five chapters illustrate the various forms of family separation in the context of economic migration and how individuals uniquely experience and are affected by family dispersal.

Section II brings together contributions that tackle family separation in the context of social and political unrest. Such crises result not just in family and individual mobility but also often in separation and the undoing of the family as a basic unit. Kristin Cheney (Chapter 6) provides a critical examination of the orphan rescue phenomenon in Uganda, where there has been a proliferation of orphanages in recent years. Drawing evidence from her fieldwork and action research, she describes how inconsistencies in notions of family among parents in Uganda and prospective adoptive families in the Global North are contributing to involuntary family separation at alarming levels. In Chapter 7, Mandi MacDonald explores adopters' subjective experience of parenthood in the context of open adoption. In these accounts, the adoptive parents identified their role as "kin-keepers," regulating their children's interaction with birth parents and safeguarding their options for relationship, In Northern Ireland, she explores how the family practices associated with open adoption, both structurally open arrangements and open family communication, facilitated occasional physical and imagined co-presence between the adopted child and his or her birth parents.

In Chapter 8, Marcela Sotomayor-Peterson and Ana Lucero-Liu provide a historical review of migration between the United States and Mexico and the experiences of transnational families living on the Sonora–Arizona border. Their work emphasizes the fact that there is vast diversity in transnational family configurations that can extend current definitions and perceptions about transnational family life. Finally, in Chapter 9, Ruth Ellingsen, Catherine Mogil, and Patricia Lester discuss family separation in the context of military deployment and the unique challenges that this type of separation entails. Military families not only navigate the challenges of separation but also the complex process of deployment, the dangers of wartime, and (ideally) reunification.

In Section III, authors discuss various circumstances of family separation in the context of personal crises. In Chapter 10, Monica Ruiz-Casares and colleagues examine child-headed households created by the HIV/AIDS crisis in sub-Saharan Africa. The unique ways that children choose to maintain the practices used by these absent parents and caregivers in regards to care and supervision, discipline, and distribution of tasks reveal a continuity of care often missed. In Chapter 11, Joyce Arditti and Jonathon Beckmeyer consider parental incarceration as a context for parenting, highlighting key intraindividual and family processes that shape incarcerated persons' parenting experiences. Maternal gate keeping, co-caregiving, and protective cultural factors are explored as they relate to incarceration. Michelle Bemiller, in Chapter 12, critiques the dominant motherhood expectation and highlights how noncustodial mothers adapt to living apart in a society that expects mothers to be primary caregivers. She examines how mothers both accept and reject the dominant definition of motherhood and how that impacts how they see themselves as mothers as well as how they parent their children from a distance.

Finally, Section IV presents research on family separation in the context of normative cultural practices and education. Although separation is often undertaken out of necessity or crises, chapters in this section illustrate contexts in which they are sometime voluntarily undertaken as part of normative care. Chapter 13 examines fosterage in Namibia. Jill Brown utilizes ethnographic fieldwork to describe a system of parenting from a distance in which 30% of children live with nonbiological "parents" even through birth parents are alive. Culturally embedded beliefs of teaching children perseverance, survival, and moral character infuse explanations of voluntary parental separation. In Chapter 14, Yvonne Bohr and her colleagues discuss the phenomenon of "satellite babies," in which Chinese migrants in North America send their infant children to be temporarily raised by grandparents in China as they cope with challenges associated with the migration experience. They argue that traditional notions of coping (e.g., by relying on extended family) persist even when the caregiving context has changed and practices might no longer be productive. In Chapter 15, Sumie Okazaki and Jeehum Kim discuss "*kirogi* parenting," which is a practice undertaken by South Korean families that sees mothers and their children temporarily migrating to Western nations so that the children can pursue better educational opportunities. In the meantime, fathers stay behind to continue their roles as breadwinners. They discuss the cultural underpinnings of this practice and the reasons for its recent decline. Finally, in Chapter 16, Edmund T. Hamann and collaborators tackle binationality and transnationalism in families caught between life in two countries. Their work examines the challenges faced by children of Mexican parents, who were born and raised in the United States, returning to Mexico for schooling. Their chapter sheds light on how various issues factor into parents' decisions about living arrangements and how sociopolitical realities sometimes make dispersal the only option for families.

By better understanding how we parent from a distance, this volume will synthesize ideas of kinship, relationships, and bonding and help the reader broaden his or her own ideas of parenting and family life. By illuminating how our ecological niche both affords and constrains parenting options to include the implications of distance, this work will ultimately broaden our definition of family. Finally, by allowing us to know and imagine family life, including parenting from a distance, as both normative and non-normative, this work can be used a tool as we leave the academy and create a place for more sound developmental science in policy affecting families and children around the world.

REFERENCES

Åhäll, L. (2012). Motherhood, myth and gendered agency in political violence. *International Feminist Journal of Politics*, *14*(1), 103–120.

Cabanes, J. V. A., & Acedera, K. A. F. (2012). Of mobile phones and mother-fathers: Calls, text messages, and conjugal power relations in mother-away Filipino families. *New Media and Society*, *14*(6), 916–930. doi: 10.1177/1461444811435397

Chasdi, E. H. (Ed.). (1994). *Culture and human development: The selected papers of John Whiting*. New York: Cambridge University Press.

Christian, J. (2005). Riding the bus: Barriers to prison visitation and family management strategies. *Journal of Contemporary Criminal Justice*, *21*(1), 31–48.

de Guzman, M. R. T. (2014). Yaya: Philippine domestic care workers, the children they care for, and the children they leave behind. *International Perspectives in Psychology: Research, Practice, Consultation* 3, 197–214. doi: 10.1037/ipp0000017

Gabel, S. (1992). Behavioral problems in sons of incarcerated or otherwise absent fathers: The issue of separation. Family *Process*, *31*(3), 303–314.

Graham, E., & Jordan, L. P. (2011). Migrant parents and the psychological well-being of left-behind children in Southeast Asia. *Journal of Marriage and the Family, 73*(4) 763–787. doi: 10.1111/j.1741-3737.2011.00844.x

Harkness, S., Mavridis, C. J., Liu, J. J., & Super, C. M. (2015). Parental ethnotheories and the development of family relationships in early and middle childhood. In L. A. Jensen (Ed.), *The Oxford handbook of human development and culture* (pp. 271–292). New York: Oxford University Press.

Hoang, L. A., Lam, T., Yeoh, B. S. A., & Graham, E. (2015). Transnational migration, changing care arrangements and left-behind children's responses in South-east Asia. *Children's Geographies, 13*(3), 263–277.

International Labour Organization. (2015). *ILO global estimates on migrant workers: Results and methodology. Special focus on migrant workers.* Accessed from http://www.ilo.org/wcmsp5/groups/public/---dgreports/---dcomm/documents/publication/wcms_436343.pdf

Ionela, V. (2013). Women's social remittances and their implications at household level: A case study of Romanian migration to Italy. *Migration Letters, 10*(1), 81–90.

Kagitçibasi, Ç. (2013). *Family, self, and human development across cultures: Theory and applications* (2nd ed.). Mahwah, NJ: Routledge

Keller, H. (2013). Attachment and culture. *Journal of Cross Cultural Psychology, 44*(2), 175–194.

Kuo, B. C. H. (2014). Coping, acculturation, and psychological adaptation among migrants: A theoretical and empirical review and synthesis of the literature. *Health Psychology and Behavioral Medicine, 2*, 16–33.

Lee, H. (2010). "I am a *kirogi* mother": Education exodus and life transformation among Korean transnational women. *Journal of Language, Identity, and Education, 9*(4), 250–264.

Levitt, P. (1998). Social remittances: Migration driven local-level forms of cultural diffusion. *International Migration Review, 32*(4), 926–948.

Madianaou, M., & Miller, D. (2011). Mobile phone parenting: Reconfiguring relationships between Filipina mothers and their left-behind children. *New Media Society, 13(3)*, 457–470. doi:10.1177/1461444810393903

Parreñas, R. S. (2001). *Servants of globalization: Women, migration and domestic work.* Stanford, CA: Stanford University Press.

Pillai, V. K. (2013). Child fosterage among Zambian families. *Vulnerable Children and Youth Studies, 8*(4). 362–365.

Shwalb, D. W., & Shwalb, B. J. (2015). Fathering diversity within societies. In L.A. Jensen (Ed.), *The Oxford handbook of human development and culture* (pp. 602–617). New York: Oxford University Press.

Smith, D. E. (1993). The standard North American family: SNAF as an ideological code. *Journal of Family Issues, 14*, 50–65.

Stenum, H. (2011). *Abused domestic workers in Europe: The case of au pairs.* Brussels: Directorate General for Internal Policies, European Parliament.

Swaroop, S. R., & DeLoach, C. D. (2015). Voices of trauma and resilience: Cultural and gender distinctive responses to war and displacement in Pakistan. *Psychology and Developing Societies, 27*(1), 1–30.

White, A. (2017). Polish families and migration since EU accession. Bristol, UK: Policy Press.

Whiting, B. B. & Edwards, C. P. (1988). *Children of different worlds: The formation of social behavior.* Cambridge, MA: Harvard University Press.

Whiting, J. W. M., & Whiting, B. B. (1975a). Aloofness and intimacy of husbands and wives: A cross-cultural study. *Ethos, 3*(2), 183–207.

Whiting, B. B. & Whiting, J. W. M. (1975b). *Children of six cultures: A psychocultural analysis.* Cambridge, MA.

United Nations Population Fund. (2015). *Migration overview.* Retrieved from http://www.unfpa.org/migration.

Yoon, E., Chang, C. T., Kim, S., Clawson, A., Cleary, S. E., Hansen, M., . . . Gomes, A. M. (2013). A meta-analysis of acculturation/enculturation and mental health. *Journal of Counseling Psychology, 60*, 15–30.

SECTION I

Economic Migration and Family Dispersal

1

Scattering Seeds in Las Orquideas

The Role of Kin Networks in Ecuadorian Parental Emigration

HEATHER RAE-ESPINOZA

Globalization and mobility reconfigure families with historical continuities and modern innovations. Each migrant's journey reflects a connection to family traditions and new ideas, impacting the parental ethnotheories that weave through societal values and personal emotions. As migrants decide to go, plan their voyages, and maintain connections, echoes of critique and support resonate from home to abroad, impacting returns and future personhoods. Looking at the role of migration through the focal point of one household's extended family, I hope to explain the complexity of life for migrant families in each step of their sojourn. As parents emigrated and children stayed, the experience of dispersing and maintaining ties differed across households. These qualitative representations encourage analyses of families in their kin networks and dynamic sociocultural settings while also building systematic connections between the cases for understanding parenting at a distance.

In this chapter, I describe the process of parental emigration, including (1) the role of motivations, (2) the arrangement of childcare, (3) the complexity of transnational bonds with both economic and social remittances, and (4) the changing landscape of future plans. Illustrating the intricacies of migration, I describe the experiences of the Mendoza family, focusing on segments of the family that stay in Ecuador and thus offering an understanding of the context for the émigrés' departures and continuing family ties. Then, I describe four cases of parental emigration in the Mendoza kin network to demonstrate the variability that exists in migratory trajectories. In conclusion, I argue for a wider perspective on how families reconfigure across distance.

MIGRATION JOURNEYS

In deciding to migrate, macroeconomic factors structured motivations. Rampant inflation with dollarization, political corruption, and marketplace instability impacted daily lives throughout Ecuador. Long-standing historical roots in rural-to-urban migration made migration an effective and affective solution to economic stagnation. With a legacy of migration and intensifying economic deprivation, migration increased to a point that news reports referred to an exodus of the economically active population. The population in their prime years of economic activity was also in their prime years of parenting practice. The increasing cost of childrearing with private schools meant émigrés were often parents. It may seem having a family would increase stability and decrease the likelihood to migrate, but, in fact, emigration was seen as a way to assure that children's needs are met. Economic advancement seemed best achieved elsewhere.

Noneconomic Motivators for Migration

Determining who emigrates and who stays entails an understanding of noneconomic migration motivators. Noneconomic migration motivators, such as exiting a bad relationship, seeking social acceptance, or living somewhere more "modern" (Giménez Romero, 2003) solidified the convergence of factors propelling emigration. Such noneconomic motivators, while veiled by families' discussions of macroeconomic conditions, often divided those who coped in Ecuador from those who emigrated. For women already criticized for life choices that resulted in single motherhood and economic deprivation, migration could mean avoiding unkind social interactions in traditional homesteads while resolving financial difficulties. They compared the faraway stigma of migrating with the nearby stagnation of staying. Even with the opportunity to make these autonomous choices, their migration journeys met limitations. Meeting locally informed, gendered expectations shaped decisions to migrate even while global policies created restrictions on an individual's ability to meet those expectations. Local parental ethnotheories focused on a mother as a necessary, irreplaceable presence in a child's life, yet limited returns on tourist visas and delayed timetables for family reunification visas could extend separations. Restrictions placed on autonomy do not erase autonomy itself; global restrictions can shape, but not prevent, personal decisions. Within the increasing regimentations of person and movement, culture and self dually inform migratory decisions. Individual motivations and macroeconomic and political pressures all differentially impact personal practice. Yet we can easily miss the role of subjectivity because migrants may keep personal factors hidden to avoid the circulation of critique.

PARENTAL ETHNOTHEORIES

Parental ethnotheories play a formative part in arranging childcare for planned migration journeys. Not only can parenthood encourage migration to meet children's economic needs, but parenthood can also shape the timing, destination, and length of journey. In Ecuador, migrants often prefer that children stay with female kin, especially maternal kin, and thus be assured of the kind of childcare and schooling available. Further, émigrés may undertake difficult journeys with plans for only temporary absences. Ethnotheories prioritize continuity for children, especially in childcare, homes, and schools. A prevailing cultural logic from rural homesteads privileges distributive care, where grandparents care for grandchildren while their parents worked in the field or nearby cities. These practices were reconfigured in urban houses in a way that both challenged and confirmed gendered expectations. Females took on economic duties as migrants or stayed as the heads of households, countering typical roles (Herrera, 2004).

Shifting gender roles can lead to stigmatized family structures (Ladd-Taylor & Umansky, 1998). Although female kin were still primarily the caregivers for children, when migration was undertaken temporarily for children's economic care and extended family assured children's physical care, families faced less stigma even when mothers emigrated. This delicate negotiation to (re)position family structures shaped children's experiences in kin networks. In the later descriptions of daily life, the émigrés' plans for the distribution of tasks and responsibilities resemble accepted practice while accommodating new routines that spanned the globe in response to shifts in the traditional caregiving context to parent at a distance. These decisions for the family unit simultaneously represent continuing norms and new ideals for a child's ecocultural niche.

LEGALITIES OF CARE

The complicated legality of documents meant families might need to make multiple arrangements for childcare, meeting different cultural models with varying degrees of success. Whereas the legacy of distributive care preferred multiple caregivers from the maternal side, custody laws informing Ecuadorian exit visas focused on nuclear families. In order to emigrate, a parent had to assure the Ministry of International Departures that any children would remain in permanent, stable care, preferably with one caregiver, for the duration of the journey. This contrasted with local practices, which might transition care through a network of related households to better meet children's disciplinary, educational, and social needs. As such, legal documents encouraged expeditious lies and falsehoods, with émigrés indicating absent parental figures to secure a visa when children might actually have extensive care from extended family. Navaro-Yashin (2007) suggests that "a nuanced study of law and the illegal in the domains of document production would ask that we . . . [invent] new frameworks for analysis" (p. 93). Instead of legal or illegal migration, this often meant that aspects of each migration journey weaved in and outside the law. The cases here represent a range of experiences in the (re)production of affective and effective childcare practices, often subject to legal and personal critique. As nation-states extend visas to other nations' economically advantaged and educated populations, these judgments move from the global to the local; the criteria become evaluations of those who cannot migrate to support their family simply because they cannot support their families. The relationship between documents and people as facets of law and statecraft inform these emotional valuations of selves and families as people migrate.

REMITTANCES, CONNECTIONS, AND RUPTURES

Kin networks maintain ties through remittances across distances with instabilities and continuities. As Boccagni (2012) indicates, Ecuadorian mothers continue to mother across the distance through sending remittances, communicating frequently, and having a deep affective connection to their children. The cases here show how these connections create everyday ruptures, where the émigré is both between and belonging to both places in unique ways. Émigrés transmit social and economic remittances. This status can depend on their subjective experiences with and prior to emigration.

First, in regard to economic remittances, kin networks are reshaped and reiterated through continuing and new expectations. Goldring (2004) indicates that key dimensions to understanding remittances are the "norms and logic(s) that regulate remittances; the uses of remittances (income versus savings); the social and political meanings of remittances; and the implications of such meanings for various interventions" (p. 799). The Mendoza cases demonstrate the complexity of these dimensions. Families have certain ideas regarding how soon, how frequent, and how large remittances should be. Even deciphering how remittances should be transferred can be challenging, often living here and there in the reconfiguration of kin. While some émigrés may need a period of adjustment before remitting money, the families that stay may also struggle to adjust. Caregivers may wish to hire someone to complete the tasks the émigré previously accomplished (Cornelius, 1991). Further, what remittances fund can cause debate and critique for all involved. Debts incurred from migration, especially in the face of increasing restrictions, need to be repaid. Should extended families' medical needs come before the émigrés' child's school expenses? How do expectations for funding a nuclear, urban family counter notions of extended, distributive care? The expectations for remittances can increase as perceived deprivations arise, turning desires into necessities and extending migratory journeys. While research has shown that when women receive remittances we see improved impacts on children's health, this gendered association has not been strongly supported in Ecuador (Göbel, 2013). This may be because more recent, undocumented emigration has entailed debts that need to be repaid first or because many Ecuadorian transnational families do not experience the same food insecurity that can characterize other migrant populations. A collective approach to family practices can reveal how the economic transfers reverberate through kin networks.

Second, social remittances alter parenting practices. Social remittances refer to the information and cultural values that migrants' actions and activities transmit between nations. As émigrés attempt to maintain and reinvent their parental roles, they contest, alter, and reaffirm parenting practices. These experiences will depend on their position in the family prior to emigration along with the care arrangements they set up. Levitt and Lamba-Nieves (2011) write that prior experiences influence actions abroad and connections back home with social remittances that reconfigure families. The affectionate role of a grandparent may extend while a mother's duty to secure goods for her child resonates across oceans. Children's care can simultaneously maintain traditions and challenge notions of parental authority. Often, the intergenerational transmission of values specifying particular kinship duties countered the international transmission of values emphasizing the excellent care of the children of émigrés. Traditionally in Ecuador, grandparents provide affection while parents focus on a balance of discipline and acquiescing to requests (Rae-Espinoza, 2010). Instead, transnational families redistributed tasks so that grandparents became conduits for parental discipline and monetary support while émigré parents offered extensive affection to compensate for time spent parenting at a distance. Interestingly, the resolution to transmitting possibly contradictory values usually entailed an emphasis on the ties across nations that matched long-standing practices, such as balanced discipline from abroad. Thereby, social ties altered parenting practices while simultaneously reinforcing them in a transnational ecocultural niche.

Through these transnational connections, dialogs on children's futures and family futures develop as a changing landscape. Motivations to emigrate for children's well-being can be questioned when financial needs are met; however, families' expectations for continued financial support upon return can delay a successful reunion, often represented with establishing a business in Ecuador. Discourses can change to the child joining the parent abroad when an adult because that would assure the child's success. Global restrictions on visas and unaccompanied minors, along with local restrictions on custody and passports, structure these trajectories. In addition to the economic and legal difficulties that prevent the return of migrants (Hochschild, 2002), we should not overlook individual psychological factors. Emotional adjustment abroad can vary greatly and alter whether and when someone returns. Returns are not necessarily permanent, with temporary reunions, extended journeys, and others going abroad common exceptions to original plans. Thus, reunions are sometimes separations, and separations can be reunions as well. An émigré's return may remind individuals of the connections they are missing or tarnish romanticized images as nostalgia gives way to reality. The meaning of success determines return journeys as pride and price both play parts.

Importantly, each part of the migration journey, from decisions to migrate, arranging care, and maintaining connections to planning reunions, can face a shifting discourse of critique. The negotiated reality of migratory journeys connects and disconnects with valued and stigmatized subjectivities (Rae-Espinoza, 2012). A number of interested parties, such as children, intermediaries, and caregivers, along with community members, may comment, interpret, and spurn migrants' decisions. Their family lives become public rhetoric. Children are called "abandoned," "left behind," or "neglected" from parental emigration, regardless of the actual care received. For this reason, migrants reconfigure their family structure in accord with valued notions of children's lives. In the cases herein, family members differed in their interpretations of émigrés' practices, sometimes in ways that diametrically opposed children's actual experiences.

In the following section, I discuss the life in this global city of an extended family, the Mendozas. The Mendoza kin network represents how families operate across distances in a myriad of emigration experiences with Las Orquideas as a global hub. The life of Eduardo Mendoza, his wife Marisol, and their daughter Briana reveal how migration impacts the cultural practices of an entire kinship network. Migration status alone cannot sufficiently depict the developmental niches of the children of émigrés. One child struggled in moving from home to home when his mother went to Italy and his father went to the United States; one child's life improved when her mother migrated to Italy and she stayed with her grandparents; another barely noticed his father's multinational trek to England; and, last, three siblings faced abuse from their paternal grandmother when their parents migrated to Spain. When children stay after parental emigration, the ruptures in everyday life and the everyday life in ruptures differentially impact children's ecocultural niche. Even when some aspects of life change, others will remain the same across a multitude of variations, formed in and informed by their cultural setting. Children may find that someone different picks them up from the same classroom on school days, a new caregiver may make a long-standing favorite dish, the previous visits to grandparents can extend to a new permanent address with similar daily routines, or a distant father remains at a distance while comments on his value change dramatically. This ethnographic description of the family demonstrates the importance of understanding local perspectives on kin networks and parental ethnotheories to see how parenting from a distance adapts to local settings.

THE MENDOZA FAMILY

In the Mendoza kin network, rural-to-urban and international migration weaves through parenting goals rather than interrupting them. When Eduardo's parents Tercero Mendoza and his wife Lucía met as teenagers in a small village in the province of El Oro, to the south of Guayaquil, they did not plan a family that would span the globe. Instead, they were caught up in local views. Lucía's landowning family did not approve of Tercero's working-class, alcoholic father. However, over the course of a half-century of marriage, Tercero has proved to be a good provider, loyal husband, and respectful man. The Mendoza family is well-respected in the village because of Lucía's descent from hacienda owners and because of the devotion of their six children.

Representing long-standing preferences for multigenerational rural homesteads, Tercero and Lucía have four houses on their land. Each of their widowed mothers has a small one-bedroom wooden home. Lucía and Tercero mainly live in another wooden house, the one in which they raised their children. A fourth concrete house primarily functions as a guesthouse, even though their children contributed to and oversaw its construction to benefit their parents. The furnishings reflect their children's desire to equip their parents with modern conveniences. However, Lucía still cooks over wood rather than using the electric stove. To the children, the unused appliances are not a waste of money because the parents have all they need. Tercero and Lucía have found no need for modern conveniences as they engage in the same daily activities that they have pursued for decades. Twice a week, he climbs a mountain behind the village where their cattle are at pasture. Lucía lovingly prepares a care package for his nights away. She usually stays behind, caring for their mothers and her grandchildren with the help of her youngest daughter, Luisa.

The youngest of the six children, Luisa keeps her mother company while her father Tercero is away. Luisa married a classmate, and they live down the street from her parents. She works as a teacher, and her husband sells wares out of their house. These endeavors do not pay well, but they receive support from her older siblings in the form of both international merchandise and funds. When Luisa's second child was born shortly after her first, her oldest brother Eduardo paid for an intrauterine contraceptive device. Luisa graciously accepts help without making requests. She does not see herself as stuck in the village, a remnant of the past, or "left behind" but, because her family owns a considerable amount of land, as the continuation of her family's presence in the community.

In contrast, the firstborn daughter and second child, Patricia, voices displeasure at her siblings' activities. She attended school in the village and married a man from the neighboring small town, where they now have an auto parts store. Her rural-to-more-urban migration once indicated an accomplishment, but now she appears to have "stayed home" in comparison to her globe-trotting siblings. Although Patricia and her husband can support their three children, she asks her distant siblings to purchase items for her home to help their parents, things like her own washing machine. Patricia also requests items that she says she cannot get for her children in the small town, like expensive sneakers or funding for an elaborate birthday party. Patricia justifies these requests by saying that her nieces and nephews with émigré parents have these things since she takes care of her parents. The siblings acquiesce because if they refused to help their parents they would be neglectful. Her siblings Kingner and Cynthia comment that Patricia makes requests that her parents would never venture to ask, and, as a result, sometimes contact lags to avoid her appeals.

Firstborn Eduardo went to high school in Guayaquil after attending elementary school in the village. Eduardo went to college for engineering and eventually completed a master's degree. He received significant support from his parents—funding for college, for his home, and for his wedding. Eduardo and his wife Marisol had similar upbringings in small farming villages and moved to Guayaquil for further education. Marisol received an associate's degree in bookkeeping.

Eduardo and Marisol settled in a new development in Las Orquídeas because Eduardo had an uncle there, even though it was far from his employment at the military base in the south of Guayaquil. They prioritized proximity to extended family over employment. Located at the northernmost point of Guayaquil, Las Orquídeas was named for a nearby botanical garden of orchids. In a decade's lapse, the once desolate lots and dirt roads leading to Las Orquídeas became wall-to-wall homes with iron-barred windows and relentlessly speed-bumped streets. Las Orquídeas represents the nation's and the city's rampant development, fear of crime, and disparate economic mobility. While those in Las Orquídeas bought their plot of land and small 500-square-foot two-bedroom concrete homes at the same time and for around the same price, the homes now differ markedly. Some have expanded into three- or four-story mansions, while others have become increasingly rundown with skinny, rickety slat fences held together by rusted wires. The inconsistent homes and diverse families in this neighborhood represent consistent characteristics of kin and connectedness in the lives of the children of émigrés. Class propels emigration, and emigration propels changes in class status at home. The Mendoza family is a focal point for describing the variable experiences of those who stay; furthermore, the family is also a focal point for describing the variable experiences of those who emigrate.

Eduardo and Marisol's lives in Las Orquídeas include international migration as well. As a naval engineer for fourteen years, Eduardo often worked overtime, including working on boats in Peru where he vacationed with his wife and daughter Briana. Marisol invested their extra income into the home and property to prevent Eduardo from spending it on consumables. They purchased their own home, modern appliances, land at the beach, and the house next door to theirs in Las Orquídeas. He returned his parents' gracious support, purchasing major appliances for his parents' home and supporting his younger siblings. This cycle of investing in a first son so he can invest in the following children is a common parental practice.

Unfortunately, after corruption at the shipyard, Eduardo was fired as a scapegoat. He could no longer fulfill his role in the cycle to support his family as the future patriarch and even needed some help, including money for an operation for Marisol. Marisol and Eduardo put the second home they bought on the market, thankful for the rampant inflation in real estate following dollarization. Marisol's foresight in investment and continuing frugality allowed her to run her household when they no longer had an income. They both sought employment in Guayaquil that would not cost more in transportation and childcare than they would earn. Eduardo's options were usually well beneath his qualifications, required too far a commute, or did not pay as promised. Marisol supplemented their income and saved money on clothing through sewing. She made casual clothes, couch covers, and graduation gowns for the neighbors. Marisol had a natural talent for sewing, and she had augmented her skills with an educational series in the Sunday paper. She worried that this pursuit took time away from her four-year-old daughter, Briana. Much of Marisol's time was taken up helping the émigrés in her family and their children. Neither Marisol nor Eduardo felt that they could return to their family homesteads once having been urban migrants with educations gained from familial investments, nor could they emigrate internationally. Instead, they shouldered responsibility for the transnational branches of their family tree.

FIRMLY PLANTED OR UPROOTED CHILDREN?

This home in Las Orquideas is the trunk for several transnational branches of the Mendoza family tree. Each émigré represents a different motivation to emigrate and different arrangements of childcare, destinations, and plans for return. Kingner Junior stayed when his parents Kingner and Rosenda emigrated; Ramona stayed when her mother Cinthya emigrated; Roberto stayed when his father Fernando emigrated; and Norman, Isabella, and Shakina stayed when their parents Liliana and Luis emigrated. Following Harkness and Super's (1996) developmental niche, I aim to connect physical and social settings, prevailing customs about childcare, and parental ethnotheories to the reconfiguration of Ecuadorian families experiencing emigration.

Rosenda and Kingner's Divorce

Considered economic migrants geopolitically, Kingner Junior's parents provide an example of the role of interpersonal experiences and potential criticism of migration decisions and transnational ties (see Figure 1.1). Financial deprivation did not motivate his parents' journey. Even though their journey differs in the role of financial motivation, it still represents common threads in Ecuadorian migration. For example, Kingner began with an initial rural-to-urban migration that resulted in multidirectional journeys involving complicated legality, uneven social and economic remittances, and expectations informed by cultural practices of parenting and family. The various destinations and transitions meant the building and severing of ties for his son Junior.

Kingner (number 10 in Figure 1.1) was Tercero and Lucía's youngest son and fourth child. Although Kingner admits that he was his father's favorite as the youngest boy, he laments that he did not receive the educational opportunities that his older brother Eduardo received. After serving a government-mandated year in the military, his paternal uncle helped him enlist in a selective military force in the province of Guayas. As he rose in the ranks, his girlfriend Rosenda (9) became pregnant. Rosenda's father, a high-ranking officer, threatened Kingner with discharge if he did not marry Rosenda. Kingner's family did not attend the wedding. Kingner questioned paternity at first, but became a proud father when his son, Kingner Junior (25), was born. Rosenda made considerable efforts to

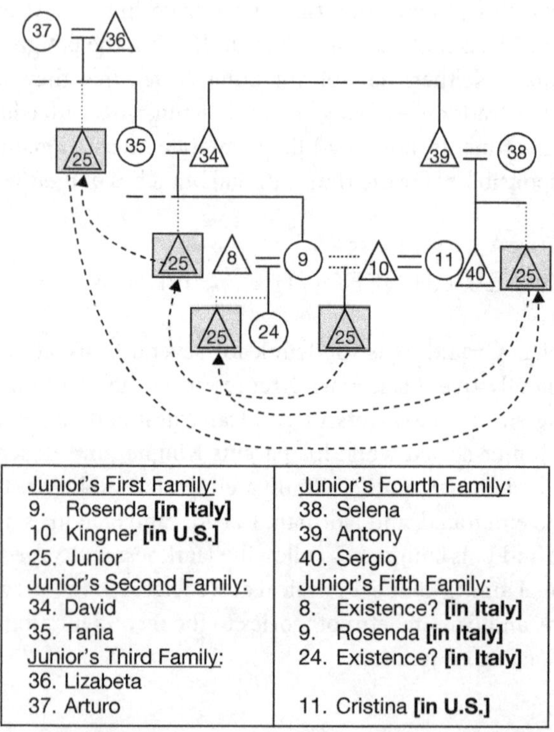

Figure 1.1. Junior's kinship chart.

accommodate her husband, but Kingner never fully embraced the marriage and arguments continued. He was envious of his brother Eduardo's educated wife.

To avoid his wife's requests to reciprocate affection, Kingner purposely accepted deployments outside Guayaquil, which required living in the barracks. Because he enjoyed village life and had no objections to rural placements, as the other officers did, he was continuously placed away from home instead of within the normal monthly rotation. Kingner supported his wife economically and visited his son, but Rosenda felt like a single mother.

After two years deployment in villages, Kingner began a relationship with a US citizen named Cristina (11) who was visiting her extended family in Ecuador on a college break. After three months of courtship, he proposed to Cristina. Kingner had been saving to begin a bus company for his parents' village, but spent it all to get a divorce from Rosenda. In Ecuador, contested divorces are time-consuming and nearly impossible for young couples with children (to prevent broken homes). To obtain her consent for divorce, Rosenda insisted that Kingner buy her a ticket to Italy, where she could join a cousin. Rosenda told others after she emigrated that a corpulent, rich foreigner seduced her husband.

For a parent to get an exit visa without a return ticket, children (who are listed on an Ecuadorian passport) need legalized substitute care. Since

Rosenda had no return date or plans to bring her son with her to Italy, the divorce papers gave Kingner full custody of Junior. However, Rosenda still exerted authority over Junior's care and forbade Kingner from bringing him to live at Kingner's parents' house or to live with him. Instead, Junior went to live with Rosenda's parents, Tania (35) and David (34), in a smaller city an hour from Guayaquil. Rosenda's mother Tania expected Kingner to financially support Junior and the household where Junior resided, as he would do if Rosenda had not emigrated. Notably, Tania did not expect remittances from Rosenda as Junior's mother.

I met two-year-old Junior in 1999 at Tania's house. When we arrived, Junior was outside playing in the dirt wearing only a diaper. Kingner was upset. He had bought Junior new clothes on his last visit, including the sneakers that Junior's cousin was wearing, and his son had vision problems that meant he should avoid getting dust in his eyes. Kingner took his son to the store for new clothes—something he said that a woman should do—before they went to the park. Rosenda's brother supervised Kingner on such outings. Kingner told me that Rosenda's family feared he would kidnap his son and then they could not live off his money and enjoy criticizing him. This criticism from Rosenda's female kin contrasted strongly with Rosenda's previous spousal attentiveness and acquiescence. Saying that he was a terrible husband and bad father insulted both his manhood and his family by implying that his own parents had improperly raised him. Thus, Kingner never brought his parents to visit Junior, and the divide deepened.

However, Rosenda's father David did not criticize Kingner. He felt his daughter erred in consenting to the divorce, emigrating, or caring about what he saw as a harmless affair with Cristina, who had returned to college for her last semester. Rosenda's behaviors disrespected her father's actions to assure her marriage and proved Kingner was right in his initial refusal to marry Rosenda—she lacked the commitment to be a good wife. Charismatic Kingner had become a respected member of the force. Even though David did not criticize him, he did not defend Kingner, and Kingner continued to suffer his ex-mother-in-law's tirades.

Kingner and Cristina's marriage a few months later started a complicated migration journey. Enjoying stable employment and social prestige in Ecuador, Kingner had never planned on emigrating. Several Ecuadorians told me that they gathered documents and kept contact information just in case an opportunity arose. Unlike his siblings, Kingner did not have a passport. In the spring of 2000, the Ecuadorian government limited passports to stem an exodus of workers. Utilizing military connections, paying bribes, and seeking his passport in a province with less demand, it still took Kingner three months to get a passport. (The wait in Guayaquil was said to be more than a year.) Furthermore, because he was listed as having full custody of his son, he could not obtain an exit visa without bribes. Also, Kingner could not receive a tourist visa to the United States because, once married to a citizen, the embassy considered him a risk for overstaying his visa. (The couple did not know that a fiancé visa was much quicker and cheaper when they chose to have an extravagant wedding event at an Ecuadorian beach resort.)

Since a spousal visa to the United States took at least 1.5 years to obtain, Kingner and Cristina decided to live on the border, in Ciudad Juarez, and sought a Mexican tourist visa. She had family on the other side of the border in El Paso, Texas, and considered having Kingner cross without documents. Even though expeditious, a Mexican visa application was daunting as well—it required the couple to purchase property temporarily, bribe bank officials to falsify account balances drained from previous bribes, buy perjured statements from employers attesting to Kingner's continued employment, and falsify car titles. Legal visas requiring illegal actions were not unique to this case.

Kingner had difficulty in Mexico. He could only remit small amounts to his son from undocumented factory work. Without any contacts in Mexico, the charismatic military leader felt socially isolated. His Mexican visa did not allow him to return to Ecuador, but he was still waiting for his US visa. His delayed journey and limited remittances exacerbated the critiques Junior heard from his maternal grandmother, and she would not let Kingner speak to his son on the phone. She reported Kingner to the Institute for Children and Families for not sending child support, which meant that he could not return to Ecuador without first legally addressing their complaint. This would be expensive, time-consuming, and difficult to counter. Even though Kingner remitted more than the national minimum to his son, he did not have documentation to prove this: instead of using expensive money wiring services, Kingner had sent Marisol an ATM card on a US checking account. His brother Eduardo risked his own safety in getting cash to Junior.

Once Kingner could provide for his family with stable employment in the United States, he still experienced a series of emotional and financial difficulties. Remittances were never enough for his own family or Rosenda's mother. The intermediary arrangement with Marisol meant that he helped his parents and Eduardo's family in addition to Junior. Kingner's proceeds from investments in family businesses turned into loans, and he purchased Eduardo's land at the beach. He was annoyed that Texans thought he was a poor Mexican and felt discouraged seeing the wealth around him. In the United States, he worked in manual labor, a stigmatized pursuit in Ecuador. Furthermore, Kingner was unaccustomed to Cristina's expectations, especially considering Rosenda's acquiescence and the *machista* behaviors he picked up from his Mexican co-workers. Menjívar (2003) identified a similar trend in immigrant couples: men engage in employment that reinforces male-dominated views, while women adopt more egalitarian ideals that lead to marital strife. Also, Kingner wanted to bring Junior to the United States to assure his medical care and education, but even his own family would not help him bring Junior to live with a stepmother. Parental ethnotheories view stepmothers as inevitably cruel to stepchildren, who become domestic servants.[1] Fathers cannot protect children while at work.

Rosenda's migration journey and perception differed from Kingner's. While she sent no money, her care arrangement met motherly expectations to assure balanced discipline in accord with Ecuadorian parental ethnotheories (Rae-Espinoza, 2010). Rosenda had a passport, did not need a visa, and had friends abroad; she adjusted well to Italy. Rumors began to spread that Rosenda adjusted too well—she was said to be pregnant. This signified no plans for return to her son. Also, others speculated that if she could care for a child abroad, then she should have brought Junior to Italy. After this, Rosenda's choices—leaving Kingner when she agreed to divorce and starting a family without Junior—reflected negatively on her parents. Because these rumors spurred further battles between Rosenda's parents, Rosenda's mother decided to join her in Italy. Tania's emigration expanded the critique because Rosenda had not assured her son's care with Tania, had not brought Junior when she could, and had a mother lacking character. Tania was a topic of gossip—a married, older woman with grown children, a daughter abroad, and a home lacked approved motivations to emigrate; for this reason, her journey was interpreted as a desire to partake in a life of vagrancy and avoid the duties to maintain her lineage that occupy the days of other senior women.

Kingner did not learn of Tania's emigration plans until after Junior had gone to live with Tania's aged parents (36, 37) in a rural area without a school or a telephone. There, now five-year-old Junior's vision problems deteriorated, and he risked permanent blindness without an operation. Kingner remitted money for the necessary operation and Junior's caretakers' expenses while in Guayaquil for the operation. Rosenda did not send any money. Since the visual difficulties were generally attributed to the mother's genetic contribution and as caused by poor childcare, Rosenda's lack of funding was seen as neglectful. After the operation, the great-grandparents could not fulfill the therapy requirements to alternately cover one eye at a time for set times and to keep the child away from dust; Junior soon needed a second, painful operation.

At that time, Rosenda's father's brother Antony (39) and Antony's wife Selena (38) took Junior into their home. They had a son (40) who was a year older. They did not know much about Junior's past but believed that he lacked maternal care due to the same emigration that harmed Antony's brother David. Seeing Rosenda's maternal relatives as the cause for distress with their kin, Selena was open to Kingner's involvement with Junior. Kingner greatly appreciated renewing ties with his son. Hoping to demonstrate his concern for his son, Kingner paid for the second operation and sent his wife Cristina to Ecuador to help. Cristina reported to Kingner that Selena took excellent care of Junior. During that time, Selena taught Junior the alphabet, which he did not yet know given his lack of schooling and vision problems. Since mothering in this ecocultural niche does not usually include academic instruction, many commended Selena's efforts. Junior realized this, too, and when they visited his great-grandparents, he insisted on sleeping with his new parents, Antony and Selena.

Trying to rebuild his paternal ties, Selena brought Junior to visit in Las Orquídeas when she visited nearby kin and picked up remittances. Selena told Marisol stories connecting Junior to his father. When Junior was chosen to escort a princess at school, he refused to smile because he had wanted to escort the girl's twin. She laughed that the stubborn boy was already choosing mates based on personality rather than looks—like his father leaving his attractive Ecuadorian wife. Junior grew more comfortable with his paternal kin and chimed in during conversations. He asked the ages of different paternal relatives[2] and sometimes confused photos of his Uncle Eduardo for Kingner. Both brothers had prominent ears, a characteristic he knew about his father. When his Aunt Marisol asked Junior who Dumbo looked like, he quickly responded "my father." After a minute, Junior reported that he had his father's ears and his mother's eyes.

Appreciative, Kingner treated Selena's family like kin, loaning money for their business and sending gifts. They built a collaborative relationship. Selena's family informed the Institute for Children and Family that the report against Kingner for neglecting his child should be revoked since the claimant had relinquished the care of the child to them and they received support beyond the national minimum. In this way, Kingner could visit Ecuador to see his son. Kingner and Cristina returned the next month, in February, for a second honeymoon on Valentine's Day and for Junior's sixth birthday.

Kingner and Cristina's return meant changes in Junior's care. When Marisol passed on Selena's story to Cristina that Junior wanted to celebrate his birthday at the neighbor's house because he thought that was where birthday parties happened, Cristina was aghast that Junior had never celebrated his birthday. She decided to throw a lavish party with balloons, cake, ice cream, a clown, party favors, and hats. Following US parental practices, Cristina brought Junior to six bakeries to find the Spiderman sheetcake with Incredible Hulk candles that he wanted. Rather than just indicating a small treat that jumps into sight on social outings as is customary (Rae-Espinoza, 2010), Cristina expected Junior to request something he may have never seen to suit it exactly to his desires. Kingner diligently drove around two cities to collect party supplies, as he did for his wedding to Cristina a few years earlier.

At the party, Junior followed Cristina's request to greet each guest with party hats. When Junior refused to leave his post awaiting arrivals to pose for photos, Rosenda's maternal family was unhappy. While normally female kin assist in distributing food, Rosenda's family spent their time commenting on Cristina instead. When Cristina helped distribute food to compensate for their protest, the comments grew louder. They told Junior that they would send photos to his real mother, who loved him. Cristina and Kingner hid their pleasure that party photos would reach Italy to counter Rosenda's claims that Kingner was neglectful.

After the birthday party and other extravagant bonding trips, both Junior and his father cried when they separated a few weeks later. The return had made Junior think that every day with his father would be like a holiday. Selena told me that Junior had not cared if his father called before, but he missed him afterward. When Kingner opened the discussion of bringing Junior to the United States, Selena told Kingner that she wanted permanent custody, thus altering the longstanding legal status in his divorce papers. Even though living with distant relations, Junior was considered to be in trustworthy care. When Rosenda heard that Kingner was going to sign over custody with the understanding that Junior could visit, Rosenda filed for a reunification visa and brought him (and his remittances) to Italy. Junior did not want to go, but he listened to Selena, who said that he should be with his mother. While difficult for Selena's family, all agreed that Junior had always belonged with his mother.

Junior went through multiple transitions from the sole recipient of his mother's affection, to distributive care in a smaller town with older cousins, to being alone in a rural area, back to a smaller town with an older brother, and then to Italy with his mother and possibly a baby sister. With these changes, the commentary on his parents changed as well. While Kingner was originally criticized, covering the two operations, party, and monthly payments relabeled him as a provider. At first, Rosenda was accepted for placing Junior in the care of her mother, but she was later censured when her mother joined her in Italy. In the end, the father completed his economic obligations, and the mother cared for Junior. Although Kingner preferred his parents or himself caring for Junior, this ecocultural niche favored care from maternal kin.

Cinthya's Social and Global Mobility

In contrast to Junior, Cinthya's daughter Ramona (Figure 1.2) experienced few changes in care after her mother's emigration. Still, interpersonal experiences and potential criticism impacted migration decisions and transnational ties. The story also begins with rural-to-urban migration and ends with a reunion as separation. Cinthya's emigration began to avoid criticism, yet criticism returned when she did.

Tercero and Lucía's fifth child Cinthya (7) attended the village elementary school and went to high school in Las Orquideas, staying at Eduardo's house. While in Guayaquil, she became pregnant with no marriage prospect. (Luisa, the youngest, was not sent to school in Guayaquil.) Only Marisol knows the identity of the father, although both Eduardo and Kingner have suspicions. Unable to support her daughter, Cinthya returned to her parents' home with her daughter Ramona (23). Tercero and Lucía cared for Ramona from infancy, and Ramona soon saw Cinthya as her sister.

When I met Ramona in 1999, at her grandparents' house, we played for hours while her grandmother tended house. The three-year-old entertained me as her

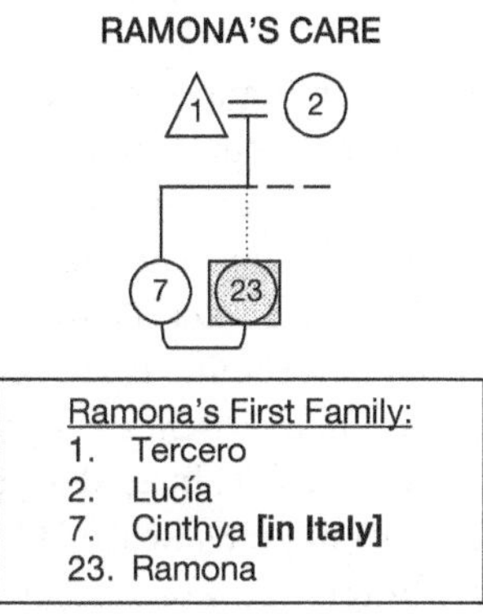

Figure 1.2. Ramona's kinship chart.

guest, showing me her stuffed animals, freely mixing differently sized dolls with animal figures and toy cars. When invited to attend a political rally in town to meet key community leaders, I agreed, not realizing that Ramona had already booked me for her nighttime television watching. Ramona asked to join me, but her grandmother told her she could not go because the foxes were out. She acquiesced but whispered to me to beware of foxes. Many visitors had left and not returned.

Ramona's mother Cinthya tried a few different careers, like selling Avon cosmetics, but she found few opportunities in the village and could not return to the city unmarried. One initiative that began to pay off was seeking documents for those abroad, beginning with her brother Kingner's ex-wife Rosenda, and then for others who requested her assistance. *Tramitadores*, or people who seek documents for others, are a fixture of Ecuadorian government offices. At the Civil Registry, Department of Justice, and Department of Motor Vehicles, men with plastic briefcases charge a small fee to help people find forms or stand in appropriate lines. Rather than being an expert at a particular locale, Cinthya was an expert on a particular person at any office. As émigrés paid her to retrieve documents, the power of income abroad became alluring.

Cinthya quickly fulfilled her desire to emigrate legally in a few months, at the end of 2000. She was familiar with the paperwork from helping others, had a passport, and Rosenda knew a family looking for a nanny in Italy. It may seem odd that Cinthya followed her brother's ex-wife, but, according to Wilson (2012), "migrant networks expand in urban centers through marriages of a family's offspring" (p. 1161), connecting people to unknown destinations abroad through affinal ties. However, Rosenda's expectation that Cinthya pay the rent and bar tabs for both of them as gratitude countered Cinthya's preference to send money home. Without a bank account with which to transfer or save money, Cinthya sometimes paid $30 to send $100. Her brother Kingner in the United States warned Cinthya that she needed to worry about establishing herself in Italy. Her brother Eduardo in Guayaquil told her that she should buy a home in Ecuador, perhaps the one he was selling, and return soon. Yet Cinthya continued to send most of her money to her parents. By emigrating, Cinthya's status transitioned from a stigmatized single mother who returned disgraced to her village to a woman in a cosmopolitan city with her own means of support.

With frequent phone calls and remittances, no one could critique Cinthya's devotion. Cinthya's diligent remittances countered her ex-sister-in-law Rosenda's claims that it was impossible for her to send money when Kingner paid for Junior's second operation. Cinthya reported that Rosenda exhausted herself looking for handouts rather than work. Rosenda found Cinthya a job (and expected money for the effort) but never found herself employment. To the dismay of both Cinthya's family and Rosenda, Rosenda's boyfriend recognized Cinthya's initiative and the two began a relationship. Instead of gaining someone new to depend on through helping Cinthya migrate, Rosenda lost someone she depended on. Cinthya's family was fearful that she would again forego advancement for a man who disrespected her, as Ramona's father had done.

Five-year-old Ramona was not told much about her mother's emigration, just that Cinthya would return and that Ramona could not go because of the foxes. Ramona did not change schools or even bedrooms when her mother emigrated. Her grandparents physically cared for her, and her mother financially cared for her because of the child's absent father. Ramona did not ask Cinthya to return when she called, but she did ask her to send presents. When Cinthya decided to emigrate, Ramona already referred to her grandmother as Mama and had always referred to her grandfather as Papa. Ramona's grandmother Lucía said other children teased Ramona, saying "Those are not your parents. They're your grandparents. Your mom is in Italy and who is your father?" Ramona offered no recollection of such teasing. In my research, many transnational families expressed concern that the child's family arrangements led to confusion: children would not learn appropriate roles if they did not understand the distinction between a grandmother and a mother. Lucía worried that Ramona would misunderstand family relationships, especially when Ramona mistook kin terms. However, Ramona selected kin terms systematically, moving herself into her mother's generation.

Ramona experienced surprising stability in parental emigration. In fact, it was not until Cinthya's return visit in 2003 that changes occurred. After a tearful meeting at the airport in Guayaquil, Cinthya told her parents, her daughter Ramona, Eduardo, and Marisol how life was different in Italy. No one expected Cinthya's thick Italian accent, and Lucía was shocked to see thong underwear and skimpy outfits in her daughter's suitcase. Cinthya shared photo albums of herself on the beach. Perceiving disapproval, Cinthya claimed that the airline lost the suitcase with more sensible clothing and photos. Her family thought Cinthya had begun to devalue her country and values. Her siblings mocked her in unity. For a month, whenever Marisol offered me a drink, she would apologize that sparkling water does not flow from the tap like in glorious Italia.

Cinthya's changes were not only reflected in her attire and attitude toward Ecuador, but also in her spending habits as well. While small treats to prevent antisocial behavior are part of Ecuadorian parental ethnotheories (Rae-Espinoza, 2010), Cinthya spent money differently. She bought expensive clothes at the elite mall for herself that she lauded as unique and modern, like something she would find in Italy. She segmented the family when she chose to buy lavish presents for some and nothing for others. When the family realized how much money she spent on herself rather than on her future, her sainted remittances seemed comparatively slight. However, Kingner reported that, when returning, others had the expectation that he spend lavishly to demonstrate his success even though he never spent that way in the United States.

Cinthya stayed at Marisol's house in Las Orquideas, as she had previously, but as an international woman rather than a high school student. Ramona did not mind Cinthya leaving her at Marisol's house to shop or visit, nor was she was anxious about Cinthya's presence. Ramona was used to Cinthya coming and going to government offices and social engagements from an early age. Ramona did not demonstrate the same affection toward Cinthya as she did toward Lucía, but she did not cling to anyone in particular either—not the mother who had been gone or the grandmother who cared for her. She just played with her cousin on the floor. Unlike some émigrés' children, Ramona did not fear that her mother would take her away from a new home or forget to bring her to their new home. Ramona could see her mother eventually rejoining the family where she had always lived—with her grandparents. On her visit, Cinthya did not stay in the cement guesthouse but in her room in the old wooden house with her parents.

Ramona adjusted to having two caregivers during Cinthya's extended visit. When Ramona requested a possession or told a story, she addressed Cinthya, whereas when she wanted food or care, she spoke to Lucía. As Junior did with Kingner, Ramona came to enjoy the new kind of care she received from Cinthya. Rather than meaning abandonment to Cynthia, emigration meant an even greater devotion because of the items she could provide her child. Cinthya consented to provide rather large items without concern for providing physical care or balanced discipline. In fact, Cinthya did not even expect Ramona to formulate socially appropriate requests, thus countering the primary goal of consenting small prizes for children. Lucía was in a difficult situation: she did not agree with her daughter Cinthya's permissiveness, but she wanted her granddaughter Ramona to learn family roles. A grandmother provides affection and does not interfere with maternal care, such as discipline. If Lucía stepped in because Cinthya was not mothering appropriately, she would no longer be grandmothering appropriately.

After a traumatic event, Ramona transferred her requests for affection to her mother as well. On a trip back to Las Orquideas from the village just before Christmas, the bus Cinthya and Ramona was on was hijacked at gunpoint. Although no one was hurt, the thieves fired a gun and stole their luggage. Cinthya said these bags contained all the Christmas presents she had brought back. (Marisol wondered why she traveled back and forth with presents, thinking that they might have been stolen earlier, along with Cinthya's appropriate clothing.) Then Ramona stayed close to her mother instead of playing with her cousin, and Cinthya showered Ramona with even more gifts. As a guest in Las Orquideas, Cinthya made it clear that the toys she bought belonged to Ramona, placing them on top of the refrigerator in their original packaging. She would re-bestow her gifts when Ramona requested them, but they were not given to Briana.

Marisol's daughter Briana did not complain when her cousin Ramona hoarded her new toys, even though Briana shared her room and toys with all the cousins who came to visit. Yet Christmas was especially injurious to Briana's usual good demeanor. Briana asked Santa for a Barbie computer that she saw in a toy store. Marisol and Eduardo could not afford the $80 toy for their daughter, so they told Briana that the store ran out. Cinthya could afford the toy and bought one for Ramona, who had never seen one. Ramona did not know how to play with the computer, but rejected Briana's offer to show her. Cinthya tried to explain the toy by play typing on it—she did not realize that it was electronic, and Marisol sent someone to the store to get batteries. Rather than encouraging Ramona to share, Cinthya suggested that Briana sit next to her cousin and watch. Both cousins were disappointed: Briana did not get to play with the toy she wanted, and no one wanted to watch Ramona play with it. Cinthya was disappointed as well when no one lauded her as the holiday heroine for getting the computer thanks to her hard work in Italy. It seemed unfair to her that her unemployed brother Eduardo was still viewed as the family success.

When it was time for Cinthya to return to Italy, separation was difficult for Ramona. The eight-year-old no longer believed that foxes would get her, and small rewards in the form of social outings offered no enticement compared to big, individual rewards. Cinthya ingratiated Ramona for a month without discipline or expectations of appropriate social behavior. When Cinthya first emigrated, Ramona was lucky to keep the same life; this time, her mother's departure meant that she had to go back to that same life. Just as with Junior after Kingner's visit, the meaningful reunion made Ramona miss her mother. Ramona spent time away from her grandparents, with whom she had always lived, to reunite with her mother Cinthya. Then she separated from her mother and returned to her grandparents' home. Reunion can be a separation, and a separation can be a reunion.

While she originally planned a five-year journey, Cinthya now hopes to stay in Italy. She said that Ramona should complete her studies in Ecuador and then decide if she wants to come to Italy also. The family admires Cinthya's ambition, but dislikes her lack of future focus. Even Kingner, who plans to stay in the United States, is disappointed in Cinthya for her apparent superiority. Cinthya spent to demonstrate the value of her migration, not realizing that it was *because* she spent so much that people questioned her migration. Cultural values support a woman migrating to support her child, but Cinthya's attempt to demonstrate her earning power through luxury purchases reinterpreted her motivations as selfish consumerism rather than familial devotion. While the family originally understood her choice as the best option for her, Cinthya's demeanor implied that she saw emigration as the best option overall.

Fernando's Separation

Roberto's case has similarities to and differences from the previous cases (see Figure 1.3). Emigration did not change his care, with international emigration occurring as an extension of rural-to-urban-to-rural journeys. However, the critiques continued long-term perspectives on his father Fernando, and no reunion concludes his story. This reveals the complex ways that personal experiences intertwine with financial motivations to shape migration decisions and transnational ties for social and economic remittances.

Tercero and Lucía's third child Fernando (12) grew up in the shadow of his older brother, Eduardo, who received an education, and of his younger brother, Kingner, who was the favorite. Fernando left his village earlier and with less education than his siblings to work as a truck driver bringing products from the southern coast to Quito. He lived near the village for the first ten years of his marriage to Nydia (13). While migration for opportunities is understood, his movement to a similar village (off the route from his village to the city) was seen

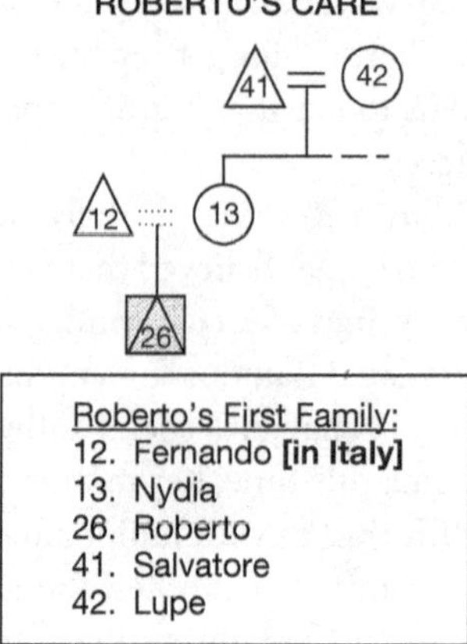

Figure 1.3. Roberto's kinship chart.

as rebellion. As a long-haul trucker, his home could be almost anywhere, but he left his wife Nydia and son Roberto (26) alone instead of with his family.

With rising gas prices and excessive personal spending on drinking and entertainment, Fernando's trucking business went bankrupt and he turned to even heavier alcohol abuse. When Roberto was four, Fernando's wife Nydia moved in with her parents (41, 42) near Quito. Without his wife and son, Fernando had no need to keep a home and began living in his truck full-time, as he used to do when he was on the road. He spent some time with his mother Lucía while Tercero was away taking care of the cattle. She cooked for him and washed his clothes. It seemed inappropriate that his aging father made the exhausting journey to the pastures while his son sat at home drunk or, even worse, wasted time with unacceptable women rather than attempting to win back his wife. To rectify this, Kingner remitted money to invest in more cattle, hoping that his brother would see the enterprise as worth his time. As a result, if Fernando worked, it spoke well of his brother Kingner, but if he did not, it spoke poorly of Fernando. Fernando was once again in the shadow of his siblings. Kingner's remittances kept their father's business running and Cinthya's remittances kept their mother's house running. Noting his condemnation and their respect, Fernando asked Kingner for money to join Cinthya in Italy. With promises of paying Kingner back, Fernando emigrated.

Fernando's emigration did not require any changes in childcare, homes, or schools for his son—Roberto already lived with his mother and maternal grandparents near Quito. As a truck driver, Fernando would leave for long periods and only visit occasionally, often late at night. After emigration, Fernando called his son more than he had while on the road or when separated from his wife. He found work quickly in Italy, painting houses for Cinthya's boyfriend, and began sending remittances to Nydia the first month. However, not everything was perfect. His remittances were unstable because, he said, Cinthya's boyfriend did not pay what was due or kept large finder's fees. Nydia did not complain because she received more than when he was a truck driver and thought Fernando chose to emigrate to take responsibility for his family and win her back. He spoke of continuing on to England for better employment opportunities.

However, when Nydia found that Fernando's mistress had migrated to England a year earlier, she was upset. Nydia resented the fact that he was unwilling to resolve his alcoholism and support his family while in Ecuador, even after he lost her. She began complaining about the remittances. Once, Fernando sent items for his son in a care package that Cinthya sent for Ramona. When it arrived at Fernando's older sister Patricia's house in a nearby city, Patricia asked Fernando for one of the shirts in the box for her own son. Fernando had no choice but to agree and experienced some of the same complexities that Kingner did with intermediaries involved in remittances. Nydia was insulted to receive leftovers from Cinthya's package; Fernando felt he had gone above and beyond, buying clothes as a mother would, but had received no gratitude. He would have to pay more to send packages separately to Quito, and he felt financial pressure to send money (as did Cinthya) to his family to cover what Kingner had invested in cattle and in his journey.

The critique of émigrés often reconfigured family relationships at home. Fernando's son Roberto started asking his father for money when he called, and Fernando's calls lagged. Fernando's parents claimed such disrespect was Nydia's selfish influence because she felt spurned. However, Fernando's parents asked what Nydia expected after leaving her husband. The mistress bought Fernando presents and chased him. Fernando did not leave his wife—his wife moved to Quito. The interpretation of migratory timelines informed critiques on morality, social obligation, and personal value in accord with long-standing values.

When Fernando continued to want to go to England, his family questioned his motivations. He claimed that the reason he wanted to leave was not for the mistress, but because he could no longer tolerate watching how Cinthya's boyfriend treated her. She moved out of the place she shared with Fernando to live with her boyfriend and his parents. Fernando claimed that she paid their rent instead of helping her own brother. Paying rent on his own was expensive, and his remittances stopped. By traveling to England, he could remit more money to his son (perhaps by sharing rent with a mistress) and not watch his sister being disrespected. He had thought about returning to Ecuador, but this was not truly an option. He emigrated to save enough money to restart his trucking business in Ecuador, and he still had not paid Kingner any money for his loan. If he returned short of that goal, he would be seen as a failure who disrespected both Kingner who funded his trip and Cinthya who received him. He could not stay in Italy, return to Ecuador, or move to England without disrespecting his family.

Fernando began drinking heavily again. Missing work and arguing about finders' fees, he did not get as much work painting houses. With Cinthya sending money and even affording to return, he had trouble claiming that earning a living was difficult in Italy. The assumption was that men should earn more than women, but in fact women's domestic work was better paid and more reliable. When Cinthya returned to Ecuador, Fernando's mistress came to Italy and brought him back to

England. Fernando said he could not watch Cinthya's boyfriend cheat on her with Rosenda anymore. Upon hearing this, Cinthya said Fernando had always wanted to be in England but knew Kingner would not give him money to emigrate to his mistress. With freedom to send remittances on his timeline rather than Cinthya's, he mainly sent them on birthdays and holidays. As Nydia and Roberto's anger increased, his phone calls diminished. Fernando's family blamed his weaknesses on the mistress, and they never got to know his son Roberto. Occasionally, Nydia would ask Marisol for small amounts of money from Kingner or Cinthya. She said it was their fault that her husband had emigrated. She did not come to Las Orquideas but had Marisol transfer the money to her bank account.

Fernando did not detail a particular timeline for his journey or to repay Kingner's loan. He mentioned restarting his trucking business, but his future plans usually did not connect to his son. His son was in maternal care, and Fernando sent money when he could. Avoiding comment on the dispute between Cinthya and Fernando, Eduardo said that Fernando needed someone to be with, as Kingner had. In interviews in Guayaquil, I was told that cheating was inevitable when a spouse emigrated alone because it was too expensive and too lonely not to cheat. It was not known if Fernando would return to Ecuador or Italy or stay in England.

Liliana and Luis's Continued Bond

Eduardo's siblings Cinthya, Kingner, and Fernando weren't the only transnational migrants to depend on his household in Las Orquideas in the transitions of transnational ties. Marisol's sister[3] Liliana and Liliana's husband Luis also migrated to Spain. Motivated by increasing financial needs, Liliana and Luis extended their rural-to-urban migration internationally. Their journey and eventual reunion closely modeled cultural ideals for children's care with transnational ties, even if it did not resemble any ideal in actualilty.

Marisol's younger sister Liliana (19) met Luis (20) in the rice-farming town where they were raised (see Figure 1.4). They had two children, Norman (31) and Isabella (32), shortly after they wed. Seeking work, the couple moved to Guayaquil. When their third child, Shakina (33), was on the way four years later, Luis again felt he lacked sufficient employment for his family. He migrated to Spain a few months after Shakina was born. With a contact abroad, he could support his family immediately as a taxi driver. Liliana moved back to their village with the children, in a reverse of rural-to-urban migration, and bought a small house with his remittances. Luis had difficulty adjusting to life without his wife, so Liliana decided to join him in Spain when Shakina turned two.

When Liliana planned for childcare during her emigration, she asked her sister Marisol to take her three children since Liliana and Marisol's mother was deceased. Marisol said she could take Shakina, since she was the same age as her own daughter Briana, but she could not take all three children. Marisol said she could not in good conscience take in children for whom she was unable to provide all the necessary care. Wanting to keep the children together, Liliana moved her

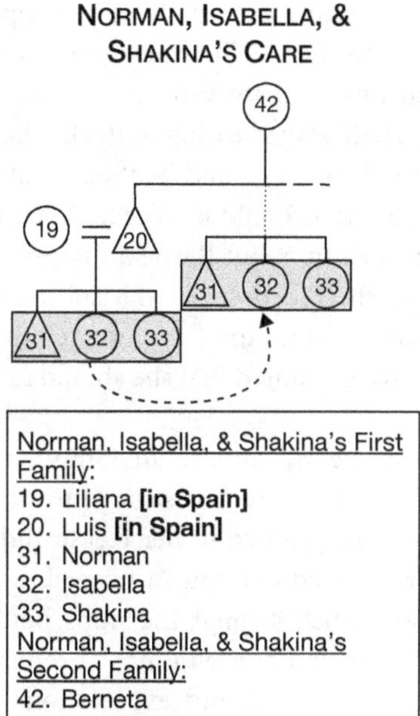

Figure 1.4. Norman, Isabella, and Shakina's kinship chart.

mother-in-law (42) Berneta into her house. When Liliana left in 2001, she told eight-year-old Norman and seven-year-old Isabella that she would send for them. Since Liliana followed Luis, the children trusted a progressive chain of emigration.

This housing arrangement quickly changed. The Spanish mafia became upset when items turned up missing on one of Luis's taxi routes (perhaps unknown to him), and Luis and Liliana were forced into hiding as a gardener and a maid at a country golf resort. The children's grandmother Berneta said the mafia called her, and she insisted that Luis relocate her to a large house where she had previously lived with her other grandchildren so that she would not be forced to reveal his whereabouts. No amount sufficed to cover the expenses in the new home, and Berneta told me that others should take care of her so she could care for their children.

Marisol again ended up handling remittance transfers and visits. Luis remitted money via Marisol, just as Kingner did. Rather than an ATM card on his account, however, Marisol had to transfer money in person. She would take a bus to the mall, wait in line at one bank, carry the money from one bank to the next, and then wait in line at a second bank to deposit the money into Berneta's account. Marisol worried that someone would follow and rob her on this task, as had been reported on the news. Marisol picked up packages from Spain, traveled by bus across the city with her daughter, and hosted Berneta to receive the packages.

On one of these visits in Las Orquideas in 2003, I met four-year-old Shakina with Berneta and Berneta's sister. Instead of introducing Shakina to me or encouraging her to greet Marisol, as would be customary, Berneta's sister simply told me that Shakina did not talk. Shakina eventually played separately with my games, but did not interact with me then. When her grandmother entered the room, Shakina stopped playing, hunched forward, and looked down. After an hour, Shakina soiled herself. Berneta stayed eating in the kitchen. Her great-aunt asked Shakina why she did not tell someone and, without waiting for a response, used the accident as proof that Shakina could not speak. Marisol said that the diarrhea might be from a stomach infection, but Berneta disagreed. She said Shakina was always "that way" because she did not eat. Marisol dressed Shakina in Briana's clothes—even though Shakina "does that," no other clothes were brought for her. Shakina stared off as Marisol explained that she should let her know if she wanted to use the bathroom.

Shakina sought care from peers, rather than adults, as Weisner and Gallimore (1977) indicated for children who are accustomed to sibling care. When Briana returned from school, Shakina pointed to her feet to indicate to her cousin that she wanted shoes. Briana realized her cousin needed a belt, too. Briana yanked Shakina around a bit to get the belt through the loops, but Shakina neither resisted nor cooperated. Sibling care in and of itself is not a problem when the appropriate social supports exist for the context and expectations for children. However, I eventually learned that Shakina's siblings lacked appropriate social support.

At lunchtime, Shakina did not in fact eat a normal amount. Once Marisol had prepared soups for the children's lunch, Marisol fed Briana while asking about her day. She asked Briana not to talk with her mouth full, so Briana had to eat diligently to tell her story between spoonfuls. Berneta and her sister sat next to where Marisol had placed Shakina to be fed and gave her two mouthfuls. Berneta then said her arthritis prevented her from feeding Shakina, and Shakina did not want soup anyway. Marisol fed Shakina, who ate silently with some coaching. Then Shakina told Marisol that she had to go to the bathroom, confirming Marisol's concern about a stomach virus. Berneta asked for money—the remittances she had just received did not include money for medical care. With money from Marisol, Berneta and her sister went to the pharmacy around the block and were away for two hours, leaving Marisol to take care of the toiletry concerns and lunch clean up. While they were gone, Shakina whispered to Marisol that she wanted to live with her, which was not news to Marisol. Shakina's older sister Isabella had previously asked to move in, and Marisol told me she regretted not taking them, believing that it would have been easier and better for the children, instead of taking care of Berneta so she could neglect the children at exorbitant prices.

Eventually, the children told me about their experiences at Berneta's house, but it took longer to earn their confidences than with other children. The siblings had created an insular adult-free world. One day in Las Orquideas, Norman and Isabella tried to convince Marisol to let them go outside. Without practice, they were not good at eliciting consent like other children. At first they said they wanted to go to the park. When that was denied since the park was dirty and dangerous, they said they wanted to go to the store to buy yogurt. Unfortunately, there was some in the fridge. When Marisol left the room, I suggested they just tell the truth, assuming that they wanted to talk to someone outside. Norman then confessed that they wanted to steal mangoes from the neighbor's tree. Isabella hushed him and denied any secretive inclinations. Norman shrugged and said it was against my job to tell. Isabella quickly contextualized their mission: the mangoes fell to the ground to spoil, and they really liked mangoes. When I said that it would be hard to convince Marisol to let them outside and *not* watch their activity, she relaxed her shoulders. Isabella embraced this trust and eventually told me about their lives.

Norman and Isabella tried their best to take care of Shakina. They prepared food for themselves and Shakina that didn't require cooking, like salads, cereal, and sandwiches. However, her siblings provided care on an as-requested rather than as-needed basis. For example, Norman and Isabella said that they did not need to pick lice off their little sister, like they did for each other, because she did not like it. Care was not to assure well-being but as a way to do what they were asked. Instead of going to school, the children spent the day doing housework or running errands. Liliana sent money earmarked for private schools, but the grandmother said she could not afford it. Berneta took Shakina out of public kindergarten because "she was not learning anyway." Isabella was removed from school, too. According to her grandmother, paying for transportation to and from school was unnecessary since Isabella soon would be going to Spain, even though she did not have a passport. The children's chores were not child-appropriate according to Ecuadorian parental ethnotheories. While shopping for dinner ingredients at a neighborhood *bodega* is a regular practice for older children, Norman complained that he was sent repeatedly for chips and candy for his cousins instead of going just once. Isabella never had to go. She defended herself by saying that she was hand-washing clothes and taking care of Shakina, so he had to go. She complained to me that Berneta and her cousins messed up the house after she cleaned it. Like Cinderella's evil stepsisters, Isabella's cousins cut up or took the clothes her mother sent. Isabella was beaten with a hair brush if she complained about her cousins. When Norman stood up to their grandmother for hitting Isabella too hard, Berneta kneeled on his throat and threatened to kill him if he told anyone how she treated them. Even with bruises as evidence and his sister's testimonials, he still did not confirm the abuse to me.

With stories about the children's "care" reaching Spain, the complicated reunion process was expedited. Children cannot fly without adult supervision, and guardians cannot receive family reunification visas, even if only to board a plane. As such, many children cannot travel either accompanied or unaccompanied. When the children's mother Liliana found that a distant cousin received a work visa for Spain, she asked the woman to accompany her children. When Berneta found out, she accused the couple of being ungrateful after she cared for their children if they left her, her sister, or her other grandchildren behind. Berneta refused to comply with any paperwork, even though she received money for the children's passports three times. Liliana acquiesced and paid for visa applications for the additional relatives. When only the three children were approved for family reunification visas—as both Marisol and Liliana knew would happen—Liliana caught the next flight back to Guayaquil to get them passports. She was afraid that Berneta might go into hiding with the children or harm them if word spread. Berneta was asked to come to Las Orquideas with the children for a visa interview. At Marisol's house, the children greeted their mother with tearful, long embraces and were surprised with the news that they were going to Spain. The children had not been told earlier, to prevent them from telling Berneta. Liliana told the children they would live their lives in Spain and return to Ecuador to retire, if they wanted.

Still, not all was easy. Shakina was afraid to go to Spain: she was told that the proper Spanish would hit her for misbehaving. Norman thought the hole in the ozone was directly over Spain, so people age faster. In contrast, Isabella was happy—she said it was worth leaving everything she owned, even her favorite bathing suit. Her mother would buy her new things. She was also happy that her "ungrateful" grandmother and cousins were not going since they had treated her so badly. The children refused to return to their grandmother's house to gather their things, and Berneta was no longer welcome in Marisol's house.

Liliana had difficulties, too. She felt guilty for leaving her children and mourned anew the loss of her own mother, who would have been a wonderful caregiver. Liliana was unsure of her fit with her self-sufficient children. The older siblings cared for Shakina, telling her she could not have soda or threatening to get the belt if she did not eat. On one occasion, as Marisol helped Briana with her homework, Shakina started scribbling on a piece of paper. Liliana asked Shakina what she was doing, modeling her older sister Marisol's mothering, and Shakina nonverbally indicated that she was waiting for her sister. Isabella came over, squinted at the line, and then decided which letter it most resembled. Liliana had to figure out how to care for Shakina, and Shakina had to figure out how to join social dynamics with a once again reconfigured family.

When the passports came a few weeks later and it was clear that they were going to Spain, the children's psychosocial health improved. Norman stopped his plans to escape. He hung around the house, conversing freely with adults. Although a little embarrassed, he once asked for his mother's help to reach bread on top of the refrigerator. Shakina no longer hid from people and was potty trained. Reflectively, Isabella said she was more relaxed because she could be a kid again. Even though it helped Isabella to process her experiences, Liliana asked her children not to talk about their abuse, especially to their father who would feel responsible and ashamed of his mother's behavior. The abuse meant that Liliana had abandoned her children and that Luis was not a good father. How could he be, with such a horrible mother? But in fact they had entrusted their children's care to a close family member, maintained the marital unit, returned as soon as possible, and took care of the children's economic needs. Although the children faced terrible circumstances, it was a migrant's success story.

CONCLUSION

The cases of Junior, Ramona, Roberto, and Norman, Isabella, and Shakina represent how networks function and how experiences vary in emigration through a global hub in Las Orquideas. Instead of relying on macroeconomic explanations, it is important to observe the parents' motivations to emigrate (divorce, no marriage, separation, or continuation of marriage), the kind of care afterward (changes in caregivers, in kinds of care, in homes, or in schools), the nature of transnational ties (returns, packages, telephone calls, or remittances), and changes in the émigré (attitudes toward home and abroad along with emotional adjustment). The timing of returns and reunifications is about more than finances or legal concerns, being embedded in social relationships and cultural norms in ways that might be unpredictable—reunions may be a separation, even as separations may be a reunion. For some, such as Cinthya and Fernando, presences can be absences as parents eke out unreliable employment, whereas absences can be presences as they demonstrate strong ties from abroad. These differences affect children's reactions to parental emigration and demonstrate the need for an in-depth comparative analysis of the children of parental emigration.

The experiences of the Mendoza family reveal connections to roots and to blossoming ideas as strongly felt parental ethnotheories respond to global influences on transnational families. Long-standing appreciation of migration as a way to cope with economic difficulties, especially to meet the increasing needs of growing children, spurred rural-to-urban journeys that eventually reversed and extended. While not always motivated primarily by economics, as in the case of Luis's emigration to Spain, economic considerations formed part of the justifications, discourses, and critiques they all faced. As is clear with each case's rural-to-urban-to-rural journeys, seeking a new place for successful employment met variable success. A destination may not be permanent, and perhaps may not even be long term. Fernando's preference to live on the road predated his multiple international destinations. These decisions developed from both economic and personal dynamics that fit existing parental ethnotheories. When émigrés chose who would care for their children, they looked to cultural preferences for maternal kin and distributive care. These arrangements did not always meet expectations, as the cases show in examples ranging from Shakina's unpicked lice to Ramona's Barbie computer. Sometimes plans fail to meet expectations, whereas at other times expectations change. Parenting practices, such as providing lavish gifts and parties, alter with the influence of life abroad. However, cultural norms may continue to be espoused as the kinship network seeks new agreement on conventional perspectives. Decisions like timing, destination, and length of journey all respond and react to existing and renovated parental ethnotheories on schools, discipline, and physical and emotional needs. Liliana continued to value Ecuadorian private schools from Spain, even as Berneta, who stayed in Ecuador, did not consider education worth the cost of transportation. These journeys involved the creation of documents with complicated legality and a tenuous relationship to reality, even as the documents determined connections and esteem. Kingner's full custody of Junior while his son transitioned through questionable care arrangements beyond his grasp reveals this. His social and economic remittances, which revealed his preferences, had little effect on Junior's reconfigured family and the boy's future plans with his mother abroad. For each case, their experiences adjusted to the circulation of critique in renegotiating ties.

The transnational branches of the Mendoza family offer insight into the complexities of parenting and family life from a distance. The maintenance of ties as families operate across the globe show how family can be reconfigured during migration, both as people renovate old meanings and adopt new values. Kin networks, including both those who migrate and those who stay, are impacted by each other's decisions and interpretations of ongoing ties and disruptions in daily practice. The links between rural, urban, and global settings come together in Las Orquideas as family is reconfigured.

NOTES

1. I suspect that this perspective persists because the few stepchildren seemed to be the result of extramarital affairs. With the difficulty of divorce and expectations to marry an expectant mother, Junior was unique in being from a previous marriage.
2. I think Junior may have been trying to map out kin generations since his great aunt Selena had a son who was close in age.
3. Marisol also had an older sister, Veronica, who lived with their father after being left at the altar twenty years earlier. She was prone to fits of rage or days without speaking. Marisol made Veronica simple clothes out of extra fabric when she sewed for the neighbor, and she had Veronica come to visit in Las Orquideas occasionally to give their father a break in caring for her.

REFERENCES

Boccagni, P. (2012). Practising motherhood at a distance: Retention and loss in Ecuadorian transnational families. *Journal of Ethnic and Migration Studies*, *38*(2), 261–277.

Cornelius, W. A. (1991). Labor migrations to the United States: Development outcomes and alternatives in Mexican sending communities. In S. Díaz-Briquets & S. Weintraub (Eds.), *Regional and sectoral development in Mexico as alternatives to migration* (pp. 89–131). Boulder: Westview.

Giménez Romero, C. (2003). *Qué es la inmigración: ¿Problema u oportunidad? ¿Cómo lograr la integración de los inmigrantes? ¿Multiculturalismo o interculturalidad?* Barcelona: RBA Libros.

Göbel, K. (2013). Remittances, expenditure patterns, and gender: Parametric and semiparametric evidence from Ecuador. *IZA Journal of Migration*, *2*(1), 1–19.

Goldring, L. (2004). Family and collective remittances to Mexico: A multi-dimensional typology. *Development and Change*, *35*(4), 799–840.

Harkness, S., & Super, C. (1996). *Parents' cultural belief systems: Their origins, expressions, and consequences.* New York: The Guilford Press.

Herrera, G. (2004). Elementos para una comprensión de las familias transnacionales. In F. Hidalgo (Ed.), *Migraciones: Un juego con cartas marcadas* (pp. 215–232). Quito: Abya-Yala.

Hochschild, A. (2002). Love and gold. In B. Ehrenreich & A. Hochschild (Eds.), *Global woman: Nannies, maids, and sex workers in the new economy* (pp. 15–30). New York: Metropolitan Books.

Ladd-Taylor, M., & Umansky, L. (1998). *Bad mothers: The politics of blame in twentieth century America*. New York: New York University Press.

Levitt, P., & Lamba-Nieves, D. (2011). Social remittances revisited. *Journal of Ethnic and Migration Studies, 37*(1), 1–22.

Menjívar, C. (2003). The intersection of work and gender: Central American immigrant women and employment in California. In P. Hondagneu-Sotelo (Ed.), *Gender and US immigration: Contemporary trends* (pp. 101–126). Berkeley: University of California Press.

Navaro-Yashin, Y. (2007). Make-believe papers, legal forms and the counterfeit: Affective interactions between documents and people in Britain and Cyprus. *Anthropological Theory, 7*(1), 79–98.

Rae-Espinoza, H. (2010). Consent and discipline in Ecuador: How to avoid raising an antisocial child. *Ethos, 38*(4), 369–388.

Rae-Espinoza, H. (2012). Parental emigration and conceptions of better futures in Ecuador. *Global Studies of Childhood, 2*(3), 217–229.

Weisner, T. S., & Gallimore, R. (1977). My brother's keeper: Child and sibling caretaking. *Current Anthropology, 18*(2), 169–190.

Wilson, T. D. (2012). Cumulative causation unbounded: Network expansion in rural and urban migration centers. *Anthropological Quarterly, 85*(4), 1161–1176.

2

Migration and "Skipped Generation" Households in Thailand

BERIT INGERSOLL-DAYTON, SUREEPORN PUNPUING, KANCHANA TANGCHONLATIP, AND LAURA YAKAS ■

When a household comprises grandparents and their grandchildren without the middle generation, this is called a "skipped generation" household. The prevalence of skipped generation households has been on the rise in various communities around the world because of varying underlying causes, such as crises that prevent parents from taking on the primary care of their children or migration that results in their parenting from afar (Toyota, Yeoh, & Nguyen, 2007). In this chapter, we review some of the emerging literature on the underlying causes of this type of family configuration and present findings from our own study on the experience of grandparents as caregivers for their grandchildren in Thailand.

CAUSES OF SKIPPED GENERATION HOUSEHOLDS

Researchers have generally explained the emergence of skipped generation households as either a result of a problem or "crisis" or as an economic "strategy" (Baker & Silverstein, 2012, p. 55). In Arber and Timonen's (2012) typology, crisis explanations align with the idea of grandparents as "child savers" (p. 6), where grandparents rescue children whose parents cannot care for them. In contrast, strategy explanations align with the idea of grandparents as "mother savers" (p. 7)—caring for children so that parents can work—or with Baker and Silverstein's (2012) term "family maximizers" (p. 51), a concept based on their research in China indicating that grandparents caring for children is a strategy that benefits the whole family. The literature suggests that, in many cases, skip generation households emerge in the Americas and in Africa tending more toward crisis situations, whereas in Asia it is more likely undertaken as a strategy.

Crisis Explanations

In the United States, beginning in the 1990s, there was much research analyzing the growing rates of skipped generation households. These studies cited crises such as the spread of crack addiction (Minkler, Roe, & Price, 1992), increased illicit drug use and HIV outbreaks of the 1980s (Burnette, 1997), teen pregnancy, mental illness, or parent death (Fuller-Thompson, Minkler, & Driver, 1997). Of relevance is that black Americans disproportionately faced these problems (Minkler et al., 1992) and that economic recessions were good predictors of increases in skipped generation households or households with all three generations (Scommegna, 2012). Three studies independently found that HIV resulted in increases in skipped generation households in Kenya (Ice, Sadruddin, Vagedes, Yogo, & Juma, 2012), South Africa (Nyasani, Sterberg, & Smith, 2009), and Zambia (Reijer, 2013).

Strategy Explanations

In the Asian context, research on skipped generation households generally points to the migration of working parents as a precipitating factor. Baker and Silverstein (2012) found that, in China, the term "family maximizer" made more sense than either "child saver" or "mother saver" as the decision for adult children to migrate for work and leave their children in the care of their grandparents was often a collective decision aimed at helping the whole family. In Thailand—the site of our research—the extremely high rate of internal migration for economic or educational reasons (Chamratrithirong, 2007; Huguet & Chamratrithirong, 2011), and the resultant skipped generation households, is receiving increasing attention. Knodel and Nguyen (2014) found that in rural Thailand, 12.2% of the elderly were in skipped generation households compared with 4.1% in both Myanmar and Vietnam. In some rural areas of Thailand (i.e., the Northeastern region), the proportion of skipped generation households is as high as 15% (Knodel, Teerawichitchainan, Prachuabmoh, & Pothisiri, 2015).

EFFECTS OF SKIPPED GENERATION HOUSEHOLDS

Much like explaining the causes, examining the effects or impacts of skipped generation households is usually framed as either positive or negative, costs or benefits.

Problem-Focused Research

In most of the literature, researchers are examining problems that could arise from living in a skipped generation household. In the United States, studies have shown that within grandparent-headed households (that are both skipped generation and three-generation), skipped generation households experience higher rates of poverty (Park, 2006), and grandparents (usually grandfathers) of skipped generation households delay retirement longer (Wang & Marcotte, 2007). Custodial grandparents (i.e., grandparents who are primary caregivers, either in skipped or multigenerational households) are more likely to have physical health problems and low health satisfaction (Minkler & Fuller-Thompson, 1999) and experience significant areas and degrees of worrying (Shakya, Usita, Eisenberg, Weston, & Liles, 2012). Furthermore, the burdens of these problems fall unevenly on people according to race and ethnicity (Chen, Mair, Bao, & Yang, 2015; Mills, Gomez-Smith, & De Leon, 2005). The picture painted in Africa is also dire, as HIV has claimed the lives of many in the middle generation. A study of custodial grandparents in Kenya found high levels of perceived stress (Ice et al., 2012), and, in South Africa, custodial grandparents experienced significant stress about rampant levels of poverty as well as intergenerational conflict (Nyasani et al., 2009).

In Thailand, the site of our study, there is also research alerting us to the possible problems faced by grandparents in skipped generation households. One study showed that grandparents in skipped generation families are worse off economically and physically than other grandparents (Kamnuansilpa & Wongthanavasu, 2005), and the large-scale CLAIM study (Jampaklay et al., 2012) found that the strongest predictors of caretaker mental health problems was that both of the parents of the children left behind had migrated, sent low remittances, and that the caretaker was aged 60 or over (i.e., a skipped generation household grandparent).

Cost- and Benefit-Focused Research

There is a growing realization that a problem-focused approach risks overlooking the agency, strength, and resilience of skipped generation household family members (Hayslip & Goodman, 2008; Hayslip & Smith, 2013). Hayslip and Kaminksi (2005) found that in a US population there were a variety of costs such as role confusion, poorer health, and poverty but that, ultimately, the role of caregiver was *rewarding* for grandparents. Ninety percent of the grandparents in their study said they would choose their role as primary caregiver again. In a population of skipped generation families in Zambia, Reijer (2013) also found that, although these families were particularly plagued by extreme poverty, they preferred to stay together rather than live separately and potentially fare better economically. And with regard to the health problems that many studies in this review found, one study in Taiwan actually found that grandparent caregivers (but not necessarily in a skipped generation household) had better self-rated health, fewer depressive symptoms, and reduced mobility limitations than grandparents who were not caretaking (Ku et al., 2013).

Baker and Silverstein's (2012) work in China with the "family maximizer" grandparents focuses on benefits. In their sample of Chinese skipped generation households, the decision that grandparents would provide care to grandchildren was a family strategy in which family members entered into this arrangement together with everyone's gain in mind. Grandparents received material benefits through the economic successes of the middle generation working in China's industrial cities and had enhanced psychological well-being (Baker & Silverstein, 2012).

In Thailand, there is also a trend in research that accounts for the costs while exploring the benefits (and neutralities) of living in a skipped generation household. Knodel, Kespichayawattana, Saengtienchai, and Wiwatwanich (2010) concluded that there was "little support for [an] alarmist view" (p. 811), instead finding many nuanced and variable ways that families adapt to changing social and economic circumstances. Additionally, Thang (2012) found that the Thai grandparents were "notable for the majority . . . refer[ring] to caring for the grandchildren as a pleasure . . . [and an] opportunity to prove one's usefulness" (p. 66). Similarly, Narongchai and Ayuwat (2011) concluded that living in a skipped generation household enhances close relationships between grandchildren and grandparents and that grown grandchildren often help with household chores. By using a cost and benefit approach, our study contributes to this emerging trend in research as we explore the joys, difficulties, and mixed feelings of Thai grandparents in skipped generation households.

THEMES IN THIS CHAPTER

This chapter is guided by four themes that explore family dynamics in skipped generation households with a particular focus on the left-behind grandparents.

How adult migrant children contribute to the household. It is important to understand the ways in which migrant children support the household from afar. Their role is crucial in the story of a skipped generation household, be that through remittances, food, or material goods. Their contributions or lack thereof may also affect the relationship between the migrant and those who are left behind.

How grandparents cope with separation. The grandparents who are caring for their grandchildren must also deal with the psychological effects of separation from their migrant children. We examine how visits from their migrant children, as well as the use of cell phones, help grandparents cope but can also result in more tensions.

How religion shapes grandparents' views of caregiving. In Thailand, most of the population is Buddhist, and religion plays an integral role in the lives of the people. Their religious beliefs are likely to influence the perspectives of grandparents who are caring for their grandchildren.

How grandparents are impacted. This literature review has highlighted research that focuses on the effects of skipped generation households in terms of costs and benefits. Our chapter will build on existing research to explore how these households adapt to their different circumstances and how grandparents experience their role as primary caregivers.

Study Description

Grandparents in our study were recruited from three areas of Thailand: Phitsanulok (in Northern Thailand), Khon Kaen (in Northeastern Thailand,) and Kanchanaburi (in Western Thailand). These regions (see Figure 2.1 for map) were selected because they have a high proportion of adults who migrate to other parts of the country to find employment (Jampaklay et al., 2012; Thailand National Statistical Office, 2006) and because these areas have been used in previous research (Jampaklay et al., 2012) due to the fact that they represent different regions within Thailand and thus provide some variability with respect to economic and sociocultural context. The criteria we used to identify grandparents in skipped generation households included (1) the interviewee was at least 50 years old, (2) the interviewee was a grandparent to at least one grandchild who lived with him or her, (3) both of the grandchild's parents had migrated outside of the district at least 3 months earlier and had not visited home during that time, and (4) none of the interviewee's other children lived in the household.

We used two recruitment strategies to identify interviewees who met our study criteria. One strategy was to contact the directors of community health centers at the subdistrict level[1] in each of three regions in Thailand where we planned to conduct our fieldwork. These directors then identified potential research participants who would likely qualify for the study, and they asked local village health volunteers (VHVs) to introduce us to these potential participants. The second strategy was to work directly with the VHVs or village headmen and women who knew the backgrounds of individuals in their villages and could introduce us to potential participants. Using these two recruitment strategies, we subsequently met with the potential participants in their homes, described the study to them, established their eligibility, and obtained informed consent from those who were eligible. At the conclusion of each interview, we provided study participants with a carrying bag.

CHARACTERISTICS OF THE GRANDPARENTS AND THEIR FAMILIES

We conducted interviews within 42 skipped generation households (14 households in each province) in which grandparents were caring for grandchildren while their adult children had migrated. We interviewed a total of 48 grandparents (36 grandmothers and 12 grandfathers). Most of these interviews were conducted

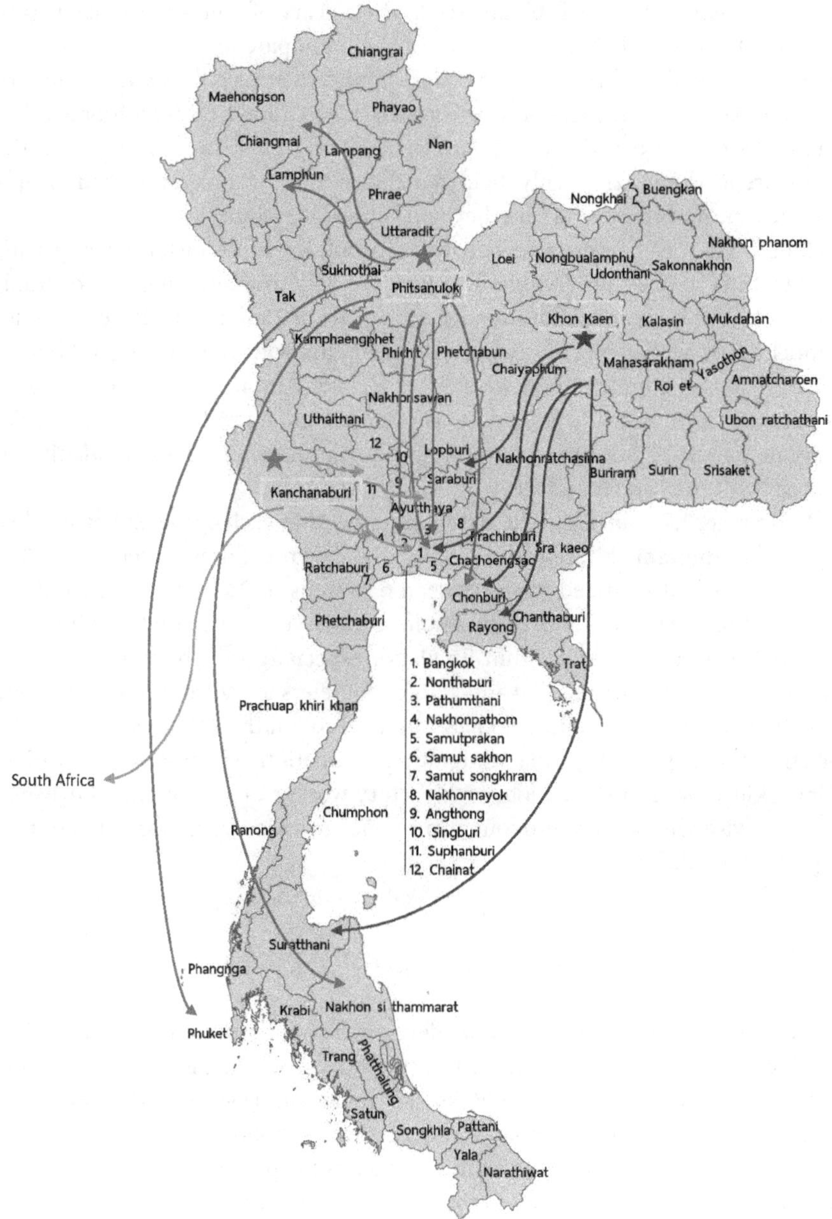

Figure 2.1. Migration patterns from regions represented in this study.

with a single grandparent (n = 36), but, when they were available, interviews were conducted with both members of the couple. This approach resulted in 36 interviews with a single grandparent and 6 interviews with couples (n = 12 husbands and wives).

Interviewees ranged in age from 51 to 82 with an average age of 62.9 years. All of them were Buddhist. Most were still married, but some were widowed and a few were either separated or divorced. Their years of education ranged from none to 14 years, and about two-thirds of the grandparents were working. They generally worked as farmers, food sellers, and basket or silk weavers. Most of the grandparents indicated that they were in fair to good health with only a few grandparents who described their health as either very bad or very good. The grandparents were fairly evenly divided between those who said they had insufficient income and those who said they had sufficient income.

Households were comprised of between two and six people (including the grandparent). Interviewees lived with one to five grandchildren (ave. number of child/household = 1.9). Grandchildren ranged in age from 7 months to 28 years. Older grandchildren were generally living in households with their younger siblings. On average, the grandchildren were 8.7 years old. Among these grandchildren, 39 were the children of the grandparents' adult daughters and 39 were children of the grandparents' adult sons. Interestingly, four grandparents had grandchildren of both adult sons and daughters.

On average, 2.7 adult children had migrated within each of the 42 households. These adult migrant children who had left their own children in the care of the grandparents had migrated from between 6 months to 23 years earlier, with an average of 9.9 years earlier per household. Almost all of the adult children had migrated to other regions within Thailand, especially to urban areas such as Bangkok, that were between 20 and 1,195 kilometers away from home. The one exception was an adult child who had migrated to South Africa. (See Figure 2.1 for a map that depicts the primary migration destinations.) They generally worked at low-skilled or semi-skilled jobs (e.g., factory workers, merchants, and drivers), and their visits home were infrequent (i.e., once or twice each year, often during important holidays).

INTERVIEW GUIDELINE AND FIELD NOTES

To address our research questions, we developed an in-depth interview guideline that focused on family dynamics within the intergenerational family (Bengtson & Roberts, 1981; Clarke, Preston, Raksin, & Bengtson, 1999; Katz & Lowenstein, 2010). We asked about the relationships between grandparents, their migrant children, and their grandchildren. In addition, we kept field notes based on our observations of what transpired during each of the interviews.

ANALYSIS OF INTERVIEWS

All the interviews with the grandparents were tape-recorded, transcribed in Thai, and translated into English. We employed several strategies, suggested by qualitative researchers, to address concerns about trustworthiness and rigor when conducting qualitative data analysis (Padgett, 2008). We used data triangulation (i.e., we analyzed responses to the open-ended questions in Thai and English and compared participant responses with our field observation notes) and observer/interdisciplinary triangulation (i.e., our team included a demographer, a social worker, and a sociologist who independently read the research materials). In addition, we had team debriefing sessions in which the investigators talked regularly about their analytic decisions and interpretations. Finally, we maintained an audit trail to document the decisions made during our team meetings.

How Adult Migrant Children Contribute to the Household

In our interviews with grandparents, there was considerable discussion about the ways in which members of each generation provided support to the other generations.

Adult Migrant Children Provide Financial Assistance

Though it is expected in Thai society for migrant children to send home a portion of their wages (remittances) to their aging parents (Knodel, Saengtienchai, & Sittitrai, 1995; Knodel & Chayovan, 2009), this expectation is particularly strong when adult children migrate and leave their children in the care of grandparents (Knodel et al., 2010). For example, a 64-year-old grandmother received remittances from the parents of her two grandchildren, one of whom was an infant. She explained her expectations about financial assistance from these adult migrants in the following way: "They have to give us (remittances) for our living expenses and their children's since we raise their kids."

A similar perspective was offered by a 52-year-old grandmother who, along with her 57-year-old husband, was caring for three grandchildren. All of these grandchildren, two of whom were infant twins, were the children of their eldest daughter. The grandmother explained that, although all three of her children sent home remittances, only the eldest daughter sent home money on a regular basis. Her daughter's willingness to send home an adequate amount of money was a deciding factor in the grandmother's willingness to provide the care.

The receipt of remittances from their migrant children sometimes played a crucial role not only in grandparents' ability to provide care to their grandchild but also in their ability to survive. Some of these grandparents were ill and unable to work; they counted on financial assistance from their migrant children to make ends meet. A 63-year-old grandmother had taken care of her grandson since he was an infant. As an adult, the grandson had migrated, and she now cared for the 3-year-old son of her grandson. The grandmother was in poor health and had problems with her eyesight. Though she received a small old age pension, she relied heavily on the money that her migrant grandson and his wife sent home. She observed that the remittances were sufficient and added, "But if (my grandson's) father does not send me money, it would be difficult . . . I'm afraid that he will starve. I can't work. If his parents don't send money, we will starve."

Adult Migrant Children Provide Food and Material Goods

In addition to financial support, adult migrant children brought or sent food and material goods for the household. A 56-year-old married grandmother with two migrant children listed the numerous kinds of goods that her children brought: "When they visit they bring supplies for the house, laundry soap, cooking oil, cocoa, powdered energy drink, etc."

Migrant children also provided the grandparents with appliances that helped make their housekeeping tasks easier. The 63-year-old grandmother who provided care to her 3-year-old grandson's son was an example. The grandson tried to make his grandmother's caregiving tasks easier by providing her with home appliances. The grandmother pointed out, "He bought the fridge and washing machine for me to use." Similarly, a 57-year-old grandmother with two migrant sons cared for a 5-year-old grandchild. She talked about the numerous ways in which the grandchild's father provided material support. He had helped to furnish her house and bought her a refrigerator and a cell phone.

Another important source of material help that migrant children provided was medicine for the grandparents. A 74-year-old grandfather and his wife cared for two grandchildren (both aged 11), one of whom was the son of his migrant daughter. He talked about the way in which this daughter attended to his health care needs, "Every time she comes, she brings me medicine. All for my health. A lot of medicines."

Adult Migrant Children Serve as a Source of Anticipatory Support

For grandparents, exchanges were also sometimes conceptualized in terms of anticipatory support; that is, assistance they expected to receive in the future. Some grandparents were quite confident that support from their adult migrant children would be forthcoming in the future. For example, a 66-year-old grandfather who, along with his wife, was caring for their 14-year-old granddaughter had two sons, both of whom had migrated. When asked if he anticipated support from his migrant sons, the grandfather replied, "I've certainly talked with my sons about it. So I am more confident that my sons will take care of us."

Other grandparents may not have had direct conversations about the future, but they were nevertheless hopeful that they could count on their migrant children. To illustrate, a 68-year-old grandmother who, along with her husband, was caring for their son's 1-year-old child talked about her expectations of future support in relation to her son's sense of filial responsibility, "We hope he takes care of us. We are his parents." Another grandmother, aged 56, was caring for three grandchildren with the help of her husband. She talked about anticipated support based upon the migrant daughter's long-range plans, "In the back of my mind, I hope they will. Our daughter has built a house nearby and should return later on."

For some grandparents, the ability to anticipate support from their migrant children was complicated by factors that made it difficult to predict the future. A 67-year-old grandmother, along with her husband, was caring for a 15-year-old granddaughter. Both grandparents were in poor health. The grandmother talked about her migrant daughter's willingness to look after her; however, the daughter wanted the grandmother to come live with her. The grandmother had mixed feelings about this anticipated caregiving arrangement and said, "She wants me to sell the land and go to live with her there. I can't decide yet. I'm attached to this place. I don't want to leave." The situation of a 67-year-old widowed grandmother was so precarious that she could not allow herself to anticipate support from her migrant children. Her five migrant children sent home remittances but not on a regular basis. Some months there was enough money, and some months there was not. When asked if she anticipated support in the future from the parents of the four grandchildren for whom she was caring, the grandmother replied, "Sometimes [I] thought about that, but I never hoped that any of my children would care for me. And I'm not sure whether they could take care of me or for how long."

How Grandparents Cope With Separation

Dealing with the separation from their migrant children was a challenge for the grandparents in skipped generation households who missed the closeness that resulted from daily interactions with their adult children. The married 66-year-old grandfather who cared for his 14-year-old granddaughter sadly acknowledged, "it's quiet" without his migrant son in the house. Despite their separation, many grandparents and migrant children maintained connections. Two of the most common ways of coping with separation were visits home from the migrant child and contact via cell phone.

Coping With Separation by Visits Home

Visits from their migrant children helped ease grandparents' feelings of loss and separation. Some families had developed a pattern of visitation in which the migrant children returned to the home of their parents on a regular basis. For example, a married 64-year-old grandmother looked after two grandchildren (aged 10 months and 5 years). Her son, the father of the younger child, consistently visited as she said, "Once a month."

For some families, rather than visiting on a regular basis, visits home were timed around specific holidays. In Thailand, adult children commonly visit their parents during Thai New Year or Songkran in April, Father's Day in December, Mother's Day in August, and then during the important religious holidays such as the beginning or end of the Buddhist Lent (Knodel et al., 2010; Knodel & Saengtienchai, 2007). Adult children in our skipped generation families were no exception to this normative pattern of holiday visits. In some cases, the migrant children visited on more holidays than did their siblings who had not left their children behind in the care of grandparents. An example was the married 52-year-old grandmother who was caring for infant twins and the 9-year old son of one of her migrant children. She explained the differential holiday visiting patterns among her three migrant children: "Once a year. All three come near New Year's. The parents of the twins come at Songkran as well." The married 56-year-old grandmother with two migrant children described how her son's visits had increased since he left his child behind in her care, "(My son) comes more often now to visit (his child). Before it was twice a year for New Year's or Songkran. Now he comes every holiday."

For other families, the visits occurred on an as-needed basis, especially when the grandparents or their children were sick or required help. A grandfather, aged 74, and his wife, aged 72, had four migrant sons all of whom worked at a considerable distance from the family home. The grandparents lived with three grandchildren (aged 9, 11, 28) and explained, "If we are sick, they drive here immediately. . . . Each family drives a separate car. . . . The trip takes 2 days and one night. They don't get to sleep. They stop over at the gas station for 2 hours. They don't stop driving the whole day." Another example was the 67-year-old widow caring for four grandchildren whose financial situation was very precarious. She had recently been in a motorcycle accident. When her migrant children heard about the accident, they returned as quickly as they could. This as-needed pattern of visitation also occurred when the grandchildren were ill. This same widowed grandmother who was caring for four grandchildren explained, "When their child is sick—I call them and say I need help. . . . Then they will come."

The importance of family visits was highlighted in a few situations in which migrant children did not visit on a regular basis or as promised. One grandmother, aged 62, lived separately from her husband who was a Buddhist monk. She cared for the two children (aged 6 and 11) of her migrant son and two children of her migrant daughter (aged 16 and 17). Both of these adult children were divorced and experiencing financial problems. Their visits home were infrequent and irregular. The grandmother did not feel that she could count on her children for help. She expressed her worry and frustration when she stated, "Some years they come, some years not. It's unpredictable. I'm telling you the truth." Another example was the 63-year-old widowed grandmother who cared for the 3-year-old son of her grandson. Her grandson was inconsistent in his visits home, and it upset her when he did not visit as promised: "Sometimes. During Buddhist Lent, he (the grandson) said that he would come, but didn't come. He said he would come during the New Year." Such cases illuminate the grandparents' need for continuity and predictability in the visits of their adult children.

When adult children did not visit on a regular, predictable, or as-needed basis, grandparents were hurt but tried to make sense of their children's behaviors by using a variety of rationalizations. One such rationalization focused on their children's work responsibilities and the expense associated with visits home. A 51-year-old married grandmother who cared for three grandchildren (aged 2 to 10) rationalized her adult children's infrequent visits, ". . . only three times a year. It's expensive to travel from Rayong or Chonburi roundtrip." Similarly, the widowed 57-year-old grandmother with two migrant sons said that, though she would like her sons to visit more often, she thought that they needed to keep working and save money for their own children's education. She explained, "They come but not that often since they have work obligations and the cost of travel is expensive." Another rationalization focused on changes in their adult child's living preferences since they had migrated. To illustrate, a widowed 63-year-old grandmother who was caring for her 9-year-old grandson was hurt by the irregular and brief visits of her migrant daughter. She tried to explain that her daughter "does not stay overnight; never has since she first left. She and her husband are too used to urban living."

Coping With Separation via Cell Phone Contact

Another vital source of connection was cell phone contact. In Thailand, the use of cell phones is now widespread due to improvements in cell tower technology and increased affordability (Knodel et al., 2010; Knodel & Saengtienchai, 2007). While in the past migrant families had to rely on letter writing, this form of communication is now seldom used. A widowed grandmother, aged 58, explained that when her two daughters first migrated several years ago, they communicated via letters. However, now things have changed: "after we had cell phones there was no need to write."

Also available on cell phones in Thailand is a service called "Line," which has a video function that allows the speakers to talk and to see each other. One 62-year-old widowed grandmother with two adult migrant children lived with her 16-year-old grandson. She explained, "Nowadays, there are mobile phones and Line for communication. Using Line for talking is free so we talk almost every day. We can also see each other. After they (her migrant children) finish work, they call me."

Having a cell phone allowed grandparents to be in contact and remain close with their migrant children. For example, a 52-year-old grandmother and her 60-year-old husband cared for three grandchildren, aged 8 months, 5 years, and 6 years. While their migrant children were only able to visit once each year, they sometimes called multiple times each day. Several grandparents talked about how having contact via cell phone allowed them to maintain a sense of emotional closeness with their migrant children. A widowed grandmother, aged 58, had two migrant daughters and now lived with her 9-year-old grandson as well as her own parents. She described her feelings of connection to her two migrant daughters, "Yes, very close . . . like they've never moved away. We talk on the phone a lot." The 51-year-old grandmother who cared for three of her grandchildren (aged 2 to 10) was another example. She had two migrant sons and said about her relationship with them, "I feel close to them even without touching. That's because we share our happiness and hardships every day. Our feelings for each other haven't changed. Even though we can't see each other, the telephone can fill that gap."

Talking to their migrant children on the phone helped diminish grandparents' worries about their adult children's well-being. A 64-year-old widowed grandmother was caring for two of her grandchildren, aged 7 and 15. Four of her adult children had migrated. The migrant son who was the father of the two grandchildren visited home only once per year while some of her other migrant children came home even less frequently. The grandmother had a cell phone and called her migrant children when she had money on her account. She explained plaintively, "I need to hear their voices."

Contact via cell phone also enabled grandparents to share their daily lives with their migrant children. Respondents reported that much of the content of their calls revolved around describing their activities during the day. For example, a married 64-year-old grandmother cared for the 8-year-old daughter of her youngest daughter. She felt particularly close to this adult daughter with whom she connected through regular phone calls: "We talk about ordinary things, food, troubles, happiness, health, the weather, money, and savings . . . things like that." Migrant children showed their concern for their parents by asking about their day-to-day activities. The 74-year-old grandfather who cared, along with his wife, for two grandsons (both aged 11) described the content of his phone calls with his migrant daughter who was the mother of his grandson and with his migrant sons. He said, "They will ask, 'Are you going to bed?' 'What did you eat rice with?' 'How are you?' My older son usually asks about my health. 'How are you?' The one in Petchaboon is like this. He does not speak much. 'That's all.' . . . My daughter first asks, 'What did you cook today?' 'What are you doing?' "

In *Migration and New Media: Transnational Families and Polymedia,* Madianou and Miller (2012) discuss the importance of such phone conversations, as well as texts and emails, in maintaining contact about everyday life. Conversations about "ordinary things"—the minutiae of life—are examples of what anthropologist Bronislaw Malinowski (1923/1989) called "phatic communion" (p. 315), or conversations that function to establish or maintain social contact not convey information. Colloquially, this is known as "small talk," and it is an important part of family life enabled by the cell phone.

The crucial role of the cell phone in maintaining family ties was reinforced by those who did not have easy access to such technology. One example was the husband, aged 74, and his wife, aged 72, who had four migrant sons and cared for three grandchildren (aged 9, 11, and 28). The grandmother talked about her inability to use the cell phone as a means of contacting her migrant children and indicated that, "I don't know how to call. They only call me." For some, the cell phone was related to frustration when the call was disconnected because their prepaid service had run out. An 82-year-old grandmother had been caring for her 23-year-old grandson since he was 15 days old. The grandmother was very poor and could not afford the cost of initiating phone calls. Instead, she directed her grandson to call his father and request that he return the call. However, even this approach led to frustration because when her son called back, "we get cut off because there isn't enough money in the phone account."

It is important to note that the cell phone, while vital to family connections, also can contribute to family tension. One source of family tension was when migrant children called home and asked to talk to some family members but not others. A 77-year-old grandfather provided most of the care for his 4-year-old grandson because his younger wife still worked outside the home. The grandfather described how phone calls worked when his migrant daughter called home: "Usually she [the migrant daughter] calls her mother." The following comment about this pattern of contact suggested that it made him feel overlooked and possibly jealous: "Once in a long time, she will talk with me." Similarly, a 60-year-old grandfather, along with his wife, cared for two grandchildren (aged 7 and 8). He also seemed to feel hurt when his migrant daughter, the mother of the grandchildren for whom he was caring, asked to speak to the grandmother rather than to him. Perhaps as an effort to cover his wounded feelings, the grandfather reported about her phone calls, "We don't talk very much now. I let her talk to her mother."

Another source of tension was when the purpose of the call from the migrant child focused solely on asking for additional assistance. In one instance, a married 67-year-old grandfather was caring for two granddaughters (aged 14 and 27) as well as a great-granddaughter (aged 5). His oldest son migrated several years ago, was divorced, and continued to have financial difficulties. The grandfather was frustrated that this son called home only when he needed money. The grandfather acknowledged that the migrant son "never calls. If he does, it is only to ask for a loan."

A third source of tension was when the grandparents' expectations about contact with their migrant children were not met. For example, a 52-year-old widowed grandmother was caring for two grandchildren, a 3-year-old grandson and a 13-year-old granddaughter. She had considerable contact with her migrant son who was the father of the grandson but much less contact with her migrant daughter, her granddaughter's mother. The grandmother felt abandoned by her migrant daughter who rarely visited or called. The grandmother observed with frustration, "She is undependable. Some months, she won't call at all." A similar narrative that was suggestive of family tension was related by a 55-year-old grandmother who, along with her 60-year-old husband, cared for their 5-year-old grandson. Their adopted daughter, the grandson's mother was divorced from her husband and made little effort to be in touch with her parents or her son. To make matters worse, the daughter had changed her cell phone number, making it impossible for the grandmother to contact her migrant daughter.

Again, grandparents coped by rationalizing when their adult children's phone contact did not meet their expectations. The most typical rationalization was that their children were working and were too busy to call home. For example, the 62-year-old grandmother whose husband left home to be a Buddhist monk worried about her two migrant children. They were both divorced and experiencing economic problems. She described her efforts to be in touch with them: "We communicate by phone. Sometimes they call me, or I call them. But they don't always answer. . . . I just called them 2–3 days ago but could not get through. They were working." Similar was the situation of the 74-year-old grandfather and his wife who were caring for two grandchildren (both aged 11), one of whom was the son of a migrant daughter and the other the son of a migrant son. While the daughter called frequently, the son did not. The grandfather noted that this migrant son "calls once a month. He is very busy."

How Religion Shapes Grandparents' Views of Caregiving

All of the grandparents in our sample were Buddhists. Not surprisingly, a number of them made references to their religious beliefs as they talked about the ways in which they viewed their role as grandparents in skipped generation households. Here, we focus on the grandparents who incorporated concepts from Buddhism—especially karma, merit-making, and acceptance—as they discussed their caregiving roles.

Believing in Karma

Central to Buddhism are the concepts of incarnation (i.e., each individual is reborn multiple times) and karma. According to the law of karma, each action has a consequence that will be experienced in this life or the next. Good deeds will result in beneficial consequences (e.g., health, happiness, affluence, spiritual growth), whereas bad deeds will result in negative outcomes (e.g., sickness, suffering, and impoverishment). Related to the law of karma is the belief that one's current situation is the result of one's good and bad deeds from this life and previous lives that have accumulated over time (Ingersoll, 1966; Kirsch, 1977; Pfanner & Ingersoll, 1962; Podhisita, 1998).

Several grandparents reported that their belief in karma provided a reason for why they were looking after their grandchildren. A couple who was caring for their 11-year-old grandson used the concept of karma to explain why it made sense for them to be caring for him. The grandmother (aged 56) explicitly talked about caregiving as part of a "circle of karma." She explained that when she and her husband were first married and had their sons, their parents lived with them and helped raise the sons. By thinking of caregiving in terms of her karma, the grandmother was framing her situation in terms that provided meaning and structure to her caregiving role. Her husband (aged 61) referred to karma in an implicit way when asked who was happier—older people who cared for their grandchildren versus those who did not care for grandchildren. He reasoned, "I guess those who care for their grandchildren are happier because we must be good enough to have the opportunity to do it. We feel proud and happy to have children and grandchildren. We don't think they're our burden. They bring us happiness really." The grandfather's observation that "we must be good enough to have the opportunity" was probably an indirect reference to his karma. For him, the fact that he was caring for his grandson was most likely an indication that his accumulated good deeds had resulted in good karma that, in turn, made him worthy of this caregiving role.

Similar was the grandmother (aged 62) whose husband had left to become a Buddhist monk, and who was caring for four grandchildren. She explained that she had talked to her husband about her caregiving situation and he had told her, "it was not a bad fate but meritorious." In this case, her husband helped the grandmother to see her caregiving role as a reflection of her karma. That is, because she had good karma, she had been given the opportunity to take care of her grandchildren.

A belief in karma also appeared to shape the thoughts of a grandfather who talked about how lucky he was to have grandchildren who were well-behaved and loving toward each other. This was the grandfather (aged 74) with four migrant sons who, along with his wife (aged 72) was caring for one son's three children (aged 9 to 28). The grandfather noted, "Some people have children and grandchildren who misbehave. Our children and grandchildren don't do anything bad, so our mind is at ease. It's hard to find anything better than this." His contentment is likely associated with the Buddhist belief that having children who are well-behaved or poorly behaved is a result of the parents' karma. According to Smuckarn (1998), Thai parents who have children who behave badly believe that this is a result of the parents' bad deeds in a previous life. For this grandfather, a belief in karma seemed to provide him with a sense of satisfaction. He understood that his own good karma had resulted in his well-behaved and loving grandchildren.

Making Merit

Intertwined with karma are two additional concepts that are key to Thai popular Buddhism. One concept is *bun* (i.e., doing good deeds and the resulting good outcomes) and the other is *bap* (i.e., doing bad deeds and the resulting bad outcomes). Good deeds contribute to merit, and bad deeds contribute to demerit. Each person's accumulation of merits and demerits throughout their multiple incarnations are how Thai Buddhists explain the good and bad events that occur in daily life. To accumulate more merit, Buddhists participate in merit-making activities that generally have a religious focus but can also be nonreligious. Religious activities include a variety of activities that support the temple (e.g., providing food, donations, and gifts to the monks), meditating, or praying. Nonreligious activities may involve taking care of others or shared activities, such as digging wells and building roads for the community. *Bun* and *bap* are related to the "law of karma" in that all deeds, whether bad or good, will have a consequence. Thus, merit-making activities (i.e., the doing of good deeds) are seen as an investment, which will result in good outcomes in the future (Ingersoll, 1966; Kirsch, 1977; Pfanner & Ingersoll, 1962; Podhisita, 1998).

Some of the grandparents we interviewed talked about caring for grandchildren as a merit-making activity. That is, the care that they were providing could be seen as a good deed that would have a positive consequence for them in the future. The 61-year-old grandfather who described his caregiving role as a result of his good karma also saw caregiving as an opportunity to make more merit. He stated very simply that caring for his grandchildren was "a source of merit and happiness." For this grandfather, caring for his grandchildren provided him with the opportunity to increase what Kirsch (1977) refers to as a "store of merit" (p. 246).

A 59-year-old widowed grandmother who was caring for four grandchildren (aged 4–9) began to cry as she talked about the stress associated with her responsibilities. She had expected that the children's parents would send her remittances, but they had not. She observed that other people she knew had suggested that her caregiving situation was the result of bad karma from misdeeds she had committed with the children's families in a previous life. The grandmother was not sure that she agreed with this interpretation; however, she was clear on one thing: "I care for these children as merit-making." In this way, the grandmother appeared to be trying to make sense of and find meaning in a very difficult situation. She reasoned that if she was not able to get financial support for providing her grandchildren's care, she would think of her caregiving role as a way of merit-making. She took this line of thought one step further by stating, "I just hope I can raise them to be self-sufficient and then they can perhaps help me out." This perspective probably allowed the grandmother to anticipate that her efforts to care for the grandchildren would provide her with an increased "store of merit" for this life or the next and with the possibility of direct assistance later in this life.

Another grandmother made the connection between merit-making, good, health, and caregiving in a somewhat different sequence of causes and effects. This was the 58-year-old widow with two migrant daughters who was caring for one daughter's son (aged 9) as well as her own parents. According to this grandmother's perspective, her accumulation of merit had resulted in her good health, which in turn allowed her to care for both her grandson and her parents. As she described her efforts to make merit, she explained, "I haven't committed any sins, but am always making merit by giving alms to the monks. I also help the poor and those in need. I'm sure I received my good health in return." Her beliefs also helped frame the connection between her good health and her caregiving. As she explained, "*Sathu* [thanks to the Bhudda]. I pray for my good health. Angels in heaven probably want me to be healthy so I can take care of my parents and grandchild." For this grandmother, her religious beliefs provided an understanding of the connection between her merit and her caregiving. She reasoned that the merit she made from both her religious and nonreligious good deeds had resulted in good karma that was reflected by her good health. Furthermore, it was her good health that allowed her to be a caregiver for her grandchildren and her parents.

It is important to note that the grandparent's beliefs about making merit were not always a source of gratification in relation to caring for grandchildren. Indeed, beliefs about the importance of merit-making occasionally clashed with caregiving roles. One example was the 64-year-old married grandmother who was caring for two grandchildren (aged 10 months and 5 years). She enjoyed the companionship of her grandchildren but was also frustrated because her caregiving responsibilities limited freedom to participate in activities outside the home that would allow her to make more merit. As she said, "What I regret most is not being able to get out and participate in community activities like merit-making."

Accepting Life Circumstances

According to Buddhist teaching, suffering is a fundamental aspect of the human condition that arises from an attachment to permanence and an inability to accept change. A belief in karma provides the perspective that suffering is the consequence of past misdeeds. This perspective can facilitate individuals' ability to accept difficult situations as beyond their control. An acceptance of difficult circumstances may, in turn, result in greater personal equanimity, a characteristic that is revered within Buddhism (Limanonda, 1995; Podhisita, 1998; Rahula, 1959).

A focus on accepting the difficulties associated with caring for grandchildren emerged several times during our interviews with the grandparents. For example, the 51-year-old married grandmother who cared for three grandchildren (aged 2 to 10) talked about how surprised she had been when she learned that her oldest son, who had not yet finished school, had gotten his girlfriend pregnant. After the birth of her son's child, the grandmother agreed to care for the child. She and her husband were now caring for two additional grandchildren. The grandmother acknowledged that caring for three grandchildren was challenging, but most of her narrative focused on an acceptance of her caregiving role. She said, "it's not easy to take the role of the parents again after you've raised your own kids because we're old people now, but we must accept it." The way in which she was able to accommodate to her role appeared to be influenced by the Buddhist perspective on acceptance of difficulties and by "letting go" of expectations and worries. As the grandmother explained,

> No, I don't dwell too much on the problems. We are bound to have grandchildren. We have to live. We can't all have a rosy world. We can't control the future. What we can do is make the best of today and deal with the future when it comes because we don't know what the future will bring. I do my best today and go to bed and don't live in a dream world [and wish for things]. Just live for today.

A 67-year-old married grandmother who cared for her 15-year-old granddaughter provides another example of acceptance. The grandmother was in poor health, and so she was no longer able to provide much physical care for her granddaughter. She was not eager to be a caregiver but saw her role in relation to lack of merit and explained her reasoning in the following way: "Those who don't have to raise grandchildren have merit. We don't have merit so we need to raise grandchildren." For this grandmother, her religious views appeared to help her understand why she was responsible for providing care to her granddaughter.

The 62-year-old grandmother whose husband had left to become a Buddhist monk and who was caring for four grandchildren provides an additional illustration of acceptance. While caring for her grandchildren, this woman was also coping with financial problems and with her own poor health. She spoke of her health (e.g., fainting episodes), her poverty, and her caregiving in relation to her karma. When the interviewer asked about her fainting spells, the grandmother replied, "I accept it as my fate, my karma." She also replied to the interviewer's question about how much longer she would continue to be able to provide care with a similar response, "I don't know. It depends upon my karma." Her acceptance of her situation was further developed in her description of her financial situation, "we have so little and are not well off like others. But I was born like this, so what can I do?" Her ability to view her situation as a result of her own karma appeared to provide this grandmother with some degree of equanimity while she coped with a confluence of difficulties.

Although our respondents attempted to accept the burdens associated with caregiving, the suffering of some was still apparent. Their pain seemed to be most acute when their adult children were irresponsible and contributed to their caregiving difficulties. For example, a 59-year-old grandmother was separated from her husband. Her son and daughter-in-law had divorced and left their children (aged 8 and 11) behind with her. The grandmother talked about how disappointed she was in her son's behavior. He drank, mistreated his children, and was critical of his mother's efforts to make merit by making donations to the monks. She plaintively summarized her reactions to her son and her caregiving situation by stating,

> It makes me sad. I didn't raise him to be like this . . . he never listens to anybody anymore. It must be some bad karma from a previous life. So I accept my fate that I have to take care of his children. Otherwise, who will take care of them?

How Grandparents Are Impacted

As the grandparents described the ways in which caring for grandchildren affected their lives, they talked about a number of negative as well as positive reactions. Here, we examine first their negative feelings and then turn to their positive feelings. Finally, we discuss the ways in which most grandparents had a mixture of both positive and negative emotions about their roles as caregivers to grandchildren.

Negative Feelings

During the course of our interviews with the grandparents, there were a number of commonly mentioned negative emotions associated with their caregiving responsibilities.

Worries About Own Health and Future of Their Grandchildren

Some of the grandparents worried about their own health and how this could impact their grandchildren. For example, a 72-year-old widowed woman was caring for two grandsons, aged 9 and 13. Her daughter rarely visited or sent home remittances, and, despite her own physical disabilities, the older woman tried valiantly to make ends meet by working cutting lemon grass. When the interviewer asked the grandmother how she felt about raising two grandchildren, she responded, "Struggle only. I think I'll struggle until I die." The older woman worried about her grandsons' future. She felt strongly that they should not go to live with their mother, whom they barely knew. Rather, she thought, they should live with their uncle instead. In this case, the older woman's worries about her own health were exacerbated by her concerns about the future welfare of her grandsons.

Similarly, the 77-year-old grandfather whose wife worked full time had reluctantly taken over the care of his infant grandson when his daughter called to ask for help. The grandfather worried about how his eventual death would impact his grandson, who was now 4 years old. He reported that his grandson was unruly and that he was concerned that neither his wife nor his daughter would be able to manage the child. This grandfather had a back-up plan for his grandson's future: send him to a Buddhist temple in the provinces and have him ordained as a monk. In this way, the temple could serve as a safety net if, upon the grandfather's death, the family could not take care of him.

Worried About Ability to Meet Financial Costs

Many of the grandparents had counted on remittances from their migrant children in order to support their grandchildren. For a variety of reasons (e.g., unplanned pregnancies, low-paying jobs, divorce, remarriage, expenses associated with a new family), these remittances generally did not come often enough or were not substantial enough for the grandparents to make ends meet. As a result, our respondents expressed concerns about not having enough money to cover basic needs such as milk and diapers for the younger grandchildren. To illustrate, a grandmother and grandfather, both aged 59, talked about feeding their infant grandson rice water and sugar when they were unable to afford milk. For those with older grandchildren, financial worries were often related to not having enough money to pay for school-related expenses.

Another example was the 64-year old widow who called her migrant children when she had money in her cell phone account. With the understanding that they would be sending home remittances, she had given each of them her blessing when they asked if they could leave home. The grandmother had hoped that, with their financial support, "I wouldn't have to do the arduous fieldwork." Unfortunately, her hopes were not realized, and she eventually had to continue the backbreaking fieldwork while also caring for two of her grandchildren (now aged 7 and 15) who came to live with her. Although her two sons (i.e., the fathers of the grandchildren) helped by paying for her cell phone and buying household appliances, the money they sent home was not enough to meet her expenses. Instead, in addition to working in the fields to raise rice and sugarcane, she needed to borrow money. Worries about her financial condition emerged throughout her interview. She worried that her poor health made it hard for her to work which, in turn, made it difficult to financially support her grandchildren. She worried that, despite the fact that they were good students, there would not be enough money to pay for further education. When asked how the government might help, the widowed grandmother said that she would like a scholarship for her grandchildren to continue their schooling. As she observed, "We could use help with the computer and internet costs. It's not like before with paper and pencil."

A similar case was the 52-year-old widowed grandmother who was caring for two grandchildren (aged 3 and 13), both of whose parents had migrated. Her son, the father of the younger grandchild, called, visited, and sent remittances, but her daughter, the mother of the older grandchild rarely visited and did not send home any money. Though the grandmother received some support from her daughter's estranged husband, who sent regular remittances to cover the costs of the granddaughter's schooling, the grandmother's financial situation was precarious and she worried: "will her father stop sending support? I am getting older by the day and have nothing to spare in case of urgent need. Her father is a playboy and just might disappear."

Feeling Trapped by Their Responsibilities

Another source of frustration was a feeling of being limited due to their caregiving responsibilities. Some of the grandparents regretted missing opportunities to socialize, travel, work, or go to the temple. The 59-year-old grandmother who was separated from her husband and was caring for two grandchildren (aged 8 and 11) was one example. They were the children of her son, who had a drinking problem and was divorced from his wife. The remittances that the grandmother received from her son were inadequate. She felt unsupported by her son and former daughter-in-law as she struggled to raise their children. When the interviewer asked if she had anticipated being the primary caregiver for her grandchildren, the older woman described her feelings of entrapment, "I thought it would be easier. I thought it was good that my son had a wife and family. And I could be free to go places, like Myanmar with a tour group. . . . Now, with these two grandchildren and their parents gone, I can't go anywhere."

Similar was the 64-year-old married grandmother who cared for two of her grandchildren (aged 10 months and 5 years). Her teeth blackened by betel nut, this grandmother continued to work and care for her grandchildren while talking to the interviewer. She cut fish, gave her younger grandchild a bath, and then gave her a bottle. Though she was receiving remittances on a regular basis and the family income was sufficient, the grandmother lamented her inability to participate in activities, especially those related to the local Buddhist temple. She stated, "It is like I am imprisoned here."

Positive Feelings

Even while grandparents described their negative emotions about caring for their grandchildren, they also elaborated on their positive feelings.

Sense of Purposefulness

Feeling that their life had additional meaning was one positive aspect of caregiving. Grandparents talked about how being involved in their grandchildren's daily activities provided them with a sense of purpose. For example, a married 60-year-old grandmother was caring for three grandsons (aged 8, 11, 22). When the interviewer asked if caring for these grandchildren was more happiness or more burden, the grandmother replied,

> It's more happiness than a burden. That's because there would be no other relatives in the household otherwise. With the grandchildren, we

> have activities to do such as bathing them and preparing them for school in the morning. Without that it would just be me and my husband with nothing to do.

Another example was the married 52-year-old grandmother who cared for infant twins and a 9-year-old grandson. Even though she acknowledged that it was difficult caring for twins, she also emphasized the sense of purposefulness that she experienced as compared to those older people who had no grandchildren. She observed, "The woman without grandchildren just sits around doing nothing." Later she added, "The neighbors over here are also my age but without grandchildren. They've said they wish they had grandchildren to care for."

Enjoy Companionship of Grandchildren

Perhaps most striking in interviewees' responses was the frequent mention of how enjoyable it was to have grandchildren in the house. Several grandparents noted their "warm feelings" toward their grandchildren and a deep appreciation for their companionship. To illustrate, a 51-year-old widowed woman was caring for two granddaughters (aged 5 and 6). One was her daughter's child, and the other was her son's child. She had a close relationship with both of her granddaughters and spoke of the numerous ways in which she enjoyed her caregiving role. The grandmother asserted that she thought it was good that she was raising her grandchildren. When the interviewer asked why she felt this way, the grandmother explained, "It's not lonely. . . . It's good because I have company. If I don't have both of them, I will be alone." The older woman went on to say that when one of her granddaughters was gone, she felt lonely. Recently, her daughter had asked to take both girls home with her for the summer holiday, but the grandmother had refused her request saying that she wanted to have at least one of her granddaughters at home with her. When her daughter took her own daughter home for the summer holiday and left the other child behind, the grandmother said, "I missed my grandchild terribly. . . . There are usually three of us."

Other grandparents elaborated on the ways in which their grandchildren added laughter and joy to their lives. The grandmother (aged 56) and grandfather (aged 61) who were caring for their 11-year-old grandson both agreed that their grandchild's companionship helped fill a void in their own relationship.

> INTERVIEWER: So if you compare your situation to others your age who do not care for a grandchild, who do you think is happier?
>
> GRANDFATHER: I think people like us would be happier having their grandchild with them. Just living by yourself would be too lonely.
>
> GRANDMOTHER: We don't talk much to each other because he goes to work and I go to the fields. So with [grandson] here, there is someone to talk with.

Ambivalence

While we have distinguished thus far between the positive and the negative feelings of the grandparents, few of the grandparents had only one set of emotions. In fact, of the grandparents in the 42 households in our study, 40 had a mixture of positive and negative feelings; two were completely positive; and none was completely negative. Here, we highlight some of the ways in which the grandparents talked about their ambivalence in relation to caring for their grandchildren.

When asked to compare the feelings of older people who were caring for grandchildren with those who were not caring for grandchildren, some of the grandparents spoke in terms of "a different kind of happiness." One was the 60-year-old married grandmother who was caring for three grandsons (aged 8, 11, and 22). She was concerned about her oldest grandson's drinking and drug use. When asked to compare her situation to that of older people who were not caring for grandchildren, the grandmother remarked, "They have a different happiness in being able to sleep when they want or go where they want to when they want to. But we have grandchildren to take with us when we go somewhere. So it is a different kind of happiness." The 67-year-old widow who was caring for four grandchildren (aged 3 to 12) spoke about her mixed feelings in a similar way: "The grandparent who does not have to care for their grandchildren should be happier. They can go where they want to, whenever they want. But if you have to care for grandchildren you have to be on-call and constantly mind them. But you receive their love as a result. So it is a different kind of happiness."

A 63-year-old grandmother and a 66-year-old grandfather were caring for two grandchildren (aged 5 and 7). The grandmother began by describing her positive feelings about caring for her grandchildren but gradually acknowledged her negative feelings as well.

INTERVIEWER: Some people say it is happiness to raise one's grandchildren while others say it is a burden and source of suffering. How do you feel?

GRANDMOTHER: I feel happiness raising them. I enjoy talking to them. If they weren't here I wouldn't have anyone to talk with.

INTERVIEWER: And how would you feel if you didn't have them to raise?

GRANDMOTHER: It would be silent in the house.

INTERVIEWER: Do you like a quiet house?

GRANDMOTHER: Yes.

INTERVIEWER: So, which would you choose, raising your grandchildren or living alone?

GRANDMOTHER: In fact, I would prefer not to. I am too lazy to talk to little children. But when I was asked to raise the children, I had to do it.

INTERVIEWER: So if you could choose, you wouldn't?

GRANDMOTHER: If I could choose, I wouldn't. Raising my own children was hard enough. Raising grandchildren makes my life difficult again. I was young and strong when I raised my children but now I am old. I am old and do not want to raise grandchildren.

Another respondent, a 62-year-old grandmother whose husband was a monk, also described the mixed feelings that she experienced in caring for her four grandchildren. The grandmother's husband had entered a Buddhist monastery many years ago, leaving her to care for the four grandchildren by herself. Her migrant children did not send home sufficient remittances, and the grandmother had to borrow money from neighbors to care for her grandchildren. The interview with this grandmother highlighted both the negative and the positive emotions associated with caregiving.

INTERVIEWER: How old was the young one when his mother left the child with you?

GRANDMOTHER: One year old.

INTERVIEWER: Did the child cry for his mother?

GRANDMOTHER: Yes, sure. We cried together. I didn't have enough money to support them. In the past, we cultivated crops in the hills. We didn't make much, couldn't save much. And when the grandchildren were born, I did not have the time or energy to do work outside the home.

INTERVIEWER: Some say that when people take care of their grandchildren, they experience happiness. Others say it is suffering. How do you feel about that?

GRANDMOTHER: I have never felt it was suffering. I am happy being with my grandchildren. If it was just me and my husband living alone, that would be tough. I may have some physical suffering but not in my heart. In the morning, I hear the children calling, "Mother, Mother." At night, we hug and feel warm. Neighbors have said that it might be a struggle raising my grandchildren but there will be satisfaction seeing them succeed, fulfilling my hopes.

In sum, while grandparents in skipped generation families step in to provide care, it is simplistic to characterize their feelings about their roles as positive or negative. Instead, they generally experience a combination of positive as well as negative feelings in relation to their caregiving responsibilities.

CONCLUSION

This chapter focused on skipped generation households in Thailand in which adult children have migrated and left grandchildren in the care of grandparents. We find that grandparents living in such households experience a mixture of costs and benefits resulting from the situation. For the most part, adult migrant children continue to contribute to their households in a variety of ways such as remittances, food, and material goods. However, the absence or inadequate levels of such material support can have distressing consequences for the grandparents, who bear additional responsibilities as caregivers. We have also examined modes of coping strategies used by skipped generation household members as they attempt to deal with separation from each other. Many adult migrant children remain in contact through cell phones and occasional visits. Such contact generally helps the grandparents to cope by maintaining feelings of closeness in the face of separation. However, in families where phone calls and visits are minimal or nonexistent, grandparents may attempt to rationalize their adult children's lack of contact but are more vulnerable to feelings of loneliness and abandonment.

Finally, we have considered the ways in which grandparents experience the costs and benefits of caregiving for their grandchildren. Almost all of the grandparents experience a mixture of negative and positive feelings about their caregiving role. On the one hand, grandparents feel worried and overwhelmed by their responsibilities. In some cases, these costs are very high as the grandparents struggle with few financial resources and/or their own poor health. On the other hand, grandparents enjoy their grandchildren's companionship and derive a sense of purpose from their caregiving role. Religion plays a pivotal role in the way in which grandparents think about caregiving. Buddhist concepts such as karma, merit-making, and acceptance help provide meaning to their role of primary caregiver to grandchildren.

Our study adds to the literature on the strengths and resilience of grandparents as caregivers (Hayslip & Goodman, 2008; Hayslip & Smith, 2013). These grandparents play an active role in supporting their children and their grandchildren. Nonetheless, the grandparents are often dealing with significant hardship as well as worries about their present and future ability to care for their grandchildren. They are also bound by their culture. It is this cultural context, and not just their economic situation, that plays a significant role in influencing how grandparents, adult children, and grandchildren cope with long-distance caregiving. Our research points to the ways in which cultural and religious beliefs are intertwined as grandparents care for their grandchildren without the regular presence of the middle generation. The case of skipped generation families may indeed be non-normative in the traditional picture of Thai family life. Nonetheless, cultural norms of collective and intergenerational caregiving, as well as religious conceptions around karma, merit-making, and acceptance of life circumstances, appear to soften the difficulties of separation and the burdens of caregiving.

This chapter provides a picture of the increasingly common phenomenon of skipped generation households. Our findings highlight the complexity of the underlying causes and consequences of adult children's mobility, the grandparents' role as caregiver for the children left behind, and the role of cultural context and deeply embedded cultural and religious beliefs in interpreting the phenomenon and coping with challenges. Understanding issues faced by skipped generation households identifies areas that need to be addressed as practitioners and policymakers attempt to support the vital role that grandparents play when adult children migrate and must parent from afar.

ACKNOWLEDGMENTS

We want to thank Kanchana Theinlai and Wannee Hutaphat for their significant contributions to this study and Jasper Ingersoll for his helpful feedback on this chapter. We also wish to acknowledge funding support for the Skipped Generation Households in Thailand Project from the University of Michigan (School of Social Work, Center for Southeast Asian Studies, and Thai Studies) as well as support from the Institute for Population and Social Research, Mahidol University.

NOTE

1. The official name is Tambon Health Promoting Hospital.

REFERENCES

Arber, S., & Timonen, V. (2012). A new look at grandparenting. In. S. Arber & V. Timonen (Eds.), *Contemporary grandparents: Changing family relationships in global contexts* (pp. 1–20). Policy Press: University of Bristol.

Baker, L., & Silverstein, M. (2012). The wellbeing of grandparents caring for grandchildren in China and the United States. In S. Arber & V. Timonen (Eds.), *Contemporary grandparents: Changing family relationships in global contexts* (pp. 51–70). Bristol: Policy Press.

Bengtson V., & Roberts, R. (1981). Intergenerational solidarity in aging families: An example of formal theory construction. *Journal of Marriage and the Family*, *53*, 856–870.

Burnette, D. (1997). Grandparents raising grandchildren in the inner city. *Families in Society*, *78*(5), 489–499.

Chamratrithirong, A. (2007). Research on internal migration in Thailand: The state of knowledge. *Journal of Population and Social Studies*,*16*(1), 1–20.

Chen, F., Mair, C. A., Bao, L., & Yang, Y. C. (2015). Race/ethnic differentials in the health consequences of caring for grandchildren for grandparents. *Journals of Gerontology, Series B: Psychological and Social Sciences*, *70*(5), 793–803.

Clarke, E., Preston, M., Raksin, J., & Bengtson, V. (1999). Types of conflicts and tensions between older parents and adult children. *Gerontologist*, *39*(3), 261–270.

Fuller-Thompson, E., Minkler, M., & Driver, D. (1997). A profile of grandparents raising grandchildren in the United States. *The Gerontologist*, *37*(3), 406–411.

Hayslip, B., & Smith, G. (2013). *Resilient grandparent caregivers: A strengths-based perspective.* New York: Taylor & Francis.

Hayslip, B., Jr., & Goodman, C.C. (2008). Grandparents raising grandchildren. *Journal of Intergenerational Relationships*, *5*(4), 117–119.

Hayslip, B., Jr., & Kaminksi, P. L. (2005). Grandparents raising their grandchildren: A review of the literature and suggestions for practice. *The Gerontologist*, *45*(2), 262–269.

Huguet, J. W., & Chamratrithirong, A. (2011). *Migration for development in Thailand: Overview and tools for policymakers.* Bangkok: International Organization for Migration.

Ice, G. H., Sadruddin, A., Vagedes, A., Yogo, J., & Juma, E. (2012). Stress associated with caregiving: An examination of the stress process model among Kenyan Luo elders. *Social Science & Medicine, 74*, 2020–2027.

Ingersoll, J. (1966). Fatalism in village Thailand. *Anthropological Quarterly, 39*(3), 200–225.

Jampaklay, A., Vapattanawong, P., Tangchonlatip, K., Richter, K., Ponpai, N., & Hayeeteh, C. (2012). *Children living apart from parents due to internal migration (CLAIM)*. Institute for Population and Social Research, Mahidol University.

Kamnuansilpa, P., & Wongthanavasu, S. (2005). Grandparents' relationships with grandchildren in Thailand. *Journal of Intergenerational Relationships, 3*(1), 49–66.

Katz, R., & Lowenstein, A. (2010). Theoretical perspectives on intergenerational solidarity, conflict and ambivalence. In M. Izuhara (Ed.), *Ageing and intergenerational relations: Family reciprocity from a global perspective* (pp. 29–56). Portland, OR: Policy Press.

Kirsch, A. T. (1977). Complexity in the Thai religious system: An interpretation. *The Journal of Aging Studies, 36*(2), 241–266.

Knodel, J., & Chayovan, N. (2009). Intergenerational relationships and family care and support for Thai elderly. *Ageing International, 33*, 15–27.

Knodel, J., Kespichayawattana, J., Saengtienchai, C., & Wiwatwanich, S. (2010). How left behind are rural parents of migrant children? Evidence from Thailand. *Ageing and Society, 30*, 811–841.

Knodel, J., & Nguyen, M. (2014). Grandparents and grandchildren: Care and support in Myanmar, Thailand and Vietnam. *Ageing and Society, 35*(9), 1960–1988.

Knodel, J., & Saengtienchai, C. (2007). Rural parents with urban children: Social and economic implications of migration for the rural elderly in Thailand. *Population, Space, and Place, 13*(3), 193–210.

Knodel, J., Saengtienchai, C., & Sittitrai, W. (1995). Living arrangements of the elderly in Thailand: Views of the populace. *Journal of Cross-Cultural Gerontology, 10*, 79–111.

Knodel, J., Teerawichitchainan, B., Prachuabmoh, V., & Pothisiri, W. (2015). *The situation of Thailand's older population: An update based on the 2014 Survey of Older Persons in Thailand* (Report No. 15–847). Population Studies Center University of Michigan.

Ku, L. J. E., Stearns, S. C., Van Houtven, C. H., Lee, S. Y, D., Dilworth-Anderson, P., & Konrad, T. R. (2013). Impact of caring for grandchildren on the health of grandparents in Taiwan. *Journals of Gerontology, Series B: Psychological Sciences and Social Sciences, 68*(6), 1009–1021.

Limanonda, B. (1995). Families in Thailand: Beliefs and realities. *Journal of Comparative Family Studies, 26*(1), 67–82.

Madianou, M., & Miller, D. (2012). *Migration and new media: Transnational families and polymedia*. New York: Routledge.

Malinowski, B. (1923/1989). The problem of meaning in primitive languages. In C. K. Ogden & I. A. Richards (Eds.), *The meaning of meaning* (pp. 233–96). Orlando, FL: Harcourt.

Mills, T., Gomez-Smith, Z., & De Leon, J. (2005). Skipped generation families: Sources of psychological distress among grandmothers of grandchildren who live in homes where neither parent is present. *Marriage & Family Review, 37*(1-2), 191–212.

Minkler, M., & Fuller-Thompson, E. (1999). The health of grandparents raising grandchildren: Results of a national study. *American Journal of Public Health, 89*(9), 1384–1389.

Minkler, M., Roe, K. M., & Price, M. (1992). The physical and emotional health of grandmothers raising grandchildren in the crack cocaine epidemic. *The Gerontologist, 32*(6), 752–761.

Narongchai, W., & Ayuwat, D. (2011). *Patterns of co-resident of skipped- generation in Isan migrant family*. Paper presented at the 12th Graduate Research Conference, Khon Koen University (in Thai).

Nyasani, E., Sterberg, E., & Smith, H. (2009). Fostering children affected by AIDS in Richards Bay, South Africa: A qualitative study of grandparents' experiences. *African Journal of AIDS Research, 8*(2), 181–192.

Padgett, D. K. (2008). *Qualitative methods in social work research* (2nd ed.). Los Angeles: Sage.

Park, H. (2006). The economic well-being of households headed by a grandmother as caregiver. *Social Service Review, 80*(2), 264–296.

Pfanner, D., & Ingersoll, J. (1962). Theravada Buddhism and village economic behavior: Burmese and Thai comparison. *The Journal of Asian Studies, 21*(3), 341–361.

Podhisita, C. (1998). Buddhism and Thai world view. In A. Pongsapich (Ed.), *Traditional and changing Thai world view* (pp. 31–62). Bangkok: Chulalongkorn University Press.

Rahula, W. (1959). *What the Buddha taught*. New York: Grove Press.

Reijer, D. B. (2013). *Grandparents as parents: Skipped-generation households coping with poverty and HIV in rural Zambia*. Leiden: African Studies Centre.

Scommegna, P. (2012). *More U.S. children raised by grandparents*. Retrieved from Population Reference Bureau website: http://www.prb.org/Publications/Articles/2012/US-children-grandparents.aspx

Shakya, H. B., Usita, P. M., Eisenberg, C., Weston, J., & Liles, S. (2012). Family well-being concerns of grandparents in skipped generation families. *Journal of Gerontological Social Work, 55*(1), 39–54.

Smuckarn, S. (1998). Thai peasant world view. In A. Pongsapich (Ed.), *Traditional and changing Thai world view* (pp. 159–175). Bangkok: Chulalongkorn University Press.

Thailand National Statistical Office. (2006). *Thailand multiple indicator cluster survey December 2005-Fevruary 2006: Final report*. Bangkok: National Statistical Office, Ministry of Information Technology and Communications.

Thang, L. (2012). The meanings of being a grandparent. In K. Mehta & L. Thang (Eds.), *Experiencing grandparenthood: An Asian perspective* (pp. 61–75). London: Springer.

Toyota, M., Yeoh, B., & Nguyen, L. (2007). Editorial introduction: Bringing the "left behind" back into view in Asia: A framework for understanding the "migration-left behind nexus." *Population, Space and Play, 13*, 157–161.

Wang, Y., & Marcotte, D. E. (2007). Golden years? The labor market effects of caring for grandchildren. *Journal of Marriage and Family, 69*(5), 1283–1297.

3

Fictive Kinships and the Remaking of Family Life in the Context of Paid Domestic Work

The Case of Philippine Yayas

MARIA ROSARIO T. de GUZMAN, AILEEN S. GARCIA, AND MINERVA D. TULIAO ■

Consider this picture of family life we observed during our fieldwork in Quezon City, Philippines. The focus of our study was on *yayas*—women employed as domestic care workers whose primary job was to take care of children in private homes. Our participants were themselves mothers who had left their children in their rural communities while they lived and worked in the city.

> On one early morning, we observed a group having a shared breakfast of fish, rice, and vegetables. In this rather intimate and idyllic family scene, there was lively banter, laughter, chiding, sharing of stories and talk of mundane issues about children, work, and plans for the rest of the day. Although there was no table, the group of seven was seated in two rows facing each other—holding plates on their laps and eating with their hands. There is nothing unusual about this event, and it was likely repeated in many households around the country that same morning. There was nothing extraordinary about the food, the scene, nor the topics of conversation except for one thing: this meal was not occurring under the roof of a house but inside the school service jeep parked outside the Little Tykes preschool in an affluent gated community in Quezon City. The driver of this school bus service is known as Kuya Jun (note: *Kuya* is a kinship term that literally means "older brother" but is also a term used for men of higher status). He is also the owner of the vehicle,

and he is charged with bringing children and their *yayas* from their homes to and from the preschool daily. In addition to Kuya Jun, partaking in this shared meal were the *yayas* whose young wards were attending the preschool that morning. The day before this observation, we had noted that there was a small makeshift cabinet bolted onto the floor of the school bus, and this is where the *yayas* and Kuya Jun kept the plastic plates for this morning ritual.

We chose to start this chapter with a scenario to illustrate the sense of closeness and participation in reconstructed family life that migrants experience and build in their host communities. As many chapters in this volume illustrate, one of the biggest sacrifices made by laborers who relocate to take on jobs is separation from family. A rich body of work describes how economic migrants bridge physical distance and maintain family connections, for instance, by adopting alternative caregiving strategies (e.g., remittances) in lieu of in-person care (Krzyowski & Mucha, 2014; Ingersoll-Dayton, Punpuing, Tangchonlatip, & Yakas, Chapter 2 in this volume) and using mediated communication and social media to connect with family (Baldassar, Baldock, & Wilding, 2007; Madianou & Miller, 2011). However, maintaining family life can also occur in the immediate settings that migrants occupy within their receiving communities. In fact, for migrants, building close social ties and even fictive kinships is essential to adapting to their new home communities (de Guzman & Garcia, 2017). It is this type of family rebuilding—one that is established in the host community and away from biological ties—that we examine in this chapter.

In this chapter, we draw from our study on Filipina rural-to-urban migrant workers in the domestic care sector to illustrate how migrants make and remake family in the context of separation. The setting of our study is in Quezon City, Philippines, and our participants are women employed as *yayas*—domestic care workers employed to care for children. They live in their employers' homes, and most of our respondents live apart from their own children and all are living away from their nuclear families. Details of this study are laid out in an earlier paper that focused on the experience of family separation for domestic care workers and strategies they utilized to reconfigure and maintain relationships across physical distance (de Guzman, 2014). Here, we reexamine our data with a lens toward understanding how they rebuild new family life in their immediate contexts. We explore the nature of those relationships and how they reflect deeply embedded notions of family life (e.g., family roles) and implications for coping and well-being given the challenges of migration and domestic care work.[1]

DOMESTIC CARE WORKERS: A SNAPSHOT

Domestic workers are those individuals employed to work in or for private households to perform a range of services related to maintaining the home (e.g., housekeeping, gardening) or caring for individuals (e.g., children, elderly) (International Labour Organization, 2011; Domestic Workers Act of 2012,

Republic Act 10361). Worldwide, there are 52 million domestic workers, most of whom are women, migrants, and members of other historically disadvantaged groups (International Labour Organization, 2013). Domestic work is a rapidly growing and important labor sector. Although paid domestic work accounts for only 2% of jobs worldwide, domestic workers and care workers take on duties that free their employers to enter or reenter the workforce or otherwise maintain a better quality of living (Chen, 2011; Luebker, 2013). Because domestic workers and domestic care workers are often employed to carry out tasks most typically undertaken by women (Boris & Parreñas, 2010), the availability of paid domestic work can have important implications for the reentry of women into the workforce to take on more highly skilled jobs. Nevertheless, paid domestic work remains one of the most undervalued labor sectors, typically netting meager wages with inadequate workplace protections. The nature of work is carried out in private households and is largely informal, making workers less visible and more vulnerable to abuse (Chen, 2011; International Labour Organization, 2011).

Domestic work, migration, and family dispersal are all intertwined. There are no reliable figures on how many domestic workers live apart from their families; nonetheless, many domestic workers worldwide are migrants from less economically prosperous nations or from poorer regions within the same country. In the Philippines, there are 2 million domestic workers, more than 84% of whom are women, and most are employed in highly urbanized regions (e.g., Manila, Davao) but migrate from rural provinces. For example, 40% of domestic workers are working in the National Capital Region alone, and 30% of those workers report having migrated from outside provinces. Half of all domestic workers in the Philippines are married, and 40% are below the age of 35. Domestic workers in the Philippines are generally young, of childbearing age, with most experiencing extended periods of family separation in pursuit of work.

Although the challenges of family life for international economic migrants have been highlighted in recent literature (e.g., see volume by Baldasaar & Merla, 2014), implications of domestic migration on family life have been relatively neglected. This gap in research is important to address because relocation within national borders occurs at a much higher frequency, and rural-to-urban migrants tend to be more disadvantaged than their transnational peers (Laczko, 2008). Domestic migrants tend to have lower levels of educational attainment, hail from regions with higher rates of rural poverty, and have fewer years of work experience (International Labour Organization, 2013).

KEEPING TIES UNLESS YOU CAN'T: THE CHALLENGES OF MAINTAINING FAMILY ACROSS DISTANCE

Migrants vary across such domains as geographic origin and destination, religious affiliation, socioeconomic levels, migration status, and, consequently, in levels of economic and social capital and access to resources (Baldassar & Merla, 2014). Disparities in access to typical tools for maintaining family life are reflected in migrants' abilities to bridge distance and maintain ties to their nuclear and extended family, as was evident in the experiences of our respondents. For instance, remitting money and gifts is a common way by which migrants continue to provide care, fulfill obligations, and show attachment to members of family from whom they are living apart (Boccagni, 2012; Fresnoza-Flot, 2009). However, the frequency and size of remittances vary as a function of migrants' length of tenure in their host community, intention to return home, skill level, migration status, and income disparity between natal and host country (Schiopu & Siegfried, 2006; Waldinger, 2007). Reciprocal visits, which provide temporary reunification that enables migrants to maintain presence and visibility in their home community and in physically participating in meaningful life events of family members (Mason, 2004) can be largely determined by financial ability to afford the cost of travel and, for transnationals, their migration status (Fresnoza-Flot, 2009; King, Cela, Fokkema, & Vullnetari, 2014). Finally, there has been much recent scholarly attention on the impacts of mobile and communicative technology on migrants' abilities to maintain contact with family. Given the ubiquity of synchronous and instant communication tools (e.g., texts, social media), migrants' experiences of absence are now said to be limited to physical separation because families can develop "co-presence" and maintain cohesion across distance (Baldassar & Merla, 2014). Madianaou and Miller (2011) coined the term "polymedia" to refer to an ecology where there is not only availability but also diversity in various technologies for communication, such that the task for migrants is no longer finding access to communication but instead choosing the appropriate and preferred technologies for specific purposes (e.g., delivering news vs. sharing intimate stories) and relationships.

For migrants in our study, access to the three most typical tools for maintaining family life across distance was limited. The use of cell phones was constrained by the relatively high cost of purchasing usage minutes and, for some, their inability to purchase cell phone units for family in rural villages. Because of the high cost of transportation relative to their income and the long commute times, our participants reported that reciprocal visits were infrequent and short at best. Connecting via remittances and sending care packages was similarly done but also much limited compared to the transnational Filipino experience of sending large packages (i.e., *balikbayan* boxes) filled with goods that not only provide for basic needs but also communicate care (McCay, 2016). Although participants reported remitting practically their entire salaries for the care of their children, these amounts were often just enough to cover basic needs.

Additionally, respondents reported barriers that stemmed from issues not directly tied to material resources. For mothers whose children were too young to engage in meaningful conversation or exchange texts, our respondents reported that phone calls did not do much to promote a sense of connection or communication. "They put the phone near the baby and she just listens to my voice," one mother recounted. Without regular physical and face-to-face contact, our respondents did not feel that they could connect with their young infants and toddlers who then were growing up without a sense of connection to their mothers. Others found phone calls to simply serve as reminders of the toll that separation was taking on their relationships with their children. "It is painful to call . . . I hear her calling my own mother '*nanay*' [i.e., mother] . . . she calls her father '*tatay*' [father] and her grandmother '*nanay*,'" one noted in describing her hesitance in calling her daughter.

Moreover, in many cases, alternative caregivers (e.g., migrants' siblings, mothers-in-law) exerted high levels of control over migrants' access to their own children, sometimes blocking communication to retaliate over arguments or as a means of control to solicit favors or additional funds. Sometimes, various family members with more direct access to the children or who could mediate between the migrant and the caregivers were able to control information that affected their ability to reach their children. Sheila (age 27) describes a complicated situation with her estranged husband whose mother (i.e., Sheila's mother-in-law) was caring for her child in a rural province while Sheila was working in Manila:

> I came home to visit my son recently and my mother-in-law acted angry. She goes, "why are you here?" So I asked my ex-husband, "what did you tell her?" And he said nothing. I said, "maybe you turned the situation upside down." Maybe he told her that I left him when in fact he left me for another woman and I didn't choose that. I just had to accept that he left. And I send money every month (through the ex-husband). It is for the care of our child but I don't think he gives it all to her (mother-in-law). He feeds himself with it.

Similarly, Ime (41 years old) sometimes considers leaving work all together to be with her daughter but notes that her mother-in-law simply "doesn't want to return" her daughter. Given more than 10 years of being the primary caregiver, her mother-in-law had grown very attached to her daughter, and Ime suspects that she does not tell her daughter that it is she who sends money for her daughter's care. Moreover, her mother-in-law has complete control over information about her daughter and the amount of long-distance contact they can have. She notes,

> She [mother-in-law] only remembers to call me when she [daughter] is sick. Sometimes they'll call me and say, "your daughter is sick, she has a fever, we don't have money, we need money." Just like that. It makes me think, when they need something, they call me.

Thus, migrants in our study had meager financial resources and were often at the mercy of those providing care for their children (e.g., mothers-in-law, siblings). Over time, many lost the ability to meaningfully connect with their children. Several participants noted that maintaining family life involved providing for the basic care of their children and not actual presence or connection. As one of our participants poignantly noted, the experience of being a mother from a distance as a *yaya* meant only that they gave birth to a child and not more. Migrants in our study were not participants in the more interconnected world more often highlighted in the literature on transnational family life and do not have the means to maintain "co-presence" with family that higher resource migrants are increasingly achieving today (Baldassar & Merla, 2014).

THE NEED TO REBUILD FAMILY RIGHT HERE AND RIGHT NOW

Given the centrality of family in traditional Filipino society and the traditional caregiving role that mothers play in caring for their children (Alampay, 2014), separation from family resulted in severe emotional burdens for our respondents. Because the desire to be with biological kin was constrained, the business of "family life" was then fulfilled in the very context of their paid domestic work and by connecting with peers in the neighborhoods in which they worked. Our respondents built tight and close connections within their new communities in ways that mimicked family life both in intimacy and structure. Consistent with findings of other scholars, the building of fictive kinships in the context of migration was an important form of coping, self-care, and as a means of establishing social capital in a situation where they otherwise would have had very limited resources (e.g., Bryceson & Vuorela, 2002; Cox & Narula, 2003; Ebaugh & Curry, 2000; Kim, 2009).

Family Life With Peers

Away from their families, migrants often seek a sense of family and build close connections in their places and communities of work (Bryceson & Vuorela, 2002; Kim, 2009). For instance, Filipino mothers working as domestic helpers in Singapore report trying to cope with family separation by regarding non-kin relations in their new places of work as family (Asis, Huang, & Yeoh, 2004). Somewhat similarly, McCay (2016) describes how Filipino migrants in London seek the company of co-ethnics to provide them with a sense of closeness and belonging as a form of self-care and coping that they deemed necessary to deal with the physically and emotionally demanding tasks of domestic care work. Consistent with those studies, our respondents formed close relations with peers in their neighborhoods who were also in paid domestic employment, such as other *yayas*, housekeepers, and drivers. As we illustrated at the beginning of this chapter, domestic care workers in our study built family life among other workers in their communities, developing close ties and even recreating everyday family rituals in modified ways to literally fit the physical spaces they occupied. In the afternoons at the local park within our study site, it was not uncommon to see *yayas* having *merienda* (a light afternoon meal) together as their wards played. Outside the local preschool, the *yayas* and drivers spent time together while waiting for their wards who attended 3–4 hours of instruction—passing time by sharing meals, gossiping, and sharing in banter and talk that similarly reflected closeness and familiarity.

Our field notes outside the local daycare captured this sense of closeness that was easily discernable from observations:

> Nannies typically congregate outside while the children are in school. Some nannies said that they don't really live nearby so they have to stay here and wait for their wards, while others do live nearby but opt to stay anyway. Some nannies joke, "*nakakalabas lang pag pumasok*" (we can only go out when the kids go to school). At 10:30 AM, approximately six nannies and three males (one is the school bus driver, one is a private car driver, one other is unknown) are gathered outside and appear to be very familiar with each other. When I approached to talk about the study, they knew immediately who among them had children and encouraged each other to participate. They were kind enough to let us use the school bus in which several of them were sitting earlier, to use for the interview. They said it would be better for privacy and to keep away from the hot sun.

Yayas described these close and fictive kinships as another "consolation prize" and a sense of family in lieu of their own kinfolk who were many miles away. And, just like family, the ties are close and deeply embedded. Individuals spend time together whenever possible, they share intimate information and seek each others' countenance, and they report being able to relate to each others' plight given their shared experience. In December, the *yayas* told us of their plans for an out-of-town holiday trip—a rendezvous that was to be made possible because Kuya Jun volunteered both the use of his jeep and his services to drive for the group. Due to what turned out to be a high cost for the trip (e.g., cost of gasoline, food, and lodging) and several of the *yayas* being called upon by their employers to work during the holidays, they were unable to carry through with their plans. Nonetheless, several *yayas* mentioned that they remained cautiously hopeful to have at least this one dream of a family trip fulfilled some day; nonetheless, others said that they suspected that this plan for an out-of-town trip together would "remain a dream."

Cultural Context Reflected in Family Life With Peers

That cultural context shapes family life is well acknowledged and supported in the scholarly literature. A rich body of research has documented systematic cross-cultural differences in such aspects of family life as parental beliefs, expectations and socialization goals (e.g., Keller et al., 2006), family configuration and household patterns (Therborn, 2009), and everyday settings of children and family members (Weisner, 2014). Less has been written about how cultural context informs the formation of fictive kinships and how social structures and roles therein reflect cultural notions of family life. In the case of *yayas'* reconstructed family life with peers, at least two characteristics of Filipino family life are evident. First, the Filipino family is characterized by the extended nature of its membership, with the extension of family descending both bilaterally and through the *compadrazgo* system, where relations are established through close friendship, shared experiences, obligations, and reciprocal ties or formalized through religious rites such as baptism (Guevarra, 2010; Medina, 2001; Szanton, 1979). As such, the process of considering non-kin as family, with all the implied obligations and roles, is typical within the Philippine context. Our respondents had substantial shared experience with their peers in the community, and they relied on each other for practical and emotional support—all of which contributed to close friendships and family-like relationships (Espiritu, 2003).

Second, hierarchies emerged based on age and length of tenure in the community. Kuya Jun, the local school service driver, held much authority in this reconstructed family, with *yayas* identifying him as their advisor, organizer of get-togethers, mediator of disagreements, host of daily breakfasts, and occasional lender of money. Felicidad was another individual to whom many *yayas* deferred. She had facilitated the recruitment and hiring of several young women to work in the neighborhood, many of whom are her younger relatives. Felicidad provided guidance and advice to the younger and newly arrived *yayas*, helping them navigate the new terrain of paid domestic work, employer–employee relations, and the challenges of family separation. Anna, a young woman of about 20 years, tells us that it was Felicidad who provided her guidance and comfort whenever she began to doubt her decision to leave her child. It was Felicidad who encouraged her to stay on the job and reminded her of the need to earn money to send for the care of her infant.

Hierarchies based on age and social status and the identification of leaders is typical in Filipino families. Local Filipino scholars have described such important roles within families as the *taga-salo* or the unofficial leader who typically steps up when a member needs financial support or reconciles disagreements among members. *Taga-salo*, which literally translates to "the one who catches," is usually the eldest in the family. Bulatao (1998, as cited in Udarbe, 2001) noted that it is typical within families for the emergence of an *Ate* or *Kuya* (i.e., literally translated, these mean "older sister" or "older brother," respectively; but figuratively these mean someone of higher status) who mediates fights or bears greater responsibility in the group. Kuya Jun and Felicidad fulfilled their roles as the *Kuya* and *Ate* for the *yayas*. The *yayas* in turn played their roles in deferring to the leader, for instance, by seeking and heeding their advice and asking for assistance (e.g., loans). *Yayas* report that when disagreements arose, the *taga-salo's* mediation and direction were respected.

Family Life With Employers

The ambiguous boundaries between personal and professional worlds and the potentially exploitative nature of paid domestic work has been documented in numerous studies and rich ethnographic accounts in numerous countries such as India (Ray & Qayum, 2009), South Africa (Ally, 2009), and the United States

(MacDonald, 2009). Living under the same roof, helping raise another's child, participating in meaningful family rituals (e.g., meals, vacations), and establishing close personal relationships with employers easily engender closeness on the one hand but also make it difficult to negotiate one's rights as an employee, and the ambiguous boundaries can further reinforce social hierarchies (Stiel & England, 1997; Tappert & Dobner, 2015). And although close employer–employee relations may be mutually beneficial and engender reciprocal respect (i.e., personalism), it can also result in the exploitation and maintenance of asymmetrical power relations between employer and employee (i.e., paternalism/maternalism; Arnado, 2003).

The blurring of personal and professional boundaries was clearly evident from our discussions with *yayas* in our study. Our respondents referred to their employers using kinship terms (e.g., "*Ate*" or older sister and "*Kuya*" for older brother), as is typical in Philippine households employing domestic workers. It should be noted, however, that the use of such terms does not necessarily reflect "family-like" relationship but that it is customary in Philippine households. Respondents spoke of the positive treatment they received and directly mentioned being considered as "part of the family" in their places of employment. Respondents described this situation as positive and ideal—a setting that netted multiple benefits. At the most basic level, being "part of the family" endowed respondents with practical benefits such as humane working conditions and basic rights, which may not always be available given the lack of general oversight of this labor sector in the Philippines. One respondent noted that, as a family member, she was never suspected nor accused of stealing—a difficult experience that many of her peers had undergone in other households. This respondent also reported that she was never scolded for lack of frugality in use of household supplies, telling us, "when things like laundry soap or pantry items run out, they just put it on the grocery list." Another respondent noted that she had gotten close to the family and, as such, she could request periodic vacations to see her own children without fear of immediately being replaced. She notes, "Even when I leave for 2 months for a vacation, they wait for me, they don't just get a replacement."

Most respondents reported receiving gifts and other tangible rewards: pay advances and being able to borrow or ask for additional money, as well as gifts and items for their own children, such as toys and clothes that their wards had outgrown. Others reported being treated with kindness and empathy: employers asking how they were doing and inquiring about their physical and emotional well-being. "They ask how my children back home are doing," one reported. Another *yaya* noted that her employer was a single mom to a son and, as such, treats her like a co-parent rather than as a *yaya*. She reports that her employer solicits her advice and gives weight to her recommendations. Another respondent, Shelda, had recently been hospitalized, and it was her employers who paid for her care and stayed by her bedside until she was discharged, showing not just financial support but also emotional care more typically seen among family members.

Clearly, participants saw "being part of the family" as beneficial and essential to having a positive work experience and for basic protection of their rights, consistent with findings by Arnado (2003), who similarly examined the experiences of Filipina household workers in the Philippine setting. One respondent, Marivic (mid-20s) described her employment situation as such: "I'm lucky I encountered them. They don't treat me like *ibang tao*." Note that the delineation between "*ibang tao*" (different from us) versus "*hindi ibang tao*" (not different from us) is highly significant in Filipino society and to a large extent dictates levels of interaction, intimacy, and behaviors (Pasco, Morse, & Olson, 2004). Being *hindi ibang tao* evokes mutual trust and reciprocal obligations and interactions that are beyond mere civility or surface-level harmony (Pe-Pua & Protacio-Marcelino, 2000). Participants who felt that they were treated as *hindi ibang tao* spoke of this experience with pride—telling us that they ate the same food as the family, that they were told they were essential members of the family, and that the family could no longer function as a family without the *yaya*'s presence. For example, Marina reports that her employer tells her that if her children were ever to visit her in the city, they could come and stay at that home, saying, "you are not different from us after all."

In contrast, those who were treated as *ibang tao* (i.e., different from us) were resentful. One *yaya* described how she not only ate separately from her employers but also was given food that was different from what the family ate. To retaliate, she indicated, "I would just steal their food . . . so I can taste what they are also eating." Another respondent, Malumi, contrasts her previous employer, who treated her simply as paid help, versus her current employer, who treats her like family. Of her previous employer she says,

> Whenever something happened to their child, they blamed me. Even inside the house and the couple was eating and the toddler was walking around, and she wasn't that good at walking yet. When she stumbled, there you go they would blame me [sobbing]. They told me that this is exactly why they hired a *yaya*. It's not that they spoke to me in a bad way. But I couldn't speak up because I'm just working as a domestic . . . they don't see that I'm with that child all day. When they come home, they just go to sleep. Sometimes, they check on the child. And if they see anything, like a red spot . . . there you go.

And, of her current employer who treats her like family, Malumi describes how and why she has persisted for several years under their employment. Early on in her tenure as *yaya*, she had fallen seriously ill and needed immediate treatment that was anticipated to be complicated and costly. Malumi describes her current employer's response:

> That is why I sort of have *utang-na-loob* [debt of gratitude] to them. . . . At the hospital, I was told I had some cysts on my fallopian tubes. I didn't plan to have an operation there. They put me under observation for a month if they could take the cysts out. And then my employer told me he would take care of the whole thing—to go ahead and get the treatment at the hospital. At first they were just going to observe but my boss said to get the full treatment.

> They paid for everything. They said I shouldn't go to the rural hospitals because I might just die. You know, I didn't have money. So the whole thing, they said to go ahead and get the operation done. She [the boss] was nice. Other things like my transportation fare, every year [i.e., after visiting home], they pay. They'd even say "you haven't been home for a year," like that.

Scholars have pointed out that such blurring of boundaries between personal and professional worlds can pose high risks for exploitation, allowing employers to impinge on the rights of employees or encroach on their personal space (Arnado, 2003; Bakan & Stasiulis, 1997). Indeed, research has shown how paternalism and maternalism, or employers' endowment of benefits and "like family" treatment to domestic workers, can foster an environment that makes it difficult for workers to negotiate personal space and employment rights (Lan, 2003). How does one then explain the generally positive regard of porous boundaries between personal life and work reported here? In the Philippine setting, closely bonded relationships outside the family are typical, and delineations between *hindi ibang tao* and *ibang tao* weigh heavily. Moreover, although the limited empirical work and news accounts of such blurring of personal–professional spheres in Philippine domestic work suggest high potential for exploitation absent these clear boundaries (see, e.g., the recent article "My Family's Slave," Tizon, 2017), the case of *yayas* may be unique. Paid domestic work in childcare entails entrusting the *yaya* with the care, health, and well-being of one's children. Discussions with our respondents suggest that the "like family" relationship obligates not just the employee to the employer, but also vice versa. That is, a "debt of gratitude" or *utang na loob* is felt by both employer and employee. For example, *yayas* indicated that they were well aware of how employers find it difficult to find reliable and trustworthy people with whom they could leave their children. They talked about the difficult demands that caring for a child entails and how the work of being a *yaya* is not for everyone. One *yaya* told us that her employers tell her how lucky they are to have found her, such that they could leave for even a day or two and entrust her with their child. Ime, who we referenced earlier, told us that she was the fourth in a line of *yayas* hired to care for Johnny, a 5-year-old boy who other *yayas* had found difficult to handle. Another *yaya*, Marivic, talked about the challenges of caring for her ward, who was 5 years old at the time of the interview:

> I took care of her when she was so small. She was premature. I took care of her way back. So there, that's why they [employers] are so thankful to me. Because I persisted. I really put in a lot of effort in caring for their child, even as a baby. When she was a newborn, they [employers] would even sometimes leave because they didn't want not to be able to sleep. . . . And she was difficult to care for. She wouldn't eat. I had to feed her with a dropper. . . . But I did it. I lasted. . . . That's why they like me. They ask me, they say "*Ate* [older sister], just don't leave." They let me go on vacation and they ask, "you will come back, right?" They will not get a replacement.

Other *yayas* reported being told that they were so essential in the household that they could "ask for anything" so long as they did not leave. Several others witnessed the difficulty that the households experienced when they took days off and reported knowing that they were indispensible in the household.

Nonetheless, the "like family" treatment that *yayas* receive from their employers also resulted in a sense of obligation that tied respondents to their employers in ways that went beyond simple employee duties. Earlier, we noted Shelda's experience with her employer who stayed by her bedside during her confinement at the hospital. Shelda describes her "payment" for this family-like treatment this way:

> The others, they say, "This *yaya* is so lucky. She was hospitalized and her boss paid for it. Where do you see this? I wish we could find something like this!" And my boss says, "just promise that you'll take care of these kids and we'll be okay" [i.e., payment is paid]. And I say, "you can see, I'm doing just that." And they are pleased because they see that even if I have something scheduled already and if they say, "we have to go somewhere," I will move my plans. So there you go. Even when I've delayed my plans again and again, I'll still do it. Because they are important. And I love their child.

Shelda's description mirrors the experiences of many of our other respondents. Several *yayas* noted changing their plans and cutting their vacations short if their employers needed them, and they would comply out of sense of debt for being treated well and for being considered part of the family. "It hasn't even been an hour of my day off, and they text me when they can't pacify her, asking me to come home," says Marivic. Similarly, Maria, a mother of three, tells us that although she had intended to visit her own children during the Christmas season, she would be unable to do so because her employers scheduled an out-of-town road trip and asked that she come along because she is the only one who can pacify her ward. During earlier visits home, she had on several occasions cut her trip short to the dismay of her own children, who would say things like "there she goes again, mom is leaving again," because her ward and the other domestic workers employed in the same household would call her on the phone and beg for her to return. She tells us that there is little she can do given how close she is to her ward and how much her employers rely on her.

For other respondents, being considered part of the family and their sense of closeness with their wards and employers tied them to their jobs even when they sometimes considered leaving. Marivic describes how she is so close to her employer and ward that although she sometimes considers returning to her children for good, she feels unable to do so:

> Sometimes when she [employer] scolds me, she will tell me later, "sorry about that, I just had so much on my mind, I'm so busy." But that's very rare. She's usually just very quiet when she has problems at work. I understand when she doesn't talk to me. I totally understand because sometimes she has to stay over at work . . . she and her husband. And then they sometimes say

> that even a full month they could leave their child with me, she really trusts me. After all, I saw her grow up. I have a good relation with her [daughter]. She obeys me. She doesn't disobey. Sometimes, I think of leaving but I don't know how I would tell them. Yes, I plan to leave some time, but I don't know how to tell them because they haven't given me bad treatment. They even ask me how my kids are. They give me so much . . . anything I ask for. They say, "when you need money, let us know."

Respondents did not report making conscious efforts to make clearer delineations between personal and professional spheres with regard to time commitments, workload, or pay. The one area in which respondents did report trying to clarify boundaries was in exercising caution with regard to closeness with their wards. *Yayas* reported being very emotionally close to their wards and treating them as their own children (see de Guzman, 2014). Our observations of their interactions corroborate those assertions, as is reflected in our field notes:

> Nannies appear to be very familiar with the kids. Teachers talk to them about the homework assignments, and some nannies discuss with each other what they need to review with the kids. . . . Some nannies at drop off tell the kids "I love you" and "kiss *yaya*," and nannies also tease the kids in a *malambing* (teasingly affectionate) way. For example, there was a birthday party so some of the kids were leaving with a piece of cake and the nannies would say "*pahingi naman*" (i.e., give me some). Nannies appear to dote on the kids for the most part—wiping their faces, etc.

Yayas take on tasks of an intimate nature (e.g., bathing, feeding), and many spend more hours in close proximity with the child than do the parents. As such, several of our respondents noted that, in the household, the *yaya* and ward were sometimes closer than the child and parent:

> That's why I cannot easily take a day off. "No more day off for *yaya*," she [the ward] says. So when I do take a day off, I have to escape at night. And my boss says, "don't let her notice that you're leaving." So I say, "bye, good night!" and they ask me to pretend that I'm about to go to sleep so she [ward] won't come to my bedroom to check. Her dad says that if this child were to chose between mommy, daddy or *yaya*, that she would say "I want to go with *yaya*." And they're fine with that. They're pleased by that. But they tell me that it's okay as long as I don't leave.

Whereas Sheila expressed no concern over her extreme closeness to her ward, nonetheless, most other participants reported making conscious efforts to establish emotional distance from the children they care for. Several respondents alluded to discouraging the children from engaging in behaviors that reflected very close and intimate relations that they deemed appropriate only within a parent–child relationship. Ime, for example, talks about how her 5-year-old ward often hugs her and tells her that he loves her. They have grown so close that Ime notes missing him and longing to be with him when she goes home to visit her own child, who she has not been able to see grow up. At the same time, her ward calls her on the phone and cries, begging her to come back whenever she takes days off. When her ward tries to give her a kiss, Ime tells him "only on the cheeks, not the lips" and explains that kisses on the lips are only appropriate for one's parents. Furthermore, her ward expresses wanting to sleep beside her at night but that she encourages him to stay in the same bedroom with his parents as this is where he "should sleep."

Yayas' motivations to distance themselves from their wards were complex. Some reasoned that being too close simply "wasn't right" and could not explain further. For some, the main motivation was that they did not want to encroach on the parent–child relationship. Ime, for example, talks about how she disagreed with some of the parents' ways, such as the late bedtime for her ward. However, she respected the parents' rights to make decisions for their own children. Related to this sentiment, other *yayas* thought it was not right for parents to give up caregiving for their children completely. One *yaya* complained that her employer spent so little time with her ward and returned the child to her as soon as the child fusses. Marivic's description captures some of these sentiments:

> They [employer and ward] are close. It's not like other kids who don't get to see their parents. I teach her not to be distant from her mom. I teach her ways. There are kids who have fits or who don't notice when their parents come. I don't want her mom to say she's [ward] too close to me. They do spend time together.

Finally, some *yayas* hinted at the guilt that they felt in becoming so close to their wards while at the same time depriving their own children of their care and attention. "It is tough. I started taking care of Johnny when he was 7 months when the last *yaya* left. Now my feelings for him are deeper than my feelings for my own child."

IMPLICATIONS AND CONCLUSION

In this chapter, we sought to explore the remaking of family life in the host communities of rural-to-urban workers employed in paid domestic care work. Our study illuminates four main points. First, despite the growing ubiquity of communicative media and mobility that allows many migrants to maintain family ties across distance, access to these resources remains limited for many. There is vast diversity in the experiences and status of migrants (e.g., migration status, geographical location) and, consequently, in their access to economic and social resources, which in turn have important consequences for their ability to maintain family ties. For our respondents, access to typical tools for maintaining long-distance family life was highly constrained.

Second, given the challenges of maintaining family ties across distance, many domestic workers recreate family life in their new communities. We focus on two reconstructed family groups here: family that is co-constructed with other domestic workers in their receiving communities and family that they build with their employers. These fictive kinships were an important source of social support and sense of family life that respondents deemed important given their own separation from kinfolk and the heavy demands of their work.

Third, we suggest that becoming "one of the family" within the employer's household is essential for migrants' positive job experience in the Philippine context. To this end, we examined how *yayas* conceptualize, interpret, and evaluate the notion of being part of the family in the context of their paid domestic work. And although social hierarchies and power differentials were still clearly evident, the "one of the family" experience tied both the employer and employee to the relationship, providing mutual benefits such as job security, material gifts, and emotional assurances for the employee and, in turn, high job quality, loyalty, and trustworthiness in caring for the children for the employer. It is perhaps for these many benefits that respondents did not express a desire to establish emotional distance from their employers. However, for a complexity of reasons—a sense of propriety, notions of what is best for their ward, and personal guilt over caring more for their ward than their own child—several respondents noted trying to set emotional boundaries between themselves and their wards even though the *yaya*-ward relationship tended to be very close and emotionally connected.

Finally, the need to incorporate the cultural context and culturally embedded notions of family life in understanding separation and the remaking of family was evident in our findings. Because family life and culture are inextricable and intimately intertwined, the experience and consequences of separation must also be examined in light of the broader cultural and social context. Traditional family roles (e.g., *taga-salo*) were evident in relationships with other domestic workers who reconstructed family life in ways that reflected hierarchies and roles within their fictive kinships. Similarly, family life built with employers reflected asymmetrical power relations that were complicated by traditional Filipino notions of extended family, *utang na loob* (debt of gratitude) and implications of in-group (i.e., *hindi ibang tao* or not different from us) versus out-group (i.e., *ibang tao* or different from us) distinction for personal and professional relationships within the sphere of paid domestic work.

It goes without saying that family life does not occur in a vacuum. Chapters in this volume challenge us to extend our thinking to include a wide range of configurations of family that emerge as a result of physical separation in contemporary life. Our findings illustrate a rich complexity of family life—how it is dynamic as it shifts in response to societal change but also somewhat constant in its underlying traditional notions and cultural beliefs about roles and obligations embedded therein. Our findings also illustrate how family life in its reconstructed form benefits its members, providing a deep sense of social support, satisfaction, and personal and social capital, as well as empowering individuals in their roles (e.g., as employer or employee), but nonetheless also ensnaring members into obligations that result in the loss of personal boundaries. Exploring and acknowledging such complexities in family life is essential as we begin to unpack and better understand contemporary family life in all its forms in the age of migration, mobility, and globalization.

NOTE

1. Interviews were conducted in Filipino, transcribed and analyzed in the original language. Quotes presented here were translated from the original transcripts.

REFERENCES

Alampay, L. P. (2014). Parenting in the Philippines. In H. Selin (Ed.), *Parenting across cultures: Childrearing, motherhood and fatherhood in non-Western cultures* (vol. 7, pp. 459–474). Dordrecht, the Netherlands: Springer. doi:10.1007/978-94-007-7503-9.

Ally, S. (2009). *From servants to workers: South African domestic workers and the democratic state*. Ithaca, NY: Cornell University.

Arnado, J. M. (2003). Maternalism in mistress-maid relations: The Philippine experience. *Journal of International Women's Studies*, *4*(3), 154–177.

Asis, M. M. B., Huang, S., & Yeoh, B. S. A. (2004). When the light of the home is abroad: Unskilled female migration and the Filipino family. *Singapore Journal of Tropical Geography, 25*(2), 198–215.

Bakan, A. B., & Stasiulis, D. (1997). Introduction. In A. B. Bakan & D. Stasiulis (Eds.), *Not one of the family: Foreign domestic workers in Canada* (pp. 3–28). Toronto: University of Toronto Press.

Baldassar, L., Baldock, C. V., & Wilding, R. (2007). Communicating across borders. In L. Baldassar, C. V. Baldock, & R. Wilding (Eds.), *Families caring across borders: Migration, ageing and transnational caregiving* (pp. 108–136). New York: Palgrave.

Baldassar, L., & Merla, L. (2014). Introduction: Transnational family caregiving through the lens of circulation. In L. Baldassar, & L. Merla (Eds.), *Transnational families, migration and the circulation of care: Understanding mobility and absence in family life* (pp. 3–24). New York: Routledge, Taylor & Francis Group.

Boccagni, P. (2012). Practising motherhood at a distance: Retention and loss in Ecuadorian transnational families. *Journal of Ethnic & Migration Studies, 38*(2), 261–277. doi:10.1080/1369183X.2012.646421.

Boris, E., & Parreñas, R. (2010). Introduction. In E. Boris (Ed.), *Intimate labors: Cultures, technologies, and the politics of care* (pp. 1–12). Stanford, CA: Stanford University Press.

Bryceson, D., & Vuorela, U. (2002). Transnational families in the twenty-first century. In D. Bryceson & U. Vuorela (Eds.), *The Transnational family: New European frontiers and global networks* (pp. 3–29). Oxford: Berg.

Chen, M. A. (2011). Recognizing domestic workers, regulating domestic work: Conceptual, measurement, and regulatory challenges. *Canadian Journal of Women and the Law, 23*(1), 167–184.

Cox, R., & Narula, R. (2003). Playing happy families: Rules and relationships in au pair employing households in London, England. *Gender, Place and Culture, 10*(4), 333–344.

de Guzman, M. R. T. (2014). Yaya: Philippine domestic workers, the children they care for and the children they leave behind. *International Perspectives in Psychology, 3*(3), 197–214.

de Guzman, M. R. T., & Garcia, A. S. (2017). From bonds to bridges and back again: The making of a Filipino community in Poland. *Journal of Ethnic and Migration Studies.*

Domestic Workers Act of 2012, R. A. 10361, 15th Cong. (2012). Retrieved from http://www.gov.ph/downloads/2013/01jan/20130118-RA-10361-BSA.pdf

Ebaugh, H. R., & Curry M. (2000). Fictive kin as social capital in new immigrant communities. *Sociological Perspectives, 43*, 189–209. doi:10.2307/1389793.

Espiritu, Y. L. (2003). *Homebound: Filipino American lives across cultures, communities, and countries.* Berkeley: University of California Press.

Fresnoza-Flot, A. (2009). Migration status and transnational mothering: The case of Filipino migrants in France. *Global Networks, 9*, 252–270. doi:10.1111/j.1471-0374.2009.00253.x.

Guevarra, R. P. (2010). Compadrinazgo. In H. Ling & A. Austin (Eds.), *Asian Americans: An encylopedia* (Vol 2, pp. 267–268). New York: Routledge.

International Labour Organization. (2011). *Decent work for domestic workers: Convention 189 and Recommendation 201 at a glance.* Retrieved from http://www.ilo.org/wcmsp5/groups/public/-ed_protect/-protrav/-travail/documents/publication/wcms_170438.pdf.

International Labour Organization. (2013). *Domestic workers across the world: Global and regional statistics and the extent of legal protection.* Retrieved from http://www.ilo.org/wcmsp5/groups/public/-dgreports/-dcomm/-publ/documents/publication/wcms_173363.pdf

Keller, H., Lamm, B., Abels, M., Yovsi, R., Borke, J., Jensen, H., . . . Chaudhary, N. (2006). Cultural models, socialization goals, and parenting ethnotheories. *Journal of Cross Cultural Psychology, 37*(2), 155–172.

Kim, E. C. (2009). "Mama's family": Fictive kinship and undocumented immigrant workers. *Ethnography, 10*(4), 497–513. doi:10.1177/1466138109347000.

King, R., Cela, E., Fokkema, T., & Vullnetari, J. (2014). The migration and wellbeing of the Zero Generation: Transgenerational care, grandparenting and loneliness amongst Albanian older people. *Population, Place and Space, 20*(8), 728–738.

Krzyżowski, Ł., & Mucha, J. (2014). Transnational caregiving in turbulent times: Polish migrants in Iceland and their elderly parents in Poland. *International Sociology, 29*(1), 22–37.

Laczko, F. (2008). Migration and development: The forgotten migrants. In J. DeWind and J. Holdaway (Eds.), *Migration and development within and across borders: Research and policy perspectives on internal and international migration* (pp. 7–11). Geneva: International Organization for Migration.

Lan, P-C. (2003). Negotiating social boundaries and private zones: The micropolitics of employing migrant domestic workers. *Social Problems, 50*(4), 525–549.

Luebker, M. (2013, January 9). *Domestic workers make an important contribution to national economies* [Video file]. Retrieved from http://www.youtube.com/watch?v_eFRuxuJoJ_g

Macdonald, C. L. (2009). *Shadow mothers: Nannies, au pairs, and the micropolitics of mothering*. Berkeley: University of California Press.

Madianou, M., & Miller, D. (2011). Mobile phone parenting: Reconfiguring relationships between Filipina migrant mothers and their left-behind children. *New Media and Society, 13*(3), 457–470.

Mason, J. (2004). Managing kinship over long distances: The significance of "the visit". *Social Policy and Society, 3*(4), 421–429. doi:10.1017/S1474746404002052.

McCay, D. (2016). *An archipelago of care: Filipino migrants and global networks*. Bloomington: Indiana University Press.

Medina, B. T. G. (2001). *The Filipino family* (2nd ed.). Quezon City, PH: University of the Philippines Press.

Pasco, C. Y., Morse, J. M., & Olson, J. K. (2004). Cross-cultural relationships between nurses and Filipino Canadian patients. *Journal of Nursing Scholarship, 36*(3), 239–246.

Pe-Pua, R., & Protacio-Marcelino, E. (2000). Sikolohiyang Pilipino (Filipino psychology): A legacy of Virgilio G. Enriquez. *Asian Journal of Social Psychology, 3*, 49–71.

Ray, R., & Qayum, S. (2009). *Cultures of servitude: modernity, domesticity, and class in India*. Stanford, CA: Stanford University Press.

Schiopu, I., & Siegfried, N. (2006). *Determinants of workers' remittances: Evidence from the European Neighboring Region*. Working Paper Series 688. Retrieved from the European Central Bank website: https://www.ecb.europa.eu/pub/pdf/scpwps/ecbwp688.pdf?f31c4dfff2b68deec59ef90384bc8e4f

Stiell, B., & England, K. (1997). Domestic disctinctions: Constructing difference among paid domestic workers in Toronto. *Gender, Place, and Culture, 43*(3), 339–359.

Szanton, M. C. B. (1979). The uses of compadrazgo: Views from a Philippine town. *Philippine Sociological Review, 27*(3), 161–180.

Tappert, S., & Dobner, M. (2015). Being a member of the family? Meanings and implications in paid migrant domestic and care work in Madrid. In M. Kontos and G. T. Bonifácio (Eds.), *Migrant domestic workers and family life: International perspectives* (pp. 276–299). Basingstoke, UK: Palgrave Macmillan.

Therborn, G. (2009). Family. In R. A. Shweder, T. R. Bidell, A. C. Dailey, S. Dixon, P. J. Miller, & J. Modell (Eds.), *The child: An encyclopedic companion* (pp. 333–338). Chicago: University of Chicago Press.

Tizon, A. (2017, June). My family slave. *The Atlantic*. Retrieved from https://www.theatlantic.com/magazine/archive/2017/06/lolas-story/524490/

Udarbe, M. H. (2001). The Tagasalo personality. *Philippine Journal of Psychology, 34*(2), 45–65.

Waldinger, R. (2007). Between here and there: How attached are Latino immigrants to their native country? *Pew Hispanic Center*. Retrieved from http://www.pewhispanic.org/files/reports/80.pdf

Weisner, T. S. (2014). Culture, context and child wellbeing. In A. Ben-Arieh, F. Casas, I. Frønes, & J. E. Korbin (Eds.), *Handbook of child well-being: Theories, methods and policies in global perspectives* (pp. 87–104). Netherlands: Springer.

4

Changing Country, Changing Gender Roles

Migration to Norway and Transformation of Gender Roles Among Polish Families

NATASZA KOSAKOWSKA-BEREZECKA, MAGDALENA ŻADKOWSKA, BRITA GJERSTAD, JUSTYNA ŚWIDRAK, ANNA KWIATKOWSKA, GUNHILD ODDEN, OLEKSANDR RYNDYK, KUBA KRYŚ, AND GUNN VEDØY ■

Work (labor) and family migration from Poland to Norway is a relatively new trend that has intensified immensely since Poland joined the European Union in 2004. Since 2009, Polish migrants have been the largest immigrant community in Norway. As of 2015, there were 91,000 registered Polish citizens living in Norway, accounting for 14% of all foreign citizens residing in the country (Statistics Norway [SSB], 2015; General Statistic Office Poland [GUS], 2015).

In recent years, it has become evident that Polish migrants dominate not only economic migration to Norway but also family reunions. In 2014, Polish migrants accounted for 16.2% (2,621 of 16,212) (SSB, 2015) of family-related entries to Norway. This trend likely has changed the gender structure of the Polish immigrant population in Norway. At the same time, there is scarce evidence that Polish migrant women pursue professional careers and participate in the labor force in Norway according to their education, skills, needs, and aspirations. Recent studies indicate that, to the contrary, Polish female migrants fail to use opportunities to advance the social standing of their families and community (Eldring & Alsos, 2010). Women's underrepresentation in the Norwegian labor market can be linked to men's lack of sufficient involvement in childcare and household duties—a gender gap within domestic life that is especially visible among less gender-egalitarian countries, such as Poland (Kosakowska-Berezecka et al., 2016; Safdar & Kosakowska-Berezecka, 2015).

Gender (in)equality is established and maintained at different but intersecting levels, from the more proximal individual and family levels to the more distant cultural level, and it is manifested in the norms and values shaping the family roles of men and women. Gender (in)equality can be observed in the rituals and practices of couples who struggle to reconcile work with family life and can be analyzed through the lenses of women's and men's internalized beliefs concerning socially accepted gender roles (Cross & Madson, 1997; Heilman, Wallen, Fuchs, & Tamkins, 2004; Rudman, Moss-Racusin, Phelan, & Nauts, 2012). We argue in this chapter that men and women themselves justify the existing status quo and allocations of power and status that lead them to feel entitlement to certain roles and social pressure to perform gender-congruent tasks and duties. Gendered attitudes, along with gendered practices, lead to the cultural devaluation of women's work at home of men who are strongly focused on family life and put more effort into a gender-congruent sphere and, consequently, unequal responsibilities at home (cf. also Jost & Kay, 2005; Laurin, Kay, & Shepherd, 2011; Pratto & Walker, 2004; Wood & Eagly, 2012).

Research suggests that acculturation in minority–majority contexts within plural Western societies over time opens new opportunities for individuals and couples to break out of traditional minority-based stereotypes of gender relations, gendered identities, and the division of domestic and income-generating labor (Berry, 1997). Labor market dynamics, government policies, and the dominant values and norms in the majority culture can come together to offer opportunities for both men and women to mobilize support outside and inside their diaspora environment to choose alternative career strategies and to renegotiate arrangements of childcare and household divisions (Fandrem, Sam, & Roland, 2009; Gjerstad, Johannessen, Nødland, Skeie, & Vedøy, 2012). Therefore, it is interesting to analyze the differences in patterns and practices of gender equality within Polish families in two countries that rank differently on gender equality indices: the home country of Poland and the host country of Norway.

In this chapter, we present the results of both qualitative and quantitative interdisciplinary Polish–Norwegian studies conducted from 2013 to 2016. This study involved more than 150 in-depth, longitudinal interviews with couples in Poland and in Norway and interviews with 20 public-sector servants and 11 employers in Norway. We analyzed attitudes toward gender equality and men's and women's practices concerning parental role division and household duties in both Poland and Norway ($N = 1{,}500$).

We describe only selected results from our wider research project that focuses on cultural and personal factors that lead to change in gender roles when migrant couples from a less gender-egalitarian country (Poland) move to a more gender-egalitarian country (Norway). We present studies making the following comparisons: (1) across countries, we compare governmental policies which might relate to couples' practices within domestic and parental duties arrangements. This comparison allows us to see how couples make use of existing policies in their respective countries (Poland and Norway). (2) Among Polish couples living in Poland (home country) and Norway (host country) and Norwegian couples, we analyze possible differences in gender-equality arrangements within domestic and parental duties. Finally, (3) across countries, we analyze differences in men's and women's views of the prescriptive and proscriptive elements of their gender roles that justify gender-(un)egalitarian parental roles and household duties division. This comparison sheds light on the regulatory function of the self-judgment of men and women and its influence on their willingness to share parental tasks and household duties. With this threefold comparison (encompassing the cultural, couple, and individual perspectives), we analyze the experiences of couples who reconcile family and professional roles while living in a new cultural context.

Our project contributes to the literature on gender equality as we show how well-established practices within family roles can change when migrating couples enter a host country where the social and political environment encompasses cultural cues promoting gender equality. We also investigate what factors facilitate and hinder the transition to a more gender-egalitarian family model. Finally, consistent with the themes in the current volume, our study investigates how gendered conceptions of parenting and family life shift or remain constant in the context of migration.

GENDER EQUALITY AND GENDERED ROLES IN POLAND AND NORWAY

The content of masculinity and femininity is strongly embedded in cultural contexts and contains both prescriptive and proscriptive indicators of what roles women and men should perform (Heilman et al., 2004; Hofstede, 2001). Cross-cultural comparisons by Hofstede (2001) and the multinational GLOBE project (House, Hanges, Javidan, Dorfman, & Gupta, 2004) show that gender egalitarianism within social and family relations is one of the most salient ways across which societies differ. *Gender egalitarianism* refers to the degree to which a society minimizes gender role differences and promotes gender equality in both public and family life (House et al., 2004). In countries scoring low on gender egalitarianism, the traditional division of gender roles (men acting as the main breadwinners and women as the main caretakers) is observed, whereas in countries scoring high on gender equality, women and men enjoy more freedom to move across the lines of gender stereotypes. Their parenting and household practices tend to be less gendered and more gender egalitarian, with both partners involved in domestic labor (Emrich, Denmark, & den Hartog, 2004). In this way, the gender equality level of a country affects women's and men's strategies for sharing parental roles and household duties (Greenhaus & Allen, 2011; Lyness & Kropf, 2005).

Gender Equality and Division of Labor

Gender equality is one of the flagship standards of Scandinavian nations and Norway, in particular. Neither a woman working on a forklift nor a man eagerly taking parental leave to care for a young child would be a surprise to Norwegians

(Living and Working in Norway, 2010). Systemic tools to foster gender egalitarianism not only strengthen women's position in the job market but also foster men's active involvement in family life. In 1993, Norway became the first country in the world to introduce the father's quota of the total parental leave (*fedrekvote*), which constitutes a number of weeks that have to be used by the father or they are lost—a total of 4 weeks when it was originally introduced. When Poland introduced a fathers' quota (*urlop ojcowski*) of 2 weeks in 2010, Norway already offered 10 weeks for fathers (Brandth & Kvande, 2015). In Poland, parental leave (*urlop rodzicielski*) for fathers was introduced only more recently in 2013. Of the 315,800 individuals who used parental leave the next year, only 5,200 were men (1.65%) (Michoń, Kurowska, & Kotowska, 2015). In Norway, less than 4% of fathers took some parental leave (*foreldrepengeperioden*) in the years before the introduction of the father's quota. In 1997, only a few years later, the take-up rate was more than 70%, and approximately 90% of eligible fathers took leave of some length (Brandth & Kvande, 2015).

With regard to domestic labor division, Norwegian men contribute the most to housework and related chores (180 minutes a day, their female partners 210 minutes) in comparison to fathers in 34 Organization for Economic Cooperation and Development (OECD) countries analyzed (Better Life Index, 2014). In contrast, Polish women spend on average 296 minutes daily, whereas men spend 157 minutes daily on housework and care of family members (OECD, 2014). Thus, when migrating to Norway, Polish couples move to a society where gender equality is more visible than in their home country. Does it influence the distribution of chores and childcare?

Differences in the male and female share in parenting and household chores constitute a visible gender gap in the family. Tai and Treas (2013) found an almost universal division of chores into male-typed (e.g., yard work, minor repairs) and female-typed (e.g., laundry, meal preparation, cleaning, sick care, and grocery shopping) tasks based on data from 32 countries. The latter group of duties consists of chores that are strongly avoided by men, who risk losing their masculine status by undertaking them (Vandello & Bosson, 2013; Kosakowska-Berezecka, Korzeniewska, Kaczorowska, 2016). For fear of not being perceived as manly enough, some men refrain from performing female-typed activities such as housework (Vandello & Bosson, 2013; Caswell, Bosson, Vandello, & Sellers, 2014; Kosakowska-Berezecka et al., 2016; Schneider, 2012). Even if men do not have breadwinner status in the family, they are not more likely to do these tasks at home (Brines, 1994). Men do not take up a share of household obligations that would allow women more time to be more visible in the labor market (Kosakowska-Berezecka et al., 2016). Clearly, domestic work is infused with gendered meanings (Poortman & Van der Lippe, 2009).

Gender-Typing of Tasks

We conducted a study among Polish and Norwegian students to examine the extent to which various household activities are gendered (i.e., considered male- or female-typed). We presented participants a list of various domestic activities (e.g., taking care of children, removing dust from furniture, cleaning the house, vacuuming, fixing things around the house) and asked them to assess whether they were male- or female-typed. Results showed that female- (e.g., cleaning the house) and male-typed tasks (e.g., fixing things around the house) were seen as less gendered in Norway than in Poland (Kosakowska-Berezecka, Jurek, Besta, & Seibt, submitted). We followed up this study by testing the hypothesis that if tasks were less female-typed, men might be more willing to take them on. Furthermore, because domestic activities are less gendered in Norway, we hypothesized that Norwegian men would be more willing to share these tasks with their partners than were Polish men. Indeed, our findings suggested that Norwegian men overall were more willing to undertake household duties than were their Polish counterparts. Analyzing perceptions of domestic duties contributed to our understanding of persistent gender inequalities in the division of household labor.

Changing Contexts, Changing Perceptions

We speculate that changing cultural contexts (i.e., from less to more gender egalitarian nations) can make gendered perceptions more neutral (Oyserman, 2011). We conducted a study among Polish migrant couples from Pomerania who migrated to the Rogaland region in Norway[1] (19 heterosexual couples) and Polish citizens living in the Pomerania region (21 heterosexual couples). The interviews were conducted in February and March 2014 and February 2015. All interviewees, who ranged in age from 22 to 53, cohabitated, and not all were married. The average length of relationship was 6.2 years for Polish couples in Poland and 8.8 years for Polish couples in Norway. The average time spent in Norway was 4.6 years. The interviewed families had one, two, or three children. Some couples did not have children when the project began. All the families had a declared dual-career relationship model, and the majority of participants had higher education degrees. Depending on the family situation (age of children), some worked part-time.

Among various themes of analysis (e.g., work–life balance, everyday life practices, parental roles, gender relations, relationship history, migration narratives, strategies of domestic duties division, and comparisons of Polish and Norwegian cultures), we examined how parental roles and household duties are perceived and realized in Norway. Results suggest that Polish couples do notice gender equality in Norway, especially with regard to the labor market. Respondents emphasized that professions are less gender stereotyped and that both women and men seem to have similar opportunities for obtaining jobs outside their gender-congruent domains. As one female informant stated,

> First of all, people say there is [gender] equality in Poland, which is not true, and I am the best example of that. I wanted to be a car mechanic.

> They did not accept me to school because they were not able to provide a separate toilet room for me. Here, women drive trucks with pear-shaped drums or lorries—well, they sometimes do that in Poland, too. They work on garbage trucks; streets are paved by women. So there is equality here. And women are able to earn as much as men here. And there is this flexibility in professions; there are no typically male or female professions. And it is so amazing when you see a concrete mixer and such a little, tiny woman driving it. (Agnieszka, 32 years old, mother of three children, 1.6 years in Norway)

Similarly, one couple discussed the issue of domestic duties, which they perceived as more gender-neutral in Norway. As Edyta (32 years, mother of three children, living 3 years in Norway), noted, "There are things Darek does better than me . . . and some I do better than he does. . . . For example, Darek cleans windows better, and I cook fish sticks better." Another respondent opined,

> What do I dislike? Ironing. I hate to iron. My husband irons. He irons babies' nappies and vests—he did this because I did not. . . . Of course, when he was at work. . . . Well, when I left it—if I had to, I did, but when I didn't, he liked it. Then he would sit, take the ironing board and iron. And I don't like ironing. (Marta, 50 years old, mother of two, 25 years in Norway)

De-gendering domestic practices and labor activities and professions is clearly present in Polish migrants' stories about their new lives in Norway. Respondents first describe the process of de-gendering as a part of cultural shock after migration. However, the longer they stay in Norway, the more they become accustomed to the cultural cues promoting gender equality in Norway and, as a result, de-gendered their practices (Żadkowska, Kosakowska, Ryndyk, in press), as described by two informants. Marcin (36 years old, father of two, 10 years in Norway), stated, "There is no rule here. I start to vacuum; I vacuum. My wife starts, she does it."

Echoing Marcin's sentiments that household duties are more easily divided equally between partners in Norway and that such tasks are seen as more gender neutral, Marek (36 years old, father of two, 5 years in Norway) notes,

> I do everything [*laugh*]. The spouse is with a kid now, so there's not much time to manage everything. We try to share. For example, cleaning and stuff like that, we try to do it together, but I take out the rubbish. I shop when I come back home from work; we live in a place where there's no grocery nowhere near. Generally, since the beginning of our relationship, we made decisions like that: I cook; the wife takes care of the papers. I manage meals, prepare food; the spouse cares for bills, recipes, guarantees and things like that—bureaucratic division. (Marek, 36 years old, father of two, 5 years in Norway)

MIGRANT WOMEN'S AND MEN'S SUBJECTIVE SATISFACTION WITH GENDER ROLES

A couple's experience of migration and implementation of more gender-egalitarian practices within family life can be mediated through various factors such as gender, education level, and professional social status in the host country (Castles & Miller, 2011). These processes can have gendered impacts on migrants' satisfaction with their perceived gender identities and their willingness to adopt more gender-egalitarian practices.

The second sample in our study, therefore, consisted of 15 Polish families residing in Norway, with partners holding jobs considered to have lower social status in Norwegian settings. Three women worked as assistants in kindergartens, four in informal or formal cleaning, two in catering, and two in production. In addition, two women were unemployed. One participant worked as a teacher, and another worked as a nurse. Regarding education, the women had rather high levels of education in Poland. Eight women had higher education at either the master's or bachelor's level, four had professional education, and three had high school as their highest achieved qualification. Those who were employed worked either full-time (8) or part-time (5) and had either temporary (6) or permanent (7) contracts. The women working in cleaning and catering often had to accept inconvenient working hours, some starting work very early in the mornings and others finishing work late at night. In addition, some had to work on the weekends.

Satisfaction With Gender Roles

Our findings suggest that Polish men in Norway for this subset in our study seemed to reaffirm their masculinity through better opportunities for work and income, whereas Polish women reported feeling less feminine. Polish men's accounts of masculinity and what it takes to be a man are largely embedded in the conceptualization of men as the primary breadwinners of the family, which they reaffirmed in their current situation. Migration to Norway presented them with opportunities to continue performing jobs similar to those they held in Poland but with considerably better remuneration. Being able to support their families gave them an opportunity to fulfil their masculine identities, as the case of Tomek illustrates:

> But a typically *true man* [emphasis added], I have become one only here. For in Poland I earned minimum wage as a construction worker. (Tomek, in his mid-30s, father of one, 4 years in Norway)

The men appeared to be largely averse to any changes that could threaten their job security. When asked whether they would like to change their jobs, most stated that they would not and explained that the remuneration and responsibilities of their positions were satisfactory to them. In contrast, changing jobs in cases when their wives held a temporary or part-time contract, we argue, could threaten the family's financial security and, thus, the husband's fulfilment of his role as the primary breadwinner. To see what can happen to a man who cannot provide for his family, the case of Bartek, the only man unemployed at the time of the interview, can be illustrative. He noted, "Now I have become [a housewife]. I've become *a housewife* [emphasis added]" (Bartek, early 30s, father of one, 2 years in Norway), suggesting that housewifization or womanization of the man can occur as an outcome of his failure to provide for the family.

Regarding female informants' perceived sense of femininity, the female participants complained about lack of opportunities to fulfil themselves professionally and to feel feminine. One respondent complained, "I always wear sports outfits here. To be honest, *I lack occasions* [emphasis added] when I can feel like a woman [here]" (Anna, 45 years old, mother of two, 1 year in Norway).

Interestingly, our informants' accounts seemed to largely relate being a woman to the construction of feminine appearance in public rather than to motherhood. Participants talked about how much they missed wearing fine clothes, high heels, and make-up in Norway:

> I thought I would never use sports shoes on a daily basis. I never wore sports shoes in Poland! [laughing] I always wore high heels. . . . I believed I would never wear such clothes in my life! Now I do not care that much anymore [about how I look]. I still wear a bit of mascara, but it is not because I think of what others think about me. I do it for myself. *I [then] feel like a woman* [emphasis added]. (Sylwia, 40 years old, mother of two, 8 years in Norway)

When asked to discuss the differences between Polish and Norwegian women, interviewees state that women in Norway are less feminine. Migration, thus, leaves a mark on Polish women's perceptions of and satisfaction with their own femininity. Gender stereotypes prescribe that women look feminine and visibly care about their looks—an expectation clearly less salient in Norwegian versus Polish culture.

Generally, informants seemed puzzled when asked about gender equality. In some cases, a clear distinction can be drawn between their attitudes towards gender equality in the abstract and in their families. For instance, Tomek talks about gender equality with admiration rather than skepticism:

> Well, I like it [gender equality], because women [want to] try it. Not that she wouldn't do it because it is too hard for her. What matters is that she comes and tries. If she tries and realizes that it is too hard for her, I can understand it for *men are made for physical work* [emphasis added]. But think how many women drive lorries here! Or excavators? Or in general, jobs that I, myself, would rather not dare to do. They dare it! (Tomek, mid-30s, father of one, 4 years in Norway)

At the same time, he expressed a desire for a situation where his wife would not need to work at all and that he could provide for her:

> I wish one day I could earn so much that [my] wife did not have to work. But I know that—it is possible, I can achieve it—but she won't give up a job she likes. And if she did not work, she would get bored. (Tomek, mid-30s, father of one, 4 years in Norway)

Although our informants reported equally sharing their duties at home, this division had a clear gender dimension. Women largely cooked meals and cleaned, whereas men mainly contributed by buying groceries and doing some cleaning and other housework:

> When [my] wife cooks dinner, I try to clean a bit or, for example, start a fire in the fireplace or, similarly, bring wood to make it warm in the house, and so on. (Pawel, early 30s, father of three, 8 years in Norway)

Female respondents stated that, due to their better Norwegian language skills, they mainly helped their children do homework. Polish men, if they helped, normally did so with homework subjects less demanding of language skills, such as mathematics. Overall, we argue that the couples in our study divided their household chores into gendered dimensions rather than shared them.

Generally, the effects of migration on women's and men's experiences seemed to be closely related to changes in their social status in their host country. Whereas Polish men tended to gain higher social status as a result of migration to Norway, Polish women experienced a decline. This tendency should not be generalized as it can be mediated by many factors, such as partners' education levels, previous work experience, language skills, and, thus, their opportunities for stable, gainful employment.

After migration from Poland to Norway, most of the interviewed women seem to have moved into a lower social status than in Poland. However, in Poland, being unemployed might not have necessarily equated to a low social status as long as they had a high level of education and a husband running his own business or sending money from abroad. Consequently, female participants often complained about their hectic work schedules and lack of opportunities to practice Norwegian and reported being unable to fulfil themselves professionally. These complaints were especially pronounced among those employed in the cleaning and catering sectors. Even Kasia, who was working as a nurse in Norway, stated that she was not satisfied with her job and had experienced a decline in her social status:

> At this moment *I am not fulfilled professionally* [emphasis added]. I came back to work in a lower position. What I did in Poland has nothing to do with the situation here. In Poland, I had a lot of *responsibility* [emphasis added], and I worked more creatively, but there was no money in it. . . . I have

> recognizable qualifications because I have an EU diploma. I am highly specialized in one area: diabetology. *I am qualified to teach* [emphasis added] others in this profession, and I did such things. Here, *I went back* [emphasis added] to the basics of nursing. (Kasia, 40 years old, mother of two, 1 year in Norway)

As mentioned, migrants' language skills are an important factor that can mediate the dynamics of their social status in the new country. Cleaning was the first job in Norway for most of the female participants. As they learned Norwegian and gained other necessary, country-specific skills, some transitioned into better jobs, such as kindergarten assistants and teachers. Kasia's comments illustrate how important language skills can be as a strategy to regain social status lost due to migration:

> I can fulfil my needs professionally, but I need to learn Norwegian better. For now, I am working, not too hard, and I earn fairly good money for Norway. I don't know how long it will take me, but I want to do something else. I know that, when I insist and push harder in terms of the language, I will be able to do what I want. (Kasia, 40 years old, mother of two, 1 year in Norway)

The accounts given by the Polish men in this sample feature very different dynamics in perceived social status and sense of work–life balance. The men seem to have gained higher social status and report being very satisfied with their professional and family situations. The jobs they performed in Norway did not differ much from those they had in Poland as most continued working in the construction industry after migration. An important difference, however, arose in the work environment, which is highly regulated and monitored in Norway. Working 7.5 hours a day, instead of 10 hours, while earning decent wages and being entitled to paid sick and paternal leave and other welfare provisions contributed to higher job satisfaction among the men. For example, Piotr states the following about working in Norway:

> Norway is such a country that, [when] one works here, one works for 7.5 hours a day, [and] one has a *normal job* [emphasis added]. If one can save here, one can manage to save for holidays or, let's say, in general. It's different here. If one has *more time* [emphasis added] for kids, then one acts differently, right? And when one comes home after 14 hours of work, what can you expect from him? (Piotr, 37 years old, father of two, 8 years in Norway)

Some of the men used to run their own businesses in Poland, which they described as very demanding in the time and effort they had to invest. Working late in the evenings and during the weekends was common. Working fewer hours resulted in more free time, which the men reported spending with their families and children. For some, migration to Norway meant a transition from being self-employed to becoming an employee, and, interestingly, they seem rather satisfied with this change. Kris compares working in Poland and Norway:

> Back in Poland, I was very stressed because I run my own business. In the past 8 years, I used to have my own firm. However, here I am mentally relaxed when working. I do not have to think and worry that I won't make the ends meet. Instead, I know that every 2 weeks there is money coming to my [bank] account. Living here is less stressful. (Kris, early 30s, father of one, 2 years in Norway)

Analyses of interviews with highly educated, dual-career families suggest that Polish male informants undertook childcare duties, shopping, cleaning, cooking, and washing dishes more willingly than Polish men living in Poland. Differences between Polish couples in Poland and Norway are evident not only in the number of duties that men performed but also in their conceptualizations of those tasks. When asked about household duties, Polish men and women in Norway simply described what they did, whereas Polish couples in Poland explained their duties as gendered obligations congruent with social expectations. As Dorota states,

> It all comes from the fact that, for example, bathing and vacuuming are more difficult things. You have to lift something, or it takes more time, and I cannot work too much. Because there are lots of different things I have to do around, so I don't do harder things. My spine aches immediately, I have to sit down and rest then, and that's it. In the kitchen, you also stand and do everything, because in your family also—women were [in the kitchen] more.... And it's the same with me. It just emerged naturally in our family. (Dorota, 37 years old, mother of one, living in Poland)

When describing their family life in Norway, Polish men emphasized the advantages of governmental policies, such as paternity leave and leave to care for a sick child—both of which they are highly willing to use. Similar solutions are available to fathers in Poland, but they see themselves as less entitled to these benefits as they felt obliged to maintain the breadwinner model. This situation is described by Paweł:

> It is nice about Norway that, as a father, I was with children by myself. I did everything; I just had to. I was changing diapers, feeding the baby, putting babies to bed. Everything had to be done, step by step. I really liked it. I do not regret it. It made me get used to it. A man got used to do it. I had developed a system, tick, tack. When she or he [the babies] was sleeping, I had some free time, and it was great. I regret there is no such a solution in Poland.... Well, there is, only 2 weeks as far as I know—it is nothing. Here, we have 3 months off work to take care of the child. (Paweł, 36 years old, father of two, 6 years in Norway).

These notions are echoed by Jacek (30 years old, father of one, living in Poland):

> For economic reasons, we decided I would stay with our son, and she [his wife] would continue to work. . . . And as I think now about all the people around me, only the financial situation matters. . . . In my friends' families, men earn more than women, and you have to go on, to survive. Let us be honest: what is taken into consideration in our country are mainly economic factors. It seems I am the only father on parental leave as generally, girls take it. (Jacek, 30 years old, father of one, living in Poland)

Differences in the distribution of household duties and parental roles are also evident in the narratives of Polish couples living in Norway and in Poland. These differences in family roles are especially visible among Polish men and women who are in dual-career relationships and have higher education degrees and high social status in the host country. It seems that these factors can provide a form of cultural capital enabling the de-genderization of family roles. Of course, these results are derived from interviews with Polish migrants. In our project, we also wanted to explore whether Norwegians perceive these family roles performed by Polish couples as egalitarian.

GENDER EQUALITY WITHIN POLISH FAMILIES IN THE EYES OF NORWEGIAN CIVIL SERVANTS

Public servants are street-level bureaucrats who act as agents between the individual citizen and the government and public policy (Lipsky, 2010). We conducted 22 personal interviews with a total of 30 public workers in three municipalities in the county of Rogaland, Norway (one city and two semirural municipalities). Our main focus was on health care and education, with 12 interviewees from the health care sector and 10 from schools or kindergartens. The interviewees answered questions about the welfare services needed by Polish migrants and notions of differences and similarities in gender equality between Polish work migrants and Norwegians. The bilingual teachers were all Polish migrants and might have reflected on these issues more than other informants.

General Views

Civil servants' views of Polish migrants and gender equality varied. A general picture is that civil servants in the city municipality noticed only nonsignificant differences between Poles and Norwegians and perceived practices in both family types as more or less gender equal. Public workers in the two semi-rural municipalities call Polish families more traditional than Norwegian families. Informants describe typical families as those in which the mother brings children to school and is the prime caregiver in the home, while the father is the breadwinner and prioritizes working. Civil servants find that childcare in Polish families is undertaken by mothers and extended family to a higher extent, whereas in Norway, childcare involves public institutions, such as schools, kindergartens, and different types of after-school activities, to a greater extent.

We found some nuances in civil servants' observations, particularly related to changes in practices when women gain employment. The story told is that dual employment results in more gender equality in the home. A bilingual teacher states the following:

> According to me, there is gender equality in Norway. In Poland, there is more expressed a female and a male gender role. However, I think that we like it. I do not think we want to—maybe, maybe we do not want gender equality. Maybe some want it because we have different opinions. Poles have different opinions.

The civil servants report that they rarely talk about gender equality when meeting Polish work migrant families. But it has become an issue in some situations in the education sector. Teachers state that they sometimes stress that both parents have to keep track of children's homework and participate in parent–teacher conferences. Another group of teachers finds it important to signal to their students that both sexes are equally valuable. In the health care sector, some midwives share that Polish men want to be involved when the woman is pregnant, whereas others would like to see more men join in consultations. Midwives also sometimes raise gender issues when the pregnant woman is tired or sick, and the message is that she is entitled to help in the home from her partner. Another civil servant brought to attention gender equality when a stroke left a man unable to be the breadwinner in the family as he had been.

Civil servants generally were not eager to talk about gender equality in encounters with Polish families. This reluctance might emerge because the Norwegian way of thinking about and practicing gender equality is considered the norm and is not up for discussion. Gender equality simply is taken for granted. Additionally, gender equality in the family can be understood as a private practice and an inappropriate topic for civil servants.

GENDERED IDENTITY AND WILLINGNESS TO SHARE PARENTAL ROLES AND HOUSEHOLD DUTIES

Most individual barriers that prevent men and women from adopting gender-equality ideologies result from cultural gender stereotypes (Rudman & Fairchild, 2004; Rudman et al., 2012). Men and women's self-descriptions are built on notions of femininity and masculinity, which reflect the content of culture-specific gender stereotypes and norms. Although cross-cultural studies show evidence for certain variations in the concepts of femininity and masculinity in different cultural contexts, two dimensions of agency and communality have characterized gender differences in most cultures: men need to be strong, agentic, and professionally successful; and women have to be caring, communal homemakers (see Diekman & Eagly, 2000; Eagly & Mladinic, 1989; Safdar & Kosakowska-Berezecka, 2015; Williams & Best, 1990). Thus, domestic work and professional life have gendered meanings. Housework and childcare are seen as women's and not men's work, and, conversely, careers and the provision of financial stability to the family is men's and not women's work. These beliefs are likely to become part of men's and women's gender identities and limit men's social role development within the household and women's within public sphere (Kaufmann, 1995; Szlendak, 2009; Żadkowska, 2011).

Consequently, changing one's gender role can be a threat to one's gendered self-concept. Fear of losing one's masculinity can act as a strong deterrent to men's involvement in household duties and childcare. Men's agentic self is strongly embedded in the context of contemporary masculinity and, as such, is the core of the stereotype of "real men." A threat to men's gender identity can influence their attitudes toward parental roles and their willingness to share household duties. Men will not undertake a large share of domestic and family obligations for fear of being perceived as not manly enough (Kosakowska-Berezecka et al., 2016).

Therefore, comparing the self-descriptions of Polish men in Poland and Norway can lead to interesting conclusions about the factors influencing their willingness to share household duties and become more involved fathers. In a quantitative, self-report study with 480 individuals living in heterosexual romantic relationships (60 Polish couples in Poland, 120 Polish couples in Norway, 60 Norwegian couples in Norway), we examined partners' willingness to share household duties (e.g., willingness to work at least as hard as one's partner), their real share of household duties (e.g., whose responsibility the household chores [laundry, cooking, cleaning, etc.] primarily are), perceptions of self (agency and communality; Laurin et al., 2011), and attitudes toward gender equality (Glick & Fiske, 2001; Van Zomeren, Spears, Fischer, & Leach, 2004). We also asked respondents to what extent they felt responsible for various household tasks, especially those (stereo)typically regarded as female (e.g., looking after children, elders, or sick family members; cleaning; washing; cooking).

Agency, Communality, and Gender Stereotyped Tasks

Our results show that being less communal and relatively more agentic helped to dissolve gender stereotypes about appropriate behaviors for both women and men. Male and female participants with higher levels of agency and lower levels of communality felt less responsible for female tasks than those perceiving themselves as less agentic. This difference is in accordance with predictions based on gender stereotypes: female tasks do not belong to individuals with non-female attributes that are agentic (male) traits. However, this effect was evident only in the sample of Poles living in their home country. Poles in Norway who describe themselves as more agentic were more willing to take responsibility for female household tasks (Kwiatkowska, Świdrak, & Krys, forthcoming). These findings suggest that agentic self-perception, enhanced by a reduced burden of communal traits, can make people feel free to take on any tasks regardless of the gender of the individual or the task gender. Such an indifference to task gender likely is possible only in Norway; that is, in an egalitarian culture. The more highly gendered Polish culture does not offer space for such shifts.

Acculturation and Willingness to Share Household Duties

Polish migrants' willingness to share household duties may depend on their adopted acculturation strategy. Migrants can adopt various acculturation strategies, and, according to Berry (1997), their choices may be explained by their attitudes toward maintaining relationships with the host country and their cultural identity during the migration experience. To these ends, an individual can adopt one of four acculturation strategies: (1) integration, (2) assimilation, (3) separation, or (4) marginalization. In *integration*, one combines close connections with the society of origin and the society of settlement. *Assimilation* entails rejecting one's cultural identity and embracing the host country's culture. *Separation* means the opposite reaction: one maintains strong cultural identity and does not develop connections with the host society. In *marginalization*, the least adaptive strategy, an individual rejects both the old and the new group identity (Berry, 1992).

Although acculturation is a mutual, reciprocal process through which both host and immigration groups pass, there are migrants for whom the adoption of a specific acculturation strategy results in major differences in the migration experience (Berry, 1997). We took a closer look at Polish migrants in Norway and analyzed how different acculturation strategies interfaced with gender equality issues.

Sharing household duties constitutes an egalitarian practice (Ogolsky, Dennison, & Monk, 2014). We find several differences in Polish women and men's approaches to sharing housework with their partners, depending on which acculturation strategy they adopt. Women who identified separation or integration as their acculturation strategy expressed the highest willingness to share their household chores with their partners. Women who reported feeling unattached to either Poland or Norway were the least willing to share household duties. Among men, the most important factor seemed to be whether an individual manages to adapt to Norwegian society, as men who feel integrated into Norwegian culture report the highest willingness to share household duties. Men who assimilated into Norwegian culture (i.e., rejected their Polish identity) were significantly more interested in sharing household duties. Male participants who used the marginalization or separation strategy did not wish to share household chores with their partners. It is possible that these men have had no opportunities to observe Norwegian egalitarian practices and consequently preferred the traditional division between female and male responsibilities.

Furthermore, given that separation from social networks in the home country makes migrants' lives harder, it is fruitful to adopt the strategy aimed at smooth acculturation with Norwegian society. Among men, openness to Norwegian society is correlated with higher willingness to share household duties. Men who rejected opportunities to observe egalitarian Norwegian practices maintained a stereotypical division of male and female responsibilities (Świdrak, Krys, & Kwiatkowska, in preparation).

CONCLUSION

This chapter focused on one of the manifestations of gender equality, that is, the egalitarian arrangement of parental roles and household duties that allow men and women equal share. Household arrangements appear to be more gender egalitarian among Polish couples in Norway than Polish couples in Poland, likely due to policies allowing men and women equal share in parenting and household duties and less-gendered meanings of domestic labor in Norway. This process might also be fostered by changes in perceptions of gender identity, which also differed by gender. That is, Polish men in Norway seemed to increase their sense of masculinity with better opportunities to fulfil the role of breadwinner, whereas Polish women in Norway experienced a decline in their sense of femininity because Norwegian feminine norms, which they tend to adapt, are different from Polish ones.

Nevertheless, as observed, childcare and household duties are perceived as less gendered in Norway than in Poland. According to our findings, men are more willing to undertake typically feminine household duties in Norway, where there is a higher level of gender equality and a smaller gap in household duties division compared to Poland. Gender is not a fixed set of roles but an ongoing, fluctuating collection of activities, created through interaction and shaped by a given cultural context. Understanding the perception of activities according to gender stereotypes is important to understanding who takes responsibility for housework. If men believed that parenting and housework are less feminine, they might see engaging in these activities as less threatening to their masculinity. When perceived as gender neutral, involvement in such an activity does not undermine a man's gender identity (masculinity). In contrast to egalitarian Norwegians, Poles exhibited visible support for traditional gender roles, which might threaten understanding of gender egalitarian attitudes.

We also find that in encounters between Polish migrant families, civil servants rarely interfered in gender issues nor on how migrant families choose to organize their household, with only a few such occasions mentioned during the interviews. In the education sector, gender issues are raised when equal opportunities for the students are an issue. In the health sector, gender equality seems to be mentioned only when a lack of equality threatens health. We find that civil servants address issues of gender equality not in general but only when they perceive that the migrants' practices interfere with their professional responsibilities as teachers or health care workers.

The de-genderization of practices is present in Polish migrants' stories about their new life in Norway. The longer they stay in Norway, the more they become accustomed to cultural cues promoting gender equality and de-gendered social roles. Changes in family roles are especially visible among Polish men and women who are in dual-career relationships, have higher education degrees, and have high social status in the host country. These factors seem to constitute a form of cultural capital enabling more egalitarian family roles.

Differences between Polish couples in Poland and in Norway are especially observed in the number of duties that men perform and in the contextualization of these tasks. Polish men and women in Norway simply describe what they do and avoid the context of gender differences in these descriptions, whereas Polish couples in Poland place the narrative of everyday practices in the context of gender differences and social expectations. The process of de-gendering parental and domestic activities is fragile and can be reversed, for example, by the outsourcing of domestic duties. These duties then usually fall upon women hired to take care of a household, which redraws the female task order (Fjell, 2010). The de-genderization process should be thus fostered by policies that maintain the norm that partners are equally involved in childcare and household chores.

Implications and Future Directions

Several promising future lines of research can be drawn from our study. One important direction reflects the reality of many families touched by migration—how concepts of gendered roles within family life are manifested when only the mother or father works and lives in another country for an extended period of time. If one of the parents experiences different gender norms of the host country and sees its benefits (e.g., as in the case of Polish men and women in Norway), to what extent are members willing to implement new strategies and more gender egalitarian approaches within the family?

Focusing specifically on women, another interesting theme of research would involve the analysis of the emancipatory effect of migration on women. In our research, we have come across two types of female migration that might relate to research of families experiencing being apart: Polish women who migrate to join their partner/husband (sometimes coming with their children and in some cases having children in Norway), and Polish women who migrate alone (without intention to join husband in Norway, with or without children). Both types of migration to a more egalitarian, sociodemocratic country open up opportunities to women that they wouldn't have in Poland. Having a fresh start, some women take this challenge and follow a path of "emancipation" in which they modify their expectations about life. As a result, they begin to feel that, when planning their life, they no longer have to follow social expectations. Some of them become more focused on their careers and demand more from men, thus manifesting a more gender egalitarian approach in their practices and attitudes (Herzberg, 2015).

On the other hand, the separation from social networks in one's home country makes migrants' lives harder, which in turn undermines their ability to tackle problems arising during migration. The cultural shock caused by division of gender roles previously unknown to migrants or the de-gendering of female and male roles in a family and in the whole society may be a source of additional stress undermining the quality of life for migrants. Therefore, inconsistency between migrants' expectations toward gender roles and the roles ascribed to genders in the hosting society may—and should—be taken into account when policies supporting migrants are designed. The stimulation of sensitivity to gender role flexibility and awareness of one's own gender role schemas (brought from the home country) may facilitate the migrant's functioning in the host culture and therefore may benefit both the migrant and the host society. In encounters with migrant families, civil servants will thus benefit from knowledge about how gender issues come into play in the migration process in order to have a better understanding of the migrant's situation. This knowledge should reflect that migration-related gender issues are relevant at the societal level for relations within the families and for the migrant's individual experiences.

As several other chapters in this volume note, it appears that breaking ties from other, even more distant extended family members (e.g., grandmothers) can be an additional source of stress related to gender norms. Polish grandparents typically contribute to the care of grandchildren. In Norway, Polish parents are without this support and thus often report feeling exhausted because of being without help. This lack of support constitutes a challenge more evident in interviews with the mothers. Some fathers even said that they liked being far from the extended family and being able to do what they wanted in life without too many (extended) family obligations.

Given that the majority of gender equality efforts tend to focus on women, one important implication for future policies is to focus on men. When attempting to explain national differences in the willingness to share household duties (i.e., Norwegians being more willing to share household duties than Poles), we find that one of the strongest mediators of cross-cultural difference among men is their readiness to support collective actions to foster gender equality. In other words, Norwegian men's ideological support for gender egalitarianism explains their higher willingness to share household duties in comparison to Polish men. We find no such relation among women. Our study suggests that it is men who inhibit gender equality in a family or in the society. Holter (2014) described an "emerging culture of gender equality," which he associated with improved health and well-being and lower violence, and this line of future studies may need to be extended—understanding the ways men benefit from gender egalitarianism may help make gender equality efforts more successful. We believe that these findings may support the conclusion that the key to real, at-home gender egalitarianism lies in having less stereotyped perceptions of gender roles and more positive attitudes toward gender egalitarianism.

Furthermore, we find it important to include gender equality issues and the cultural variety of gender stereotypes in school programs—from the earliest stages of education. As societies become increasingly more culturally heterogeneous, teachers, like civil servants, need to emphasize the cultural roots of gender roles. The role of education is crucial in that it forms future members of societies and may show the variety of different worldviews dominating in a given culture—including gender roles.

An example of such an education program can be found in our PAR Migration Navigator manuals for couples and for trainers who work with couples during workshops. In these publications, we share results from our Polish-Norwegian project and present knowledge that allows couples to more effectively negotiate division of household duties and parental roles, in hopes of increasing their work–life balance. Participation in the workshop based on this method helps couples avoid unconscious and automatic assumptions concerning women and men at home. Such programs and resources offer potentially fruitful supports for migrants and families.

NOTE

1. Our PAR Migration Navigator was the first research project on Polish migrants in the region of Rogaland, with the main city of Stavanger. Statistically, this region is a very important destination for Poles migrating to Norway.

REFERENCES

Berry, J. W. (1992). Acculturation and adaptation in a new society. *International Migration, 30*, 69–85.

Berry, J. W. (1997). Immigration, acculturation, and adaptation. *Applied Psychology: An International Review, 46*, 5–68.

Brandth, B., & Kvande, E. (2015). Norway country note. In P. Moss (Ed.), *International review of leave policies and research 2014*. Retrieved from http://www.leavenetwork.org/lp_and_r_reports/

Brines, J. (1994). Economic dependency, gender and the division of labor at home. *American Journal of Sociology, 100*, 652–688.

Castles, S., & Miller, M. (2011). *Migracje we współczesnych świecie*. Warszawa: Wydawnictwo Naukowe PWN.

Caswell, T. A., Bosson, J. K., Vandello, J. A., & Sellers, J. G. (2014). Testosterone and men's stress responses to gender threats. *Psychology of Men & Masculinity, 15*, 4–11.

Cross, S. E., & Madson, L. (1997). Models of the self: Self-construals and gender. *Psychological Bulletin, 122*, 5–37.

Diekman, A. B., & Eagly, A. H. (2000). Stereotypes as dynamic constructs: Women and men of the past, present, and future. *Personality and Social Psychology Bulletin, 26*, 1171–1188. doi:10.1177/014616720026200.

Eagly, A. H., & Mladinic, A. (1989). Gender stereotypes and attitudes toward women and men. *Personality and Social Psychology Bulletin, 15*, 543–558. doi:10.1177/0146167289154008.

Eldring, L., & Alsos, K. (2010). *Migrant domestic workers—beyond regulation regimes?* Paper presented at the 9th European Congress of the International Industrial Relations Association (IIRA), University of Copenhagen.

Emrich, C. G., Denmark, F. L., & den Hartog, D. N. (2004). Cross-cultural differences in gender egalitarianism: Implications for societies, organizations, and leaders. In R. J. House, P. J. Hanges, M. Javidan, P. W. Dorfman, & V. Gupta (Eds.), *Culture, leadership, and organizations: The GLOBES study of 62 societies* (pp. 343–394). Thousand Oaks, CA: Sage.

Fandrem, H., Sam, D. L., & Roland, E. (2009). Depressive symptoms among native and immigrant adolescents in Norway: The role of gender and urbanization. *Social Indicators Research, 92*(1), 91–109.

Fjell, T. I. (2010). Doing gender equality. Cleaners employed in Norwegian middle class homes. In L. W. Widding Iskasen (Ed.), *Global care work. Gender and migration in Nordic societies* (pp. 99–118). Lund: Nordic Academic Press.

General Statistic Office Poland. (2015). Retrieved from https://stat.gov.pl/obszary-tematyczne/ludnosc/migracje-zagraniczne-ludnosci/informacja-o-rozmiarach-i-kierunkach-emigracji-z-polski-w-latach-20042015,2,9.html

Gjerstad, B., Johannessen, Ø. L., Nødland, S., Skeie, G., & Vedøy, G. (2012). *Regional integreringspolitikk og praksis—Kunnskapsstatus og utviklingsmuligheter* (Regional integration politics and practice—Knowledge status and development possibilities). SIK report 2012:1, Stavanger.

Glick, P., & Fiske, S. T. (2001). An ambivalent alliance: Hostile and benevolent sexism as complementary justifications for gender inequality. *American Psychologist, 56*, 109–118.

Greenhaus, J. H., & Allen, T. D. (2011). Work-family balance: A review and extension of the literature. In J. C. Quick & L. E. Tetrick (Eds.), *Handbook of occupational health psychology* (2nd ed., pp. 165–183). Washington, DC: American Psychological Association.

Heilman, M. E., Wallen, A. S., Fuchs, D., & Tamkings, M. M. (2004). Penalties for success: Reactions to women who succeed at male gender-typed tasks. *Journal of Applied Psychology, 89*, 416–427.

Herzberg, M. (2015). Emigration as an emancipatory project. Narratives on experiences of Polish women in Norway. *Current Issues in Personality Psychology, 3*(3), 175–184. doi:10.5114/cipp.2015.53191.

Hofstede, G. (2001). *Culture's consequences: Comparing values, behaviors, institutions and organizations across nations*. Thousand Oaks, CA: Sage.

Holter, Ø. G. (2014). "What's in it for men?": Old question, new data. *Men and Masculinities, 17*, 515–548. doi:10.1177/1097184X14558237.

House, R., Hanges, P., Javidan, M., Dorfman, P., & Gupta, V. (2004). *Culture, leadership, and organizations. The GLOBE study of 62 societies*. Thousand Oaks, CA: Sage.

Jost, J. T., & Kay, A. C. (2005). Exposure to benevolent sexism and complementary gender stereotypes: Consequences for specific and diffuse forms of system justification. *Journal of Personality and Social Psychology, 88*(3), 498–509. doi:10.1037/0022-3514.88.3.498.

Kaufmann, J-C. (1995). *Trame coniugali. Panni sporchi e rapport di coppia*. Bari, IT: Edizioni Dedalo.

Kosakowska-Berezecka, N., Besta, T., Adamska, K., Jaśkiewicz, M., Jurek, P., & Vandello, J. A. (2016). If my masculinity is threatened I won't support gender equality? The role of agentic self-stereotyping in restoration of manhood and perception of gender relations. *Psychology of Men and Masculinity, 17*(3), 274–284. dx.doi.org/10.1037/men0000016

Kosakowska-Berezecka, N., Jurek, P., Besta, T., Korzeniewska, M., & Seibt, B. (submitted). De-gender them! Gendered division of household labour and men's willingness to share it—cross-cultural comparison of Polish and Norwegian male students.

Kosakowska-Berezecka, N., Korzeniewska, L., & Kaczorowska, M. (2016). Sharing housework can be healthy: Cultural and psychological factors influencing men's involvement in household maintenance. *Health Psychology Report, 4*(3), 189–201. doi:10.5114/hpr.2016.62232.

Kwiatkowska, A., Świdrak, J., & Krys, K. (forthcoming). The role of communion and agency in dissolving migrants' gender stereotypes.

Laurin, K., Kay, A. C., & Shepherd, S. (2011). Self-stereotyping as a route to system justification. *Social Cognition, 29*(2), 360–375. doi:abs/10.1521/soco.2011.29.3.360.

Lipsky, M. (2010). *Street-level bureaucracy: Dilemmas of the individual in public services*. New York: Russel Sage Foundation.

Living and working in Norway. (2010). Oslo, Norway: NAV Eures. Retrieved from http://www.eures.dk/JobSeeker/Landeinfo-og-jobdatabaser/Norden/Living_and_working_in_Norway_%28engelsk%29.aspx

Lyness, K. S., & Kropf, M. B. (2005). The relationships of national gender equality and organizational support with work-family balance: A study of European managers. *Human Relations, 58*, 33–60.

Michoń, P., Kotowska, I. E., & Kurowska A. (2015). Poland country note. In P. Moss (Ed.), *International review of leave policies and research 2015*. Retrieved from http://www.leavenetwork.org/lp_and_r_reports/

Organisation for Economic Co-Operation and Development. (2014). *OECD better life index*. Canada. OECD Publishing. Retrieved from http://www.oecdbetterlifeindex.org/countries/canada/

Ogolsky, B. G., Dennison, R., & Monk, K. (2014). The role of couple discrepancies in cognitive and behavioral egalitarianism in marital quality. *Sex Roles, 70*, 329–342.

Oyserman, D. (2011). Culture as situated cognition: Cultural mindsets, cultural fluency, and meaning making. *European Review of Social Psychology, 22*, 164–214. doi:10.1080/10463283.2011.627187.

Poortman, A. R., & Van der Lippe, T. (2009). Attitudes toward housework and child care and the gendered division of labor. *Journal of Marriage and Family, 71*, 526–541.

Pratto, F., & Walker, A. (2004). The bases of gendered power. In A. H. Eagly, A. Beall, & R. Sternberg (Eds.), *The psychology of gender* (2nd ed., pp. 242–268). New York: Guilford.

Rudman, L. A., & Fairchild, K. (2004). Reactions to counterstereotypical behavior: The role of backlash in cultural stereotype maintenance. *Journal of Personality and Social Psychology, 87*,157–176. doi:10.1037/0022-3514.87.2.157.

Rudman, L. A., Moss-Racusin, C. A., Phelan, J. E., & Nauts, S. (2012). Status incongruity and backlash effects: Defending the gender hierarchy motivates prejudice against female leaders. *Journal of Experimental Social Psychology, 48*, 165–179. doi:10.1016/j.jesp.2011.10.008.

Safdar, S., & Kosakowska-Berezecka, N. (Eds.). (2015). *Psychology of gender through the lens of culture. Theories and applications*. Cham, CH: Springer International. doi:10.1007/978-3-319-14005-6.

Schneider, D. (2012). Gender deviance and household work: The role of occupation. *American Journal of Sociology, 117*(4), 1029–1072.

Statistics Norway, SSB. (2015). Retrieved from http://www.ssb.no/en/befolkning/statistikker/innvbef

Świdrak, J., Krys, K., & Kwiatkowska, A. (unpublished manuscript). Work-Life Balance Mediates Between Acculturation Strategies and Life-Satisfaction.

Szlendak T. (2009). O naskórkowej (lub kosmetycznej) przemianie męskości. In M. Sikorska (Ed.), *Być rodzicem we współczesnej Polsce: Nowe wzory konfrontacji z rzeczywistoscią* (pp. 62–76). Warszawa: Wydawnictwo Uniwersytetu Warszawskiego.

Tai, T., & Treas, J. (2013). Housework task hierarchies in 32 countries. *European Sociological Review, 29*(4), 780–791.

Vandello, J. A., & Bosson, J. K. (2013). Hard won and easily lost: A review and synthesis of theory and research on precarious manhood. *Psychology of Men & Masculinity, 14*, 101–113. doi:10.1037/a0029826

Williams, J. E., & Best, D. L. (1990). *Measuring sex stereotypes: A multination study.* Thousand Oaks, CA: Sage.

Wood, W., & Eagly, A. H. (2012). Biosocial construction of sex differences and similarities in behavior. In J. M. Olson & M. P. Zanna (Eds.), *Advances in experimental social psychology* (Vol. 46, pp. 55–123). London: Elsevier.

Van Zomeren, M., Spears, R., Fischer, A. H., & Leach, C. W. (2004). Put your money where your mouth is! Explaining collective action tendencies through group-based anger. *Journal of Personality and Social Psychology, 87*, 649–664.

Żadkowska M. (2011). Mąż uczniem żony. O podziale obowiązków domowych na podstawie socjologii pary Jeana-Claude`a Kaufmanna. In M. Świątkiewicz-Mosny (Ed.), *Rodzina—kondycja i przemiany*. Kraków: Wydawnictwo Uniwersytetu Jagiellońskiego. (Husband—a wife student. Domestic duties division according to Jean-Claude Kaufmann sociology of couple).

Żadkowska, M., Kosakowska-Berezecka, N., & Ryndyk, O. (2018, forthcoming). Two worlds of fatherhood—comparing the use of parental leave among Polish fathers in Poland and in Norway. In K. Slany, P. Pustulka, E. Guriye, & M. Ślusarczyk (Eds.), *Transnational Polish Families in Norway: Social Capital, Integration, Institutions and Care*, Warsaw: Peter Lang International Academic Publishers.

5

Parental Migration and Well-Being of Left-Behind Children From a Comparative Perspective

YAO LU

Increasing globalization and urbanization worldwide have profoundly altered the state of the family in many societies. Hundreds of millions of people migrate internally (within a country) or internationally (across countries) to seek better life prospects (Lucas, 1997; Massey et al., 1998). More than 214 million people in developing nations live outside their home countries, sending back a total of $330 billion in remittances (United Nations, 2009; Ratha, 2009). Internal migration and remittances occur at even higher rates (International Organization for Migration, 2005). Global migration is projected to accelerate further in the coming decades. As a consequence, a sizeable fraction of children is affected by parental migration (United Nations International Children's Emergency Fund [UNICEF], 2007) who either accompany their migrant parents (migrant children) or, more often, are left behind by one or both parents (left-behind children) to circumvent the costs and uncertainties associated with migration. Conservative estimates suggest that more than 200 million children from developing countries are affected by migration (Organization for Economic Cooperation and Development [OECD], 2006; Whitehead & Hashim, 2005), with 15–30% of all children living in households with emigrant parents across Africa, Asia, and Latin America (Afsar, 2003; Bryant, 2005). China alone has 61 million left-behind children, mainly as a result of internal migration (All-China Women's Federation [ACWF], 2013).

Migration is a distinct form of family transition and one that is likely to have important effects on child development. Especially relevant for children, migration patterns have changed to involve more women and longer distances (Donato & Gabaccia, 2015). Migration leads to the disruption of family life and deprivation of parental presence, either of which may have detrimental implications for child well-being. However, migration often brings considerable economic improvement to original households through remittances (earnings from migrant workers to families they leave behind), which tends to benefit children. Overall, out-migration potentially confers both benefits and costs for children. Not only are there immediate impacts on children's welfare, but there may be long-term consequences for their transition to adulthood and adult socioeconomic status, which in turn may facilitate intergenerational mobility or reinforce social reproduction.

Migration research can be a productive way of elucidating the mechanisms through which family dynamics influence children's development (Stark, 1991). Studies of the consequences of migration for sending communities have long focused on macrolevel economic outcomes. A burgeoning literature has begun to examine the impact of emigration on the microworlds of families, especially on the well-being of children left behind (Dreby, 2010; Hoang & Yeoh, 2012; McKenzie, 2005; Parreñas, 2005; Toyota, Yeoh, & Nguyen, 2007). This strand of research has contributed to our understanding of how much variation there is in family structures in developing countries, as well as how new forms of family shape children's development. Yet the overall effect of parental emigration is not clear-cut because of potentially countervailing psychosocial and economic processes. Thus, to date, this literature has yielded inconclusive findings, reporting a positive, negative, or neutral relationship between migration and children's well-being.

In this chapter, I contend that this line of research should move beyond the debate of whether children benefit or suffer from parental out-migration and instead develop a more contextualized understanding by identifying the circumstances under which children benefit or suffer from migration. To this end, I first provide a conceptual framework for understanding the multifaceted consequences of parent migration for children left behind. I further delineate a comparative perspective that helps uncover the heterogeneity of the impact by different dimensions of child well-being, by the type of parental migration (domestic or international), and by the broader context of origin communities.

CONCEPTUAL FRAMEWORK

The conceptual framework for examining the developmental consequences of parental migration for left-behind children is displayed in Figure 5.1. It is informed by several strands of literature on child development in the context of parent–child separation, parental employment, and childcare arrangements, as well as by a growing literature on the economic impacts of migration.

The literature on family dissolution and parental employment demonstrates the critical consequences of parental absence, with high levels of parental input improving a wide range of child outcomes and parental absence exerting detrimental impacts on children (McLanahan & Sandefur, 1994; Waldfogel, 2010). In this respect, family separation resulting from out-migration inevitably leads to changes in family life and could put strains on family relationships (Dreby, 2010;

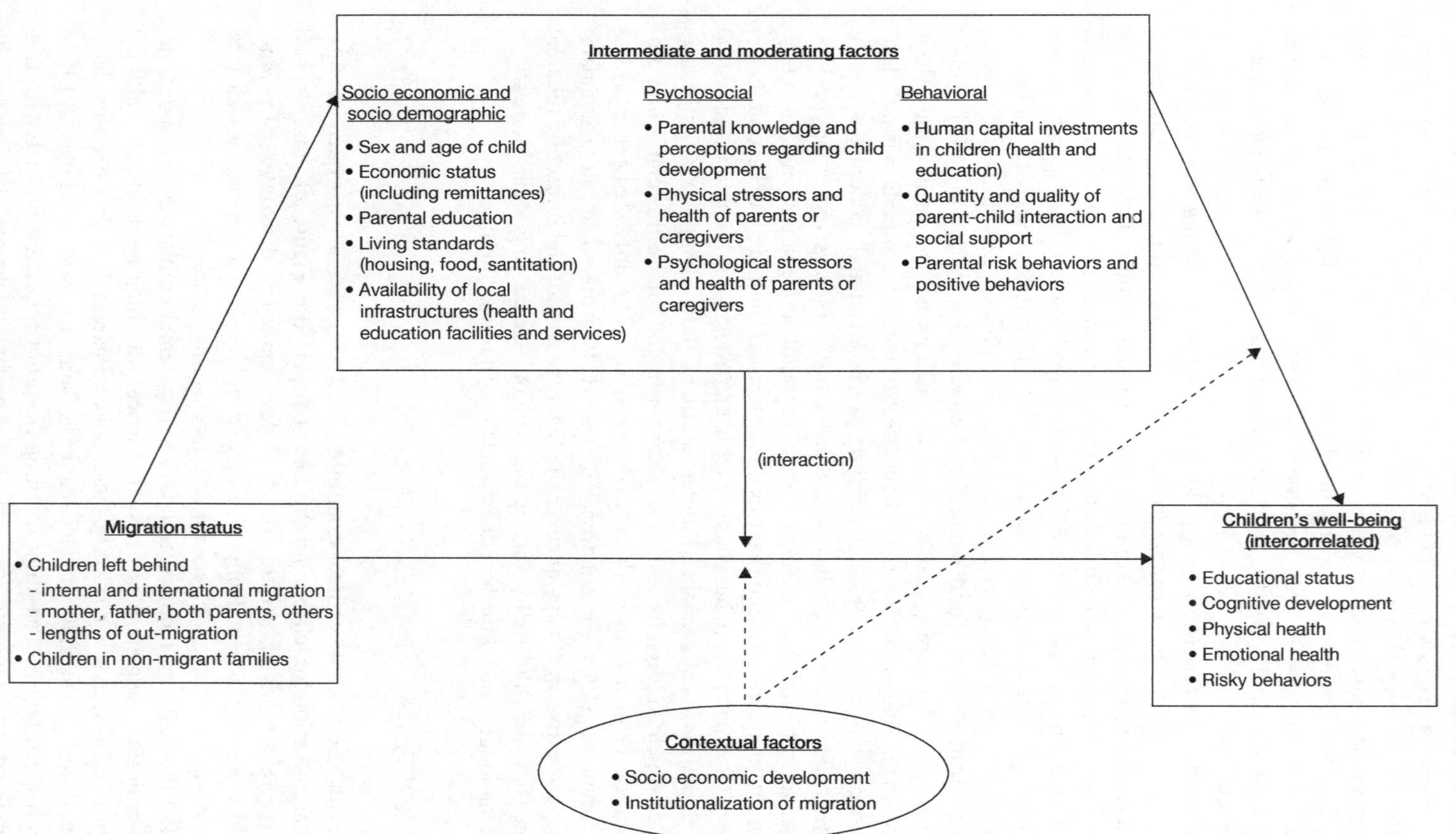

Figure 5.1. Children's well-being as a function of parental migration status.

Parreñas, 2005). The literature on the economic impact of migration perceives migration as a household strategy for improving household economic welfare (Stark & Bloom, 1985). Specifically, a large fraction of migrants' incomes is devoted to remittances, which reduce the economic vulnerability of the original families (Azam & Gubert, 2006; Semyonov & Gorodzeisky, 2008). A synthesis of these bodies of literature suggests that the impact of parental out-migration is multifaceted, as will be discussed in more detail later.

First, an extensive literature regarding family structure and child well-being, especially in Western societies, provides conclusive evidence of the detrimental consequences of parental absence for a range of child outcomes (McLanahan & Sandefur, 1994). Parental availability and engagement in children's lives improves children's social and educational outcomes, even after ability and family background are taken into account (Epstein, 2001). In contrast, single parenthood is linked to lower child development, indicated by reduced physical and psychological well-being and cognitive development and lower educational attainment (Amato & Cheadle, 2005; McLanahan & Sandefur, 1994). Parental work arrangements are also related to the development of children, with full-time employment having a detrimental effect for children, though mainly in early childhood (Waldfogel, 2010). The repercussions of family disruptions can be buffered by high-quality alternative childcare, or alternatively, exacerbated by low-quality care. In developed societies, marital dissolution is the primary source of parental absence (Amato & Cheadle, 2005; Potter, 2010). In the developing world, however, family disruption often arises when one or both parents migrate for work.

The adverse impact of parental absence noted in the broader family literature also arises in the context of migration. Parent–child separation due to out-migration leads to reduced parental input essential for children's development (Dreby, 2010; Graham & Jordan, 2011; Hoang & Yeoh, 2012; Parreñas, 2005; Suarez-Orozco, Todorova, & Louie, 2004; Toyota et al., 2007). When parents migrate, children inevitably experience prolonged periods of separation involving reduced parental input and supervision. The remaining parent or caregiver almost certainly faces additional household responsibilities and emotional burdens (Lu & Treiman, 2011), thus further occasioning a decline in the quantity and quality of care provided to children (Hildebrandt & McKenzie, 2005). The parent or caregiver left behind may also encounter emotional distress (Lu, 2012). Such distress not only aggravates parenting deficits but may also be inadvertently transferred to children and weaken their overall well-being. Parent–child separation can also lead to the absence of traditional authority figures and the breakdown of essential social control in the household (Parreñas, 2001). Children themselves may endure not only the emotional costs of separation from parents but also increased household responsibilities (Jones, Sharpe, & Sogren, 2004). Whereas migrants and families left behind continue to share strong bonds of collective welfare, the family separation inevitably leads to changes in family relations (Parreñas, 2001), a situation that is sometimes hard to remedy even after migrant parents return. Children left behind often feel a lack of affection and attention and therefore develop resentment toward their parents (Nazario, 2007). Migrant families sometimes seek to cope with the separation by turning to extended kin for support. These and similar resources may help alleviate some family constraints, but this is not consistently the case (Parreñas, 2001). This could be due to a lack of supervision authority among nonparent family members as well as a lack of education among older relatives (e.g., grandparents).

Second, parental out-migration is distinct from many other types of parent–child separation (e.g., divorce, parental death), which are commonly accompanied by declines in economic well-being (Garfinkel & McLanahan, 1986). Households with migrants often receive substantial remittances, which can benefit children's development (Hildebrandt & McKenzie, 2005; Semyonov & Gorodzeisky, 2008). This is predicted by the "new economics of labor migration" that links migration and the families left behind (Stark & Bloom, 1985). This theory contends that migration decisions are made collectively by families in order to diversify risks and maximize household economic welfare. This is particularly true in less-developed societies, which often have inadequate credit systems and little institutionalized provision for insurance against crop failure, illness, or loss of productivity in old age. Thus, families send some of their members to work as wage labor while others tend the fields, generating surplus capital from the savings of the migrant workers. In this sense, remittances can play a crucial role in reducing the level of poverty and economic uncertainty (Adams, 2006; Azam & Gubert, 2006).

From the perspective of child development, these economic gains serve as a critical means for enhancing family income and standard of living, allowing for more resources to be allocated toward children's education and health (Amuedo-Dorantes, Sainz, & Pozo, 2007; Antón, 2010). These remittances can be used to keep children in school, to pay for supplementary educational services and other school supplies, and to enhance children's learning ability by affording health care and nutritious food. They also can improve utilization of health services and other forms of health-seeking behavior by directing more resources to health-related investments. Remittances may also help mitigate the time and energy constraints of the remaining caregiver (Brown & Poirine, 2005), enabling them to dedicate more time to childcare, and to reduce the household's demand for child labor (thus reducing economic pressure on children to leave school) (Brown & Poirine, 2005; Lu & Treiman, 2011). The family's improved economic status may also bring nonpecuniary psychological benefits. Given the widely documented protective effect of economic resources on mental health (Kahn, Wise, Kennedy, & Kawachi, 2000), remittances may mitigate the stressful circumstances resulting from the out-migration of some family members. In the long run, as migration becomes an integral feature of a community, it can lead to concomitant improvements in local infrastructure and broader local development, which are conducive to child development health (Taylor et al., 1996).

These economic benefits may not be ubiquitous, however, especially in the initial stage of out-migration when left-behind households receive limited or no remittances in tandem with reduced household labor (Kandel, 2003). There is generally a time lag between migration and receipt of remittances and improvement in household welfare. Because of this time lag, one immediate aftermath for families left behind is financial hardship, which may compel caregivers to shift more time from childcare into home production and also force families to reduce spending on children. If out-migration creates an unmet need within the household for domestic duties, children may shift their time into home production, resulting in schooling interruptions. The time lag between out-migration and improved household welfare tends to increase over the past several decades—especially for families of undocumented migrants—as a result of the rising costs and difficulties of out-migration. Even at later stages of out-migration, some households continue to experience large fluctuations in remittances (Amuedo-Dorantes & Pozo, 2010; De Brauw & Mu, 2011). Moreover, there is a long-standing debate on whether households spend remitted earnings on productive investments that may contribute to poverty reduction and economic development, such as investment in health, human capital, and entrepreneurship. Some suggest that a large share of remitted earnings is used for recurrent expenses and consumer goods (Canales, 2007). Others document that remittances are used for facilitating small business and agricultural investment (Woodruff & Zenteno, 2007) or for investing more in children's education (Lu & Treiman, 2011).

Third, beyond financial remittances, emigration can bring about social transfers of knowledge, attitudes, and practices (i.e., "social remittances," Levitt, 1998; Lindstrom & Munoz-Franco, 2006), which may confer both benefits and costs on the well-being of the people left behind. Such transfers often take place as a result of migrants' exposure to destination contexts, which can lead to greater information, increased awareness of parental investment in children, and probably also a new set of lifestyles. These social remittances can have direct effects on children, and they can also reinforce the impact of monetary remittances. However, social transfers may also confer costs on children's well-being. For example, they may bring about unhealthy lifestyles as migrants adopt a new set of behaviors that are commonplace in host societies. Migration can also diminish children's educational aspirations if migration appears to be a more viable and alternative route to economic success than education (Kandel & Kao, 2001). As a result, migration of family members may increase the likelihood that children will forgo school and migrate in search of employment. Furthermore, families may anticipate that children will eventually migrate to obtain low-skilled work; in these situations, adults may reduce educational expenditures and children may decrease the effort they invest in school (Kandel, 2003).

Because migration potentially confers both benefits and costs for children, the key in understanding the effect of migration on children hinges on the balance of these multifaceted processes. This raises an important question about what conditions shape the relative balance between the positive and negative aspects of parental migration. This question, until now, has not been well understood and is thus the focus of this chapter.

Despite the general conceptual framework just provided, there tends to be considerable heterogeneity in the role of parental migration. One example of such heterogeneity is the relationship between migrants and children. A number of earlier studies use a composite measure of household migration status (Hildebrandt &

McKenzie, 2005; Lopez-Cordoba, 2005) that captures common situations where migrants are household members other than the parents (i.e., siblings, other relatives). This strategy obscures the very different experiences children endure when their parents (as opposed to other nonparent family members) migrate. A more negative impact of migration seems to occur when parental migration status is distinguished from migration of other family members (Lu, 2012). This is because migration of other family members gives rise to economic improvements from remittances without incurring family disruptions due to parental migration. Migration becomes more disruptive when key parents are the migrants, largely overshadowing the positive effect of migration.

The impacts of migration can also differ by whether mother, father, or both parents migrate. Out-migration of mother or both parents often leads to significantly worse outcomes than out-migration of fathers. This is because mothers assume greater caregiving roles. Mothers are often charged with being the main caregivers of their children, and fatherhood is linked with authority and protection. In the context of migration, these differences may mean that whereas the out-migration of fathers leads to the lack of a male role model and disciplinarian figure, the absence of mothers tends to incur substantial disruptions in everyday life and may be more detrimental for children (Parreñas, 2005). Women also have a greater propensity to invest in children than do men, especially when they are empowered to manage resource allocation (which can happen when the male family member has migrated). This suggests that the presence of mothers could reinforce the positive economic impact of migration on children.

Other heterogeneous effects of migration, such as by different dimensions of child well-being, by the type of parental migration (domestic or international), and by the broader context of origin communities, are less adequately understood and will be discussed in length in the subsequent sections. Attention to these differences helps us understand how the positive and negative processes associated with migration balance under distinct contexts. To the extent that the role of parental migration plays out similarly across outcomes, types of migration, or contexts, these comparisons facilitate the development of broader generalizations about the consequences of out-migration for children. Equally important, a comparative perspective allows the identification of differences in the effect of parental migration across settings.

DIMENSIONS OF CHILD WELL-BEING

The psychosocial costs due to parental migration are likely to have especially adverse effects on the aspects of child social, psychological, and cognitive development that hinge strongly on parental emotional and social input (Ehrle & Moore, 1999; Paxson & Schady, 2007). These negative feelings and experiences likely result in emotional and behavioral repercussions for children that are not easily reparable (Lahaie, Hayes, Piper, & Heymann, 2009). Children left behind may be especially susceptible to emotional instability, behavioral problems, and lower cognitive development and academic performance. By contrast, migrants' financial and social transfers can have beneficial effects for children, especially with respect to educational opportunities and physical health, both of which depend heavily on household material resources in developing settings (Buchmann & Hannum, 2001; Smith & Haddad, 2000). Remittances represent the core mechanism for these dimensions of child development.

Mixed evidence from previous research suggests possible heterogeneous effects by the outcomes examined. With respect to educational attainment of left-behind children, the area that has received the most scrutiny, studies often suggest an overall negative or neutral effect of parental migration (Acosta, 2006; Arguillas & Williams, 2010; Borraz, 2005; Creighton, Park, & Teruel, 2009; Halpern-Manners, 2011; Kandel, 2003; Kandel & Kao, 2001; Lahaie et al., 2009; Lopez-Cordoba, 2005; McKenzie & Rapoport, 2006; Nobles, 2011). As for children's school enrollment, the picture is more optimistic, suggesting that migration is positively associated with children's school attendance (Adams, Cuecuecha, & Page, 2008; Curran, Cadge, Varangrat, & Chung, 2004; Hanson & Woodruff, 2003; Lu & Treiman, 2011; Macours & Vakis, 2010). These results suggest that the potential beneficial impact of migration is largely overshadowed by the social costs of family separation. Such social costs are clearly reflected in educational outcomes (less so in enrollment) because educational attainment is closely linked to parental nonmaterial resources (while enrollment is more closely tied to family material resources). Children with migrant parents receive less adequate supervision and academic assistance and live in a home environment less conducive to learning. These children also might develop emotional and behavioral problems. All these factors could manifest in school-related problems and hinder children's school progress in ways that are not easily offset by improved economic resources from remittances.

The findings are generally more positive for children's health outcomes. Lopez-Cordoba (2005) found that the receipt of remittances is associated with lower rates of infant mortality in Mexico. Hildebrandt and McKenzie (2005) demonstrated that the presence of US migrants in the household lowers the risks of infant mortality and low birth weight, though it lowers the probability that children are breastfed and fully vaccinated. Frank and Hummer (2002) demonstrated that having a US migrant in the household has a positive effect on birth weight in Mexico. Carletto, Covarrubias, and Maluccio (2011) provided similar evidence for a positive impact of migration to the United States on the height-for-age of children left behind in Guatemala. Similar positive impacts of migration on the nutritional status of children are found in Ecuador (Antón, 2010) and rural Nicaragua (Macours & Vakis, 2010). The importance of migration and remittances is particularly salient in times of crisis, mitigating declines in child growth during a food crisis in El Salvador (de Brauw, 2011). But other studies suggest the opposite. Kanaiaupuni and Donato (1999) found higher rates of infant mortality in Mexican communities with high levels of migration, although this negative effect diminishes as the level of remittances increases. Nobles (2007) found that parental migration outside the community is associated with lower height-for-age.

Overall, this line of work on health shows a positive relationship because health is closely related to the material resources of the households. But the beneficial effect can be reduced for young children, for whom parenting practices are especially crucial. Lu (2014, 2015) studied the educational attainment and physical growth of children in two countries, Mexico and Indonesia, and found that in both settings the growth of left-behind children is more positively associated with parental migration than is education.

The socioemotional and behavioral well-being of children left behind has received less attention, largely due to data limitations. The emerging evidence has painted a rather pessimistic picture, pointing to the detrimental impacts of parental migration on children's psychosocial development. Jordan and Graham (2012) represent one of the most comprehensive studies to date. This study examines the well-being of children left behind by overseas migrant parents in three southeast Asian countries (Indonesia, Philippines, and Vietnam) and shows that children left behind reported less happiness across the three settings.

INTERNAL VERSUS INTERNATIONAL MIGRATION

Both internal and international migration are common occurrences that result in widespread family separation in different parts of the world. Previous research suggests that internal and international migration are alternative strategies in response to broad social and economic forces and can be studied under a unified framework (Castles & Miller, 1998; DeWind & Holdaway, 2008; Pryor, 1981). Whereas internal and international migration share fundamental processes, they are likely to incur different levels of family disruption and economic return, which in turn have potentially different ramifications for children.

The existence of border restrictions means that international migration implies longer durations of family separation and less frequent contact between parents and children than internal migration (DeWind & Holdaway, 2008), which tends to result in substantial disruptions in caregiving practices and reductions in parental support. Although many international migrant parents expect separations to be brief, they typically drag out for years (Nazario, 2007). By contrast, internal migration is more likely to be circular and usually generates shorter episodes of separation.

International migration can often generate a higher level of remittances, although families left behind by international migrants may face more fluctuations in remittances than do families of internal migrants. Because international migration often entails a longer period of adjustment than internal migration, the time lag, initial economic difficulties, and fluctuations of remittances confronting left-behind families of international migrants tend to be greater (Kandel, 2003). These constraints may be intensified for families of undocumented immigrants as a result of the high costs of illegal immigration and the precarious conditions illegal immigrants face (Durand & Massey, 2006). Therefore, it is worth noting that although international migration can generate a higher level of remuneration than internal migration due to differences in wage rates between sending and receiving nations, it is not always the case.

On balance, international migration of parents, especially undocumented international migration, may be more detrimental for children due to the greater difficulty both in returning home for visits (thus longer episodes of separation) and in transferring money across countries. Placing the results from previous studies in the context of internal versus international migration helps reconcile seemingly inconsistent findings that depict a positive, neutral, or negative effect of parental migration. A negative impact of parental migration on education and health is often found in the context of international migration (Creighton et al., 2009; Halpern-Manners, 2011; McKenzie & Rapoport, 2006; Nobles, 2011). The net impact tends to be less adverse and may even turn positive in cases of internal migration (Adams et al., 2008; Anton, 2010; Curran et al., 2004; Lu & Treiman, 2011; Macours & Vakis, 2010).

In one of the few existing studies directly comparing the effect of internal and international migration of parents, Lu (2014, 2015) shows that children of international migrant parents generally fare worse than those of internal migrant parents. This is the case with respect to both health and educational outcomes and for two different settings studied (Mexico and Indonesia). International out-migration tends to have a more deleterious or less positive effect on children than internal migration, especially for education. Internal migration can sometimes play a negative role, such as when either the mother or both parents migrate, but this is less consistent and often to a lesser degree. This difference is presumably due to the longer duration of family disruption and fluctuations in remittances. While improved material resources from remittances may generate some positive effects, this is mostly seen in children left behind by internal migrant parents. For international out-migration, the substantial disruptions in household and childcare arrangements present important hurdles for migrant families, which can offset or even reverse the potential benefits resulting from migrants' remittances.

DOES CONTEXT MATTER?

The balance of underlying processes of parental out-migration, and thus the net effect of migration, is contingent on context. Although there tend to be some broad similarities in migrant-sending areas, these settings differ in potentially important ways—for example, in terms of the level of socioeconomic development and the institutionalization of migration (World Bank, 2005). Such differences could affect the link between parental migration and children's development.

The comparative family research sheds some light on the contextual factors shaping the importance of family resources for children's development. Lockheed, Vail, and Fuller (1986) found that basic material inputs were most important for children's well-being in resource-poor settings with inadequate or highly variable resources but were less so in contexts that have achieved a certain minimum level of basic resources. In comparison, research in developed societies has shown that family economic resources have a relatively small effect on children's outcomes, which is partially attributed to the public spending and welfare that help provide for families' basic needs (Aughinbaugh & Gittleman, 2003). Similarly, in developing societies, government educational spending may reduce the direct costs of schooling, thereby reducing the importance of family resource constraints for investment in children (Lloyd, 1994; Post & Pong, 1998). Following this proposition, one may expect that the economic benefits accrued from migration have a greater impact on children's development in settings with limited public spending on human capital (e.g., education, health) than in settings with more generous public resources. This is because, in more resource-constrained settings, these material resources can tip the balance regarding how much the family can invest in children's human capital.

Previous research, mostly based on single settings, displays considerable discrepancies with regard to the impact of migration, This implies that the relationship may vary by contexts that affect the relative importance of the underlying psychosocial and economic processes. Existing research has demonstrated a negative outcome of parental migration in Mexico (Creighton et al., 2009; Halpern-Manners, 2011; McKenzie & Rapoport, 2006; Nobles, 2011), a migrant-sending region that is comparatively more developed than many other poorer sending areas. In contrast, the association tends to be less adverse and may even turn positive in more resource-constrained settings such as less-developed countries in Asia, Africa, and Latin America (Adams et al., 2008; Curran et al., 2004; Lu & Treiman, 2011; Macours & Vakis, 2010). For example, South Africa's long history of racial stratification created dramatically unequal access to education, and many blacks have had to resort to migration to better their livelihoods and those of the next generation. In this context, remittances can tip the balance and allow the family to provide necessary economic resources for children in deprived households.

Lu (2014, 2015) examines the education and health of children in two distinct settings, Mexico and Indonesia, using highly comparable data. The studies find that the effect of parental migration is more detrimental and less beneficial for children in Mexico than in Indonesia. One plausible explanation hinges on the different levels of development and public spending. In the more resource-constrained Indonesia, where educational and health resources are limited, additional economic resources from remittances can provide necessary resources for children. This economic benefit may offset much of the disruptive consequences of parent–child separation. The potential benefits conferred by remittances are constrained in Mexico, which has achieved a moderate level of economic development and better public provisions on human capital. This results in a net negative relationship between parental migration and child well-being. To be sure, with a two-country comparison, it is difficult to definitely pin down the contextual factors shaping the cross-country difference. Nonetheless, these results provide suggestive evidence for the importance of a contextualized understanding of the effect of parental migration on children.

The cultural and institutional context of sending regions can be equally crucial and can determine the specific context underlying migration. Cultural context can shape the normative expectations of parenting behavior and the ways in which parental absence is internalized. Although empirical evidence is only emerging, there is some indication that the deleterious effects of parental absence due to migration may be ameliorated in communities where migration becomes a normative family strategy and when the care-providing role is extended beyond the nuclear family unit (Parreñas, 2005). Institutional context also matters. A special case is China, where the life circumstances of internal migration bear great resemblance to those of international migrants (especially undocumented migrants) to the United States and other industrialized societies (Roberts, 1997). This is attributed to China's unique institutional arrangements that result in various structural and social barriers facing migrants. This context has important implications for understanding how migration shapes the developmental prospects of children left behind in a domestic scene.

DISCUSSION AND FUTURE DIRECTIONS

Parent–child separation due to migration has become increasingly prominent in developing countries. This chapter discusses a conceptual framework for understanding the effects of parental migration on children and identifies several conditions that can shape the impact. In emigrant families, the well-being of children can be understood as both a socioeconomic process and a psychosocial process stemming from family separation. Whereas the overall impact of parental out-migration may not be as ubiquitously deleterious as that of marital dissolution, the social costs of family separation resulting from migration are real and can overshadow potential benefits. This strand of research contributes to our understanding of family structure variations in developing countries, as well as to how a distinct form of family structure resulting from migration influences child well-being. Existing findings suggest that it is difficult to draw sweeping conclusions about whether the role of parental migration for children is beneficial or harmful; instead, its role should be understood within the specific context in which migration occurs.

I highlight the importance of a comparative perspective in understanding the relationship between parental migration and children's development. This perspective helps illustrate the circumstances under which children either suffer or benefit from parental migration. A synthesis of previous research suggests that the relative balance of the economic and psychosocial processes arising from parental migration is contingent on several factors: (1) Who is the migrant? Out-migration of parents, particularly mothers, often leads to worse child well-being than migration of fathers or nonparent family members. (2) Which dimensions of child development are affected? Parental migration tends to have an especially adverse effect on children's psychoemotional and behavioral well-being (sometimes spilling over to educational outcomes) because such well-being hinges strongly on parental emotional and social input. (3) Where do migrant parents go? International migration of parents seems to have a somewhat more adverse and less beneficial impact on children than does internal migration because of the longer episodes of separation and greater difficulties in transferring stable remittances. (4) What is the origin context? The influence of parental migration tends to be contextualized within the larger socioeconomic sphere within which migration occurs. The existence of different developmental stages and institutional systems across settings means that a different set of social and economic conditions exist in different locales. Instead of viewing parental migration as having a homogeneous influence on children, the comparisons I emphasize in this chapter suggest that the impact of parental migration should be interpreted within the specific context that surrounds the process of migration.

Thus far, existing evidence shows that parental migration has not given children left behind as much of a developmental advantage as their parents had hoped. This is disheartening because the sheer number of children affected by parental out-migration is growing worldwide, and one of the primary reasons for migration is to improve children's life chances. Unfortunately, the success of this strategy is limited because few families left behind are prepared for the unintended consequences of the resultant family disruptions. The plight of these children presents major challenges not only to their own development, but also to the social and economic development of the society in which they live.

These findings highlight a need to rethink the strategies of leaving children behind for labor migration and, when family separation due to migration cannot be avoided, to devise migration strategies that mitigate the negative impact on children (i.e., shorter distance domestic migration instead of cross-country migration). The solution is not to impose stringent mobility restrictions, but to devise effective programs that simultaneously address the psychosocial costs of migration and promote regular economic transfers. One strategy could be to boost the amount and regularity of remittances by diversifying transfer methods and reducing transfer costs. Also, families of out-migrants may benefit from programs that facilitate regular contacts between migrants and families left behind, such as those that lower the cost of communication and transportation services. This strategy may be especially effective because it could help reduce the distress encountered by both migrants and their children. Programs that provide good-quality substitute child care or that provide support for remaining caregivers may also be useful.

Future research based on different types of comparisons pertinent to migration will be especially useful in advancing this line of inquiry. The focus should be on exploring the heterogeneity of the effect of migration and on understanding the conditions giving rise to these heterogeneous effects. Larger scale cross-national comparisons, especially those with rich information on family psychosocial and economic processes as well as on a wide array of child outcomes, would be especially useful in illuminating the mechanisms underpinning the effect of parental migration, establishing commonalities across settings, and identifying factors that account for the cross-setting differences.

ACKNOWLEDGMENTS

The author gratefully acknowledges support from the National Institute of Child Health and Development (1K01HD073318).

REFERENCES

Acosta, P. A. (2006). *Labor supply, school attendance, and remittances from international migration: The case of El Salvador* (Research Working Paper No. 3903). Geneva: World Bank.

Adams, R., Cuecuecha, A., & Page, J. (2008). *The impact of remittances on poverty and inequality in Ghana* (World Bank Policy Research Working Paper No. 4732). Geneva: World Bank.

Adams, R. H. J. (2006, May). *Migration, remittances and development: The critical nexus in the Middle East and North Africa.* Presented at United Nations expert group meeting on international migration and development in the Arab region, Beirut.

Afsar, R. (2003, June). *Internal migration and the development nexus: The case of Bangladesh.* Paper presented at the Regional Conference on Migration, Development and Pro-Poor Policy Choices, Dhaka, Bangladesh.

All-China Women's Federation. (2013). *Research report on the current status of rural left-behind and urban migrant children in China* [in Chinese]. Retrieved from http://acwf.people.com.cn/n/2013/0510/c99013-21437965.html

Amato, P., & Cheadle, J. (2005). The long reach of divorce: Divorce and child well-being across three generations. *Journal of Marriage and Family, 67*(1), 191–206. doi:10.1111/j.0022-2445.2005.00014.x.

Amuedo-Dorantes, C., & Pozo, S. (2010). Accounting for remittance and migration effects on children's schooling. *World Development, 38*(12), 1747–1759.

Amuedo-Dorantes, C., Sainz, T., & Pozo, S. (2007). *Remittances and healthcare expenditure patterns of populations in origin communities: Evidence from Mexico* (Working Paper 25). Inter-American Development Bank.

Antón, J. (2010). The impact of remittances on nutritional status of children in Ecuador. *International Migration Review, 44*(2), 269–299.

Arguillas, M. J. B., & Williams, L. (2010). The impact of parents' overseas employment on educational outcomes of Filipino children. *International Migration Review, 44*(2), 300–319.

Aughinbaugh, A., & Gittleman, M. (2003). Does money matter? A comparison of the effect of income on child development in the United States and Great Britain. *Journal of Human Resources, 38*(2), 416–440. doi:10.3368/jhr.XXXVIII.2.416.

Azam, J., & Gubert, F. (2006). Migrant remittances and the household in Africa: A review of evidence. *Journal of African Economies, 15*(suppl 2), 426–462.

Borraz, F. (2005). Assessing the impact of remittances on schooling: The Mexican experience. *Global Economy Journal, 5*(1), 1–9. doi:10.2202/1524-5861.1054.

Brown, R. P., & Poirine, B. (2005). A model of migrants' remittances with human capital investment and intrafamilial transfers. *International Migration Review, 39*(2), 407–438. doi:10.1111/j.1747-7379.2005.tb00272.x.

Bryant, J. (2005). *Children of international migrants in Indonesia, Thailand, and the Philippines: A review of evidence and policies.* (Innocenti Working Paper No. 2005-05). Florence, IT: UNICEF.

Buchmann, C., & Hannum, E. (2001). Education and stratification in developing countries: A review of theories and research. *Annual Review of Sociology, 27*(1), 77–102.

Canales, A. I. (2007). Remittances, development and poverty in Mexico: A critical view. *New Perspectives on Remittances from Mexicans and Central Americans in the United States, 4*, 59–101.

Carletto, C., Covarrubias, K., & Maluccio, J. A. (2011). Migration and child growth in rural Guatemala. *Food Policy, 36*(1), 16–27. doi:10.1016/j.foodpol.2010.08.002.

Castles, S., & Miller, M. J. (1998). *The age of migration: International population movements in the modern world* (2nd ed.). London: Macmillan.

Creighton, M. J., Park, H., & Teruel, G. M. (2009). The role of migration and single motherhood in upper secondary education in Mexico. *Journal of Marriage and Family, 71*(5), 1325–1339. doi:10.1111/j.1741-3737.2009.00671.x.

Curran, S., Cadge, W., Varangrat, A., & Chung, C. (2004). Boys' and girls' changing educational opportunities in Thailand: The effects of siblings, migration and village location. *Research in Sociology of Education, 14*, 59–102. doi:10.1016/S1479-3539(03)14004-9.

De Brauw, A. (2011). Migration and child development during the food price crisis in El Salvador. *Food Policy, 36*(1), 28–40.

De Brauw, A., & Mu, R. (2011). Migration and the overweight and underweight status of children in rural China. *Food Policy, 36*(1), 88–100.

DeWind, J., & Holdaway, J. (2008). *Migration and development within and across borders: Research and policy perspectives on internal and international migration.* Geneva: International Organization for Migration.

Donato, K. M., & Gabaccia, D. R. (2015). *Gender and international migration: From the slavery era to the global age.* New York: Russel Sage Foundation.

Dreby, J. (2010). *Divided by borders: Mexican migrants and their children.* Berkeley: University of California Press.

Durand, J., & Massey, D. (2006). *Crossing the border: Research from the Mexican Migration Project.* New York: Russell Sage Foundation.

Ehrle, J., & Moore, K. A. (1999). *1997 NSAF Benchmarking measures of child and family well-being: Report No. 6.* Washington, DC: The Urban Institute.

Epstein, J. L. (2001). *School and family partnerships: Preparing educators and improving schools*. Boulder, CO: Westview Press.

Frank, R., & Hummer, R. A. (2002). The other side of the paradox: The risk of low birth weight among infants of migrant and nonmigrant households within Mexico. *International Migration Review, 36*(3), 746–765.

Garfinkel, I., & McLanahan, S. S. (1986). *Single mothers and their children: A new American dilemma*. Washington, DC: The Urban Institute.

Graham, E., & Jordan, L. P. (2011). Migrant parents and the psychological well-being of left-behind children in southeast Asia. *Journal of Marriage and Family, 73*(4), 763–787.

Halpern-Manners, A. (2011). The effect of family member migration on education and work among nonmigrant youth in Mexico. *Demography, 48*(1), 73–99. doi:10.1007/s13524-010-0010-3.

Hanson, G., & Woodruff, C. (2003). *Emigration and educational attainment in Mexico* (Unpublished manuscript). San Diego: University of California Press.

Hildebrandt, N., & McKenzie D. (2005). The effect of migration on child health in Mexico. *Economia, 6*(1), 257–289.

Hoang, L. A., & Yeoh, B. S. (2012). Sustaining families across transnational spaces: Vietnamese migrant parents and their left-behind children. *Asian Studies Review, 36*(3), 307–327. doi:10.1080/10357823.2012.711810.

International Organization for Migration (IOM). (2005). *Internal migration and development: A global perspective* (Migration Research Series 19). Geneva: Author.

Jones, A., Sharpe, J., & Sogren, M. (2004). Children's experiences of separation from parents as a consequence of migration. *Caribbean Journal of Social Work, 3*(1), 89–109.

Jordan, L. P., & Graham, E. (2012). Resilience and well-being among children of migrant parents in south-east Asia. *Child Development, 83*(5), 1672–1688. doi:10.1111/j.1467-8624.2012.01810.x.

Kahn, R. S., Wise, P. H., Kennedy, B. P., & Kawachi, I. (2000). State income inequality, household income, and maternal mental and physical health: Cross sectional national survey. *BMJ, 321*(7272), 1311–1315.

Kanaiaupuni, S. M., & Donato, K. M. (1999). Migration and mortality: The effects of migration on infant survival in Mexico. *Demography, 36*(3), 339–353.

Kandel, W. (2003). *The impact of U.S. migration on Mexican children's educational attainment*. Washington, DC: Economic Research Service, U.S. Department of Agriculture.

Kandel, W., & Kao, G. (2001). The impact of temporary labor migration on Mexican children's educational aspirations and performance. *International Migration Review, 35*(4), 1205–1227.

Lahaie, C., Hayes, J. A., Piper, T. M., & Heymann, J. (2009). Work and family divided across borders: The impact of parental migration on Mexican children in transnational families. *Community, Work & Family, 12*(3), 299–312.

Levitt, P. (1998). Social remittances: Migration driven, local-level forms of cultural diffusion. *International Migration Review, 32*, 926–948.

Lindstrom, D. P., & Munoz-Franco, E. (2006). Migration and maternal health services utilization in rural Guatemala. *Social Science & Medicine, 63*(3), 706–721.

Lloyd, C. (1994). *Investing in the next generation: The implications of high fertility at the level of the family*. New York: Population Council.

Lockheed, M. E., Vail, S. C., & Fuller, B. (1986). How textbooks affect achievement in developing countries: Evidence from Thailand. *Educational Evaluation and Policy Analysis, 8*(4), 379–392. doi:10.3102/01623737008004379.

Lopez-Cordoba, E. (2005). Globalization, migration, and development: The role of Mexican migrant remittances. *Economia, 6*(1), 217–256.

Lu, Y. (2012). Household migration, social support, and psychosocial health: The perspective from migrant-sending areas. *Social Science & Medicine, 74*(2), 135–142. doi:10.1016/j.socscimed.2011.10.020.

Lu, Y. (2014). Parental migration and education of left-behind children: A comparison of two settings. *Journal of Marriage and Family, 76*(5), 1082–1098.

Lu, Y. (2015). Internal migration, international migration, and physical growth of left-behind children: A study of two settings, *Health & Place, 36*, 118–126.

Lu, Y., & Treiman, D. J. (2011). Migration, remittances and educational stratification among blacks in apartheid and post-apartheid South Africa. *Social Forces, 89*(4), 1119–1143. doi:10.1093/sf/89.4.1119.

Lucas, R. (1997). Internal migration in developing countries. In M. R. Rosenzweig & O. Stark (Eds.), *Handbook of population and family economics* (vol. 1B, pp. 722–798). New York: Elsevier.

Macours, K., & Vakis, R. (2010). Seasonal migration and early childhood development. *World Development, 38*(6), 857–869. doi:10.1016/j.worlddev.2010.02.012.

Massey, D., Arango, J., Hugo, G., Kouaouci A., Pellegrino A., & Taylor J. E. (1998). *Worlds in motion: Understanding international migration at the end of the millennium*. New York: Oxford University Press.

McKenzie, D., & Rapoport, H. (2006). *Can migration reduce educational attainment? Evidence from Mexico* (Policy Research Working Paper No. 3952). Washington, DC: World Bank.

McKenzie, D. J. (2005). Beyond remittances: The effects of migration on Mexican households. In C. Özden & M. Schiff (Eds.), *International migration, remittances and the brain drain* (pp. 123–147). Washington, DC: World Bank.

McLanahan, S., & Sandefur, G. (1994). *Growing up with a single parent: What hurts, what helps*. Cambridge, MA: Harvard University Press.

Nazario, S. (2007). *Enrique's journey*. New York: Random House.

Nobles, J. (2011). Parenting from abroad: Migration, nonresident father involvement, and children's education in Mexico. *Journal of Marriage and Family, 73*(4), 729–746. doi:10.1111/j.1741-3737.2011.00842.x.

Nobles, J. E. (2007). *The effects of Mexican migration on sending families* (Doctoral dissertation). University of California, Los Angeles.

Organization for Economic Cooperation and Development (OECD). (2006). *Starting strong II. Early childhood education and care*. Paris: Author.

Parreñas, R. (2001). *Servants of globalization: Women, migration, and domestic work*. Stanford, CA: Stanford University Press.

Parreñas, R. (2005). *Children of global migration: Transnational families and gendered woes*. Stanford, CA: Stanford University Press.

Paxson, C., & Schady N. (2007). Cognitive development among young children in Ecuador: The role of health, wealth and parenting, *Journal of Human Resources, 42*(1), 49–84.

Post, D., & Pong, S. L. (1998). The waning effect of sibship composition on school attainment in Hong Kong. *Comparative Education Review, 42*(2), 99–117.

Potter, D. (2010). Psychosocial well-being and the relationship between divorce and children's academic achievement. *Journal of Marriage and Family, 72*(4), 933–946. doi:10.1111/j.1741-3737.2010.00740.x.

Pryor, R. J. (1981). Integrating international and internal migration theories. In M. M. Kritz, C. B. Keely, & S. M. Tomasi (Eds.), *Global trends in migration: Theory and research on international population movements* (pp. 110–129). New York: Center for Migration Studies.

Ratha, D. (2009). *Dollars without borders: Can the global flow of remittances survive the crisis?* Retrieved from http://www.foreignaffairs.com/articles/65448/dilip-ratha/dollars-without-borders

Roberts, K. D. (1997). China's "tidal wave" of migrant labor: What can we learn from Mexican undocumented migration to the United States? *International Migration Review, 31*(2), 249–293.

Semyonov, M., & Gorodzeisky, A. (2008). Labor migration, remittances and economic well-being of households in the Philippines. *Population Research and Policy Review, 27*(5), 619–637.

Smith, L. C., & Haddad, L. (2000). *Explaining child malnutrition in developing countries: A cross-country analysis* (Research Report 111). Washington, DC: International Food Policy Research Institute.

Stark, O. (1991). *The migration of labor*. Cambridge, MA: Basil Blackwell.

Stark, O., & Bloom, D. (1985). The new economics of labor migration. *American Economic Review, 75*(2), 173–178.

Suarez-Orozco, C., Todorova, I. L. G., & Louie, J. (2004). Making up for lost time: The experience of separation and reunification among immigrant families. *Family Process, 41*(4), 625–643.

Taylor, E., Arango, J., Hugo, G., Kouaouci, A., Massey, D. S., & Pellegrino, A. (1996). International migration and community development. *Population Index, 62*, 397–418.

Toyota, M., Yeoh, B. S. A., & Nguyen, L. (2007). Bringing the "left behind" back into view in Asia: A framework for understanding the "migration–left behind nexus". *Population Space & Place, 13*(3), 157–161.

United Nations. (2009). *International migration*. New York: Author.

United Nations International Children's Emergency Fund (UNICEF). (2007). *The state of the world's children 2007*. Retrieved from https://www.unicef.org/publications/files/The_State_of_the_Worlds__Children__2007_e.pdf

Waldfogel, J. (2010). *What children need (The family and public policy)*. Cambridge, MA: Harvard University Press.

Whitehead, A., & Hashim, I. (2005). *Children and migration: Background paper for DFID migration team*. London: Department for International Development.

Woodruff, C., & Zenteno R. (2007). Migration networks and microenterprises in Mexico. *Journal of Development Economics, 82*(2), 509–528.

World Bank. (2005). *Human development report 2005*. Retrieved from http://hdr.undp.org/en/data.

SECTION II

Sociopolitical Crises and Family Separation

6

The Making of "Orphans"

How the "Orphan Rescue" Movement Is Transforming Family and Jeopardizing Child Well-Being in Uganda

KRISTEN E. CHENEY

While global political and social unrest is causing a great deal of family separation, the main issue affecting families in Uganda and other parts of Africa remains chronic poverty. However, Western humanitarian responses tend to focus on targeting particular figures. One of its favorites is "the orphan." The Western demand for experiences with orphans—from sponsorship to volunteering at orphanages to intercountry adoption—has created a multimillion dollar industry. Rather than helping reduce the number of orphans, however, this orphan industrial complex has generated even more "orphans" by driving the unnecessary institutionalization of children with families (Cheney & Rotabi, 2014). In part, this is achieved by birth parents' and guardians' obfuscation of institutionalization with other traditional forms of child circulation as a parenting strategy; mainly, however, it is achieved by creating a scenario that makes the option of parenting from a distance seem appealing. Once a child goes into a childcare institution, it can be very difficult to get him or her back out—such that parents sometimes lose their parental rights altogether. I thus argue that what I call the "orphan industrial complex" itself is in fact a greater threat than AIDS, war, or other reasons that adoption agencies are marketing as the explanation for the proliferation of orphanages. And it is creating a climate in which childcare institutions create a convenient excuse for poor caregivers to put their children in such institutions. We have seen the effects of institutionalization on families, children, and child protection systems—albeit by different means—in, for example, former communist and socialist regimes such as Romania and other Eastern European block countries (Cartwright, 2005; Misca, 2016). Not only did it cause massive family separation and severe developmental delays in institutionalized children, but the child protection systems suffered the vagaries of the free market. Under such circumstances, the intercountry adoption trade may even take on elements of organized crime (Cheney & Rotabi, 2014). Many childcare experts in Uganda now feel the same is happening there, where Western demand for orphans is driving the establishment of childcare institutions, sometimes for the express purpose of exploiting children and their families (Walakira, Ddumba-Nyanzi, & Bukenya, 2015). This chapter therefore exposes the effects of the global political economy of intercountry adoption on Ugandan families, bringing it into conversation with ethnotheories of parenting to consider the local effects of international "orphan rescue" efforts on families in Uganda. This, I claim, comes with profound implications for family preservation, family welfare, and child protection.

THE GROWTH OF THE ORPHAN INDUSTRIAL COMPLEX IN UGANDA

In *The Child Catchers*, journalist Kathryn Joyce details the recent development of a growing American evangelical "orphan movement" (Joyce, 2013). Drawing on narratives of child saving (in the literal and Biblical senses), pastors across the United States are preaching a theology of global orphan rescue. Based on interpretations of Biblical passages like James 1:27, congregants are given biblical mandates to "look after orphans and widows in their distress" and to minister to "the least of these" as an expression of their "pure religion." Appropriate expressions of this could include volunteering at orphanages, the establishment of orphanages, or even adoption—particularly from countries in the Global South. In fact, adoption has come to be seen as a way for conservative Christians to actuate their pro-life politics and evangelize by saving a child—literally and spiritually—from his or her origins and bringing the mission into their own homes.

Despite churches encouraging many US women with unintended pregnancies to have the children and give them up for adoption, the demand for healthy infants to adopt has consistently outpaced the domestic supply. So, just like other potential adoptive parents, evangelicals turned their attention abroad, where adoptions are typically quicker, cheaper, and easier to frame as a humanitarian act. Despite the global standards established by the Hague Convention on Intercountry Adoption that was promulgated in 1993 and the United States' ratification of it in 1994, the US—which accounts for almost half of intercountry adoptions worldwide—and other receiving countries in Europe tend to adopt children from nonsignatory, poorer countries with weak regulatory systems, in effect trending toward a "free market" adoption process (Cheney, 2014).

These developments, coupled with more secular interest in international orphan voluntourism and the popularity of celebrity adoptions, have spurred the growth of a global multimillion dollar "orphan industrial complex" that funds the creation of orphanages in poor communities around the world, particularly in Africa. While the number of intercountry adoptions has dropped worldwide over the past decade, they are on the rise in Africa (African Child Policy Forum,

2012), despite the number of children without parents also decreasing (Cheney & Rotabi, 2014).

In Uganda, where I have conducted ethnographic fieldwork with children for 20 years, this trend has manifested in the proliferation of foreign-supported orphanages that encourage poor parents to place their children in care and even relinquish their children for adoption to meet the demands of a very profitable "orphan rescue" movement. Despite the Western portrayal of Uganda as a war-torn country littered with AIDS orphans, Uganda largely weathered the perfect storms of protracted civil war in the 1970s and '80s and the apogee of the AIDS epidemic in the 1990s and 2000s without resorting to institutional care; children who lost their parents were largely cared for by a strong extended family support network and an ethos of socially distributed care (Brown, 2009; Weisner, 1997). Development aid was thus channeled into strengthening this traditional social safety net such that relatively few children fell through the cracks (Cheney, 2017).[1] Redirecting resources into community-based care, which is more effective and efficient than institutional care, thus largely averted the "orphan crisis."

This started to change with the growth of the orphan industrial complex in the 2000s. Uganda became one of several African countries targeted by the orphan movement for humanitarian intervention, which started pushing the notion that institutional care is the best place for children deemed to be without sufficient care. As a country with few travel restrictions (visas for most Westerners are available upon arrival), Ugandans are also highly receptive to—and even welcoming of—evangelizing missions: there is little or no oversight and few restrictions to missionary activities, including the establishment of orphanages. While there are no official statistics, practically every plane coming into the country from the United States and Europe during the summer high season carries a missionary group in matching t-shirts as well as individual volunteers—many of whom come either to build or to work in already-established orphanages.[2] Some volunteers are motivated through the volunteering experience to adopt in Uganda.

It takes 3 years to finalize an adoption order in Uganda—essentially meaning that foreigners have to be resident in Uganda for 3 years before they could take an adopted Ugandan child out of the country. However, a loophole was discovered in 2007: an American family with a Ugandan child under their temporary legal guardianship obtained a visa for the child from the US embassy and discovered that they could finalize an adoption of the child in the US courts. The Ugandan High Court also started granting legal guardianships of Ugandan children to foreign families, despite knowing that the families intended to finalize adoptions outside of their legal jurisdiction (Namubiru Mukasa, 2013). Word quickly got around the global adoption community, which has a strong web presence. With popular African adoption destinations either drastically reducing the number of adoptions (as in Ethiopia) or closing their intercountry adoption programs altogether in the face of mounting evidence of systemic corruption and child trafficking (as in the Democratic Republic of the Congo), the intercountry adoption community turned their attention toward Uganda (Cheney, 2014).

As a result, the number of orphanages has risen by more than 400% since 2009. There are now estimated to be as many as 900 orphanages hosting about 50,000 children (Walakira et al., 2015). Only about 30 of these childcare institutions are licensed by the Ministry of Gender, Labour, and Social Development (MGLSD), whose responsibility it is to ensure child welfare. Furthermore, about 80% of the children in care are known to have living, locatable relatives capable of caring for them (Riley, 2012). Poverty tends to be the push factor, while childcare institutions themselves—by their very existence in poor communities but also by their own recruitment techniques—provide significant pull factors that draw children out of the community and into their institutions. Rather than rescuing "orphans," then, the orphan industrial complex in Africa actually *manufactures* orphans for Western intervention and profit (Cheney & Rotabi, 2014).

How does the international orphan rescue movement actually result in the unnecessary institutionalization of children with families, and what does that mean for the future of family in communities targeted for such interventions? Drawing on ethnographic fieldwork and action research with child protection and alternative care professionals in Uganda, the rest of this chapter considers how intercountry adoption as a force of globalization and mobility is not only resulting in questionable adoption practices and the unnecessary institutionalization of children but is also more broadly reconfiguring family life and parenting in Uganda.

IF YOU BUILD IT, THEY WILL COME: THE PROLIFERATION OF ORPHANAGES IN UGANDA

In Uganda, 80% of the funding for private childcare institutions is estimated to come from foreign donations (Walakira et al., 2015, p. 8)—surely from well-meaning individuals who want to help meet the needs of orphans. When you build an orphanage in a poor community, however, it quickly gets filled with the children of the poor, who are easily drawn into such childcare institutions. Childcare institutions are commonly painted in bright child-friendly colors and cartoon characters—much the same as crèches and daycare centers. Intermediaries and recruiters erroneously convince parents that childcare institutions are the best place for their children, often with the promise of free schooling. This is particularly appealing to poor families who cannot otherwise afford to enroll their children in school. Child protection professionals[3] in Uganda told me that churches often play a role in encouraging children into childcare institutions with which they are affiliated, and people tend to be more willing to entrust their children to a faith-based institution. One consultant who had traveled around the country surveying childcare institutions told me about meeting a social worker in a newly established faith-based childcare institution. Upon completion of the brand new facility, the foreign directors of the project reportedly told her that they wanted 50 babies in the home by the end of the year. "Fifty!?" she replied in shock. "But there aren't 50 babies abandoned in the whole country in a year, let alone in this district!" They countered that they did not really care how she did it, as long as she filled the home with babies. To their supporters, a full home was a good home. Yet studies on institutionalized children's development have established quite the opposite (Dozier, Zeanah, Wallin, & Shauffer, 2012). It is estimated that, especially in the case of young children, for every 3 months they spend in institutional care, they can lose as much as 1 month developmentally (Dozier et al., 2012). UNICEF has therefore called for the placement of children younger than 3 years in institutions to be "restricted to a short-term emergency measure . . . not exceeding 6 months, and only as a last resort" (UNICEF, 2011, p. 3).[4]

Although some children find their way into childcare institutions due to abandonment, abuse, and neglect, many more end up in institutions because their families experience an emergency or crisis that requires some short-term parenting assistance. However, increasing numbers of parents and guardians of young children report being approached by adoption agency and orphanage intermediaries when they are at their most vulnerable, and there are indications that persistent inducement, coercion, and fraud is frequent. Jenny's story is one example of the way childcare institutions may attempt to deceive and coerce parents into relinquishing children for profitable intercountry adoptions.[5]

Jenny's Story

I met Jenny in Kampala on a rainy day in October 2015 through the director of an organization that was assisting to resettle her after her ordeal with a childcare institution. Her voice quavered, but she was determined to tell me her story in order to warn others.

Jenny was a poor woman working as a housekeeper for an Indian family in 2011. She is circumspect about whether it was actually consensual, but she had sexual relations with her boss before he fired her. When Jenny contacted him to inform him that she was 3 months pregnant with his child, he got very angry and told her never to call him again. "Go away and die!" he said as he hung up the phone.

Jenny soon discovered that she would have twins. She gave birth to 2 healthy and beautiful girls. Having no income and nowhere to go (her only family lived deep in the village and was too poor to help her), she approached Watoto Babies Home, an organization run by Canadian missionaries Gary and Marilyn Skinner who currently hold thousands of children in "children's village"-style childcare institutions around the country in what amounts to a massive homeschooling project. But Watoto staff wanted her to leave her children with them until they were 18 years old. She refused, so Watoto referred her to a childcare institution in Kampala run by Dutch missionaries. She lived there with her babies for several months before the social worker[6] informed her that they had found a Belgian couple to help her. She pulled out a file and showed Jenny pictures of the Belgian couple, "a rich doctor and nurse." Jenny asked how exactly the Belgian couple would help her, and the social worker explained that they would give her the money to set up her own hair salon and give her clothes. They would also come get the twins, take them to Belgium, and put them in school—but they would come back for holidays after several months. Jenny recognized that they were talking about adoption, though the social worker never used that word. She refused, saying she did not want to relinquish her daughters for adoption; she just wanted some help getting on her own 2 feet but that she wanted her daughters to stay with her.

Jenny then met a woman who ran a foundation that helped prevent family separation and even disrupted unethical adoptions. The foundation recognized that Jenny was in imminent danger of losing her children to international adoption, so they gave her the funds to start her own hair salon. She settled in the community and worked on establishing her business while her daughters stayed at the orphanage for another few months. Her business started thriving, so the foundation helped pressure the childcare institution to release her daughters, and they came to live with her in August 2012. Every few weeks, however, the social worker from the childcare institution would visit her and take pictures of her daughters, claiming that the photos would help find a sponsor for the twins. This continued for nearly 3 years, but it never yielded any assistance.

In 2014, Jenny's salon was doing very well, her daughters were thriving in her care, and it seemed she was holding her own. But then Jenny started a new relationship with a man who impregnated her with a third daughter. After the baby was born, he told her he wanted to move closer to his family, so, in December 2014, he suddenly sold off her salon equipment, kept the money, and moved her to his family's village. He became increasingly abusive just as he had made her reliant on him, and, in early 2015, he told her to take her children and get out of his house. Once again having no money and nowhere to go, Jenny found herself in another desperate situation—this time with three daughters. She had lost the foundation's number, her boyfriend was threatening her, and she had grown very thin. She called the social worker from the childcare institution to see whether any financial assistance had come through. It had not, but the social worker offered her sympathies and convinced Jenny to let her take the twins back into the childcare institution for a while. They were crying for their mother every day in the orphanage, and the social worker kept telling Jenny that the twins would be better off if she sent them out of Uganda. Jenny still refused and even threatened to report the social worker to the police, but the childcare institution had her daughters, so she did not report them for fear of losing her children.

One day, the social worker called her telling her to come quickly to the childcare institution; the MGLSD was apparently coming to the childcare institution to check on the case, so she gave Jenny some supplies and told her to go hide in the village. She went to her father's family for a week, until the social worker said the coast was clear. When she returned and wanted to get her children out of the childcare institution, however, the social worker presented her with official adoption papers. She showed Jenny the file, with more pictures of the Belgian couple, copies of the twins' birth certificates, and even passport applications for the twins. The social worker even more forcefully tried to convince Jenny to go to court and relinquish her children and tried to trick her into signing relinquishment papers, but Jenny, being uneducated, could not read the papers and so refused to sign anything.

In May 2015, the foundation heard through contacts at the Ministry that the twins were back at the childcare institution and they were pushing the adoption to Belgium ahead. However, they could not find Jenny anywhere. Finally, the foundation director found Jenny's grandmother using a picture she had taken during Jenny's resettlement several years beforehand. They went to the same community with the photo and asked around until they found the grandmother. The foundation director told the grandmother that the childcare institution was still trying to have her great-granddaughters adopted to Belgium, and the grandmother was livid. She put the foundation staff back in touch with Jenny, and they went to see her with people from the Ministry. Jenny told them the whole story of her hardships. She started crying and told them that the social worker at the childcare institution wanted to sell her children to the Belgian couple. She asked them to take her immediately to the childcare institution to help get her children out of the home. With the support of the Ministry and the foundation, she was finally able to get the children released from the childcare institution. The foundation hid her and her daughters—from both the childcare institution and her abusive boyfriend—in a "safe house" for several months, then they helped her rent a new home and reestablish her business. The new salon is now named after the organization that helped prevent her children from being adopted. They are also working on contacting the twins' father to ask him for child support.

If it were not for the foundation's intervention, the twins would likely be in Belgium by now—despite Jenny's consistent objections to their adoption. But other people's children have slipped away from them just as easily due to increasing demand for healthy young children for intercountry adoption. Initially, for example, Belgium would only adopt from the Dutch-run childcare institution. When the two women who founded it returned to the Netherlands, however, they promised the Ministry and the foundation that the childcare institution would no longer do intercountry adoptions but would resettle all the children in the home either with known family or with foster families. However, after the closure of the Democratic Republic of Congo to intercountry adoptions, the Belgian embassy started pushing them to make more of the children available for adoption, and several children have since gone from the childcare institution to Belgium. The same social worker who harassed Jenny for several years to give up her children is now apparently running the Dutch childcare institution. It is thought by the foundation staff that she is in collusion with a probation and social welfare officer from the district Jenny is originally from, funneling children from the district into the childcare institution. In another case, they convinced a little boy's family from the same district to relinquish him for adoption by a Dutch couple by lying that the boy would come back. The Netherlands has now stopped allowing adoptions from Uganda due to alleged corruption, and there are rumors that the childcare institution is transitioning into a vulnerable mothers and children's home—but that is exactly how Jenny was repeatedly separated from her daughters, and there were other women with young children residing at the home at the same time that Jenny was living there—including other mothers with twin babies. "Twins are big business at the moment," the foundation director told me. Being half-Indian, Jenny's twin girls were also lighter skinned than most Ugandan children available for adoption—another "selling point." "[B]ut they don't understand the curse in Uganda that comes upon a parent who lets twins go," the director continued. "They will be haunted forever."

Exacerbating the situation is the fact that most childcare institutions currently operating in Uganda make little or no effort to reunite children in their facilities with their families. After parents and guardians are encouraged to institutionalize their children, some are then prohibited from visiting them in the orphanage and/or coerced into relinquishing them to foreign adoptive parents. Many institutions likewise actively discourage children's contact with their families in an effort to keep them in the orphanage, either to use them to raise funds—foreign child sponsorships being the main source of funding for childcare institutions in Uganda (Walakira et al., 2015: viii)—or to make them available for international adoption. As soon as a child comes into the care of a childcare institution, protocol demands that they seek a care order from the district probation and social welfare officer. However, a leaked 2014 UNICEF report found that of the adoption files they reviewed, only 26% had care orders, and these were applied for only *after* an adoption process had begun, meaning that "pursuance of a care order is motivated by a prospective interest in adoption and legal guardianship with regard to a specific child, and not necessarily as a result of due process" (Among, 2014: viii). In a set of practices David Smolin has described as "child laundering," children's records are often expunged of information about surviving relatives and extenuating circumstances in an effort to render the child more "adoptable" to authorities and potential adoptive parents (Smolin, 2010). Prospective adoptive parents who have gone through the process have started advising others to hire a private investigator to verify the facts presented by orphanages and adoption agencies about the child to which they are matched. Often, within a very short period of time, investigators are able to find a living parent or guardian who is able and willing to take care of the child, whereas the orphanage has listed him or her as having been abandoned and/or having no traceable family. For some families, this is ample reason to call off the adoption; for others, especially under pressure by the very church communities who inculcated them with the mission of child rescue and who even helped fundraise their adoption costs, it is much more difficult to back out—especially after cultivating a longing to adopt a child over several years.

Despite the fact that there is often a relinquishing parent or guardian in many intercountry adoption cases in Uganda, my associates in child protection did not personally know of any birth families who actually gave *fully* informed consent to relinquish their children to adoption. Most times, if they had given consent, they later came to realize the actual implications of relinquishment and wished they could take it back—but by then it was often too late. Their children had already been taken abroad and there was no legal recourse.

There are also reports of prior contact with families through church-sponsored mission trips, as in the case of a missionary couple from Idaho, who claimed that the father of the girl they adopted had asked them to take his 2-year-old daughter to the United States a month after his wife's sudden death.[7] Not only does this contravene the international standards of subsidiarity in the Hague Convention on Intercountry Adoption (though Uganda has not yet ratified the Hague Convention) but it posits a permanent solution to a temporary crisis in the family—and a very expensive solution, as a simple intervention of counseling and/or temporary care for the child might have helped the father move past his grief without relinquishing his daughter. Though he may have assumed that his daughter would get a better education than he could possibly provide, he clearly had not thought through the implications of giving her to a family that would take her thousands of miles from home to live in Idaho. Neither, apparently, had the adoptive parents thought through the implications of raising an African child in one of the most predominantly white states in the United States.[8] And because the "adoption" (which was really a legal guardianship) was conducted entirely outside of the child protection system, no one counseled either party about the possible detrimental effects of such a displacement on the child. Yet intercountry adoption, according to the Hague Convention, should only take place as a last resort to long-term institutionalization and in the best interests of the child (Hague Conference on Private International Law, 1993). Unfortunately, because it is so lucrative, intercountry adoption has become a first resort in many cases in Uganda.

GLOBALIZED FOSTERING AND SPONSORSHIP WITHOUT BORDERS? OR THE LOSS OF PARENTAL RIGHTS?

To understand how Ugandan parents come to a decision to relinquish a child to intercountry adoption, it is important to put this phenomenon in the context of local parenting practices. A robust anthropological literature has detailed a long historical tradition of child circulation and fosterage in Africa (Bledsoe & Isiugo-Abanihe, 1989; Goody & Goody, 1969). Periodic shocks like colonial rule, civil war, and the AIDS pandemic have contributed to the plasticity of family formations in Uganda—but they have also strengthened a reliance on blood ties as a form of social security (Cheney, 2017). Often, strategies for child rearing are predicated on reciprocity between family members and what Weisner (1997) has termed "socially distributed care," in which childcare is shared widely across a kin network. Education is a big part of such strategies. It is not uncommon for parents in Uganda to send their children to live with a more prosperous relative, or even a close friend, who has access to better educational opportunities (for a more extensive review of reciprocity, see Ruiz-Casarez et al., Chapter 10 in this volume). But this never connotes a relinquishment of parental rights—in fact, quite the opposite. Part of the intent of such a move is to educate a child such that he or she can eventually attain better job prospects and then reciprocate by helping his or her parents and other family members to attain better housing, food, health care, and the like. They are also often expected to help the next generation with their education—not only their own children but nieces, nephews, and young cousins. Moreover, there is a postcolonial history of reliance on coveted foreign educational sponsorship, where available, which also has roots in Christian charity (Bornstein, 2001).

Hence it is not surprising that Ugandan parents and other caregivers may tend to think of intercountry adoption as a global expansion of local informal fostering practices. However, they rarely have a clear understanding of the detrimental effects of institutionalization on children (Dozier et al., 2012), nor on the implications of relinquishment and the permanency of adoption—a fact some unscrupulous intermediaries appear to be preying upon for profit. As in Jenny's story, most intercountry adoptions are presented to parents and guardians as transnational educational sponsorship and thus a fantastic educational opportunity for their children that many poor parents would jump at—not only to have the daily burden of childcare lifted from them but because of the reasonable assumption, based on what they know of fosterage and sponsorship, that the educated child will then return and help lift the rest of the family out of poverty.

Traditional patterns of child circulation, fosterage, and the plasticity of family may thus appear to fit rather neatly into emerging patterns of intercountry adoption. This causes some Ugandan parents and caregivers to believe that by placing their children in an institution, and even allowing their children to be adopted internationally, they are merely parenting them from a distance just as in informal fostering or sponsorship arrangements. However, the adoptive families from the Global North emphatically do *not* see it that way—and they are supported by both the Western legal system that favors the rigid exclusivity of nuclear family over the plasticity of African configurations of family. While domestic adoptions in the West have moved toward a more open model—one in which contact with birth families is maintained and cultivated for the adopted child's well-being, thus allowing birth parents regular participation in their children's upbringing—intercountry adoptions remain primarily closed. The adoptive family maintains little or no ties with the child's birth family, and, in any case, the adoptive family maintains control over decisions about whether to seek contact or not (Högbacka, 2014).[9] Adoptive families may limit contact with first families in order to consolidate their own nuclear family formation through cultivating attachment in the adopted child, even though this has been shown to be more difficult for the entire adoption triad—the birth family, the adopted child(ren), and the adoptive family (Richards, 2014). Adoptive parents may therefore feel threatened when birth families from abroad try to reassert their parental rights and prerogatives (which, in fact, they have legally relinquished). This is when adoptive families may cut off contact (NTV Uganda, 2013). Because parents and guardians may go into intercountry adoption thinking that it extends their family support network across borders rather than obviates their roles as parents or guardians, they understandably become alarmed when communication with their child's adoptive family gradually or suddenly ceases. According to case workers, Ugandan parents who seek recourse when they lose touch with their children are breaking down in the halls of the High Court when their records are pulled and they are told that they can do nothing because they had signed relinquishment papers, even if that happened under deceitful circumstances.

Furthermore, the reliance on blood ties as a form of social security for birth families is often foreclosed by intercountry adoption—unbeknownst to relinquishing parents or guardians. A social worker at a childcare institution in Kampala once told me about a father who visited him 20 years after having left his child at the childcare institution and relinquished his parental rights. He wanted to know what had happened to his son. The social worker pulled the file and informed the father that his son had been adopted by a couple from Italy (when intercountry adoptions were still very rare in Uganda). The father was pleased and then asked for the son's address in Italy. "I think now he can support me," he surmised. The social worker was reluctant, explaining that relinquishment meant a legal break of all parental rights. He refused to give the father the address, saying it could be very devastating for the young man in Italy. The father became belligerent, insisting that he had given the boy "a good life" by giving him up for adoption, so now he felt he had a right to expect reciprocation, to be supported in his old age by the same son he had relinquished—another way of understanding the "predictability of life" that underlies hierarchical and kin-dominated socially distributed support (Weisner, 1997, p. 35). The social worker did not relent, however, so the man took the case to court, where he lost because the court upheld that the relinquishment meant he had no right to contact the son.

REDEFINING FAMILY IN THE FACE OF POVERTY AND ORPHAN DEMAND

While intercountry adoption is but one end of the spectrum of orphan industrial complex activities that raises concern about fraud, coercion, and trafficking, there is also growing concern about how the demand for experiences with orphans is driving unnecessary institutionalization and making it all too easy for families to relinquish their parental responsibilities. This is signaled not only at the local level where guardians easily acquiesce to placing their children in an institution on the assumption that they will receive better quality care and schooling than they can give; it is also the message the courts inadvertently send when they grant legal guardianship orders to foreign adoptive parents almost solely on the basis of immediate material considerations (Namubiru Mukasa, 2013). Intercountry adoption was one of several urgent issues highlighted at a meeting I attended in July 2015 between children's rights activists and the Gender Committee of the national parliament regarding the passage of proposed amendments to the Children Act. Members of the Uganda Child Rights NGO Network (UCRNN) noted with alarm a trend toward prioritizing money as the most important measure of a child's best interests over a child's need for a loving and caring environment. This is concerning for two reasons: first, it erroneously posits poverty as a valid reason for relinquishment of parental responsibilities while it does nothing to combat poverty. Second, though the "orphan crisis" was largely averted by redirecting resources into more effective and efficient community-based care programs that kept families together, the orphan industrial complex is now pushing the notion that institutional care is the best place for children loosely deemed to be without sufficient care. This, in Christian discourse, has even translated into "fatherless" children, such that vulnerable single mothers like Jenny are at even greater risk of losing their children.[10] Child protection professionals have tried to put measures in place to counteract the effects of the orphan industrial complex, including the creation and promotion of an Alternative Care Framework, but they are consistently "outmonied" by adoption interests as well as charitable organizations establishing childcare institutions instead of following the best practices posited in the framework. Such intervention is thus not only encouraging family separation but undermining the development of an effective child protection system.

Research shows that, in the long run, even local child institutionalization has a profound impact on individual family members—most especially the children—the family unit, and the broader community culture of child rearing. While some parents and guardians may rationalize it as parenting from afar, some in fact start to view the children as "belonging" to the childcare institution rather than the family (Cheney, 2017)—as do the childcare institution staff, who tend to talk about the children in their care as "ours." Children also become accustomed to identifying with the childcare institution in which they grow up, and, even where children *are* encouraged to maintain ties with relatives, they may resist returning home on occasional visits either because they come to prefer the material comforts of the institution or because they feel alienated from their families by their experiences in the childcare institution and are anxious about how their relatives, who perceive them as privileged, will treat them (Dahl, 2014; Freidus, 2010, p. 299; Freidus, 2013, pp. 315–316; Freidus & Ferguson, 2013, p. 212). Furthermore, children who may grow up materially privileged in a childcare institution often suddenly find themselves cut off and thrust back out into the community once they turn 18 and age out of care. They then find their "privileged" childhood of little value in that it alienated them from their communities and yet did not adequately prepare them to live independently. They may then start to feel betrayed and exploited by the childcare institution (Ucembe, 2015).

As for intercountry adoption from Uganda, it is too soon to tell how Ugandan adoptees will feel about the circumstances of their adoptions as they grow up, but other international adoptees' experiences indicate that many will be outraged to discover the actual circumstances of their adoptions, especially where it involved illicit or unethical activity. They may also become resentful of the circumstances under which they grew up: often in nondiverse families, communities, and schools in which they do not always feel they belong. As one adult transracial adoptee is widely quoted as saying, "Your child should not be your first black friend."[11]

Birth parents who are later contacted by adoptees as they grow up and want to learn more about their identity may still expect fulfillment of the traditional social contract, which may make adoptees feel compromised and cause them to distance themselves again from their birth families. Other adoptees may find that while they want to reestablish family relations with their original families as they get older, they are not accepted because of the perceived privilege in which they grew up, leaving adoptees feeling betrayed and alienated from both their original and their adoptive families. As one such Ethiopian adoptee wrote in regard to her experience of international adoption, "I wasn't saved from Ethiopia; I had Ethiopia stolen from me."[12]

In order to combat the adverse consequences for parenting and family life in Uganda, we have to combat the dominant narratives of the orphan industrial complex that prevent the development of an effective child protection system, instead directing assistance toward strengthening families, not orphanages. This is not as easy as it may sound, however, as the main appeal of orphans from donors' points of view is in their separation from family (Freidus & Ferguson, 2013, p. 211). There may not be much glory in it for the humanitarian hoping to "save" orphans, but we must engage in the more difficult and long-term task of dealing with structural poverty so that parents do not feel that parenting from a distance is their only option, breaking ties with their children entirely in the process. It must be stressed to would-be orphan rescuers that family preservation and strengthening, where possible, is consistently in the best interests of children.

The Ugandan foundation that sometimes disrupts illegal and unethical adoptions like that of Jenny's twins continues to work with the biological and potential adoptive families of Ugandan children, but they also assist foreign prospective adoptive parents who find themselves in the middle of unethical adoptions. If they choose not to go through with such an adoption, the foundation supports the decision to allow the child to stay with relatives in Uganda. Some even make the decision to support the birth family of the child(ren) with whom they were matched for adoption, in effect becoming the ones who parent from afar instead of the biological family. The director of the foundation told me that she sends them regular updates on the children they did not adopt, to show them that the children are not suffering, as many of them worry. "In fact they are thriving!" she said. "It's important to show the people who've been convinced that adoption is all about rescuing children from suffering that it is indeed possible for the children to thrive, even in a little village in Uganda." She hopes that the potential adoptive parents will go on to proselytize about the success of family preservation instead of intercountry adoption.

NOTES

1. In fact, many studies showed that orphans were achieving better outcomes in schooling and health than their nonorphaned counterparts; see Lorraine Sherr et al., "A Systematic Review on the Meaning of the Concept 'Aids Orphan': Confusion over Definitions and Implications for Care," *AIDS Care*, 20/5 (May 2008 2008), 527–536.
2. I am tentatively commissioned to conduct a study in conjunction with alternative care organizations in Uganda on missionary trips to orphanages. The funders

would like us to expand the study to Kenya, South Africa, and possibly Ghana due to similar problems emerging there.

3. Due to the sensitive nature of the situation in Uganda, I avoid using the names of people in the field of child protection to protect them from recrimination by people invested in the orphan industrial complex.
4. For this and other recommendations that intercountry adoption follow protocols compatible with international adoption standards and children's rights, the adoption community—and particularly the pro-adoption lobby in the United States led by Harvard law professor Elizabeth Bartolet—has vilified UNICEF as being anti-adoption and thus actually against the best interests of children in care (http://www.ncregister.com/daily-news/unicef-blamed-for-decline-in-international-adoptions/); see Beale (2013).
5. It is estimated that intercountry adoptions/legal guardianships from Uganda currently cost about USD $40,000.
6. The term "social worker" loosely applies in Uganda, where there is no certification process for social workers, so that anyone who comes into a job in social services can call themselves "social workers," whether they have been trained in social work or not. There are currently efforts under way to professionalize the field and offer certification courses to prevent unqualified people from filling social work positions. But, for now, most people who work at childcare institutions have little or no professional qualifications.
7. Jones (2014): http://www.localnews8.com/news/family-faces-challenges-adopting-ugandan-child/30171104
8. According to the 2010 US Census, Idaho has a black population of less than 1%; see List of US States (2015): https://en.wikipedia.org/wiki/List_of_U.S._states_by_African-American_population.
9. Adoptive families have cited limited obligation to have contact with birth families as an incentive to adopt internationally rather than domestically; see Oh Myo Kim, Beaupre, and Langrehr, *Deepening the Understanding of the 'Adoption Triad' in Transnational Adoptive Families: New Research from Transracial, Transnational Adoptee Scholars*, 5th International Conference on Adoption Research (Auckland, New Zealand, 2016).
10. There are many historical and current examples of how stigmatizing single motherhood is used to justify dispossessing especially poor and minority mothers of their children and having them adopted to middle- and upper-class two-parent families. For examples, see Lydia Murdoch, *Imagined Orphans: Poor Families, Child Welfare, and Contested Citizenship in London* (New Brunswick: Rutgers University Press, 2006); Laura Briggs, *Somebody's Children: The Politics of Transracial and Transnational Adoption* (Durham: Duke University Press, 2012); and Ann Marie Leshkowich, "Rendering Infant Abandonment Technical and Moral: Expertise, Neoliberal Logics, and Class Differentiation in Ho Chi Minh City," *Positions,* 20/2 (2012), 497–526.
11. NPR (2014): http://www.npr.org/2014/01/26/266434175/growing-up-white-transracial-adoptee-learned-to-be-black
12. Lemma (2014): http://www.theguardian.com/commentisfree/2014/oct/31/international-adoption-made-me-a-commodity-not-a-daughter

REFERENCES

African Child Policy Forum. (2012). *Africa: The new frontier for intercountry adoption.* Addis Ababa: Author.

Among, H. (2014). *Study of legal guardianship and adoption practices in Uganda.* Kampala: UNICEF.

Beale, S. (2013). *UNICEF Blamed for decline in international adoptions.* Retrieved from National Catholic Register website: http://www.ncregister.com/daily-news/unicef-blamed-for-decline-in-international-adoptions

Bledsoe, C., & Isiugo-Abanihe, U. (1989). Strategies of child-fosterage among Mende grannies in Sierra Leone. In R. J. Lesthaeghe (Ed.), *Reproduction and social organization in sub-Saharan Africa* (pp. 442–474). Berkeley: University of California Press.

Bornstein, E. (2001). Child sponsorship, evangelism, and belonging in the work of world vision Zimbabwe. *American Ethnologist, 28*(3), 595–622.

Briggs, L. (2012). *Somebody's children: The politics of transracial and transnational adoption.* Durham, NC: Duke University Press.

Brown, J. (2009). Child fosterage and the developmental markers of Ovambo children in Namibia: A look at gender and kinship. *Childhood in Africa, 1*(1), 4–10.

Cartwright, L. (2005). Images of "waiting children": Spectatorship and pity in the representation of the global social orphan in the 1990s. In T. A. Volkman (Ed.), *Cultures of transnational adoption* (pp. 185–214). Durham, NC: Duke University Press.

Cheney, K. (2014). Giving children a "better life"? Reconsidering social reproduction and humanitarianism in intercountry adoption. *European Journal of Development Research, 26*(2), 247–263.

Cheney, K. (2017). *Crying for our elders: African orphanhood in the age of HIV and AIDS.* Chicago: University of Chicago Press.

Cheney, K., & Rotabi, K. S. (2014). Addicted to orphans: How the global orphan industrial complex jeopardizes local child protection systems. In C. Harker, K. Hörschelmann, & T. Skelton (Eds.), *Geographies of children and young people: Vol. 11. Conflict, violence and peace* (pp. 1–19). Singapore: Springer Science + Business Media.

Dahl, B. (2014). "Too fat to be an orphan": The moral semiotics of food aid in Botswana. *Cultural Anthropology, 29*(4), 626–647.

Dozier, M., Zeanah, C. H., Wallin, A. R., & Shauffer, C. (2012). Institutional care for young children: Review of literature and policy implications. *Social Issues and Policy Review, 6*(1), 1–25.

Freidus, A. (2010). Raising Malawi's children: Unanticipated outcomes associated with institutionalised care. *Children & Society, 24*(4), 293–303.

Freidus, A. (2013). Malawi's orphans: Children's rights in relation to humanitarianism, compassion, and childcare. In B. Derman, A. Hellum, & K. B. Sandvik (Eds.), *Worlds of human rights: The ambiguities of rights claiming in Africa* (Afrika-Studiecentrum Series, 26) (pp. 303–332). Leiden: Brill.

Freidus, A., & Ferguson, A. (2013). Malawi's orphans: The role of transnational humanitarian organizations. In D. J. Johnson, D. L. Agbényiga, & R. K. Hitchcock (Eds.), *Vulnerable children: Global challenges in education, health, well-being, and child rights* (pp. 203–215). New York: Springer.

Goody, J., & Goody, E. (1969). The circulation of women and children in Northern Ghana. In J. Goody (Ed.), *Comparative studies in kinship* (pp. 184–215). Stanford, CA: Stanford University Press.

Hague Conference on Private International Law. (1993). *Convention on protection of children and co-operation in respect of intercountry adoption.* The Hague: Author.

Högbacka, R. (2014). *Intercountry adoption, countries of origin, and biological families.* (Working Paper No. 598). The Hague: International Institute of Social Studies.

Jones, L. (2014). Family faces challenges adopting Ugandan child. *Local News 8.* Retrieved from http://www.localnews8.com/news/kifi-top-story/family-faces-challenges-adopting-ugandan-child_20160825030017132/57867442

Joyce, K. (2013). *The child catchers: Rescue, trafficking, and the new gospel of adoption.* New York: Public Affairs.

Kim, O. M., Kim, J., Beaupre, A., & Langrehr, K. (2016, January). *Deepening the understanding of the "adoption triad" in transnational adoptive families: New research from transracial, transnational adoptee scholars.* Paper presented at the 5th International Conference on Adoption Research, Auckland, New Zealand.

Lemma, T. (2014). International adoption made me a commodity, not a daughter. *The Guardian.* Retrieved from http://www.theguardian.com/commentisfree/2014/oct/31/international-adoption-made-me-a-commodity-not-a-daughter

Leshkowich, A. M. (2012). Rendering infant abandonment technical and moral: Expertise, neoliberal logics, and class differentiation in Ho Chi Minh City. *Positions, 20*(2), 497–526.

List of US states by African-American population. (2015). *Wikipedia.* Retrieved from https://en.wikipedia.org/wiki/List_of_U.S._states_by_African-American_population

Misca, G. (2016, January). *The "rescued Romanian orphans" revisited: Coming of age.* Presented at the 5th International Conference on Adoption Research ICAR5, Auckland, New Zealand.

Murdoch, L. (2006). *Imagined orphans: Poor families, child welfare, and contested citizenship in London.* New Brunswick, NJ: Rutgers University Press.

Namubiru Mukasa, S. (2013). *Applying the principle of the best interests of the child in inter-country legal guardianship and adoption matters: Experiences of the family court in Uganda.* Rotterdam: Erasmus University.

NPR. (2014). Growing up "white," transracial adoptee learned to be black. *NPR Weekend Edition Sunday.* Retrieved from http://www.npr.org/2014/01/26/266434175/growing-up-white-transracial-adoptee-learned-to-be-black

NTV Uganda. (2013). *Taken & never returned: When adoption profits the middleman.* Retrieved from https://www.youtube.com/watch?v=yEeDL70WKOA&list=PLPz47e2di8dP7rcrKxbsqoQqQk2wZ1lrk&index=4>

Richards, S. (2014). HCIA Implementation and the Best Interests of the *Child. ISS Working Paper Series / General Series No. 597.* The Hague: International Institute of Social Studies of Erasmus University.

Riley, M. (2012). *Baseline study: The state of institutional care in Uganda.* Kampala: Ministry of Gender, Labour and Social Development.

Sherr, L., Varrall, R., Mueller, J., Richter, L., Wakhweya, A., Adato, M., . . . & Kimou, J. (2008). A systematic review on the meaning of the concept "AIDS orphan": Confusion over definitions and implications for care. *AIDS Care, 20*(5), 527–536.

Smolin, D. (2010). Child laundering and the Hague Convention on Intercountry Adoption: The future and past of intercountry adoption. *University of Louisville Law Review, 48*(3), 441–498.

Ucembe, S. (2015). *Exploring the nexus between social capital and individual biographies of "care leavers" in Nairobi, Kenya: A life course perspective.* Rotterdam: International Institute of Social Studies, Erasmus University.

UNICEF. (2011). *End placing children under three years in institutions—A call to action.* Geneva: Author.

Walakira, E. J., Ddumba-Nyanzi, I., & Bukenya, B. (2015). *Child care institutions in selected districts in Uganda and the situation of children in care: A baseline survey report for the strong beginnings project.* Kampala: Terres des Hommes Netherlands.

Weisner, T. S. (1997). Support for children and the African family crisis. In T. S. Weisner, C. Bradley, & P. L. Kilbride (Eds.), *African families and the crisis of social change* (pp. 20–44). London: Bergin & Garvey.

7

Imagined and Occasional Co-Presence in Open Adoption

How Adoptive Parents Mediate Birth Connections

MANDI MACDONALD

Adoption is a long-standing social institution that endures, in some form, across historical and cultural contexts. Adoption fundamentally alters the relationship between parent and child, changing the family identity of adopted children and shifting the responsibility for their care, along with the associated parental rights, from birth to adoptive parents. While the social function of adoption has fluctuated, currently its role is to provide an alternative family for children whose birth parents are unable or unwilling to rear them, often as a result of personal and social constraints. Worldwide, there are an estimated quarter of a million child adoptions each year, with half of these occurring in the United States, and the principle that adoption should primarily serve the child's best interests is enshrined in the adoption laws of most countries (Department of Economic and Social Affairs [DESA], 2009). Some adoption involves children moving between countries, usually from Asia and Eastern Europe to the United States and Western Europe, however, most adoptions occur within the child's country of birth through domestic adoption (DESA, 2009).

Although adoption affects a small proportion of all the world's children, it is nonetheless an emotive and at times contentious practice, raising questions about the meaning of parenthood and familial ties. In some countries, it is culturally unacceptable to terminate the relationship between parent and child, and informal provisions allow birth parents to place their children in the care of others without having to sever their own parental ties (DESA, 2009). However, most countries recognize the legal institution of adoption, and, in a Western context, within which this chapter is written, adoption is characterized by formal regulation and legal finality. It involves the complete transfer of parental rights and responsibilities from birth to adoptive parents and severance of legal ties between child and birth parent; in most cases, its effects are permanent and irrevocable. For adopted children, birth parents, and adopters, therefore, adoption has fundamental and lifelong implications for their kin relationships and family membership.

Adoption depends on demand from adults seeking to adopt as a route to parenthood often, though not exclusively, due to involuntary childlessness, and on the availability of children who are legally adoptable either because their birth parents have relinquished them or had their parental rights terminated via the legal child welfare provisions of some countries. This latter practice of public adoption, often contested by birth parents, is prevalent particularly in the United States and United Kingdom where it is used to secure permanent alternative families for children in state care for whom a return home is deemed unsafe. Although adoption delivers good outcomes for children who would otherwise remain in care (Selwyn, Meakings, & Wijedasa, 2015), it does not sit easily with human rights principles that favor family preservation and the maintenance of birth family ties. As adoption has become increasingly open, the now common practice of ongoing contact between child and birth parent might be seen to partially resolve the tension between family rights and child welfare priorities. However, while postadoption contact acknowledges the significance of birth ties between parent and child, it can entail particularly challenging emotions and relationship complexity that might mitigate against the maintenance of beneficial and enduring relationships between adopted children and their birth parents.

This chapter is interested in the complex workings of adoptive kinship and will explore, in particular, the ways that adopted children and their birth parents can remain co-present following adoption. It will focus specifically on public adoption of children who have been in the care of child welfare services, and it draws on adoptive parents' accounts of their experiences of adoption openness. The distinctive features of co-presence between children and their birth parents after adoption are that it is mediated by negotiated contact agreements and through ongoing adoptive family practices and that it is occasional, with its infrequency displaying the status and significance of birth relationships. Physical co-presence can in some cases be achieved through face-to-face contact; however, even when this not possible, birth parents can be present in the hearts and minds of the adoptive family, constituting a form of imagined co-presence. This chapter will explore how adopters achieve, delimit, and mediate imagined and physical co-presence between their child and their child's birth parent. It concludes by considering the emergence of virtual co-presence via online social media.

PROXIMITY AND DISTANCE IN OPEN ADOPTION FROM CARE

The concepts of family and parenthood presuppose more or less permanent relationships (Jallinoja, 2008). Adoption, however, entails the simultaneous breaking and making of parent–child bonds and permanently alters the kin relationships of all involved. In adoption, the legal relationship between birth parent and child is severed and a new permanent parental relationship is legally established between the child and his or her adoptive parent(s). This process effects a total and permanent transfer of legal parenthood from birth to adoptive parents, who exclusively and irrevocably assume the parental rights and responsibilities relinquished by, or removed from, the birth parents.

Adoption extinguishes birth parents' right to care for their child and relieves them of associated responsibilities for their welfare. There is no expectation that birth parents will continue to engage in parenting, and, in most cases, they would not be afforded the opportunity to do so. Nonetheless, in Western culture, there is a strong assumption that the connection between a child and his or her birth parent—a link based on biology and genetics rather than actualized caregiving—will have enduring importance even when permanently legally severed. Birth parents are assumed to remain significant long after their active parenting role has ended. Birth ties are perceived as enduring, indissoluble, and inevitable even when biological parents are not involved in the activities of parenting (Smith, Surrey, & Watkins, 2006).

Recognition that connection with their birth origins can be important to the adopted person's healthy identity formation (Triseliotis, 1973) has led to a steady evolution away from the historical practices of secrecy toward "openness in adoption" (Brodzinsky, 2006, p. 149). Adoptive parents are now advised to engage their children in open discussion of their birth histories and adoption-related issues (Morrison, 2012). In recent decades, there has also been a steady and significant increase in "open adoption" (Brodzinsky, 2006, p. 149) characterized by occasional interaction between the adopted child and their birth relatives in order to maintain active kinship links. Contact after adoption might be indirect via written communication, or direct and involving face-to-face meetings between the child and any combination of birth relatives, and it might occur with or without the facilitation of an adoption agency intermediary. This form of structural openness (Brodzinsky, 2005) upholds children's right under the United Nations Convention on the Rights of the Child to know their parents even if living separately from them (Article 7) and to stay in contact with both parents unless this might hurt them (Article 9), and it has become common practice in domestic adoption (Siegel & Smith, 2012). It is estimated that a significant minority (Neil, Cossar, Jones, Lorgelly, & Young, 2011), perhaps around one in five (Jones, 2016), of children adopted from public care in the United Kingdom have direct face-to-face contact with a birth relative, and there is evidence of a trend toward higher rates of contact generally and direct contact in particular in more recent adoptions from care in Northern Ireland (Kelly, 2012).

In open adoption, therefore, birth parents are no longer engaged in day-to-day caregiving, but their kin connection with their child is kept alive through occasional contact. The socialities and forms of co-presence involved when individuals are significantly linked to one another but are not involved in ongoing daily interaction (Baldassar, 2008; Urry, 2002) provide a useful conceptual lens through which to view adoptive kinship. Explorations of families separated by migration, for example, have highlighted the practices by which individuals create and sustain their kin networks and significant relationships across often very great geographical distances (Reynolds & Zontini, 2014) and have allowed for the identification of practices through which physically separated kin "do" family and retain the sense of being present with one another despite physical distance (Baldassar, 2008). Urry (2002) looked to family practices employed by migrants to sustain a sense of belonging when individuals are not involved in day-to-day interaction, in particular how travel facilitates occasional face-to-face meetings and the resultant physical togetherness or, as Urry (2002) terms it, the intermittent corporeal co-presence that helps sustain connections (p. 257). Family members might also employ communication technologies, engage in family rituals, or imbue artifacts with family meaning in order to experience virtual, proxy, and imagined forms of co-presence with distant kin (Baldassar, 2008). This can facilitate a sense of family belonging even in the case of complete absence when all co-present forms of interaction are unavailable—potentially permanently—as in the case of refugee families (Robertson et al., 2016). The "distant co-presence" (Baldassar, Nedelcu, Merla, & Wilding, 2016, p. 135) experienced by transnational families challenges the taken-for-granted assumption that physical proximity is necessary for the maintenance of significant social ties and demonstrates that individuals within families can continue to engage in active relationships that are sustained by expressions of care and commitment even when separated over great geographical distance.

Although open adoption entails a physical separation of birth parent from child, it can involve especially complex patterns of social, rather than geographical, proximity and distance. The intimacy of consanguinity is held in tension with the legal extinguishing of parenthood. Having lost their parental status, birth parents are, paradoxically, encouraged to maintain contact with the child precisely because of the assumed significance of their biological parenthood (Sales, 2012). This has implications for the frequency of contact as birth parents are not expected to have day-to-day engagement but instead are positioned as more occasional kin. In domestic adoption, there is further ambiguity as birth parents might live nearby, though a vast and sometimes unbridgeable social separation is created by the legal realities and relationship dynamics of adoption.

In a similar paradox, the adopted child is installed fully in a new permanent family with adoptive parents who are to provide love and everyday care as if he or she was born to them while simultaneously facilitating their ongoing connection to their original family. In law, the adopted child has no family other than his or her adoptive family. However, this situation has been referred to as a legal fiction (Smith, 2002) in that it does not accurately reflect the social and psychological reality that the child does have another family from which he or she originated and which does not cease to exist after adoption. Open adoption requires an acknowledgment of the child's dual connection and acceptance by adoptive parents that their child is "at the same time one's own child (through adoption) and another's child (by birth)" (Rosnati, 2005, p. 197). A key task for all families is to achieve a sense of belonging and the integration of its members. A further task in open adoption is to enable the adopted child to feel comfortable with belonging, albeit in very different ways, to two families (Schofield & Beek, 2006). This entails negotiation of complex relationships across the adoptive kinship network (Grotevant, 2000) that links birth and adoptive family members via their common interest in the adopted child, who is in central position and who provides the purpose and motivation for the adult relationships.

Our study draws on adopters' subjective experience of parenthood in this context of open adoption. In these accounts, the adoptive parents identified their role as "kin-keepers" (Grotevant, 2009, p. 309), regulating their children's interaction with birth parents, safeguarding their options for relationship, and leaving open the possibility of a closer engagement with birth family in the future. The discussion herein explores how the family practices associated with open adoption, both structurally open arrangements and open family communication, facilitated occasional physical and imagined co-presence between the adopted child and his or her birth parents.

THE CURRENT STUDY

This study utilized interpretative phenomenological analysis (Smith, Flowers, & Larkin, 2009) to understand adopters' experience of parenthood in the context of open adoption, and involved semi-structured interviews designed to elicit accounts of adoptive parenthood with 31 adoptive parents from 17 families, all of whom had adopted unrelated children from care in Northern Ireland between 2000 and 2006. All of the participants had some form of contact with birth parents at some stage. At the time of interviews, the children had been adopted between 5 and 11 years, and ranged in age from 9 to 14 years (see MacDonald, 2016, for a more complete discussion of the study methodology and findings).

The interpretative aspect of the study was informed by the idea of the double hermeneutic (Smith et al., 2009). In the first turn of the hermeneutic circle, the participant draws on a culturally available repertoire of explanations and meanings to interpret and make sense of his or her lived experience. The researcher then in turn draws on her own knowledge and experience to interpret the participants' sense-making efforts. In this study, the interpretative analysis was influenced particularly by concepts associated with the sociology of personal life and relatedness (Mason, 2011), which understands kinship as needing to be "made" rather than simply "given" and focuses on the "doing" rather than the "having" of family relationships (Morgan, 2011). In particular, the related concepts of family configuration (Widmer & Jallinoja, 2008) and family practices (Morgan, 1996, 2011) were employed as interpretive resources to make sense of the way participants actively constituted and sustained adoptive kinship through the subjective realities of everyday life.

In a further turn of the hermeneutic circle, this chapter draws on the idea that separated family members can experience co-presence in a variety of ways (Baldassar, 2008; Campos-Castillo & Hitlin, 2013; Urry, 2002). It examines how the family practices required by both structural and communicative aspects of open adoption—that is, contact with birth relatives and open family discussion of origins—constitute varieties of co-presence between birth and adoptive families. In particular, it identifies the imagined and occasional physical forms of co-presence between parents and children separated by adoption and how these are mediated by formal contact agreements and by the protective priorities of adoptive parents.

MEDIATED CO-PRESENCE

All of the families in this study adopted children who were in the care of public child welfare services, which is the main route to adoption in Northern Ireland. In most cases, the adoption had been formally contested by birth parents and was achieved via legislation which allowed the dispensing of parental consent. Some of the factors that precipitated the children's admission to care included neglect, abuse, domestic violence, parents' mental health problems, and alcohol abuse (McSherry, Fargas Malet, & Weatherall, 2013), and, in order for these public compulsory adoptions to be granted by the courts, the children needed to be demonstrably suffering or at risk of suffering significant harm in their birth parent(s)' care.

In this context of adoption from care, all forms of co-presence between birth parent and child were mediated, initially by the agencies making the adoption and then on an ongoing basis by the adoptive parents who were deeply invested in the child's well-being and operated from a protective stance. Even in complex situations following adoption from care, when children are having contact with a birth relative who had previously neglected or abused them, adoptive parents have identified benefits in terms of identity development and continuity of relationships for the child (Neil et al., 2011). However, they have also reported challenges in these situations that centered on the child's negative reaction to contact, the quality of interactions during contact, and the burden of managing risks, boundaries, and relationships. Many of the adoptive parents in the current study referred to explicit agreements for contact that had been negotiated with the input of social workers and judges. The intention of such agreements was to uphold the right to respect for family life of both parent and child under the Human Rights Act (1998) but to do so in a way that managed the risks that contact might potentially represent for the child.

Mostly, contact agreements had been established as the adoption was made, and the form the agreed contact took was contingent on birth parents' circumstances at that time and the extent to which they were able to accept the permanence of the adoption and the parental status of adopters. Direct contact was ruled out with some birth parents who had perpetrated abuse and who, because of this, were described as having forfeited not only their parental status but also the right to ongoing relationship with the child. For some of these families, the continued risk of actual harm to the child prohibited any face-to-face contact. In cases where children were adopted as a result of chronic neglect, it was difficult for some participants to conceive of birth parents experiencing positive change or to see the potential benefit for the child of a relationship with "unfit" birth parents. Thus, the importance given to safeguarding the child's emotional, physical, and developmental well-being, a key responsibility of parenthood, inevitably inhibited the development of relationships with birth relatives who could not demonstrate a commitment to this welfare priority. As one adoptive mother said: "Our motto was the safety of the child. We had no problem with bringing him to meet his siblings—they had done him no harm. But no, not to his birth parents who had physically harmed the child."

In some cases, birth parents' problematic lifestyles at the time of the adoption (e.g., chronic substance misuse, transience) prevented regular contact, and it was challenging to establish arrangements that could accommodate the difficult realities of birth parent's lives. Issues sometimes represented risk to the child or simply made it impossible to arrange any kind of meeting, for example, when whereabouts of the birth parent where unknown. As one adoptive parent noted, "With their problems at that time it [contact] would have been very disruptive to the children." Another explained, "They moved house and nobody knew where they had disappeared to."

Several families were unable to establish face-to-face contact because of birth parents' antagonism and explicit threats of aggression toward adopters, sometimes co-existing with a history of violent offences. In some cases, direct contact with birth mothers or siblings was ruled out on the basis of their ongoing relationship with birth fathers who presented a risk of violence. In all such cases, the reality of the situation was at odds with the anticipated benefits of open adoption, as the following quotation illustrates: "I would really liked to have met their birth mother. I don't think it could be possible, there would be too much animosity and aggression towards me."

Contact agreements imposed a degree of constraint on adoptive parents' management of family-forming and their child's dual connection. Agreeing to facilitate birth parent contact was perceived as a non-negotiable condition of their approval as prospective parents and an inevitable consequence of the "rules of the adoption." Social workers or judges were referred to as the final arbiters of openness arrangements, and adopters felt bound to comply with proposed contact plans, despite some strong misgivings. As one adoptive parent said:

> If the judge decides that that's the way it is, then that's the way it's going to be. When the judge makes his decision—his judgement—his instruction has to be followed and we understood that there was little that we could do about it.

Social work mediation of contact can also, however, be facilitative of sustained relationships between birth and adoptive families. In complex cases of contact following adoption from care, some families might receive formal help with practical arrangements, such as setting up meetings and providing transport, while for others professionals might facilitate interactions and help the individuals manage their emotional responses to contact (Neil et al., 2011). Only a few families had ongoing help with contact, but those who did valued the social worker's role in mediating the flow of emotive and evaluative information, encouraging exchanges that conveyed acceptance and respect, which helped scaffold delicate relationships between adoptive and birth parents. As one adoptive parent put this:

> I suppose we have learnt to trust her [the birth mother] because of the reports we get back from [the social worker] . . . she always says that [birth mother] would speak positively about us, she would never ever say anything really negative about us . . . she [social worker] passes the positivity from one to the other.

The process of forming a family in open adoption requires adoptive parents to create a recognizable family identity and sense of belonging while at the same time acknowledging the child's connection to his or her birth family. This disconnect between current and originating family is not exclusive to adoption since adults who have moved out of their parents' home and established their own households might frequently make this distinction (Jallinoja, 2008). What differs in adoption is the stage in the life-course when current family and family of origin cease to be one and the same and the lack of control that child and birth parent might have over how their connection is subsequently configured. Across the lifespan of a family, the dispersal of children from parents and siblings from siblings might be more or less expected as individuals follow their separate developmental trajectories. However, in adoption, the separation of child from parent occurs at a much earlier stage, and it is adoptive parents who are charged with forging and facilitating new relational habits. This requires adoptive parents to develop family boundaries that are rigid enough to provide autonomy, security and cohesion, yet permeable enough to retain a connection between the child and his or her birth parents that persists across the distance between these separated families.

Open adoption represents a particularly explicit crossing of the boundary between birth and adoptive families. In this context, the adoptive parents highlighted the importance of feeling in control of family boundaries, and, as in other studies (Dunbar et al., 2006; McSherry et al., 2008), their satisfaction with contact and the likelihood of its continued success was linked to their ability to take the initiative, retain a sense of being in charge of arrangements, and the extent to which family boundaries were respected.

While contact agreements were initially perceived as imposing constraints on parental autonomy, they subsequently became useful for helping to regulate family boundaries. The adopters emphasized the importance of keeping to the negotiated contact arrangements, or "sticking to the agreement," and keeping within clearly demarcated lines that should not be overstepped seemed to be important in the maintenance of contact. Speaking of letters they exchanged with birth parents via an intermediary in the adoption agency, known locally as "post-box" contact, one couple noted that "sticking to the rules" of contact was important "or else everything goes funny." Emphasizing also the moral imperative to keep to one's word, the father in this couple said: "We are religious in maintaining the post-box contact because we are clearly fulfilling our side of our obligations."

Some adopters spoke of an ongoing negotiation with birth parents around the parameters of contact and of having to rein-in control of arrangements and assert the terms of the initial agreement. This was particularly the case when birth parents wanted to increase the frequency or intensity of contact or involve an increasing number of different birth relatives in the visits. Over time, more family-like relationships did develop in some cases, with the range of linkages and points of contact between the adoptive and birth families going beyond what had been originally negotiated. However, the contact agreements provided a blueprint for relationships that could be referred back to when needed.

All participants expected their child to seek more intense and more independent contact with their birth parents as they matured into adulthood in order to satisfy a normative curiosity and desire to own birth family relationships for themselves. Expectations about the timing of changing relationships were supplied by age-related cultural norms, with children expected to assume a more autonomous approach to contact at age 18 years, the cultural time of coming of age and a point at which parental responsibility diminishes. It was speculated that this might entail reduced contact with some birth relatives but an increased relationship with others or new contact with relatives who were not currently known to the child, thereby further blurring the boundary between adoptive and birth families.

While the adopters stated their intention to support their children in the future to achieve their desired level of relationship, most did not have a clear plan for how they might initiate the changes to contact they believed their child would want. Furthermore, they recognized that they could not predict how birth relatives might respond to the child's future advances. The changing wishes and needs of various members of the adoptive kinship network can be out of synchrony with one another. For example, the birth parent may desire contact for reassurance of the child's welfare in the early stage of placement when adoptive parents are focused on family integration but may be less engaged several years later when the adopters' desire contact in response to their child's growing curiosity (Wrobel, Grotevant, Berge, Mendenhall, & Mcroy, 2003). The adoptive parents had a tacit understanding of this transactional nature of relationships (Neil & Howe, 2004) and spoke of having to manage children's expectations and prepare them for a range of possible reactions. As one adoptive father put this:

> Their birth mum may say "I want nothing to do with you," and we will have to cope with that. Or it may well be at the other end of the scale that they will maybe meet their birth mother and she will shower them with hugs and kisses and they will feel uncomfortable, because, "whoa, who is this person?"

Notwithstanding the value of formal agreements for managing boundaries, it was evident from adopters' accounts that they thought of birth parents in relational rather than contractual terms. In all of the accounts, children's birth relatives were present as significant figures in the adoptive parents' stories of kinship. They related to birth parents as kin of the child, acknowledging the child's family connection to "their mother," and demonstrated a strong sense of responsibility for building and maintaining links with birth parents on the child's behalf. The adoptive parents had a sense of their child's birth connections stretching into the future and felt accountable for building "kinship heritages" (Mason & Tipper, 2008, p. 154), or, in other words, laying a foundation upon which kinship might grow and evolve and leaving open the child's options for changed or renewed relationships with birth relatives in the future. Their choices about contact with birth parents was mediated by the strong sense of obligation to keep in touch that is characteristic of kin, as opposed to non-kin, relationships: culturally we have a deeply rooted sense of obligation to be together with those we categorize as family members (Jallinoja, 2008).

This sense of obligation extended beyond birth parents to include also wider birth kin. Adoptive parents engaged in a complex and nuanced form of openness in which various birth relatives were positioned differently within the adoptive family configuration through practices that both included *and* excluded various members. The proximity afforded to different birth relatives was mediated by informal, tacit rules (Jallinoja & Widmer, 2011) that guided the adoptive parents' choices about the timing, frequency, and nature of the contact they maintained with various individuals (see MacDonald, 2016, for a fuller discussion of how adoptive parents configure birth relatives as kin). The most family-like relationships were with genealogically close relatives whose behavior was consistent with adopters' strong priority for their children's protection. This meant that the closest relationships were not necessarily with birth parents, but with birth grandparents and siblings who had demonstrated concern for the child's well-being. Adopters' protective stance generated resistance toward birth parents whose behavior posed a risk to the child or who might undermine their parental status or the child's sense of uncontested belonging in their adoptive family. Concomitantly, these tacit rules allowed the inclusion of birth mothers who, in the present, were supportive of the adoption, living relatively settled lifestyles, and whose influence on the child was perceived as benign, even if their care of the child had been harmful in the past.

The label "mother" is commonly indicative of a central place within one's nuclear or close extended family. However, in none of the accounts was the child's birth mother described as occupying such a position. Relationships with birth mothers were mediated by a sense of social exhaustion (Edwards & Strathern, 2000) which mitigated against any very close engagement as, in the context of busy family lives, there was neither the time nor emotional resources to sustain the level of support and care they might need or desire. The adoptive parents struggled to find a term to adequately label the birth mother's position in their family. Most likened the relationship with the birth mother to that normally associated with more distant kin, referring to her as "sort of like a friend" or "like an aunt." This language reflected the positioning of birth mothers as a relative who one might see infrequently and toward whom family obligations were more dilute, acknowledging that they did not have the capacity to fulfil the responsibilities that close kinship would require. This was outworked by restricting the frequency and intensity of visits and letters to enable the child's birth connections to be maintained while also repositioning birth mothers into a clearly delimited role and relationship. The following quotation from one adoptive mother illustrated the complexity for adoptive parents mediating relationships with birth parents:

> Birth mum would love to see the kids every day if she could, but the kids have busy lives too, and they have to be free to get on with their lives. . . . It's not that we want to hurt anyone's feelings, and certainly if the kids wanted more contact or needed something else from it then we would look at that again. But as it is we are meeting ourselves coming back! It is hard, your heart would go out to her. I had to discuss this at length with one of the post-adoption team because it is very, very difficult to know what to do for the best, but the way it was explained was the contact is for the children it's not for birth mum and you have to see it that way round.

For this family, sticking to an agreement for infrequent contact was a pragmatic response to the demands of a busy family life but also helped to maintain relationship boundaries, positioning the birth mother as occasional kin to lessen the burden of family obligation. However, there was also a tension in this account and uncertainty as to "what to do for the best" that was fueled by empathy and a commitment to consider the children's changing needs and wishes. Their assertion that contact should primarily benefit the child reflected a foundational principle of UK child welfare law that the child's welfare should be the paramount consideration.

IMAGINED CO-PRESENCE

Adoption severs the legal link between birth parent and child, but it does not necessarily cut any emotional, psychological, or memory ties that may exist, and so the child and their birth parents may continue to remain emotionally and psychologically present to one another. All of the adopters in the current study, regardless of the type of contact experienced or not, talked about the presence of birth parents in their thoughts or "in the back of my mind." Thus, while birth parents were not physically present in everyday adoptive family life, they often occupied a significant place in the thoughts and emotions of the adoptive parents and children. Adoption commentators seeking to understand the impact of this holding multiple families in mind (Rustin, 2008) have looked to the concept of boundary ambiguity (Boss & Greenberg, 1984), recognizing that in situations where the psychological presence of a family member is incongruent with their physical absence, the resultant sense of ambiguous loss might be experienced as a source of stress (Clark, Thigpen, & Yates, 2006; Fravel, McRoy, & Grotevant, 2000; Powell & Afifi, 2005; McSherry et al., 2013). In the adopters' accounts, however, having birth parents in the heart and on the mind was not described in altogether negative terms. Indeed, the psychological or imagined presence of birth parents was often experienced constructively and was outworked in symbolic family practices that served to constitute the thought about birth relatives as part of the child's kinship network.

Through a range of symbolic and family display (Finch, 2007) practices, the adoptive families seemed to achieve an imagined co-presence with birth parents in that they retained a sense of togetherness even in the absence of frequent interaction with one another (Baldassar, 2008). In a similar vein, Campos-Castillo and Hitlin (2013) contended that, rather than the actual physical proximity of the other, "it is the *perception* of one another that renders co-presence manifest for individuals" (p. 170) and, in particular, the perception of being mutually engaged. For example, some birth parents were consciously included in family rituals such as nightly prayers, and this act of remembering constituted imagined co-presence (Baldassar, 2008): "I would have been saying their prayers at night with them and I had promised mother that whenever I say 'God bless mommy and daddy', I'll be thinking of you too."

Adoptive parents who had little actual contact could not know what birth parents thought of their children but wondered about the imagined synchronicity of feeling that is a requisite feature of co-presence (Campos-Castillo & Hitlin, 2013). As the following quotation illustrates, it was important to think that the child would be in birth parents' thoughts:

> ADOPTIVE FATHER: "All the time you would think 'I wonder where is she now, or what is she doing or is she still about or what?.'"
> ADOPTIVE MOTHER: "and whether she has had any more children or has she ever thought of (child)."

Birth parents were particularly thought about at key family moments, such as Christmas or First Communion, which are culturally reserved for family and close friends and could be understood as an indicator of their psychological inclusion as kin. Some indirect contact took the form of symbolic gestures that were commonly understood to denote "family," for example, the giving of personal mementos, such as a lock of the child's hair. Some adoptive parents also made a point of sending letters and photographs to coincide with special occasions and rites of passage in the child's life, acknowledging that, in different circumstances, these were celebrations at which birth parents would have been present. Even in the absence of frequent or regular contact, these gestures served to include the birth parents in the emotional and psychological life of the adoptive family and were a form of family display that demonstrated their inclusion as kin (MacDonald, 2015).

The geographical proximity between many of the adoptive and birth families facilitated imagined co-presence as children and adopters often came in contact with people or artifacts associated with birth parents. For example, driving past birth parents' previous or current home or encountering their name in the community served as a prompt for thinking and talking about them. However, the "strangeness" of shared geography in the absence of shared lives also created unease for some families, as one adoptive parent noted, "[Child's birth] grandfather has a business in town and he has vans on the road and I would see the name, and it would remind me of them . . . you know that there is a connection there." Similarly, another recounted, "Their lives are running parallel to ours as they only live a couple of miles away in [town] yet we don't see each other . . . so that is very strange."

Adopted children's options for imagined co-presence with birth parents were mediated by their access to information about them. As in other studies (e.g., Jones & Hackett, 2007) the adoptive parents struggled with conveying potentially distressing birth histories in ways that were sensitive to the child's feelings and stage of development. Because of the adversity that some children had experienced preadoption, and the continued difficulties experienced by some birth parents, adopters found it challenging to talk about birth origins positively and honestly. They therefore explained children's life stories in euphemistic terms, withholding some of the more "gory details" and "rough side of the story." The children's imagined birth families and understanding of their birth histories were mediated by life-story books prepared by social workers at the time of the adoption, but these, too, tended to gloss over the harsher aspects of their early lives and reasons for adoption. As two adoptive parents commented:

> In that [life-story] book there's nothing of why he came into care, you know there's none of the harder questions of oh why did my mummy not feed me, or why did my mummy not keep me clean or why did my mummy let me crawl on the road when I was only 2 . . . that's not in the book, it's the happy times.

Another recounted,

> I say, "when mummy had you she'd nobody to help her and because she was very young herself," I say "she wasn't able to do certain things you know for you. Sometimes she didn't know that you needed your nappy changed or sometimes she forgot maybe to feed you." . . . Apparently [birth father] was violent and into drugs, but I wouldn't say that to [child] at this stage.

How birth histories were discussed constituted a form of family display that fueled the children's imagination in ways that allowed for family-like conceptions of their birth parents (MacDonald, 2015). Withholding biographical truth is not exclusive to adoptive families (Smart, 2009), but, in this context, the protective distortion of facts and the "active not-knowing" (Smart, 2009, p. 559) of certain information may have facilitated imagined co-presence with birth parents and preserved connections that would otherwise have been impossible to sustain. Nonetheless, adoptive parents expressed frustration over mixing truth and imagination, and euphemistic talk had consequences for the children's imaginary of their birth parents. They referred to the child's imagined birth family being unrealistically positive and to children viewing their birth parents through a "rose tinted" lens that distorted them to appear more positive and appealing. As one adoptive father put this:

> We knew what the facts were . . . we knew that this isn't the perfect princess that [child] is talking about, but yet she seemed to idolize her as someone perfect and we knew the facts . . . that it didn't mirror what was happening in real life.

The partial and somewhat sanitized information available to the children led to an imagined co-presence that was unrealistic and idealized. Children's imagining of birth parents was likened to a form of "worship" that rendered them ill-equipped to make informed judgments about the boundaries of their relationship with birth family (MacDonald & McSherry, 2013). As the adoptive parents looked ahead to future changes in contact, or responded to unexpected and unplanned contact, they anticipated having to tell children the "full facts" and "hard realities" as a way of preparing them for new or more intensive relationships. They expected that this would be important in order to counteract romanticized notions, buffer the child against disappointment, and empower the child to make choices about his or her level of engagement with birth parents. Talking of his daughter seeking out new contact with birth parents, one adoptive father said:

> We would have to tell her all the different bits and pieces so that she just knew what she was getting into, that she wasn't going to go and see them and imagine them to be [a certain way] and then once she gets there "Oh!"

Many of the families had exchanged photographs with birth parents at some stage, and these appeared to be a potent instrument in sustaining an imagined co-presence. As in other forms of separated families, photographs fueled the family imaginary and thus helped sustain a sense of kinship. Robertson, Wilding, and Gifford (2016), for example, identified the importance of digital photography among young refugees as means of "presencing a relationship" (p. 227), with photographs serving as a proxy for absent individuals (Baldassar, 2008). In the adopters' accounts, the way that photographs were stored and presented represented a display of the particular family meaning attributed to the photographed individuals (MacDonald, 2015). The adoptive parents were aware that in birth parents' homes photographs of the children were displayed prominently on living room walls, illustrated by the following quotation:

> She [birth mother] has a collage of all the photos that I had sent her and she pointed out [child] and said this was the year that she did this, and this was the year that she did that, and this is her confirmation.

The pride of place that was given to the children's photographs by birth parents was understood to be indicative of the strength of their imagined co-presence and sense of continued belonging to them. These prominent displays were in contrast to the more private way that photographs of birth parents were dealt with in the adoptive family home, where they were understood to belong primarily to the child. As a result, photographs of birth parents were kept in dedicated albums or life-story books or were displayed in the child's room only, perhaps conveying that these were kin who belonged to the child but not to the adoptive family as a whole. Some of the children were described as making very overt displays of birth family photographs, "like a shrine," indicating their role in the child's construction of "idealized" or "idolized" birth parents.

While photographs are generally taken to be accurate representations of people and places, some adoptive parents expressed frustration that the only photographs available presented a distorted, outdated, or incomplete image of birth parents. This diminished their value as a tool for family display because, while the practice of safeguarding the birth parent's photograph emphasized their significance as kin, the actual images did not help the child understand how they should relate to that individual (MacDonald, 2015). The lack of currency and accuracy in photographs taken some time ago therefore mediated imagined co-presence. Adopters reported their children's difficulty in relating to images that were frozen in the past or imagining what their birth parent might be like in the present. Furthermore, the passage of time likely also distorted the birth parents' imagination of the child. As one adoptive mother said of her teenage son: "He's no longer the little boy that she would have remembered and hankered after, you know, he's different."

OCCASIONAL PHYSICAL CO-PRESENCE

While physical proximity might not be absolutely necessary to achieve a sense of co-presence (Campos-Castillo & Hitlin, 2013), meeting up and being physically present with one another remains important to relationships, often motivating people to travel great distances to occasionally be together (Urry, 2002). Baldassar (2008) suggested that while virtual and proxy forms of co-presence are highly valued, *physical* co-presence remains the gold standard. The sense of missing absent relatives might best be resolved through physical co-presence, allowing individuals to be experienced fully with all the senses and providing an opportunity to confirm their well-being (Baldassar, 2008). "Seeing" relatives has been found to be central to children's definitions of "family" (Davies, 2012), a form of interaction that characterizes what family members do: relatives are people we make a point of seeing.

For families that had face-to-face contact, seeing birth parents afforded a greater and more accurate knowledge of their personality and circumstances. In contrast to looking at photographs, reading letters, or hearing about them in family stories, *seeing* facilitated really knowing the birth parent, rather than merely knowing *about* them. The opportunity for the child to "see clearly" and "know exactly" what his or her birth parents were like was welcomed by the adoptive parents as it counteracted the idealizing tendencies of their imagination. The more exact form of knowing afforded by face-to-face meetings prevented children from glamorizing birth parents or developing unrealistic notions of what life with them might be like. This was an equipping knowledge that empowered children to make decisions about the nature of their relationships with birth parents. As one adoptive mother put this:

> We particularly felt that our daughter, if she didn't continue contact, would build up a fairy tale image of her birth mother and we just thought it would help to keep things grounded and help her to remember just exactly, you know, what she was like if she saw her on a regular basis. She does see now that her life is very different being with us than what it would be if she was still with [birth mother], and so I don't think she has any desire in her heart whatsoever to go and live with her.

In addition to being told the reasons that they were no longer living with birth parents, seeing this reality for themselves lessened the child's sense of "hankering after" imagined but unrealistic lives. As the preceding quotation illustrates, seeing the birth mother obviated any desire to go and live with her. In this way, face-to-face meetings were valued as an opportunity to display (Finch, 2007) the precise nature of adoptive kin relationships, helping the child understand more accurately the status of their connection to both birth and adoptive parents (MacDonald, 2015).

Occasional meetings also had the potential to ease relationships between adoptive and birth parents. Recognizing that their children were emotionally drawn to birth parents, many adoptive parents expressed a sense of insecurity in their own parental status, concerned that their child "might want her [birth mother] more than they want us." Opportunities for accurate family display via face-to-face contact helped ease concerns that adoptive family bonds might be usurped or undermined by the strength of the child's birth connections, allowing recognition of their status as "parents in the present" (Sykes, 2000, p. 28). In addition to lowering this sense of threat or rivalry, seeing birth parents was an opportunity to get to know them as real people (Grotevant, 2000), to have a more rounded view recognizing their positive qualities, and to develop empathy toward their situation (Neil, 2003).

Face-to-face meetings also provided a context in which practices of family display (Finch, 2007) could be performed, and birth parents could convey their acceptance of adopters' role as parents to the child (MacDonald, 2015). In the context of physical meetings, adoptive parents were able to display the intimacy, commitment, and effectiveness of their parental relationship with the child, and birth parents had the opportunity to recognize and validate the legitimacy of adoptive family relationships. This validation by birth parents often took the form of subtle but powerful verbal acknowledgments, for example referring to the adopters as the child's "mum and dad" or telling them "you're doing a good job."

Conversely, contact meetings have also been found to challenge adopters' parental role identity (Logan & Smith, 2005; McSherry et al., 2008), emphasizing the adoptive status of their parenthood (MacDonald, 2016). For some families, validation was not forthcoming, and birth parents continued to explicitly challenge the permanence of the adoption or expressed negativity about the adopters' parental role. In such cases, face-to-face contact was considered unfeasible, and, even in the course of letter exchanges, both adoptive and birth mothers experienced a mutual sense of threat to the legitimacy of their maternal status in what Logan and Smith (2005) have described as a "conflict of motherhood" (p. 21).

Highlighting the reciprocal nature of relationships, Logan and Smith (2005) further noted that adopters' sense of entitlement was enhanced when birth relatives expressed permission for their parental role, but this in turn was more forthcoming when adopters communicated permission for the birth relatives' ongoing involvement in the child's life. Similarly, for those who were able to maintain occasional physical contact, meetings were an opportunity to display the inclusion of birth parents into the adoptive family configuration as the child's kin. The way that meetings were undertaken, the nature of the family practices exchanged, conveyed a message about the position and status of the birth parent relative to the adoptive family.

Most face-to-face visits followed an agreed and well-established pattern but were only occasional, taking place two or three times per year. The regularity of meetings reflected the strong sense of obligation that adoptive parents expressed for keeping in touch with birth parents which, as discussed earlier, was characteristic of the sense of duty we tend to feel toward kin. However, the infrequency or occasionality of these meetings positioned birth parents on the outskirts of adoptive family life as more distant kin with whom relationship could be less intimate.

Adoption from care is made possible through the discipline and governance of defaulting birth parents (O'Halloran, 2001), and the de facto entitlement that comes with biological or "natural" parenthood can be forfeited if its inherent responsibilities are not properly fulfilled. For those families who maintained regular direct birth parent contact, open adoption created a space in which the status of the "unfit" birth parent could be reconfigured (Sales, 2012), repositioning them into another, albeit ambiguous, kinship position that permitted ongoing connection without threat to the child's welfare. While birth parents were described as having forfeited the right to engage in active day-to-day parenting, they did not necessarily forfeit the right to be an occasional visitor.

The adoptive parents welcomed the opportunity provided by contact to find out about the child's genetic heritage. One adoptive parent explained the value of birth parent contact to help develop the child's sense of self and place:

> [Child] is very confident at music, and when we wrote and said she is doing the violin, she [birth mother] came back and said "oh, that's like her great granny" . . . and it is really nice to know, that sort of stuff is nice, you know, because it sort of says to you where you sit in the world.

While they supported children knowing their roots and identifying genetic traits, adopters were more resistant to the family of origin having an ongoing social influence on the child's behavior or to their child "inheriting" the values and lifestyle norms of birth parents. Limiting the frequency and intensity of visits allowed the child's birth connections to be maintained while also repositioning birth parents into a more marginal role and relationship.

Adopters talked about their efforts in bringing the children up with a set of values and healthy lifestyles. This form of parental investment was potentially threatened by contact with birth parents who they described as living in "a different world" that was unknown to the child and to which they did not belong, one characterized by different lifestyles and values. Direct contact caused the separate worlds of adoptive and birth family to coincide, albeit briefly, and adoptive parents expressed concerns that this could undermine their moral priorities for the child. They feared that the child might assimilate birth parents' norms or cross a boundary into the other world, resulting in lifestyle choices that might be harmful, unhealthy, and inhibit the child from reaching his or her potential. As one adoptive mother said:

> The contact with the birth family has maybe given me the impetus to really try harder to try and ensure that they don't go down the route that the birth parents did. Educating them about alcohol and things like that.

While the adoptive parents were concerned that birth relatives might exert a negative influence on the child, they also felt unable to stand in the way of these relationships. Belief in the enduring importance of blood ties operated as a motivator to facilitate contact and simultaneously imposed constraints on adopters' parental autonomy, curtailing their ability to prohibit contact that they feared might be detrimental. Respecting the child's "right to know where they come from" often contravened welfare priorities, and this dilemma left adoptive parents feeling conflicted and uncertain about how best to proceed with contact. This tension was typified by the following two quotations from one adoptive mother's account:

> Everybody wants to know their roots, to know where they came from and who they look like and where they get their personality from and all this sort of stuff.
>
> I wouldn't want her to be drawn into this, em, whole thing, the whole scenario, with friends and family cos, that's different, it's a different, how can I say it, different standards and ethos of living from what she is used to. She [birth mother] is still in contact with people that are alcoholics, and her friends do drugs and stuff like that, so you wouldn't want her to get into that with relatives, that's what I would be concerned about.

For the most part, contact visits with birth relatives took place in public locations, positioning birth relatives outside of the circle of close kin who were invited into the home. The family home, as an explicitly family space, served as a physical boundary marker that delimited the membership of the adoptive family.

Two families recounted occasions when birth mothers visited their home uninvited, which was experienced as a violation of physical and symbolic family boundaries. Adoptive parents were loath to restrict their children's contact, but also keen to prevent an incursion on their private family space. While the commitment to maintaining occasional contact with birth parents reinforced the significance of this essential kin connection, keeping visits beyond the threshold of the family home demarcated birth relatives clearly as the child's kin but not of the adoptive family as a whole.

In adoptive kinship, relationships between the child and birth parents are not inevitable but rely on demonstrations of trustworthiness, care, and commitment if meaningful connections are to be sustained (Jones & Hackett, 2012). Simply being in close physical proximity does not necessarily constitute co-presence; rather, it is the subjective perception of being mutually connected that is important regardless of the physicality of the exchange (Campos-Castillo & Hitlin, 2013). Coming together to be physically alongside one another can, however, afford an opportunity to display commitment and the caring nature of the shared connection (Urry, 2002). Because adoptive parents distinguished between the role and status of birth parents pre- and postadoption (Sales, 2012), they were no longer expected to demonstrate the level of care and commitment normally required of a parent; rather, a lesser standard was expected that was consistent with their more marginal kinship position. Face-to-face contact could be maintained, therefore, with birth mothers who behaved benignly toward the child in the present despite perhaps having been neglectful in the past. Although occasional physical co-presence did not permit birth parents to perform any actual caregiving role, it was nonetheless important that they demonstrated concern and care for the child. Contact was a chance for birth mothers to display their sensitivity to the child's need for close, secure adoptive relationships; their acceptance of the adoption; and to act in a way that, if not actively nurturing, then at least did not compromise the child's welfare. The adoptive parents appeared, however, to maintain realistic expectations of how this family-like commitment might be evidenced, and simply making the effort to be "pleasant" or "chatty" and turn up reliably could be sufficient. As one adoptive mother described this:

> [Birth mum] makes a big effort because it's only once a year and she's always there, so we have nothing in recent years to be angry with her about and it's just, I think it's all those things sort of married together that developed our relationship over the years.

As the adoptive parents sought to mediate the physical co-presence between birth parent and child, this was not exclusively with the aim of restricting their influence but was also intended to scaffold and support delicate relationships. Meetings were arranged around family leisure activities, for example, an outing to a zoo, park, or restaurant. Although these encounters were infrequent, they involved a concentrated exchange of family practices, with shared enjoyment and the expenditure of time, effort, and money marking the occasion and relationship as significant. The adoptive parents also highlighted their own role as facilitators during meetings, encouraging positive interaction between child and birth parent. One couple, for example, recounted a meeting when the birth mother was feeling "fragile," and they carefully structured activities so that the children "didn't actually notice too much that she wasn't at her usual bouncy self." As they described their role in facilitating the contact:

> If we weren't there, this sounds awful, guiding them along there would be very little chatting between [child] and her mother . . . when it goes a bit flat one of us would have to go and say "what about telling your mother about Irish dancing or what about telling her about your horse riding."

Adopters talked about family life and relationships as distinct and separate from the birth parents. However, the relatively close geographical proximity of birth and adoptive families following domestic adoption in Northern Ireland presented overlapping social worlds that raised the prospect of accidental contact (e.g., through shared community and leisure spaces, shopping in the same stores). Some families made creative use of community resources to arrange contact between siblings around shared activities and leisure. However, the status of birth parents was more contested, and shared geographical location was more problematic. Adopters expressed a sense of dissonance when lives that were normally lived at a comfortable social distance and in parallel accidentally and unexpectedly converged:

> I was coming out of the health centre after a check-up, and this man looked at me straight in the face, and looked at the child and walked straight towards me, and I just knew that this person knows this baby, and it was the father. I was standing there quaking in my shoes thinking "this person is violent."

This same adoptive mother went on to describe how, in the course of further accidental meetings, she came to revise her view of the birth parents who she subsequently, and more empathically, assessed as "both nice people who just have a problem."

For this and other adoptive parents, the prospect of bumping into birth parents seemed preferable to formal meetings because it allowed a more " natural exchange," and some used this opportunity to update birth parents on the child's welfare or even to give the photographs of the children that they carried in their wallets. As another adoptive mother said:

> Some days I do wish we would bump into her . . . because for me that would be different if I just bumped into her because it hasn't been planned. I don't have that worry of the anticipation of what's gonna happen and I think it's more natural just to bang into each other . . . your expectations are different if you formalise it, you know [birth mother's] expectations of that meeting would be different, [child's] expectations and my expectations would all be

> very, very different than if we just bumped into each other because there is no expectation there, you've met up, you start a conversation . . . you can be more relaxed.

Some families feared and avoided accidental meetings, particularly when birth parents represented percieved or actual threat. When a birth parent was believed to be aggressively opposed to the adoption, adopters practiced social avoidance and restricted their use of public spaces. They described, for example, avoiding certain towns, shopping centers, or leisure activities and maintaining a closely guarded privacy by prohibiting the announcement of the child's sporting success in local newspapers. The adoptive parents talked of this aspect of their family life with a calm pragmatism, noting,

> Say [child] was on a team or anything that got recognition in the press. . . . He wants to have his photograph taken and he's getting pulled out of those photographs and that's a downer for him, but again that's life.

VIRTUAL CO-PRESENCE

Recent years have seen an emergence of the use of social media as a means for adopted young people and birth relatives to maintain their relationship or to seek each other out when no other contact arrangement was in place (Neil et al., 2013). Given the relatively recent proliferation of information and communication technologies, it is likely that adoptive families will have increasingly intensive experiences of co-presence in a virtual environment (Baldassar et al., 2016).

Newer communication technologies have begun to challenge the premise that strong relationships require face-to-face interactions, and they can support more frequent and more diverse connections across time and space (Baldassar et al., 2016). Digital communication technology can enable the types of interaction dynamics that occur in shared physical spaces to be replicated over distance (Campos-Castillo & Hitlin, 2013) and, compared to traditional postal exchanges, can afford a more intimate way for separated families to maintain a sense of togetherness. Communicating via webcam, for example, allows individuals to both see and hear one another and so involves an appeal to the senses that is missing when letters are exchanged (Baldassar, 2008).

Although there is limited research on the use of communication technology in adoptive kinship networks, studies involving children adopted from care have identified a range of difficulties associated with the use of online social media in particular. Many of the challenges and concerns have concentrated around adoptive parents' role as mediators. Particularly problematic has been the unplanned and unexpected use of social media by birth parents and adopted children, particularly in adolescence, and the potential for this contact to go unmediated, or indeed unknown, by adoptive parents (Greenhow, Hackett, Jones, & Meins, 2015; MacDonald & McSherry, 2013; Neil, Beek, & Ward, 2013).

Online social media presents a route for birth parent and adopted children to seek out and communicate independently, without the need for an intermediary. However, adopters in this study expressed concern that this constrained their ability to mediate birth connections or shield their children from potentially negative influences, particularly in early adolescence, when young people were perceived to have the digital skills to communicate with birth parents via social media but not the emotional maturity or social wisdom to manage resultant relationships (MacDonald & McSherry, 2013). Most of the supports for contact available in the United Kingdom are structural systems that support letter exchange (Neil et al., 2011), and mediation of virtual contact may not have kept pace with the use of communication technology. Virtual contact between adopted children and birth parents may not, therefore, be regulated by the clearly established agreements and mechanisms of mediation that are often put in place for more traditional contact meetings or letter exchange. Greenhow and colleagues (2015), for example, found that because virtual contact was less restricted, it therefore could become "relentless" (p. 4) and hard to stop. On a more positive note, the use of social media has been reported to be beneficial when used to complement existing contact arrangements and where adoptive parents are involved in its management (Neil et al., 2013). Within these parameters, virtual contact can offer a convenient vehicle for extending existing positive contact and widening relationships in birth family networks in a way that fits more naturally with everyday adoptive family communication practices (Greenhow et al., 2015).

CONCLUSION

In all adoption, but particularly in the case of compulsory adoption of children in public care, the status of birth and adoptive parents can be contested and their respective positions relative to one another and their child can be somewhat ambiguous (MacDonald, 2016). Notwithstanding the complexities of adoptive kinship, the discussion here illustrates the creative and nuanced ways in which birth and adoptive families can achieve imagined and occasional physical co-presence after adoption. This chapter has illuminated the experiences of adoptive parents, but there is also an ongoing need to understand the perspectives of all members of the adoptive kinship network and the extent to which they differ or converge. It is important to listen to adopted children and young people's views on open adoption and how their families are configured and to explore from the birth parents' standpoint what factors inhibit or enable meaningful connection with their children after adoption. There is also scope for further conceptualization of the use of virtual contact in open adoption (Greenhow et al., 2015), and negotiated agreements for post-adoption contact should take account of the prevalence and potential value of communication technologies. Attention should also be paid to understanding the factors mitigating the potential risks associated with unmediated and unregulated contact for children adopted from care. How to capitalize co-presence in the virtual environment (Baldassar et al., 2016) to facilitate connections between adopted children and birth parents should also be explored.

REFERENCES

Baldassar, L. (2008). Missing kin and longing to be together: Emotions and the construction of co-presence. *Journal of Intercultural Studies, 29*(3), 247–266.

Baldassar, L., Nedelcu, M., Merla, L., & Wilding, R. (2016). ICT-based co-presence in transnational families and communities: Challenging the premise of face-to-face proximity in sustaining relationships. *Global Networks, 16*(2), 133–144.

Boss, P., & Greenberg, J. (1984). Family boundary ambiguity: A new variable in family stress theory. *Family Process, 23*(4), 535–546.

Brodzinsky, D. M. (2005). Reconceptualizing openness in adoption: Implications for theory, research and practice. In D. M. Brodzinsky & J. Palacios (Eds.), *Psychological issues in adoption: Research and practice* (pp. 145–166). Westport, CT: Praeger.

Brodzinsky, D. M. (2006). Family structural openness and communication openness as predictors in the adjustment of adopted children. *Adoption Quarterly, 9*(4), 1–18.

Campos-Castillo, C., & Hitlin, S. (2013). Copresence revisiting a building block for social interaction theories. *Sociological Theory, 31*(2), 168–192.

Clark, P., Thigpen, S., & Yates, A. M. (2006). Integrating the older/special needs adoptive child into the family. *Journal of Marital and Family Therapy, 32*(2), 181–194.

Davies, H. (2012). Affinities, seeing and feeling like family: Exploring why children value face-to-face contact. *Childhood, 19*(1), 8–23.

Department of Economic and Social Affairs of the United Nations Secretariat (DESA). (2009). *Child adoption: Trends and policies.* New York: United Nations.

Dunbar, N., Van Dulmen, M. H., Ayers-Lopez, S., Berge, J. M., Christian, C., Gossman, G., & McRoy, R. (2006). Processes linked to contact changes in adoptive kinship networks. *Family Process, 45*(4), 449–464.

Edwards, J., & Strathern, M. (2000). Including our own. In J. Carsten (Ed.), *Cultures of relatedness: New approaches to the study of kinship* (pp. 149–166). Cambridge, UK: Cambridge University Press.

Finch, J. (2007). Displaying families. *Sociology, 41*(1), 65–81.

Fravel, D. L., McRoy, R. G., & Grotevant, H. D. (2000). Birthmother perceptions of the psychologically present adopted child: Adoption openness and boundary ambiguity. *Family Relations, 49*(4), 425–432.

Greenhow, S., Hackett, S., Jones, C., & Meins, E. (2015). Adoptive family experiences of post-adoption contact in an Internet era. *Child & Family Social Work.* doi:10.1111/cfs.12256.

Grotevant, H. D. (2000). Openness in adoption: Research with the adoption kinship network. *Adoption Quarterly, 4*(1), 45–65.

Grotevant, H. D. (2009). Emotional distance regulation over the life-course. In G. M. Wrobel & E. Neil (Eds.), *International advances in adoption research for practice* (pp. 269–294). Chichester, UK: Wiley-Blackwell.

Human Rights Act. United Kingdom of Great Britain and Northern Ireland. (1998). This is a legislative act which can be accessed online from: https://www.legislation.gov.uk/ukpga/1998/42

Jallinoja, R. (2008). Togetherness and being together: Family configurations in the making. In E. D. Widmer & R. Jallinoja (Eds.), *Beyond the nuclear family: Families in configurational perspective* (pp. 97). Bern: Peter Lang.

Jallinoja, R., & Widmer, E. D. (2011). *Families and kinship in contemporary Europe.* Hampshire, UK: Palgrave Macmillan.

Jones, C. (2016). Openness in adoption: Challenging the narrative of historical progress. *Child and Family Social Work, 21*(1), 85–93.

Jones, C., & Hackett, S. (2007). Communicative openness within adoptive families: Adoptive parents' narrative accounts of the challenges of adoption talk and the approaches used to manage these challenges. *Adoption Quarterly, 10*(3-4), 157–178.

Jones, C., & Hackett, S. (2012). Redefining family relationships following adoption: Adoptive parents' perspectives on the changing nature of kinship between adoptees and birth relatives. *British Journal of Social Work, 42*(2), 283–299.

Kelly, G. (2012). *Listen up—speak out: A survey of adoptive parents in Northern Ireland.* Belfast: Adoption UK.

Logan, J., & Smith, C. (2005). Face-to-face contact post adoption: Views from the triangles. *British Journal of Social Work, 35*(1), 3–35.

MacDonald, M. (2015). A picture of who we are as a family: Conceptualizing post-adoption contact as practices of family display. *Child and Family Social Work.* doi:10.1111/cfs.1224.

MacDonald, M. (2016). *Parenthood and open adoption: An interpretative phenomenological analysis.* Basingstoke, UK: Palgrave Macmillan.

MacDonald, M., & McSherry, D. (2013). Constrained adoptive parenthood and family transition: Adopters' experience of unplanned birth family contact in adolescence. *Child & Family Social Work, 18*(1), 87–96.

McSherry, D., Fargas Malet, M., & Weatherall, K. (2013). *Comparing long-term placements for young children in care.* London: British Association for Adoption and Fostering.

McSherry, D., Larkin, E., Fargas, M., Kelly, G. M., Robinson, C., Macdonald, G. M., . . . & Kilpatrick, R. (2008). *From care to where? A Care Pathways and Outcomes Report for Practitioners.* Belfast: Queens University, Institute of Child Care Research.

Mason, J. (2011). What it means to be related. In V. May (Ed.), *Sociology of personal life* (pp. 59–71). Basingstoke, UK: Palgrave Macmillan.

Mason, J., & Tipper, B. (2008). Children and the making of kinship configurations. In E. D. Widmer & R. Jallinoja (Eds.), *Beyond the nuclear family: Families in a configurational perspective* (pp. 137–156). Bern: Peter Lang.

Morgan, D. H. (1996). *Family connections: An introduction to family studies.* Cambridge: Polity Press.

Morgan, D. H. (2011). *Rethinking family practices.* Basingstoke, UK: Palgrave Macmillan.

Morrison, M. (2012). *Talking About Adoption.* London: British Association for Adoption and Fostering.

Neil, E. (2003). Understanding other people's perspectives: Tasks for adopters in open adoption. *Adoption Quarterly, 6*(3), 3–30.

Neil, E., Beek, M., & Ward, E. (2013). *Contact after adoption: A follow up in late adolescence*. University of East Anglia, Centre for Research on Children and Families, Norwich. Retrieved from https://core.ac.uk/download/pdf/29109730.pdf

Neil, E., Cossar, J., Jones, C., Lorgelly, P., & Young, J. (2011). *Supporting direct contact after adoption*. London: British Association for Adoption and Fostering.

Neil, E., & Howe, D. (2004). Conclusions: A transactional model for thinking about contact. In E. Neil & Howe D. (Eds.), *Contact in adoption and permanent foster care: Research, theory and practice* (pp. 224–254). London: British Association for Adoption and Fostering.

O'Halloran, K. J. (2001). Adoption in the two jurisdictions of Ireland: A case study of changes in the balance between public and private law. *International Family Law, 2*, 43–54.

Powell, K. A., & Afifi, T. D. (2005). Uncertainty management and adoptees' ambiguous loss of their birth parents. *Journal of Social and Personal Relationships, 22*(1), 129–151.

Reynolds, T., & Zontini, E. (2014). Transnational families: Migrant youths "doing" families across proximities and distances. *Families, Relationships and Societies, 3*(2). 251–268.

Robertson, Z., Wilding, R., & Gifford, S. (2016). Mediating the family imaginary: Young people negotiating absence in transnational refugee families. *Global Networks, 16*(2), 219–236.

Rosnati, R. (2005). The construction of adoptive parenthood and filiation in Italian families with adolescents: A family perspective. In D. M. Brodzinsky (Ed.), *Psychological issues in adoption: Research and practice* (pp. 187–210). Westport, CT: Praeger.

Rustin, M. (2008). Multiple families in mind. In D. Hindle & G. Shulman (Eds.), *The emotional experience of adoption: A psychoanalytic perspective* (pp. 77–89). Oxon, UK: Routledge.

Sales, S. (2012). *Adoption, family and the paradox of origins: A Foucauldian history*. London: Palgrave Macmillan

Schofield, G., & Beek, M. (2006). *Attachment handbook for foster care and adoption*. London: British Association for Adoption and Fostering.

Selwyn, J., Meakings, S., & Wijedasa, D. (2015). *Beyond the adoption order: Challenges, interventions and adoption disruption*. London: British Association for Adoption and Fostering.

Siegel, D. H., & Smith, S. L. (2012). *Openness in adoption: From secrecy and stigma to knowledge and connections*. New York: Evan B. Donaldson Institute.

Smart, C. (2009). Family secrets: Law and understandings of openness in everyday relationships. *Journal of Social Policy, 38*(04), 551–567.

Smith, B., Surrey, J. L., & Watkins, M. (2006). "Real" mothers: Adoptive mothers resisting marginalisation and recreating motherhood. In K. Wegar (Ed.), *Adoptive families in a diverse society* (pp. 146–161). New Brunswick, NJ: Rutgers University.

Smith, C. (2002). Adoptive parenthood as a "legal fiction": Its consequences for direct post-adoption contact. *Child and Family Law Quarterly, 14*(3), 281–301.

Smith, J. A., Flowers, P., & Larkin, M. (2009). *Interpretative phenomenological analysis: Theory, method and research*. London: Sage.

Sykes, M. (2000). Adoption with contact: A study of adoptive parents and the impact of continuing contact with families of origin. *Adoption & Fostering, 24*(2), 20–32.

Triseliotis, J. (1973). *In search of origins: The experiences of adopted people.* Boston: Beacon Press.

Urry, J. (2002). Mobility and proximity. *Sociology, 36*(2), 255–274.

Widmer, E. D., & Jallinoja, R. (2008). *Beyond the nuclear family: Families in configurational perspective.* Bern: Peter Lang.

Wrobel, G. M., Grotevant, H. D., Berge, J., Mendenhall, T., & Mcroy, R. (2003). Contact in adoption: The experience of adoptive families in the USA. *Adoption & Fostering, 27*(1), 57–67.

8

Untold Transnational Family Life on the Sonora–Arizona Border

MARCELA SOTOMAYOR-PETERSON AND ANA A. LUCERO-LIU

The term "transnational families" refers to those in which members are dispersed across international borders but sustain ties across distance and whose members spend time in one country or another (Vertovec, 2004). Research on transnational families mostly assumes long physical distances and long periods of separation (Boehm, 2011; Parreñas, 2008, 2015); however, in reality, transnational family arrangements are diverse. The US–Mexico border in Arizona is a fluid one, where contact between members is a possibility for some families. This potential of physical contact on a semi-regular basis makes these families unique. This chapter provides a portrait of transnational families from Sonora–Arizona, with the goal of illustrating the diversity of family life for transnational families.

In order to contextualize our work, we start with a brief history of migration between Mexico and the United States, followed by a review of how Mexican transnational families operate across distance. We continue with a description of the transnational families we found in the Sonora–Arizona area and present preliminary findings of *transnational* and *transborder* families with regard to parenting and family issues. Mexican transnational families are defined as those whose members live separated by an international border. The legalities of border crossing prevent members from reuniting, and thus many families experience long-term separations. In contrast, transborder families are those living near the border (e.g., within 60 miles) in contexts where there are age-old practices of border crossing, with social networks on both sides facilitating and fostering family reunions (Ojeda, 2008). We close with a discussion of the implications of the transnational experience for family well-being and discuss directions for future research.

BRIEF HISTORICAL CONTEXT OF MEXICO–US MIGRATION

In 1848, California, Arizona, New Mexico, and parts of Colorado, Nevada, and Utah (and their inhabitants, by then around 100,000 people) became part of the United States, shaping the history of migration between Mexico and the United States. At the end of the 19th century until 1929, the expansion of the railroad favored the massive transit of Mexicans to the California area, in addition to those who fled the violence produced by the Mexican Revolution of 1910. From 1929 to 1941, a saturated job market in the United States resulted in massive deportation of those workers lacking legal documentation. During and following World War II, thousands of Mexicans found jobs in the construction industry and were hired under the Programa Bracero (1942–1964) to work in agricultural fields (Vázquez & Bocanegra, 2013). This was a temporary and circular migration accompanied by bilateral agreements providing legal status to these workers (i.e., Immigration Reform and Control Act [IRCA, 1986]; Amnistia, Programa Huesped para Trabajadores Agrícolas, Programas de Reunificación Familiar [between 1965 and 1986]; Durand & Massey, 2003, cited in Secretaría de Educación Pública, 2011). During this time, the numbers of Mexican migrants in the United States remained within a range of 200,000 up to 500,000. An unprecedented increase in these numbers began in the early 1980s and continued until 2010, when the number of migrants grew from 2.2 to 12.5 million (Delgado Wise, 2014, p. 14) resulting from the dynamic of a globalized economy embodied in the Tratado de Libre Comercio de América del Norte (NAFTA) and the neoliberal policies of the Mexican government.

An important change took place as a consequence of the world financial crisis in early 2000 and the more stringent US immigration policies and tightening of the borders that developed after September 11, 2001. The financial crises in the United States fostered the return of migrants to Mexico, and a punitive policy of migrant criminalization sent back about 350,000–365,000 Mexicans each year (Márquez & Garcia, 2014). The tightening of the border caused migration flows to move from well-known crossing points to other less supervised and arguably more dangerous areas, such as the deserts of Sonora–Arizona. The risks of crossing, the tight surveillance of the border, and the increasing anti-immigrant policies reduced temporary and circular migration and fostered a pattern of longer and more permanent stays in the United States, impacting transnational families' well-being (Berumen & Santiago, 2012).

MEXICAN TRANSNATIONAL FAMILIES LIVES

Migration challenges family and individual well-being in multiple ways, as is evidenced by several chapters in this current volume. Research specifically on Mexican transnational families suggests that migration often comes at a high cost.

Fathers and mothers who leave their spouses and/or children in Mexico face the challenge of maintaining their parental and spousal roles over long distances, and minors pay the emotional costs of growing up with fractured families, with loved ones on both sides of the border (e.g., Heymann et al., 2009; Lahaie, Hayes, Piper, & Heymann, 2009).

Transnational parenting has an important impact on children. Children born in transnational families can result in cases where siblings never meet (Mummert, 2009). For those who stay behind in Mexico, the emotional consequences include feelings of abandonment and separation anxiety, among other outcomes (McGuire & Martin, 2007; Sotomayor-Peterson & Montiel-Carbajal, 2014). Mexican children born in the United States and raised by undocumented immigrants face a disadvantaged position regarding economic, social, and educational spheres of development, often resulting in limited access to services and benefits. Additionally, as these children have US citizen status, they are continuously at risk of losing their parents due to deportations and being placed in foster homes (Yoshikawa, 2011; see also Hamann et al., Chapter 16 in this volume). In cases when children migrate from Mexico accompanying their parents and consequently pay the costs of acculturative stress, studies have documented feelings of inadequacy, irritability, and even identity ambivalence as responses to growing up within a sociocultural environment distinct from Mexican traditions (Faulstich Orellana, Thorne, Chee, & Lam, 2001; Romero & Roberts, 2003).

The impact of migration on marital relationship and spousal well-being has also been studied. Marsiglia, Kulis, Perez, and Bermudez-Parsai (2011) found that Mexican-heritage women were among the Latinas who had higher frequencies of psychiatric disorders compared with their male counterparts, and Martínez and colleagues found that stress and loneliness associated with an irregular legal status were common causes for depression in a Latino sample, a third of which were Mexican immigrants (Martinez, Castañeda, Porter, Quiroz, & Carrion, 2011). Boehm (2011) and Castellanos and Boehm's (2008) ethnographic work have depicted the more intimate emotions of marital partners separated by migration. These works propose gendered effects on how marital partners deal with separation and trust issues that are socially acceptable for Mexicans, suggesting that migration north is colored by both desires and suffering, creating a painful paradox for partners.

Notwithstanding the challenges just described, many transnational families have found strategies to maintain well-being and thrive in the context of migration. In a qualitative study, Bonizzoni (2012) observed that mothers kept alive their love and care toward their children through phone calls, short visits, and through remittances they send home. These practices allow mothers to reconnect later and help reestablish a sense of intimacy once reunited. Marsiglia and colleagues (2011) suggest that culturally rooted aspects, such as resiliency and a sense of optimism connected with immigration, appeared to shelter these women from hopelessness and depression. Additionally, Moreno, Mejía, Lucero-Liu, and Sotomayor-Peterson (2013) found that coping strategies for migrants in Los Angeles included focusing on the capital aspects of separation, fostering the "sense of family" by emphasizing the hard work endured to provide for their families while maintaining communication as frequently as possible.

Other studies have explored the role that contact has on alleviating the distress of distance. In her ethnographic work, Dreby (2006) found that the amount of contact migrant mothers versus migrant fathers maintain with their children in Mexico is equal and that the most common medium of contact is the telephone. Using the 2005 Mexican Family Life Survey, Nobles (2011) found that 61% of migrant fathers maintained phone contact with their children in Mexico on at least a weekly basis. Furthermore, the amount of contact is greater than that of nonresident fathers who left their homes following divorce. Additionally, the majority of fathers in their sample helped with most of their children's expenses. As mentioned earlier, financial contributions made by migrant fathers are positively correlated with children's school outcomes. Similarly, Kanaiaupuni (2000) found that maintaining frequent contact by phone and letters reduced anxiety for both women and children who stayed in Mexico.

Madianou and Miller (2013) have proposed that the nature of family relationship is changing by means of what they termed "polymedia," which represents an ecology that has a net full of resources to keep a constant presence through real-time communication and tools such as web cameras that make virtual presence a very true reality for interpersonal relationships. Regretfully, sometimes the economic and legal constraints of migration limit the frequency of transnational interchange and make these strategies less attainable. In her ethnographic research with domestic workers in internal migration, de Guzman (2014) showed that many mothers could not contact their children by phone because they either lacked the money to pay for service or could not afford mobile phones. Menjivar (2012) highlighted the role that immigration laws have played on reunification efforts for Central American immigrants. She documented how Guatemalan, Nicaraguan, and Salvadoran mothers face unique circumstances when dealing with immigration services by obtaining temporary permits to stay in United States. These permits can later become an obstacle in their attempts to visit their children and return as policies change, thus leaving these families legally undefined, sometimes for decades.

In sum, the challenges of migration for marital and parental relationships are important variables explaining the impact of family separation due to international migration for families, and specifically for Mexicans. Nevertheless, Mexican transnational families have developed ways to cope with restraints that US immigration policies place on their lives such as redefining roles, reassessment of meanings, and heightening relational ties not only by remittances to home but also by increasing intimate contact through more accessible communication technology that has become a key factor for keeping distances shorter (Madianou & Miller, 2013).

Despite all that we already know about transnational family lives, several important gaps remain. Previous studies have highlighted that migration experiences may vary based on country of origin (i.e., Mexicans vs. Guatemalan, Salvadoran; Martinez et al., 2011; Menjívar, 2012). Such inquiries are intuitive, as immigrants from different countries deal with different immigration issues at both their places of origin and destinations. Mexico, which has a long history of a common border with the United States and complex patterns of migration, displays a rich variety of reasons behind these flows (Instituto Nacional de Migración [INM], 2012). We suspect that family experiences of Mexican immigrants from the Central and Southeast regions of the country (i.e., Oaxaca, Michoacan, Chiapas, etc.) may differ from those originating from border areas. People from the border region have shared special meanings and practices around the border for more than a hundred years, and these influence the ways in which they cope with transnational experiences. Gaps also exist in the array of family issues already explored. Whereas gender issues within marital relationships of transnational partners have received some attention (Hirsch, 1999; Pribilsky, 2004; Sotomayor & Lucero-Liu, 2017), specific aspects of marital arrangements, such as co-parenting, have been less explored. Co-parenting, or partners' sharing the duties of childrearing, may play a role in explaining how parents cope with distance. The analysis of specific cultural values that may work in favor of or against transnational experiences deserves more attention. We do not know the role that *familism* has in explaining family adaptations to distance, especially among transnational families who do not match the typical portrait of "transnational" that the literature has provided. Familism has been studied with Mexican immigrants of all generations (Sabogal, Marin, Otero-Sabogal, & Marin, 1987; Zinn, 1982), and recent findings suggest that this value interacts with family processes involved in coping and adaptation in the host community (Zeiders, Updegraff, Umaña-Taylor, McHale, & Padilla, 2015). There remains a need for more research on family issues when families are operating across distance, especially as close relationships are critical for mental and physical health and well-being (e.g., Fincham & Beach, 2010).

TRANSNATIONAL FAMILIES IN SONORA–ARIZONA LIVING NEAR THE BORDER

Families living on different sides of, but in proximity to, the border may have different experiences of migration than reported by typical transnational experiences. Thus its effects on family life may also differ. From a socioanthropological point of view, Ojeda (2008) proposes that transborder and transnational families are two different types of family, but not mutually exclusive. Based on a historical and geographical analysis of US and Mexico relationships, she defines that while transborder families form part of a regional phenomenon unique to the two nations and dating from the very moment of border creation, transnational families respond to a broader social situation tied to both the migration flow between the countries and globalization. In Ojeda's perspective, one difference is the cultural context of families living near the border (Ojeda, 2008); there is a *sui-generis* border or *fronteriza* (border line) culture along its 2,000-mile length. Despite features that are specific to each region of the border (i.e., from east to west: "Tex–Mex," "Sonora-Arizona," "Las Californias" areas), there is a shared culture for inhabitants of border cities, where cultural and social traits from both countries interact to produce a culture that is neither American nor Mexican, but a hybrid. Ojeda (2008) proposes that the *fronteriza* experience is one marked by daily international contact, conflict, and harmony and feelings of separateness between First and Third Worlds. The author suggests that this complex dynamic results in higher tolerance and adaptation to "other side" ways and ideas and favors interaction and sometimes cooperation between sides. People who live in border cities experience intense and diverse flows of migration: internally, from migrants originating from inside Mexico, and externally, from those coming from diverse countries, as well as those who settle down on the Mexican side of border and those who cross to the United States. These groups all converge at the borders, increasing the complexity of social life.

The complexity of social life at the US–Mexico border is rooted in history, beginning when a part of Mexico became part of the United States. At that point, the border was permeable, porous, and mobile. Identities and families became intertwined, leading to the daily crossing of people, services, goods, drugs, and money (Ruiz & Valdez-Gardea, 2013). The uneven socioeconomic reality of Mexico and the United States has fostered the existence of "commuters," people who live on one side and work on the other, commonly from South to North, creating a continuous crossing from one country to another seeking services, goods, and social relations. The transborder experience may be a different way to cope with migration, as compared to transnational families who respond more to globalized economies involving people from two different cultures separated geographically (Ojeda et al., 2008). We believe this is an important issue to explore. We maintain that transnational family experience must take into consideration the idea that not all Mexican immigrants are the same. The aim of our work is to delve into the diversity within transnational family life by studying Mexican transnationals from the border region.

THE SONORA–ARIZONA STUDY

In 2013, we began a study of transnational families from the Sonora–Arizona border area with support from the Programa de Investigación en Migración y Salud (PIMSA, University of California, Berkeley) with the objective of exploring family mental health and well-being within the context of Mexico–US migration. After obtaining Human Protection approval from both the University of California, Northridge in the United States and the University of Sonora in Mexico, the principal investigators and a team of graduate and undergraduate students initiated the process of recruiting participants at both sides of the border. A first phase of the study was conducted with a few transnational families recruited in the Southern area of Los Angeles. These families were originally from the Central and Southern states of Mexico, with most of them living in the United States for more than a decade and having family members in Mexico. This manuscript does not include all data collected from this first study phase because the focus of the study is on the Sonora–Arizona border. A second phase of the study recruited transnational families that could be reached in Sonora, a state in Northwest Mexico sharing a border with Arizona. The recruitment criteria included individuals older than 18 years of age, living in a marital-type relationship, and having children. Additionally, participants also must have had at least 6 months of marital separation due to migration. Our first approach to recruitment was to visit a pair of nongovernmental organizations working in the capital city of Sonora and at the border city of Nogales. We did not succeed; as the vast majority of people at these community centers or shelters were men from other states of Mexico and from Central America (i.e., San Salvador, Guatemala, etc.) and who were in transit to the United States. Some would cross for the very first time, others reported having been there for short periods of family separation. Others reported having lived in the United States for a long time with their families and been recently deported. Thus, the majority of these men did not meet our recruitment criteria.

In our recruitment effort, we also posted fliers in locations where people cashed remittance checks coming from family members in the United States and visited local schools where we knew that non–Spanish-speaking Mexican children were attending classes in a new program. The Secretariat of Education reported about 10,000 minor migrants returning to Sonora schools from 2008 to 2012 who were admitted under the Binational Program of Migrant Education (Ruiz & Valdez-Gardea, 2013). Elementary school authorities facilitated first contact with some of these families. We continued our recruitment through word-of-mouth where participants helped us contact other potential participants in various places in Sonora. Finally, we interviewed participants mostly in the central area of Sonora (i.e., cities and towns within a 3- to 5-hour drive to the US border) and the border city of Nogales, Sonora.

Description of the Families

The study recruited 119 participants who we interviewed in Sonora. One hundred fourteen were originals/residents of the area and five were interviewed while transiting through Sonora (i.e., four were from other states of Mexico and one from San Salvador). In 77 cases, the participant was the partner of the migrant (i.e., the participant stayed in Mexico), 18 participants were the migrant themselves (i.e., the participant had left Mexico and was temporarily in Mexico at the time of the interview), and 24 participants were return migrants. The latter group consisted mostly of couples who left and return to Mexico together (11 couples and 2 women). In order to avoid duplication, for the next analyses, we used only data from one member of each couple, even when data from both were available (i.e., thus 5 partners of migrants and 11 individuals from returned migrant couples were dropped from analyses). The final sample size is 103 participants categorized as 72 partners of migrants (64 female/8 male), 18 migrants (3 female/15 male), and 13 returned migrants (8 female/5 male). The majority of participants (89%) were born in Sonora or surrounding border areas.

Table 8.1 Participants' Demographic Information, $N = 103$

	Percent	Mean (SD)	Minimum	Maximum
Age		41.1 (9.5)	22	67
Marital Status				
Married	91.3			
Unmarried	8.7			
Relationship length in years		17.6 (9.6)	1	45
Months living apart from partner		62.6 (57.6)	1	288
Number of children		2.5 (1.2)	1	7
Age of youngest child		11.9 (7.3)	1	38
Migrant's employment in US*				
Temporal	17			
Part time	7			
Full time	71			
Send remittances to Mexico*				
Yes	72			
How frequently send*				
Regularly	77			

*Numbers do not add up because of missing values.

As shown in Table 8.1, we have a sample with great variability. Mean age was 41 years, with 17 years of marriage and approximately 5 years living apart from the partner (mean = 62.6 months), but the range was considerable (e.g., including very recent marriages with 1 year or less of separation, up to 24 years living apart). Most had children or young adolescents. Seventy-one percent reported that the migrant had full-time employment in United States, with a similar frequency sending remittances to Mexico. We asked participants where their family member lived in the United States to calculate the geographical distance from each other, and found that more than 50% of families were from 1 to 372 miles away, and 9.7% were approximately a thousand miles distant or more. The distribution was almost identical when we disaggregated and discharged returned migrant couples (i.e., this question was useful with returned migrant families to determine how distant they were from their residence in Mexico; see Table 8.2). We then explored how often they got in touch over long distances or had physical encounters. For this analysis, we dropped returned migrant couples because they were special cases of migration where the partners did not separate and, therefore, family contact was unaffected by crossing the international border. The remaining participants reported as follows: two-thirds of the sample (67.8%) reported contacting each other on a daily basis (overwhelmingly by telephone and internet options, see Table 8.3).

With respect to physical contact, 20% reported meeting from 4 to 6 times a year, meaning up to every 2 months; 40% met from once a month up to every

Table 8.2 Geographical Distance between Family Members, $N = 103$

	Percent	Cumulative Percent
Within 60 miles north and south of the border	22.3	22.8
120–372 miles	31.1	54.5
372–993 miles	35.0	90.1
993 miles or more	9.7	100.0

Notes: For the 13 returned migrant families, the value represents the distance from their residence in Mexico and the place where they used to live in the United States.

week or more; and 21% reported a very low frequency of physical contact (see Table 8.4). When disaggregated by distance, we found that 80% of transborder (i.e., families within 60 miles of the border) met once a month up to every week or more, 46% of the participants living up to 372 miles apart reported the same frequency of meeting (we defined them as *high-frequency transnational families*), whereas families living beyond that distance met in the same fashion 16% of the time.

These patterns of distance and family contact led us to think that transnational families from the Sonora–Arizona area were different from those reported in the literature. Research on transnational families mostly assumes long physical distances and long periods of separation. However, our findings suggest that many families and their practices are embedded within a *fronteriza* culture straddling the political division. Our transborder families (i.e., those living within the 60 miles of the border) have taken advantage of some aspects of *fronterizos* by meeting frequently and have found a way to cope with family separation due to international division. The literature is rich describing how families of Sonora–Arizona have flourished with continuous crossing and the existence of *commuters* and how they have made permeable and mobile the border's political division (Ojeda, 2008; Ruiz & Valdez-Gardea, 2013).

With this idea in mind, we wanted to explore the possibility that meeting frequently has relevance to parenting and family experiences for this unique sample.

Table 8.3 Frequency of Long-Distance Contact between Partners, $N = 90$

	Percent	Cumulative Percent
Never	0.0	0.0
1–2 Times a year	0.0	0.0
4–6 Times a year	1.1	1.1
Once a month	0.0	0.0
Every 2 weeks	5.6	6.7
Every week or more	25.6	32.2
Once a day	67.8	100.0

Table 8.4 FREQUENCY OF PHYSICAL CONTACT BETWEEN PARTNERS, $N = 90$

	Percent	Cumulative Percent
Never	21.1	21.3
1–2 Times a year	18.9	40.4
4–6 Times a year	20.0	60.7
Once a month	13.3	74.2
Every 2 weeks	11.1	85.4
Every week or more	14.4	100.0
Once a day	0.0	0.0

To do so, we narrowed our inquiry to analyze and discuss the quality of parent–child affection and discipline, whether parents are able to share parenting, if familism endorsement has a role in parenting, and to determine their level of psychological well-being—defined here as feelings of loneliness. We compare transborders and high-frequency transnationals against typical transnational families (i.e., families separated by long geographical distance and little physical contact).

Exploring Family Experiences of Transborder and Transnational Families

In this section, we present the preliminary analysis of our study. The Sonora-Arizona study questionnaire included several measures. For this work, we present data on the following measures: co-parenting was assessed with a 10-item questionnaire rated on a 5-point scale (0 = Never to 4 = Always) (Ahrons & Wallisch, 1987) with questions revolving around how often parents share their child's experiences and parenting responsibilities. A sample item assesses "Making day-to-day decisions regarding your child's life." Parent–child relationship was measured with 6 affection and 5 discipline items, modified from the MIDUS Parental Affection Scale (Brim, Baltes, Bumpass, et al., 2000). The items were measured on a 4-point Likert scale (0 = Never to 3 = Very Much) and coded so that higher scores reflected greater levels of parental affect and discipline. We computed each set of items independently as an index. A sample item for affection is: "How much do you understand your child's problems and worries?" A sample item for discipline is: "How strict are you with the rules you put on your children?" Familism was measured by a scale created by Knight et al. (2010) including three subscales, familism-support (6 items), familism-obligations (5 items), and familism-referent (6 items). We created a composite, or index, by averaging the three scores for each respondent. The three subscales were rated using a 5-point Likert scale (0 = Never to 4 = Always) with higher scores reflecting greater endorsement of familism values. A sample item is: "Parents should teach their children that the family always comes first." Finally, loneliness was measured with three items from the UCLA Loneliness Scale (Russell, 1996). The items were scored with a 5-point Likert response format (0 = Never to 4 = Always), with higher scores representing greater feelings loneliness. A sample item is: "How often have you feel abandoned?" All scales displayed good internal consistency using Cronbach alpha with coefficients ranging from .72 to .91; furthermore, measures have been previously validated for use with Mexican and migrant samples (Proulx, Helms, & Buehler, 2007; Sotomayor-Peterson, Cabeza de Baca, Figueredo, & Smith-Castro, 2013; Sotomayor-Peterson, Figueredo, Christensen, & Taylor, 2012).

Our analysis is preliminary and results must be taken with caution. We have a unique transnational sample of small size, particularly when we compare groups. Our sample is also uneven with respect to respondents, with the majority being partners of migrants and mostly women (i.e., 72 partners of migrants [64 female/8 male], 18 migrants [3 female/15 male]; see earlier description of families). Regardless, we believe our results will contribute to current knowledge on how transnational families arrange their family lives. In our analysis, we first we used *t*-tests to compare mean levels of all variables across families (i.e., transborder vs. transnationals; see Table 8.5). Second, we compared responses by type of respondent (i.e., partners of migrants vs. migrants; see Table 8.6). Finally, we performed a bivariate Pearson correlation analysis with the whole sample to identify trends of associations that can be explored by future analyses.

As depicted in Table 8.3, mean values for transborders and transnationals were in the middle-upper range on most variables, with familism endorsement at the higher value; this is consistent with countless literature reporting the importance that family has for Mexicans. Loneliness score is at the lower level ($M = 1.06$ and 1.50, range 0–4). Significance tests showed only one difference on parent–child affection ($t = -2.1$, $p < .05$), and a trend level difference for loneliness ($t = -1.8$, $p < .10$), both favoring transnationals. This is consistent with previous studies on mental health that show loneliness is an important risk factor for Mexican migrants (Marsiglia et al., 2011; Muñoz-Laboy, Hirsch, & Quispe-Lazaro, 2009). These findings seem to suggest that our transnational families are similar to those reported in the literature: those

Table 8.5 MEAN GROUP COMPARISONS OF STUDY VARIABLE ACROSS TYPE OF FAMILIES

	Transborder/ High-frequency ($N = 48$)	**Transnational ($N = 41$)**		
	Mean (S.D.)	**Mean (S.D.)**	**Mean Diff**	**<*p***
Co-parenting	2.83 (.81)	2.77 (.72)	.07	*ns*
Parent–child relationship				
Affection	2.64 (.42)	2.79 (.24)	−.15	.05
Discipline/control	2.01 (.64)	2.05 (.52)	−.05	*ns*
Familism endorsement	3.37 (.38)	3.38 (.39)	−.01	*ns*
Psychological well-being				
Loneliness	1.06 (.99)	1.5 (1.1)	−.42	.07

Table 8.6 Mean Group Comparisons of Study Variable Across Type of Respondent

	Partner of Migrant ($N = 72$)	Migrant ($N = 18$)		
	Mean (S.D.)	Mean (S.D.)	Mean Diff.	<p
Co-parenting	2.79 (.73)	2.86 (.90)	−.07	*ns*
Parent–child relationship				
Affection	2.71 (.29)	2.67 (.55)	.04	*ns*
Disciplina/control	2.07 (.52)	1.87 (.77)	.20	*ns*
Familism endorsement	3.33 (.38)	3.57 (.34)	−.24	.05
Psychological well-being				
Loneliness	1.16 (.99)	1.60 (1.20)	−.44	*ns*

who are far from their loved ones, with few or no possibilities to meet, experience more deeply the affection they share with their children and the loneliness of separation. This is found for both migrants and their partner who stays in Mexico. When comparing families by type of respondent, only familism endorsement reached significance ($t = -2.6, p < .05$; see Table 8.6) suggesting that the importance of family is stronger for those who left home, consistent with literature reports.

Finally, the correlation analysis depicted in Table 8.7 shows two significant associations between co-parenting and parent–child discipline, suggesting that partners who share childrearing have higher levels of disciplining their children ($r = .26, p < .01$) and lower levels of loneliness ($r = -.21, p < .05$). Also, the familism endorsement seems to play a role in explaining higher parent–child affection ($r = .26, p < .01$) within a family context, characterized by the special kind of separation and distance represented by an international border.

CONCLUSION

Although the study of migration from Mexico into the United States has been examined in other disciplines, it is relatively new in family studies. There are studies of transnational families comparing Latino immigrants in the United

Table 8.7 Bivariate Correlation Analysis of Study Variables ($N = 103$)

	1	2	3	4	5
1. Co-parenting		.06	.26**	.03	−.21*
2. Parent–child affection			.24*	.26**	−.13
3. Parent–child discipline				.17	.03
4. *Familism* endorsement					.13
5. Loneliness					

* $p < .05$, ** $p < .01$.

States based on country of origin under the hypothesis that the country-specific situation influences the immigration process and adaptation once in the United States (Martinez et al., 2011; Menjívar, 2012). Mexico and the United States share a long history of complex and dynamic migration (Delgado & Márquez, 2006 as cited by Vázquez & Bocanegra, 2013) that has special features for those living in the border areas. More than 150 years have passed since the political division between the countries placed inhabitants of the northern states of Mexico between two countries and cultures, blurring the border and creating a hybrid culture where people share practices and meanings around the border that are distinct from the rest of the country (Ojeda, 2008; Ruiz & Valdez-Gardea, 2013). Social networks and traditions intertwine for Sonora–Arizona transborder families, making mobile the geographical limits of the countries and thus presenting unique opportunities to overcome a restrictive border.

The Sonora–Arizona region is also a place of crossing for migrants. Here, it is possible to encounter a variety of people, some from places far from the border region and among them unaccompanied minors. Most research on unaccompanied minors from this region have found that one of the reasons for them to cross is family reunion. This literature has centered its interest on legal and political issues, human rights, and the risk and vulnerabilities encountered by crossing without a guardian and on the implications this carries for children's future and well-being (Chavez & Menjívar, 2010; Menjívar, 2012; Stinchcomb & Hershberg, 2014; Valdez-Gardea, 2008).

Our findings contribute to current understanding of how migration impacts family and parenting for Mexican transnational families. First, this work illustrates the diversity of Mexican transnational families. For transborder families, the possibility of meeting on a regular basis could explain the lower levels of loneliness they experience compared to their transnational counterparts, and this enhances their emotional well–being. The experiences of Sonora-Arizona transnationals, meaning those dealing with a typical long-distance separation and low physical contact, resemble what the literature has to say about typical transnationals. In this study, transnational families report higher levels of parent–child affection, which may be in part a compensatory response working both ways to compensate for one's own absence as well as that of a partner's. In this context, the set of significant associations among co-parenting and parent–child discipline, loneliness, and familism with affection makes sense. As family studies scholars, we largely know that good co-parental relationships influence parent–child relationships (Gable, Crnic, & Belsky, 1994). In addition, partners who share childrearing have been found to be more satisfied in their marital relationship, which, in turn, is a good predictor of overall well-being (McClain, 2011). In the same vein, previous studies have found familism to be associated with higher levels of co-parenting among Mexican-origin immigrant couples in United States (Sotomayor et al., 2012) and with more parental monitoring in Mexican parents of young adolescents (Romero & Ruiz, 2007) that could be a culturally rooted expression of care and affection.

Our findings suggest that Mexican transnational families from the border region have the special advantage of meeting more frequently compared with those from other regions of Mexico, and this greater physical contact facilitates family bonds. With regard to family dynamics, findings mirror previous research (Bonizzoni, 2012; Dreby, 2006; Martinez et al., 2011). Those participants at larger distance from their loved ones and with fewer opportunities to meet reported more intense emotional experiences. Deeper affection toward their children and stronger feelings of loneliness, regardless of whether the respondent was the migrant or the partner who stays in Mexico. Finally, a familism endorsement seemed to matter in explaining parent–child affectional relationship, especially for the party that left home.

Implications

International migration has important implications for Mexican family well-being. We have detailed the challenges around migration, as well as the ways in which transnationals have coped with distance. Still, we want to make note of the vulnerability of these families. Transnational separation implies an ambiguous loss (Moreno et al., 2013), and it has important consequences with regard to family and psychological well-being. Regardless of the possible advantages of transborder families compared with typical transnationals, all of them share challenging experiences (e.g., separation) that puts members at higher risk.

Undocumented crossing implies precarious stability for those who have been able to settle on the other side. Countless studies have shown that the Mexico–US border is a dangerous place. Criminal activity surrounds migrants in their attempts to cross, and increasing legal restrictions to obtaining work permits as well as reinforcement of borders have made it harder to reunite. Such circumstances demonstrate that parental roles depend on external forces, and the bonds they develop against distance perhaps may be terminated due to legal enforcement. Since regular contact with loved ones is critical for individual and family well-being, it should be viewed as a fundamental human right.

Finally, undocumented migration is, no doubt, a complex phenomenon, and the health and well-being of involved families is crossed by several factors far beyond any individual's resources or limitations (Castañeda et al., 2012). Social, economic, and political inequalities between countries determine the agency of the actors in overcoming the challenges of international migration. Simplistic and superficial analyses highlight poverty as the main cause of Mexican migration to the United States, obscuring the benefits to the receiving country. Delgado Wise, Marquez, and Gaspar (2013) reported that, in times of economic crisis, migrants have contributed high productivity at low cost (as cited in Marquez & García, 2014). From 2007 to 2010, Mexican migrants were responsible for 20% of the US gross domestic product (GDP; or producto interno bruto [PIB]). Another idea deserving of more thought is that the remittances sent to Mexico can be viewed as a leverage for social development. Canales (2014) found just the opposite. The total amount of remittances sent to Mexico by migrants who entered the United

States in the period from 2000 to 2012 represented just 86% of the amount of money that the Mexican government had spent on education and social reproduction for this population, before emigrating north (Canales, 2014). Thus, there is a need for broader analyses examining the uneven economic and social conditions between the origin and destination countries to better explain transnational families' well-being.

REFERENCES

Ahrons, C. R., & Wallisch, L. (1987). The relationship between former spouses. In. D. Perlman & S. Duck (Eds.), *Intimate relationships: Development, dynamics and deterioration* (pp. 269–296). Los Angeles: Sage.

Berumen, S. S., & Santiago, H. J. (2012). Reflexiones sobre migración internacional, el género y las familias transnacionales. In S. S. Berumen, N. Frias, & J. Santiago (Eds.), *Migración y familia*. Monterrey, MX: Tilde Editores.

Boehm, D. A. (2011). Deseos y Dolores: Mapping desire, suffering, and (dis)loyalty within transnational partnerships. *International Migration, 49*(6), 95–106.

Bonizzoni, P. (2012). Here or there? Shifting meanings and practices in mother–child relationships across time and space. *International Migration.* Advance online publication. doi:10.1111/imig.12028.

Brim, O. G., Baltes, P. B., Bumpass, L. L., Cleary, P. D., Featherman, D. L., Hazzard, W. R., . . . Shweder, R. A. (2000). *National survey of midlife development in U.S. (MIDUS), 1995–1996 [Computer file].* ICSPR version. Ann Harbor, MI: DataStat, INC./Boston, MA: Harvard Medical School Dept. of Health Care Policy [producers], 1996. Ann Harbor, MI: Interuniversity Consortium for Political Research [distributor].

Canales, A. I. (2014). Indicadores estratégicos sobre migración y desarrollo. In R. Delgado Wise (Coord.), *Migración y desarrollo* (pp. 53–76). Colección Hacia Donde Va la Ciencia en México. México: Consejo Nacional de Ciencia y Tecnología (CONACYT).

Castañeda, H., Holmes, S. M., Madrigal, D. S., Young, M. E. D., Beyeler, N., & Quesada, J. (2012). Immigration as a social determinant of health. *Annual Review of Public Health, 36*, 375–392.

Castellanos, M. B., & Boehm, D. A. (2008). Introduction. Engendering Mexican migration. *Latin American Perspectives, 35*(1), 5–15.

Chavez, L., & Menjívar, C. (2010). Children without borders: A mapping of the literatura on unaccompanied migrant children to the United States. *Migraciones Internacionales, 5*(3), 71–111.

de Guzman, M. R. T. (2014). Yaya: Philippine domestic care workers, the children they care for, and the children they leave behind. *International Perspectives in Psychology: Research, Practice, Consultation, 3*(3), 197.

Delgado Wise, R. (2014). Introducción. In R. Delgado Wise (Coord.), *Migración y desarrollo* (pp.13–19). Colección Hacia Donde Va la Ciencia en México. México, Mexico City: Consejo Nacional de Ciencia y Tecnología (CONACYT).

Delgado Wise, R., Marquez, H., & Gaspar, S. (2013). Ten myths about migration and development: Revelations involving the Mexico-United experience. In D. Acosta (Ed.), *Global migration: Myths and realities* (pp. 103–138). Santa Barbara, CA: Praeger.

Dreby, J. (2006). Honor and virtue: Mexican parenting in a transnational context. *Gender and Society, 20*, 32–59.

Durand, J., & Massey, D. (2003). El núcleo básico de la migración México-Estados Unidos. Premisas para entender y explicar el proceso. In *Clandestinos. Migración México-Estados Unidos en los albores del siglo XXI* (pp. 45–61). Zacatecas, MX: Universidad Autónoma de Zacatecas.

Faulstich Orellana, M., Thorne, B., Chee, A., & Lam, W. S. E. (2001). Transnational childhood: The participation of children in process of family migration. *Social Problems, 48*(4), 572–591.

Fincham, F. D., & Beach, S. R. H. (2010). Marriage in the new millennium: A decade in review. *Journal of Marriage and Family, 72*, 630–649.

Gable, S., Crnic, K., & Belsky, J. (1994). Coparenting within the family system: Influences on children's development. *Family Relations, 43*, 380–386.

Heymann, J., Flores-Macias, F., Hayes, J. A., Kennedy, M., Lahaie, C, & Earle, A. (2009). The impact of migration on the well-being of transnational families: New data from sending communities in Mexico. *Community, Work & Family, 72*, 91–103.

Hirsch, E. (1999). En el norte la mujer manda: Gender, generation, and geography in a Mexican transnational community. *American Behavioral Scientist, 42*(9), 1332–1349.

Instituto Nacional de Migración. (2012). *Estadísticas migratorias 2012.* [Monografía en internet]. México, D.F.: SEGOB/Instituto Nacional de Migración Centro de Estudios Migratorios. Recuperado de http://www.inm.gob.mx/estadisticas/Sintesis_Grafica/2012/Sintesis2012.pdf

Kanaiaupuni, S. M. (2000). *Sustaining families and communities: Nonmigrant women and Mexico-US migration* (Center for Demography and Ecology working paper). Madison: University of Wisconsin-Madison.

Knight, G. P., Gonzales, N. A., Saenz, D. S., Bonds, D. D., Germán, M., Deardorff, J., . . . & Updegraff, K. A. (2010). The Mexican American cultural values scales for adolescents and adults. *Journal of Early Adolescence, 30*(3), 444–481.

Lahaie, C., Hayes, J. A., Piper, T. M., & Heymann, J. (2009). Work and family divided across borders: The impact of parental migration on Mexican children in transnational families. *Community, Work & Family, 12*, 299–312.

Madianou, M., & Miller, D. (2013). *Migration and new media: Transnational families and polymedia*. New York: Routledge.

Márquez, C. H., & Garcia, Z. R. (2014). Retorno forzoso de migrantes mexicanos. In R. Delgado Wise (Coord.) *Migración y desarrollo* (pp.115–133). Colección Hacia Donde Va la Ciencia en México. México, Mexico City: Consejo Nacional de Ciencia y Tecnología (CONACYT).

Marsiglia, F. F., Kulis, S., Perez, G. H., & Bermudez-Parsai, M. (2011). Hopelessness, family stress, and depression among Mexican-heritage mothers in the southwest. *Health & Social Work, 36*(1), 7–18.

Martinez, T. D., Castañeda, H., Porter, M., Quiroz, M., & Carrion, I. V. (2011). More similar than different? Exploring cultural models of depression among Latino immigrants in Florida. *Depression Research and Treatment,* Article ID 564396.

McClain, L. R. (2011). Better parents, more stable partners: Union transitions among cohabiting parents. *Journal of Marriage and Family, 73*, 889–901.

McGuire, S., & Martin, K. (2007). Fractured migrant families. Paradoxes of hope and devastation. *Family Community Health, 30*(3), 178–188.

Moreno, G., Mejía, B., Lucero-Liu, A., & Sotomayor-Peterson, M. (2013, November). *Parenting and parent-child relationships in Mexican transnational families.* Poster presented at the Annual Conference of the National Council on Family Relations, San Antonio, TX.

Menjívar, C. (2012). Transnational parenting and immigration law: Central Americans in the United States. *Journal of Ethnic and Migration Studies, 38*(2), 301–322.

Mummert, G. (2009). Siblings by telephone: Experiences of Mexican children in long distance childrearing arrangements. *Journal of the Southwest, 51*, 503–521.

Muñoz-Laboy, M., Hirsch, J. S., & Quispe-Lazaro, A. (2009). Loneliness as a sexual risk factor for male Mexican migrant workers. *American Journal of Public Health, 99*, 802–810.

Nobles, J. (2011). Parenting from abroad: Migration, nonresident father involvement, and children's education in México. *Journal of Marriage and Family, 73*, 729–746.

Ojeda, N. (2008). Reflexiones acerca de las familias transfronterizas y las familias transnacionales entre México y Estados Unidos. *Frontera Norte, 21*(42), 7–30.

Parreñas, R. S. (2008). Transnational fathering: Gendered conflicts, distant disciplining and emotional gaps. *Journal of Ethnic & Migration Studies, 34*(7), 1057–1072.

Parreñas, R. S. (2015). *Servants of globalization: Migration and domestic work* (2nd ed.). Stanford, CA: Stanford University Press.

Pribilsky, J. (2004). *Aprendemos a convivir*: Conjugal relations, co-parenting, and family life among Ecuadorian transnational migrants in New York City and the Ecuadorian Andes. *Global Networks, 4*(3), 313–334.

Proulx, C. M., Helms, H. M., & Buehler, C. (2007). Marital quality and personal well-being: A meta-analysis. *Journal of Marriage and Family, 69*, 576–593.

Romero, A. J., & Roberts, R. E. (2003). Stress within a bicultural context for adolescents of Mexican descent. *Cultural Diversity and Ethnic Minority Psychology, 9*(2), 171–184.

Romero, A. J., & Ruiz, M. (2007). Does familism lead to increased parental monitoring? Protective factors for coping with risky behavior. *Journal of Child & Family Studies, 16*, 143–154.

Ruiz, P. L. F., & Valdez-Gardea, G. C. (2013, May). *El sentido del retorno a las aulas sonorenses: experiencias escolares de niños y jóvenes migrantes en la region Sonora-Arizona*. Ponencia presentada en el IV Encuentro Internacional Migración y Niñez Migrante. Migración y retorno. Retos para la familia transnacional, Hermosillo, Sonora, Colegio de Sonora.

Russel, D. W. (1996). UCLA loneliness scale (versión 3): Reliability, validity, and factor structure. *Journal of Personality Assessment, 66*, 20–40.

Sabogal, F., Marin, G., Otero-Sabogal, R., & Marin, B. V. (1987). Hispanic familism and acculturation: What changes and what doesn't? *Hispanic Journal of Behavioral Sciences, 9*, 397–412.

Secretaría de Educación Pública. (2011). *Pensar desde el otro lado. Los Desafíos de una educación sin fronteras* (1era.Edición corregida, pp. 38–42). México: Secretaria de Educación Pública.

Sotomayor-Peterson, M., Cabeza de Baca, T., Figueredo, A. J., & Smith-Castro, V. (2013). Shared parenting, parental effort, and life history strategy: A cross-cultural comparison. *Journal of Cross-Cultural Psychology, 44*(4), 620–639.

Sotomayor-Peterson, M., Figueredo, A. J., Christensen, D., & Taylor, A. (2012). Couples' cultural values, shared parenting, and family emotional climate within Mexican American families. *Family Process, 51*, 218–233.

Sotomayor-Peterson, M., & Lucero-Liu, A. A. (2017). Correlates of mental health and well-being for Mexican female partners of migrants. *International Journal of Migration, Health, and Social Care, 13*, 361–373.Sotomayor-Peterson, M., & Montiel-Carbajal, M. (2014). Exploring the psychological and family well-being of unaccompanied Mexican children migrant sent back from U.S. in the border Sonora-Arizona. *Hispanic Journal of Behavioral Sciences, 36*(2), 111–123.

Stinchcomb, D., & Hershberg, E. (2014). *Unaccompanied migrant children from Central America: Context, causes, & responses* (CLALS Working Paper Series, No. 7.). Washington, DC: American University Center for Latin American & Latino Studies.

Valdez-Gardea, C. (2008). Actores de la migración. En G. C. Valdéz (Coord.). *Achicando futuros: Actores y lugares de la migración* (pp. 459–474). Hermosillo, Sonora, MX: Colegio de Sonora.

Vázquez, R. M. A., & Bocanegra, G. C. (2013, Mayo). *El proceso de migración México-Estados Unidos: Dimensión, rutas y regiones*. Ponencia presentada en el IV Encuentro Internacional Migración y Niñez Migrante. Migración y retorno. Retos para la familia transnacional, Hermosillo, Sonora, Colegio de Sonora.

Vertovec, S. (2004). Migrant transnationalism and modes of transformation. *International Migration Review, 38*(3), 970–1001.

Yoshikawa, H. (2011). *Immigrants raising citizens: Undocumented parents and their children*. New York: Russell Sage Foundation.

Zeiders, K. H., Updegraff, K. A., Umaña-Taylor, A. J., McHale, S. M., & Padilla, J. (2015). Familism values, family time, and Mexican-origin young adults' depressive symptoms. *Journal of Marriage and Family, 78*(1), 91–106. doi:10.1111/jomf.12248.

Zinn, M. B. (1982). Familism among Chicanos: A theoretical review. *Humboldt Journal of Social Relations, 10*, 224–238.

9

The Experience of Families Separated by Military Deployment

RUTH ELLINGSEN, CATHERINE MOGIL, AND PATRICIA LESTER

Every year, millions of mothers and fathers are required to temporarily parent their children across great distance, yet we have limited empirical knowledge of the processes involved, the impact on parents and children, or the effective interventions to support these families. There are several methodological barriers to conducting research with families experiencing temporary parental absence, but, as demonstrated in other chapters of this volume, researchers are increasingly taking on the challenge of investigating families' experiences with temporary parental absence and how best to support these families. This chapter will focus on the experiences of military families with parenting from afar and the growing body of literature on this particular population, including the unique context of military life and how military families navigate relationships across geographical distances during various types of separations, particularly deployments in support of wartime operations. A parent's wartime service presents a range of challenges for the entire family, including changes in roles and routines, parental absences during key developmental milestones, and possible physical or behavioral health problems in returning service members. The experience of parenting from afar during the various phases of parental deployment will be examined through the lens of four different theoretical perspectives, and research evidence on the impact of parental deployment on family well-being will be summarized. Finally, some promising interventions designed for military families that support parenting from afar will be presented.

THE CONTEXT OF MILITARY FAMILIES

More than 2.7 million US military service members have served in the wartime operations undertaken after 9/11, including in Iraq (Operations Iraqi Freedom and New Dawn) and Afghanistan (Operations Enduring Freedom and Freedom's Sentinel), with more than 3.3 million total deployments (Tanielian, Karney, Chandra, & Meadows, 2014; US Department of Defense, 2015). Between 2001 and 2015, there have been more than 6,800 deaths and more than 52,300 injuries among US military service members in Iraq and Afghanistan (Fischer, 2015). The high operational tempo of these conflicts have placed great demands on US military personnel, requiring unprecedented lengthy and multiple deployments, shorter stays at home between deployments, and extensive involvement of the National Guard and Reserve forces. As service members have returned from combat and transitioned out of the military, they have faced well-documented challenges, such as increased risk for health and behavioral health problems, unemployment, housing problems, and other adjustment issues.

This increased demand on military personnel has also led to greater demands on US service member families and their children. For those currently serving in the Armed Forces, almost half are parents of children under 18 years old, with nearly 2 million children with at least one parent serving (US Department of Defense, 2015). Since September 11, 2001, military children and their parents have experienced the many challenges of recurrent separations, frequent moves, and high operational tempo associated with military life during war. In this context, service members and families are reported to experience a theoretical "cycle of deployment" initially conceptualized by Pincus, House, Christenson, and Adler (2001) and applied by other researchers as a framework describing a period of anticipation and preparing for deployment, a period of deployment, followed by a postdeployment return home to civilian life (DeVoe & Ross, 2012; Logan, 1987; Pincus et al., 2001; Riggs & Riggs, 2011). For service members who are parents, transitions from active combat operations to home life may present several challenges to the process of reconnecting with children and other family members after a long separation while also anticipating the possibility of another extended deployment. Furthermore, military families often have to prepare for deployments with very brief notice and uncertainty about when a deployment will end. Further complicating the experience for some families has been the requirement to extend deployments beyond the typical period anticipated by each service branch. Arguably, the most significant source of deployment stress for families is that these separations occur in the context of heightened awareness of the danger of injury and/or loss of the deployed parent. All of these factors combined pose unique challenges for parenting at a distance.

Due to advances in technology, service members and families are able to communicate more frequently and easily during deployments than during previous eras. In the past, service members and their families were limited to expensive international phone calls or letters during times of separation. The challenge is no longer finding ways to communicate, but rather choosing among the many options (e.g., phone call, video chat, text, social media). According to Madianou and Miller (2012), who coined the term "polymedia" to refer to an ecology where multiple mediated communicative technologies are available, the choice one makes about what form or combination of forms of communication to use can have emotional consequences. Consider, for example, the child who emails his father every night with a summary of his day and wakes up the next morning with a response. When the service member is out on a mission that hinders email capabilities, this child may wake to the absence of an email, which can cause concern about the safety of the absent parent. In addition, a service member or at-home parent might avoid voice communication when sharing bad news and instead use email or text to avoid hearing a negative or stress-provoking reply. Although more available and frequent communication may potentially ease some of the difficulties caused by parent–child separations across distance and over time, it may also increase both service members' and their families' awareness of the respective stressors one another are facing during deployments (Green, Buckman, Dandekar, & Greenberg, 2010; Skomorovsky & Bullock, 2016; Warner et al., 2007). Moreover, the accessibility of information about military operations in the media may also increase families' stress through greater and more direct and immediate exposure to the risks faced by service members (Green et al., 2010).

Challenges faced by military families have remained largely out of public consciousness in the United States, particularly in parts of the country where there are relatively few military installations. For those families who do live on or near a military installment, the presence of a strong military community and a family's identification with military life may protect against associated uncertainties and stressors (Chapin, 2011). The availability of resources such as health care and family support, particularly among active-duty families, may also help families deal with the stress of separation (MacDermid, Samper, Schwarz, Nishida, & Nyaronga, 2008) and may be protective for young children (Wadsworth et al., 2016). However, these resources are most commonly available to and utilized by active-duty military families. National Guard and Reserve families, whose primary role is to be available when a nation mobilizes for war, are typically not fully integrated into military life, and these families live in civilian communities (as opposed to military bases) that may not provide specific support for issues arising from deployment and extended family separations. Although community support is more readily available to families who live on or near a military installment, there is growing awareness of the need to increase awareness of and support for military families living in civilian communities, including training for clinicians about military life and the deployment cycle, online communities, and multimedia resources for military families (Kudler & Porter, 2013).

In addition to the National Guard and Reserve, other specific populations within military families are less commonly addressed in research and service delivery, including dual-service families, female service members, and single-parent service members (Kelley, Doane, & Pearson, 2011; Lester et al., 2011). Although the majority of the research has focused on traditional two-parent families where one parent is deployed, it is important to consider that military families comprise many different configurations, and each family system has its own particular issues and stresses when a loved one is deployed. For example, in single-parent families, children often go to live with new caregivers, such as extended family or nonfamily caregivers in other cities and states; thus, for some children, parental deployment means a new primary caregiver, moving to another area of the country, and leaving their homes, neighborhoods, and schools (Kelley et al., 2011). For dual-military families, attempts are made to sequence deployments so that both parents are not deployed at the same time, when possible. This creates a different challenge, in that it is less likely that parents will be home at the same time. Although children can stay in the same house, coordinated parental leadership may become more difficult and children must still adjust to different family constellations and parenting practices.

Another important consideration is that there are many types of separations that are required by a military career, all of which may create specific transitional challenges for parenting across a distance (e.g., trainings, predeployment workups, temporary duty assignments). While recent national and research attention has focused on the impact of wartime deployments for military families, particularly the influence on parenting, it is important to recognize that prolonged parental absences are a regular part of military family life, regardless of the context of war or peace.

HOW MILITARY FAMILIES NAVIGATE SEPARATION AND DISTANCE

The experiences of military families navigating deployment separation are complex, and scholars have utilized several theoretical perspectives to understand, interpret, and explain its various facets. Four theoretical perspectives are presented here as a backdrop to understanding the unique challenges of parenting from afar in military families.

Family Systems Theory

The family systems framework (Minuchin, 1985; Sameroff, 1994) posits that individual family members mutually affect one another so that an individual can be best understood in the context of the entire family system. Just as individuals within the system affect one another, relationships, such as parent–child or the couple relationship, can also influence one another (Erel & Burman, 1995). To understand the effect of deployment and other separations on military families, a family systems approach would suggest that the experiences and well-being of parents and children are inextricably linked. For example, when a service member returns with physical or psychological injuries, such as posttraumatic stress or traumatic brain injuries, the impact of these injuries may affect their children and partners both directly and indirectly through changes in parenting, co-parenting, and marital adjustment (see Paley, Lester, & Mogil, 2013, for a review). Similarly, when the at-home parent is stressed from the wear and tear of fulfilling the logistical and emotional duties of both parents over months of separation, the marital relationship is likely to be stressed. Whereas such everyday stressors can affect individual and reciprocal relationships in all families, the additional challenge for military parents lies in managing these ruptures over a distance, when they may be more difficult to repair.

Socioecological Theory

A socioecological perspective (Bronfenbrenner & Morris, 1998) builds on the family systems framework to include broader systems (e.g., government agencies, cultural values) that support and interconnect with military families. This lens provides a context for understanding how multiple ecological systems may influence the experience of parenting from afar within military families. For example, in the United States, there are several service systems that specifically support military families, such as a network of high-quality child development centers, medical treatment facilities, and family support programs (Floyd & Phillips, 2013). Some military-connected children may receive education through the Department of Education Activity (DoDEA) schools (essentially, a school district for children on certain military installations) or through the traditional public education system. Whether the child attends a DoDEA school or enrolls in a public school district, the degree to which the system is aware of and is supportive of the unique needs of military-connected children and the manner in which the family utilizes that system will have an influence on the child and the family system. Dependent family members of active-duty service members have access to health insurance and often can access networks of military medical providers that are knowledgeable about the unique needs of military families. The availability and quality of military-informed health care, school, and community service systems all influence the child's experience of deployment and separation from a parent.

Attachment Theory

Several researchers have utilized attachment theory to understand the impact of military family separations and to develop responsive interventions to address their unique needs (DeVoe & Ross, 2012; Mogil et al., 2015; Riggs & Riggs, 2011). Attachment is a motivational and behavioral system that directs the child to seek proximity with a familiar caregiver when they are alarmed, with the expectation that they will receive protection and emotional support (Bowlby, 1980). Deployment and other separations of a military parent constitute a threat to all family members' sense of safety because the secure base of an attachment figure becomes unavailable (Vormbrock, 1993). The child's typical strategies for managing distress and regulating difficult emotions may be diminished. Consequently, the child may rely more heavily on the at-home parent as a coping resource, thus compounding the demands for that caregiver's attention during a time when his or her own resources may be similarly weakened. As a result, the at-home parent may be less consistently available and attuned to the child's emotional needs. Within the context of multiple deployments or separations of a military parent, the attachment system is chronically activated (Paley et al., 2013). In the case of combat deployments, the attachment system may be further impacted by the constant worry and concern of having a loved one in harm's way.

Separation during early childhood when the parent–child attachment relationship is being developed may be particularly stressful for both parent and child (Paris, DeVoe, Ross, & Acker, 2010). This deserves special attention in the military population, given that nearly 40% of military children in active-duty families are younger than 6 years (US Department of Defense, 2015). Frequent and lengthy separations may make it difficult for infants and young children in military families to securely bond with the deployed parent and may lead to more adjustment and behavior problems (Barker & Berry, 2009; Chartrand, Frank, White, & Shope, 2008; Cozza & Lieberman, 2007). A parent who is deployed during a child's first year may mentally carry the child with him; however, the child may have no connection to or familiarity with his or her service member parent unless purposeful steps are taken. Returning home to a son or daughter who does not know you can be extremely distressing to a parent. Strategies to keep the absent parent present in the everyday life of the child through routines and rituals may help mediate these potential challenges (Mogil et al., 2015).

Ambiguous Loss Theory

An *ambiguous loss* is by definition uncertain, vague, and indeterminate (Boss, 1999). A family member may be physically absent but psychologically present (i.e., "there but not there") or physically present but psychologically absent (i.e., "here but not here"). This kind of loss may be uncertain as to its duration or even whether a loss has occurred. One result of ambiguous loss is *boundary ambiguity*, or not knowing who is in or out of the family. Boundary ambiguity is particularly salient for families in which a parent is frequently away for work, as is often the case in military families. The context of family life may be confusing as members struggle to organize and reorganize roles and responsibilities (Boss, 1999). While there are clearly several applications of ambiguous loss theory relevant to parenting in military families, little has been written about the experience of military-connected children through this lens. For example, a parent's emotional unavailability may be experienced as a loss in that the family system is now shifted. Combat-related behavioral health problems may take parenting offline, even if for fleeting moments, such as during a flashback or in a dissociative moment. In these instances, the child may feel that the parent is unavailable emotionally.

HOW FAMILIES OPERATE DURING DIFFERENT PHASES OF DEPLOYMENT

The "cycle of deployment" (Pincus et al., 2001) referenced earlier is a widely acknowledged model that is helpful in understanding the processes that families undergo when members are deployed. Since the initiation of operations in Iraq and Afghanistan in 2001, hundreds of thousands of military families have experienced the cycle of deployment many times, and their cumulative experience of multiple deployments is perhaps best described not as a "cycle" but as a "spiral" (National Military Family Association, 2005) in that the family does not enter the next deployment in exactly the same way as they entered the previous one. Earlier deployment experiences undoubtedly shape later deployment experiences, so that each deployment experience is unique. Families hone strengths and build new skills during each deployment, which may carry forward into the next deployment. They simultaneously bring with them the wear-and-tear effects of the previous deployment, which can include unresolved conflicts, relational ruptures, and misunderstandings (Paley et al., 2013). Taken together, the positive and the negative effects of each deployment shape the family's ability to successfully manage future deployments and transitions. The cycle of deployment (Pincus et al., 2001) is depicted as occurring in five distinct stages, which we describe here. We also highlight potential implications for family functioning at each stage.

Predeployment

The predeployment phase begins with the warning order for deployment and ends when the service member leaves home; the duration of predeployment can vary from several weeks to more than a year. In this phase, the service member must prepare psychologically and physically for his or her departure while the nondeployed parent faces the very different challenges of preparing to manage the household and the children alone while worrying about the deployed parent's safety. The deploying parent may experience difficulty balancing an increasingly heavy training regimen with the desire to spend time with family before departing. Concurrently, the nondeploying parent may experience conflict between wanting the service member to be prepared while also wishing for closeness. Parents must decide how and when to communicate with their child(ren) about the impending departure. From an attachment perspective, notification of deployment orders is likely to be perceived as an immediate threat to security, and, as the anticipated separation approaches, normal and expected behavior during this period includes increased anxiety and tension, as well as vacillations between anger, denial, and sadness in anticipation of loss (Bowlby, 1980; Pincus et al., 2001). Individual distress may affect the family system, causing interference with parenting and family routines and, consequently, negatively affecting individual coping. Practical matters and getting personal affairs in order may take priority in the weeks preceding the deployment, leaving little opportunity for communicating about feelings and preparing emotionally for the impending separation.

Deployment

In the deployment phase (i.e., the first month following departure), each family member is likely to experience a roller-coaster of emotions, including sadness, worry, numbness, disorientation, resentment, and irritability. The feeling as though life is "on hold" before the deployment may give way to a sense of temporary relief at the point of departure.

At home, the departure brings forth a new set of parenting challenges, including how to respond to children's distress, concerns, and questions. The impact of the deploying parent's departure can be mitigated if children feel securely bonded to the nondeploying caregiver and if that parent is able to cope effectively and maintain relatively stable parenting practices. There are reciprocal influences in the parent–child relationship and the family system, such that child attachment security assists the nondeploying parent to preserve responsive parenting practices. At the same time, varied coping responses and emotional reactions of the nondeployed parent contribute to different outcomes for themselves, their children, and family processes.

Sustainment

The sustainment stage lasts from the first month to the last month of deployment. Over time, new routines emerge, and parents develop and identify sources of support in their respective environments. The deployed parent might relinquish daily involvement in parenting or struggle with how to stay salient in the mind of their child every day. Both caregivers are likely to adopt new strategies within the constraints of technology and distance. For example, a family might "meet" online every evening or create another ritual that allows the absent parent to be a part of the child's everyday life, thus creating a relational space at a distance (Heiselberg, 2016). Families must reorganize their daily routines in order to function without the physical presence of the deployed member, but it is unclear how permanent these changes will be, if they will sustain once the parent returns home, or if they are simply a temporary strategy to manage the current deployment. Children may take on additional responsibilities, including household tasks or care for younger siblings (Chandra, Martin, Hawkins, & Richardson, 2010; Hooper, Moore, & Smith, 2014; Houston et al., 2009; Huebner, Mancini, Wilcox, Grass, & Grass, 2007; Knobloch, Pusateri, Ebata, & McGlughlin, 2015). Shifting roles can result in boundary ambiguity and confusion as families adjust when one parent temporarily exits the family system (Rodriguez & Margolin, 2015).

Uncertainty can be intensified during the sustainment phase when the service member parent is in communication with at-home family members. Real-time communication can create further ambiguity in relation to the deployed parent's participation in family functioning and decision-making (Faber, Willerton, Clymer, MacDermid, & Weiss, 2008). There is some research to suggest that newer communication technologies (e.g., email, text) may not carry the emotional cues that help children connect with their deployed parent as they would when speaking on the phone (Houston, Pfefferbaum, Sherman, Melson, & Brand, 2013). In addition, parents may be unsure of what to share with their children perhaps, in part, because the behavioral and emotional cues may be harder to decode at a distance, but also because parents are unsure what level of information is appropriate to share and how it will affect their children. An emerging literature indicates that preoccupation with child and family well-being and uncertainty about the amount and content of information that should be shared is a serious concern for deployed service members (Barker & Berry, 2009; Lester, 2012; Renshaw, Rodrigues, & Jones, 2009). Even if the deployed parent withholds information from family members about his or her experience, the level of media exposure detailing the effects of war can create a heightened sense of uncertainty about the service member's safety and his or her likelihood of return (Huebner et al., 2007).

Redeployment

The redeployment phase is defined as the month before the service member is scheduled to return home, and this is generally a period of intense anticipation by all members of the family. The expectation is for the deployed parent to return home, but it remains a situation of unpredictability and uncertainty. Although a return date is often provided, it is not uncommon for this date to be changed as deployments are extended. During this period, family members might begin to anticipate another renegotiation of roles and responsibilities, as well as reorganization of daily routines. For example, a child might have begun to co-sleep in the parental bed, but, with the anticipation of the service member parent's return, the child might begin to experience anxiety about having to return to his own bed.

Postdeployment

In the postdeployment phase (also referred to as "reintegration"), the service member's initial return home is typically a joyful event, and family members may experience a sense of relief for the safe return of their loved one. The transition back home, however, poses unique stresses as families renegotiate roles and relationships. As the family begins to reorganize to accommodate the return of the military member, stress and conflict can arise regarding major decisions, confusion in altered roles or routines, independence and control, criticism or disagreements about child rearing, and family shifts in social support (Drummet, Coleman, & Cable, 2003; Huebner et al., 2007). Families who have adjusted to new roles when a parent was deployed may experience significant stress and confusion when that parent is reintegrated and attempts to reestablish his or her roles as they existed prior to deployment (Chandra, Burns, Tanielian, & Jaycox, 2011). Often, adolescents have experienced greater freedoms (e.g., extended curfew or obtaining a driver's license) or have increased responsibilities in the family (e.g., watching younger siblings after school or preparing meals) that can be undermined when a service member returns and expects to return to an earlier time when the child was developmentally younger and unable to manage such responsibilities.

Functioning of the family system and subsystems generally does not return to the exact state that existed prior to the deployment. Frequently, the returning parent must "catch up" with his or her child(ren)'s growth and development that took place during the deployment. Some military parents may have been absent during key developmental periods (Lester et al., 2010). For example, a parent might have missed important milestones like starting kindergarten, joining a sports team, or turning 16. The returning parent can feel loss around having missed these events, and adolescents may harbor sadness or even resentment over missed milestones.

Notable challenges may exist in establishing an attachment bond between returning parents and very young children with no memory of the deployed parent. A young child initially may not recognize or may be afraid of the military parent after reintegration (Cozza & Lieberman, 2007; Saltzman et al., 2011). Other significant challenges may exist with children who were bonded to the military parent and grieved the loss of their attachment figure; these children may remain detached and ignore the returned parent for a period of time.

Transitional tasks require parents and children alike to refamiliarize with each other in new and sometimes unexpected ways, especially in instances when the service member returns home with physical and/or psychological trauma. Whereas the parent was physically absent but psychologically present while away, upon return, the parent may be physically present in the family system but absent from the family both emotionally and functionally (Dekel, Goldblatt, Keidar, Solomon, & Polliack, 2005). Furthermore, chaotic home environments and greater tension in the family may trigger or aggravate the service member or veteran's posttraumatic symptoms (Tarrier, Sommerfield, & Pilgrim, 1999), which can then exacerbate problematic family interactions.

IMPACT ON FAMILY WELL-BEING: WHAT THE RESEARCH TELLS US

Research on the impact of parental deployment on children is mixed. Whereas many studies indicate that the majority of children adjust well, there is a growing body of data indicating that cumulative exposure to deployment separations increases the risk for emotional and behavioral, academic, and other adjustment problems (Chandra, Martin, Hawkins, & Richardson, 2010; Chartrand et al.,

2008; Meadows, Tanielian, & Karney, 2016; US Department of Defense, 2010). Although research remains limited, studies indicate that children's reactions and adjustment to parental deployment may at least partly rely on their developmental stage (Stafford & Grady, 2003). For this reason, we present the current literature on child outcomes by age group.

Early Childhood

Parental deployment during the first years of a child's life may limit opportunities to develop and maintain the parent–child relationship during this critical developmental period. Infants and young children have not yet developed the cognitive capacity to understand the separation from or sudden reappearance of a deployed parent (Gorman & Fitzgerald, 2007; Rosenblum, Dayton, & Muzik, 2009). Studies on infants and young children in military families suggest that prolonged separations may hurt children's ability to securely bond with the deployed parent and may lead to more adjustment and behavior problems. In a cross-sectional study, children between the ages of 3 and 5 years who had a deployed parent had higher levels of behavior problems when compared with children whose parents were not currently deployed (Chartrand et al., 2008). Similarly, Barker and Berry (2009) found that young children with a deployed parent showed increased behavior problems during deployment and more insecure attachment behaviors (e.g., ignoring the parent or extreme difficulty in separating) at reunion than did children who had not experienced a recent deployment.

School-Age

School-aged children are often aware of the threats associated with war and the potential impact on a parent's safety during deployment. Lester et al. (2010) examined the impact of parental deployment in children between the ages of 6 and 12; results indicated that children with a deployed or recently returned parent demonstrated anxiety symptoms that were above community norms. In another study of military children between ages 5 and 12 with a deployed parent, parent-report indicated that 32% of children in the sample demonstrated clinically significant psychosocial problems (Flake, Davis, Johnson, & Middleton, 2009). Parental deployment has also been associated with academic difficulties in school-aged children.

Engel, Gallagher, and Lyle (2010) found that lengthy deployments and deployments during academic testing negatively influenced children's standardized achievement scores. In the largest longitudinal study to date, Meadows and colleagues (2016) found that, during deployment, spouses of deployed parents reported an increase in emotional problems and depression; however, they posited that other changes seen in children across the deployment cycle were likely due to maturational processes.

Adolescence

In addition to navigating the usual milestones of adolescent development, including the onset of puberty and changes in peer relationships, adolescents who experience the deployment of a parent face the additional stressors of significant changes in family life and knowledge of potential dangers to the deployed parent (for a review, see Milburn & Lightfoot, 2013). Adolescents with a deployed parent have been shown to experience greater emotional difficulties when compared with national samples; however, these changes during deployment may not persist into later periods (Chandra, Lara-Cinisomo, Jaycox, Tanielian, Burns, Ruder, & Han, 2010; Meadows et al., 2016; White, de Burgh, Fear, & Iversen, 2011). Large population-based studies of adolescents have shown that adolescents with a deployed military parent reported more thoughts of suicide, lower quality of life, and more depression than adolescents in civilian and nondeployed military families (Cederbaum et al., 2014; Reed, Bell, & Edwards, 2011). Research has also found higher rates of alcohol and drug use in adolescents with currently or recently deployed parents (Acion, Ramirez, Jorge, & Arndt, 2013; Reed et al., 2011). Engagement with other military-connected adolescents during a deployment may be protective against many of these challenges and is associated with more positive outcomes across the deployment cycle (Meadows et al., 2016).

PATHWAYS BETWEEN DEPLOYMENT AND CHILD OUTCOMES

The pathways by which deployment impacts children are not yet well understood. A recent study (Lester et al., 2016; Mustillo, Wadsworth, & Lester, 2016) examined how parental deployment may affect adjustment in young children and their families. Although the study design was cross-sectional and could not test mediational mechanisms, data indicated that greater deployment exposure was related to impaired family functioning and marital instability, suggesting that there are likely several family relational process mechanisms that mediate the association between parent deployment and youth outcomes by fostering adaptation or, alternatively, enhancing risk. In the following section, we describe four potential mechanisms—parent stress/mental health, parenting behaviors, family communication, and family role shifts—that likely impact child outcomes in the context of parenting from afar.

One possible way by which deployment impacts children's outcomes is through parental stress. Prior research has demonstrated that a substantial minority of military personnel experience significant psychosocial problems associated with deployment. Prevalence rates of posttraumatic stress disorder (PTSD), for example, have been estimated to fall within a range of 4–17% in US military veterans (Richardson, Frueh, & Acierno, 2010). Results from a population-based study of the first cohort of military service members returning from Iraq found that 20.3% of active duty and 42.4% of reserve component soldiers required mental health treatment (Milliken, Auchterlonie, & Hoge, 2007). Among military parents, PTSD symptoms have been associated with self-reported poorer parenting practices postdeployment (Gewirtz, Polusny, DeGarmo, Khaylis, & Erbes, 2010) and decreased parenting alliance (i.e., cooperation and communication) between caregivers (Allen, Rhoades, Stanley, & Markman, 2010). With a large body of evidence emphasizing the critical role of effective parenting for child adaptation among families living in stressful circumstances (Masten, 2001), one possible pathway of the negative impact of deployment on children may be mediated through its effects on parenting due to parent psychological distress.

Stress for the nondeployed parent can also be substantial. A growing body of research shows increased risk for psychological distress in this population, including elevated rates of depression, sleep problems, anxiety disorders, and acute stress reactions (Green, Nurius, & Lester, 2013; Haas, Pazdernim, & Olsen, 2005; Jensen, Martin, & Watanabe, 1996; Mansfield et al., 2010), which may impede parenting abilities. Indeed, at-home caregiver psychological distress and parenting stress have been found to be significant predictors of child functioning during and after deployment (Allen et al., 2010; Flake et al., 2009; Lester et al., 2010).

Caregivers are at risk of experiencing high levels of stress when temporarily taking on the role of a single parent during a deployment, and this in turn can impact upon parenting behaviors and the quality of relationship with one's child. One study found a decline in mother–child intimacy when the father was deployed, and the mothers' lowest levels of intimacy with their children coincided with the highest levels of child behavior problems (Zeff, Lewis, & Hirsch, 1997). Similarly, Kelley (1994) found that mothers reported less nurturance in their parent–child relationships during the time that their husbands were deployed, and less nurturance was associated with more child behavior problems. Mothers in this study also reported that they yelled at their children more before and during deployment than after (Kelley, 1994). In another study, adolescents reported increased conflict and negativity in their relationships with the at-home caregiver while the other parent was deployed (Huebner et al., 2007). The strain of parenting during a partner's deployment may lead to increased harshness of punishments or a lower tolerance for misbehavior. Multiple studies have demonstrated that child maltreatment (primarily neglect in nonmilitary caretakers) increases during periods of parental deployment, most notably in families with known maltreatment histories (Gibbs, Martin, Kupper, & Johnson, 2007; Hisle-Gorman et al., 2015; Rentz et al., 2007).

Communication

Evidence is mixed regarding the role of parent–child communication when a parent is deployed. The risk or protective quality of communication appears to depend on the information conveyed to the child. Many children find it helpful to communicate regularly, which is made easier by voice-over-internet protocols such as Skype; however, other children report that they find too much communication distressing (Skomorovsky & Bullock, 2016). On the one hand, communication about the reasons for separation can help the child make sense of conflicting messages (namely, "my parent loves me" and "my parent left me"). A child may believe that a parent is making an honorable sacrifice for others; alternatively, he or she may believe that the parent is rejecting or abandoning the family for self-interested reasons. The effects of positive attributions about a parent's absence are not well understood, although youth do report these attributions and feelings (Houston et al., 2009).

Importantly, the nature of military deployments often influences the extent to which parents share information openly with their children, and there is evidence that limiting child knowledge about deployment might be protective. Children's knowledge about their parent's deployment has been associated with anxiety surrounding the parent's safety, school problems, and feelings of anger and loneliness (Chandra, Martin, Hawkins, & Richardson, 2010; Houston et al., 2013).

Shift in Family Roles

Military families often negotiate a redistribution of responsibilities and roles during a family member's absence (Hooper et al., 2014). A frequent pattern that emerges in the context of parental deployment is that youth take on additional responsibilities, such as household chores and supervision of siblings (Houston et al., 2009; Huebner et al., 2007). In addition to taking on household responsibilities, children may take on the role of providing emotional support for the at-home parent (Chandra, Martin, Hawkins, & Richardson, 2010). Often characterized as "parentification," as the child is assuming the role previously filled by the deployed parent, this role shift can result in blurred parent–child boundaries. A considerable body of evidence suggests that parentification in childhood is often related to higher rates of psychopathology in adulthood (Hooper, DeCoster, White, & Voltz, 2011), including depression (Schier, Herke, Nickel, Egle, & Hardt, 2015) and substance abuse (Chase, Demming, & Wells, 1998).

Adolescents in particular tend to take on more responsibilities during deployment and often take pride in their new adultlike roles (Lester & Bursch, 2011; Mmari, Roche, Sudhinaraset, & Blum, 2009). Adolescents may gain personal satisfaction and value from this new role or may feel overwhelmed and resentful about additional burdens (Lester & Bursch, 2011; Mmari et al., 2009). A particularly challenging time seems to be when the deployed parent returns and family life must readjust once again—necessitating a renegotiation of roles and responsibilities in the context of becoming reacquainted. Children, particularly adolescents, may be reluctant to relinquish roles they assumed while the parent was away (Huebner et al., 2007).

SERVICES TO SUPPORT PARENTING FROM AFAR IN MILITARY FAMILIES

Many promising interventions have emerged in the past several years that emphasize family functioning and parenting in the context of military deployment. It is beyond the scope of this chapter to review all such interventions, and, as such, we offer some examples that target the pathways by which deployment impacts children highlighted in this chapter.

Communication Enhancement

Family communication is likely to be an important protective factor but, due to the unique circumstances faced by military families, can be difficult to navigate. Facilitation of positive, helpful communication in a structured manner may be a particularly important intervention strategy for military families during the course of a deployment. One example of a widely available program that facilitates communication in families before, during, and after deployments is the Sesame Street educational outreach initiative "Talk, Listen, Connect." This project includes videos, storybooks, and workbooks, as well as supplemental materials to help parents talk with young children about what to expect during deployment and offers concrete activities and techniques to maintain the parenting connection. Program evaluation data suggested that parent depressive symptoms and child aggressive behaviors declined, and parents reported increased comfort discussing deployment with their children after using the "Talk, Listen, Connect" materials (O'Grady, Burton, Chawla, Topp, & Wadsworth, 2016).

Another innovative program, "United Through Reading," facilitates the bonding experience of reading aloud together, even when parenting from afar. This program offers military service members the opportunity to be video-recorded reading books to their children at home, thus guaranteeing special and uninterrupted time with their service member parent.

Psychoeducation and Developmental Guidance

Young children are disproportionately represented in military families and present specific developmental challenges, particularly when a parent is absent. Zero to Three has established an interdisciplinary, collaborative initiative named "Coming Together Around Military Families" to address the needs of infants and toddlers affected by deployment. Several resources are available to families that provide psychoeducation and developmental guidance for parenting young children, including brochures that focus on the unique experience of parenting during deployment separation and an app designed with behavior tips and parent–child activities. This initiative also includes materials that can be used by service providers to meet the specific developmental needs of military families with young children.

Another program designed specifically for parents of young children is "Strong Families Strong Forces," a home-based reintegration program for military families with a recent deployment and young children (DeVoe, Ross, & Paris, 2012). The program emphasizes the particular needs and developmental challenges that arise when parenting young children and includes the constructs of parental reflective capacity, attachment, and developmental relevance to assist families with young children with postdeployment reintegration. Program outcomes are currently being evaluated through a randomized controlled trial.

Early Identification and Interventions to Target Parental Stress

Repeated research findings have demonstrated elevated levels of caregiver distress in both the absent and at-home caregivers, as well as strong associations between caregiver distress and child outcomes. Therefore, early identification and treatment of parent stress is essential to healthy family functioning. One example of such a program is the "Family Advocacy Program," a Department of Defense program designed to prevent partner violence, child abuse, and neglect by improving family functioning, easing stress that can lead to abuse, and working to create an environment that supports families. Another helpful resource for parents that emphasizes identification of parent stress and parent support are command-sponsored "Family Readiness Groups." These groups comprise family members, volunteers, service members, and civilian employees associated with a particular unit. The goal of these groups is to provide support and practical tools for military families, which are tailored to the specific unit's status (e.g., pre-/ postdeployment, deployed, training/sustainment).

Support of Effective Parenting Practices

The rates of child maltreatment and neglect associated with parental deployment highlight the need for parenting programs that provide families with effective parenting practices tailored to the specific challenges faced by military families. One example is "After Deployment Adaptive Parenting Tools Program" (ADAPT; Gewirtz, Erbes, Polusny, Forgatch, & DeGarmo, 2011), a group intervention designed to address the unique challenges faced by military families during reintegration, with emphasis on emotion regulation skills to improve both parenting practices and child adjustment. Program outcomes are currently being evaluated through a randomized controlled trial.

Another program with an emphasis on parenting skills is the "New Parent Support Program," offered across all branches of service. This program offers expectant parents and parents of young children the opportunity to learn effective parenting practices through parenting classes and home visits. Another parenting resource that is accessible to families regardless of geographic location is an online parenting course offered by the US Department of Veteran Affairs and US Department of Defense. "Parenting for Service Members and Veterans" offers several modules that provide parenting strategies, guidance to help parents reconnect with children after a deployment, parenting exercises, and parenting tip sheets.

Family-Centered Resilience Enhancement Intervention

Given the demands of parenting from afar in military families, building and maintaining parental and child resilience is critical, and several programs have been developed in response. One example of a trauma-informed, family-centered preventive intervention program is Families Overcoming Under Stress (FOCUS; Beardslee et al., 2011; Lester et al., 2012, 2013). Consistent with a family systems and social ecological model framework, FOCUS is designed to enhance parents' and children's functioning as individuals, as well as within and across relationship dyads and the family system (Lester et al., 2010; Saltzman et al., 2011). The FOCUS model includes four core elements: (1) standardized family assessments with provider decision-making support as a web-based tool; (2) customized trauma-informed psychoeducation and developmental guidance; (3) learning and practicing family-level skills including emotional regulation, communication, goal-setting, problem-solving, and management of separation, trauma, and loss reminders; and (4) structured family narrative to increase family cohesion, strengthen family communication, and develop perspective-taking to support one another through the frequent transitions that military families face. The FOCUS intervention was disseminated through a large-scale demonstration project and implemented at several highly deploying military installations (Beardslee et al., 2011). Longitudinal program evaluation data revealed sustained trajectories of reduced psychological health risk symptoms and improved resilience in children and parents (Lester et al., 2012, 2013, 2016).

These examples of interventions designed for military families demonstrate strong efforts to target various pathways by which deployment impacts children and families, including communication, developmental understanding, parental stress, parenting practices, and family resilience. There is a growing body of evidence to support many of these interventions, and several have been successfully disseminated to reach a wide audience. Importantly, additional intervention research is currently under way to better refine programs—specifically, to identify what works for whom and at what point in the deployment cycle.

CONCLUSION

Military service presents unique challenges for families due to a range of transitions, both expected and unexpected. In the context of wartime duty, deployments may make unpredictable and taxing demands on maintaining parenting and parent–child relationships. Although still limited, research has begun to inform our understanding of the impact of parental deployment separations, as well as identify risk and resilience processes within the family system. Future research in this area will be important to describe child and family trajectories through deployment and identify processes that buffer the impact of separation. Longitudinal research, specifically, is needed to better understand the impact of deployment, which often occurs multiple times and which has impacts at multiple levels (i.e., individual, dyadic, family, community). Longitudinal research is essential to our understanding of the cumulative effects of multiple deployments on military families and how children and parents are mutually shaped by and shape subsequent deployments and reintegration periods as a function of the strengths and vulnerabilities they carry forth to each new experience.

Research that can inform interventions to address family functioning and parenting in the context of military deployment remains necessary. Interventions that offer developmental guidance, target parent stress, support effective parenting practices, and educate families about the disruption that traumatic stress or other combat injuries can have on parenting and family life are important to mitigate their potentially serious impacts on child well-being and family functioning. Finally, interventions are needed to address specific opportunities for utilizing remote communication technologies to maintain parenting at a distance, stabilize care routines, and create rituals that allow the absent parent to remain salient in the everyday life of the family. Family separation in the context of military deployment is complex and multifaceted, and more information is needed to understand how it ultimately impacts family members individually and as a unit and how interventions can be developed to address and mitigate its impacts.

REFERENCES

Acion, L., Ramirez, M. R., Jorge, R. E., & Arndt, S. (2013). Increased risk of alcohol and drug use among children from deployed military families. *Addiction, 108*, 1418–1425.

Allen, E. S., Rhoades, G. K., Stanley, S. M., & Markman, H. J. (2010). Hitting home: Relationships between recent deployment, post-traumatic stress symptoms, and marital functioning for Army couples. *Journal of Family Psychology, 24*, 280–288.

Barker, L. H., & Berry, K. D. (2009). Developmental issues impacting military families with young children during single and multiple deployments. *Military Medicine, 174*, 1033–1040.

Beardslee, W., Lester, P., Klosinski, L., Saltzman, W., Woodward, K., Nash, W., . . . Leskin, G. (2011). Family-centered preventive intervention for military families: Implications for implementation science. *Prevention Science, 12*, 339–348.

Boss, P. (1999). *Ambiguous loss: Learning to live with unresolved grief.* Cambridge, MA: Harvard.

Bowlby, J. (1980). *Attachment and loss: Vol. 3: Loss, sadness and depression.* New York: Basic Books.

Bronfenbrenner, U., & Morris, P. A. (1998). The ecology of developmental processes. In W. Damon (Series Ed.) & R. M. Lerner (Vol. Ed.), *Handbook of child psychology: Vol. 1: Theoretical models of human development* (pp. 993–1028). New York: Wiley.

Cederbaum, J. A., Gilreath, T. D., Benbenishty, R., Astor, R. A., Pineda, D., DePedro, K. T., . . . Atuel, H. (2014). Well-being and suicidal ideation of secondary school students from military families. *Journal of Adolescent Health, 54*, 672–677.

Chandra, A., Burns, R. M., Tanielian, T., & Jaycox, L. H. (2011). Understanding the deployment experience for children and youth from military families. In S. M.

Wadsworth & D. Riggs (Eds.), *Risk and resilience in US military families* (pp. 175–192). New York: Springer.

Chandra, A., Lara-Cinisomo, S., Jaycox, L. H., Tanielian, T., Burns, R. M., Ruder, T., & Han, B. (2010). Children on the homefront: The experience of children from military families. *Pediatrics, 125*, 16–25.

Chandra, A., Martin, L. T., Hawkins, S. A., & Richardson, A. (2010). The impact of parental deployment on child social and emotional functioning: Perspectives of school staff. *Journal of Adolescent Health, 46*, 218–223.

Chapin, M. (2011). Family resilience and the fortunes of war. *Social Work in Health Care, 50*, 527–542.

Chartrand, M. M., Frank, D. A., White, L. F., & Shope, T. R. (2008). Effect of parents' wartime deployment on the behavior of young children in military families. *Archives of Pediatrics and Adolescent Medicine, 162*, 1009–1014.

Chase, N., Demming, M., & Wells, M. (1998). Parentification, parental alcoholism, and academic status among young adults. *American Journal of Family Therapy, 25*, 105–114.

Cozza, S. J., & Lieberman, A. F. (2007). The young military child: Our modern Telemachus. *Zero to Three, 27*, 27–33.

Dekel, R., Goldblatt, H., Keidar, M., Solomon, Z., & Polliack, M. (2005). Being a wife of a veteran with posttraumatic stress disorder. *Family Relations, 54*, 24–36.

DeVoe, E. R., & Ross, A. (2012). The parenting cycle of deployment. *Military Medicine, 177*, 184–190.

DeVoe, E. R., Ross, A., & Paris, R. (2012). Build it together and they will come: The case for community-based participatory research with military populations. *Advances in Social Work Research, 13*, 149–165.

Drummet, A. R., Coleman, M., & Cable, S. (2003). Military families under stress: Implications for family life education. *Family Relations, 52*, 279–287.

Engel, R. C., Gallagher, L. B., & Lyle, D. S. (2010). Military deployments and children's academic achievement: Evidence from Department of Defense education activity schools. *Economics of Education Review, 29*, 73–82.

Erel, E., & Burman, B. (1995). Interrelatedness of marital relations and parent-child relations: A meta-analytic review. *Psychological Bulletin, 118*, 108–132.

Faber, A. J., Willerton, E., Clymer, S. R., MacDermid, S. M., & Weiss, H. M. (2008). Ambiguous absence, ambiguous presence: A qualitative study of military reserve families in wartime. *Journal of Family Psychology, 22*, 222–230.

Fischer, H. (2015). *A guide to US military casualty statistics: Operation Freedom's Sentinel, Operation Inherent Resolve, Operation New Dawn, Operation Iraqi Freedom, and Operation Enduring Freedom*. Retrieved from https://fas.org/sgp/crs/natsec/RS22452.pdf

Flake, E. M., Davis, B. E., Johnson, P. L., & Middleton, L. S. (2009). The psychosocial effects of deployment on military children. *Journal of Developmental and Behavioral Pediatrics, 30*, 271–278.

Floyd, L., & Phillips, D. A. (2013). Child care and other support programs. *The Future of Children, 23*, 79–97.

Gewirtz, A. H., Erbes, C. R., Polusny, M. A., Forgatch, M. S., & Degarmo, D. S. (2011). Helping military families through the deployment process: Strategies to support parenting. *Professional Psychology, Research and Practice, 42*, 56–62.

Gewirtz, A. H., Polusny, M. A., DeGarmo, D. S., Khaylis, A., & Erbes, C. R. (2010). Posttraumatic stress symptoms among National Guard soldiers deployed to Iraq: Associations with parenting behaviors and couple adjustment. *Journal of Consulting and Clinical Psychology, 78*, 599–610.

Gibbs, D. A., Martin, S. L., Kupper, L. L., & Johnson, R. E. (2007). Child maltreatment in enlisted soldiers' families during combat-related deployments. *Journal of the American Medical Association, 298*, 528–535.

Gorman, L. A., & Fitzgerald, H. E. (2007). Ambiguous loss, family stress, and infant attachment during times of war. *Zero to Three, 27*, 20–26.

Green, S., Nurius, P. S., & Lester, P. (2013). Spouse psychological well-being: A keystone to military family health. *Journal of Human Behavior in the Social Environment, 23*, 753–768.

Green, T., Buckman, J., Dandeker, C., & Greenberg, S. (2010). How communication with families can both help and hider service members' mental health and occupational effectiveness on deployment. *Military Medicine, 175*, 745–749.

Haas, D. M., Pazdernik, L. A., & Olsen, C. H. (2005). A cross-sectional survey of the relationship between partner deployment and stress in pregnancy during wartime. *Womens Health Issues, 15*, 48–54.

Heiselberg, M. H. (2016). Fighting for the family: Overcoming distances in time and space. *Critical Military Studies, 3*, 69–86.

Hisle-Gorman, E., Harrington, D., Nylund, C. M., Tercyak, K. P., Anthony, B. J., & Gorman, G. H. (2015). The impact of parents' wartime military deployment and injury on young children's safety and mental health. *Journal of the American Academy of Child & Adolescent Psychiatry, 54*, 294–301.

Hooper, L. M., DeCoster, J., White, N., & Voltz, M. L. (2011). Characterizing the magnitude of the relation between self-reported childhood parentification and adult psychopathology: A meta-analysis. *Journal of Clinical Psychology, 67*, 1028–1043.

Hooper, L. M., Moore, H. M., & Smith, A. K. (2014). Parentification in military families: Overlapping constructs and theoretical explorations in family, clinical, and military psychology. *Children and Youth Services Review, 39*, 123–134.

Houston, J. B., Pfefferbaum, B., Sherman, M. D., Melson, A. G., & Brand, M. W. (2013). Family communication across the military deployment experience: Child and spouse report of communication frequency and quality and associated emotions, behaviors, and reactions. *Journal of Loss & Trauma, 18*, 103–119.

Houston, J. B., Pfefferbaum, B., Sherman, M. D., Melson, A. G., Jeon-Slaughter, H., Brand, M. W., & Jarman, Y. (2009). Children of deployed National Guard troops: Perceptions of parental deployment to Operation Iraqi Freedom. *Psychiatric Annals, 29*, 805–811.

Huebner, A. J., Mancini, J. A., Wilcox, R. M., Grass, S. R., & Grass, G. A. (2007). Parental deployment and youth in military families: Exploring uncertainty and ambiguous loss. *Family Relations, 56*, 112–122.

Jensen, P. S., Martin, D., & Watanabe, H. (1996). Children's response to parental separation during Operation Desert Storm. *Journal of the American Academy of Child and Adolescent Psychiatry, 35*, 433–441.

Kelley, M. L. (1994). The effects of military-induced separation on family factors and child-behavior. *American Journal of Orthopsychiatry, 64*, 103–111.

Kelley, M. L., Doane, A., & Pearson, M. (2011). Single military mothers in the new millennium: Stresses, supports, and effects of deployment. In S. M. Wadsworth & D. Riggs (Eds.), *Risk and resilience in U.S. military families* (pp. 343–363). New York: Springer.

Knobloch, L. K., Pusateri, K. B., Ebata, A. T., & McGlughlin, P. C. (2015). Experiences of military youth during a family member's deployment: Changes, challenges, and opportunities. *Youth & Society, 47*, 319–342.

Kudler, H., & Porter, R. I. (2013). Building communities of care for military children and families. *The Future of Children, 23*, 163–185.

Lester, P. (2012). War and military children and families: Translating prevention science into practice. *Journal of the American Academy of Child and Adolescent Psychiatry, 51*, 3–5.

Lester, P., Aralis, H., Sinclair, M., Kiff, C., Lee, K. H., Mustillo, S., & Wadsworth, S. M. (2016). The impact of deployment on parental, family, and child adjustment in military families. *Child Psychiatry and Human Development, 47*, 938–949.

Lester, P., & Bursch, B. (2011). The long war comes home: mitigating risk and promoting resilience in military children and families. *Psychiatry Times, 28*, 1–3.

Lester, P., Leskin, G., Woodward, K, Saltzman, W., Nash, W., Mogil, C., . . . Beardslee, W. (2011). Wartime deployment and military children: Applying prevention science to enhance family resilience. In S. M. Wadsworth & D. Riggs (Eds.), *Risk and resilience in U.S. military families* (pp. 149–173). New York: Springer.

Lester, P., Peterson, K., Reeves, J., Knauss, L. Glover, D., Mogil, C., . . . Beardslee, W. (2010). The long war and parental combat deployment: Effects on military children and at-home spouses. *Journal of the American Academy of Child & Adolescent Psychiatry, 49*, 310–320.

Lester, P., Saltzman, W. R., Woodward, K., Glover, D., Leskin, G. A., Bursch, B., . . . Beardslee, W. (2012). Evaluation of a family-centered prevention intervention for military children and families facing wartime deployments. *American Journal of Public Health, 102*, 48–54.

Lester, P., Stein, J. A., Saltzman, W., Woodward, K., MacDermid, S. W., Milburn, N., . . . Beardslee, W. (2013). Psychological health of military children: Longitudinal evaluation of a family-centered prevention program to enhance family resilience. *Military Medicine, 178*, 838–845.

Logan, K. V. (1987). The emotional cycle of deployment. *US Naval Institute Proceedings, 113*, 43–47.

MacDermid, S. M., Samper, R., Schwartz, R., Nishida, J., & Nyaronga, D. (2008). *Understanding and promoting resilience in military families.* West Lafayette, IN: Military Family Research Institute.

Madianou, M., & Miller, D. (2012). Polymedia: Towards a new theory of digital media in interpersonal communication. *International Journal of Cultural Studies, 16*, 169–187.

Mansfield, A. J., Kaufman, J. S., Marshall, S. W., Gaynes, B. N., Morrissey, J. P., & Engel, C. C. (2010). Deployment and the use of mental health services among US army wives. *New England Journal of Medicine, 362*, 101–109.

Masten, A. S. (2001). Ordinary magic: Resilience processes in development. *American Psychologist, 56*, 227–238.

Meadows, S. O., Tanielian, T., & Karney, B. R. (2016). *The deployment life study: Longitudinal analysis of military families across the deployment cycle.* Santa Monica, CA: RAND Corporation.

Milburn, N. G., & Lightfoot, M. (2013). Adolescents in wartime US military families: A developmental perspective on challenges and resources. *Clinical Child and Family Psychology Review*, *16*, 266–277.

Milliken, C. S., Auchterlonie, J. L., & Hoge, C. W. (2007). Longitudinal assessment of mental health problems among active and reserve component soldiers returning from the Iraq war. *Journal of the American Medical Association*, *298*, 2141–2148.

Minuchin, P. (1985). Families and individual development: Provocations from the field of family therapy. *Child Development*, *56*, 289–302.

Mmari, K., Roche, K. M., Sudhinaraset, M., & Blum, R. (2009). Exploring the issues faced by adolescents and their families. *Youth & Society*, *40*, 455–475.

Mogil, C., Hajal, N., Garcia, E., Kiff, C., Paley, B., Milburn, N., & Lester, P. (2015). FOCUS for early childhood: A virtual home visiting program for military families with young children. *Contemporary Family Therapy*, *37*(3), 199–208

Mustillo, S., Wadsworth, S. M., & Lester, P. (2016). Parental deployment and well-being in children: Results from a new study of military families. *Journal of Emotional and Behavioral Disorders*, *24*, 82–91.

National Military Family Association. (2005). *Report on the cycles of deployment*. Retrieved from http://www.militaryfamily.org/assets/pdf/NMFACyclesofDeployment9.pdf

O'Grady, A. F., Burton, E. T., Chawla, N., Topp, D., & Wadsworth, S. M. (2016). Evaluation of a multimedia intervention for children and families facing multiple military deployments. *Journal of Primary Prevention*, *37*, 53–70.

Paley, B., Lester, P., & Mogil, C. (2013). Family systems and ecological perspectives on the impact of deployment on military families. *Clinical Child and Family Psychology Review*, *16*, 245–265.

Paris, R., DeVoe, E. R., Ross, A., & Acker, M. L. (2010). When a parent goes to war: Effects of parental deployment on very young children and implications for intervention. *American Journal of Orthopsychiatry*, *80*, 610–618.

Pincus, S. H., House, R., Christenson, J., & Adler, L. E. (2001). The emotional cycle of deployment: A military family perspective. *US Army Medical Department Journal*, 615–623.

Reed, S. C., Bell, J. F., & Edwards, T. C. (2011). Adolescent well-being in Washington state military families. *American Journal of Public Health*, *101*, 1676–1682.

Renshaw, K. D., Rodrigues, C. S., & Joes, D. H. (2009). Combat exposure, psychological symptoms, and marital satisfaction in National Guard soldiers who served in Operation Iraqi Freedom from 2005 to 2006. *Anxiety, Stress, & Coping*, *22*, 101–115.

Rentz, E. D., Marshall, S. W., Loomis, D., Casteel, C., Martin, S. L., & Gibbs, D. A. (2007). Effect of deployment on the occurrence of child maltreatment in military and non-military families. *American Journal of Epidemiology*, *165*, 1199–1206.

Richardson, L. K., Frueh, B. C., & Acierno, R. (2010). Prevalence estimates of combat-related post-traumatic stress disorder: Critical review. *The Australian and New Zealand Journal of Psychiatry*, *44*, 4–19.

Riggs, S. A., & Riggs, D. S. (2011). Risk and resilience in military families experiencing deployment: The role of the family attachment network. *Journal of Family Psychology*, *25*, 675–687.

Rodriguez, A. J., & Margolin, G. (2015). Parental incarceration, transnational migration, and military deployment: Family process mechanisms of youth adjustment to temporary parent absence. *Clinical Child & Family Psychology Review*, *18*, 24–49.

Rosenblum, K. L., Dayton, C., & Muzik, M. (2009). Infant social and emotional development: Emerging competence in a relational context. In C. H. Zeanah (Ed.), *Handbook of infant mental health* (3rd ed., pp. 80–103). Toronto: Guilford.

Saltzman, W. R., Lester, P., Beardslee, W. R., Layne, C. M., Woodward, K., & Nash, W. P. (2011). Mechanisms of risk and resilience in military families: Theoretical and empirical basis of family-focused resilience enhancement program. *Clinical Child and Family Psychology Review, 14*, 213–230.

Sameroff, A. (1994). Developmental systems and family functioning. In R. D. Parke & S. G. Kellam (Eds.), *Exploring family relationships with other social contexts* (pp. 199–214). Hillsdale, NJ: Erlbaum.

Schier, K., Herke, M., Nickel, R., Egle, U. T., & Hardt, J. (2015). Long-term sequelae of emotional parentification: A cross-validation study using sequences of regressions. *Journal of Child and Family Studies, 24*, 1307–1321.

Skomorovsky, A., & Bullock, A. (2016). The impact of deployment on children from Canadian military families. *Armed Forces and Society, 43*, 654–673.

Stafford, E. M., & Grady, B. A. (2003). Military family support. *Pediatric Annals, 32*, 110–115.

Tanielian, T., Karney, B. R., Chandra, A., & Meadows, S. O. (2014). *The deployment life study: Methodological overview and baseline sample description.* Retrieved from http://www.rand.org/content/dam/rand/pubs/research_reports/RR200/RR209/RAND_RR209.pdf

Tarrier, N., Sommerfield, C., & Pilgrim, H. (1999). Relatives' expressed emotion (EE) and PTSD treatment outcome. *Psychological Medicine, 29*, 801–811.

US Department of Defense. (2010). *Report on the impact of deployment of members of the armed forces on their dependent children.* Retrieved from http://download.militaryonesource.mil/12038/MOS/Reports/Report-to-Congress-on-Impact-of-Deployment-on-Military-Children.pdf

US Department of Defense. (2015). *2015 demographics: Profile of the military community.* Retrieved from http://download.militaryonesource.mil/12038/MOS/Reports/2015-Demographics-Report.pdf

Vormbrock, J. K. (1993). Attachment theory as applied to wartime and job-related marital separation. *Psychological Bulletin, 114*, 122–144.

Wadsworth, S. M., Cardin, J. F., Christ, S., Willerton, E., O'Grady, A. F., Topp, D., . . . & Mustillo, S. (2016). Accumulation of risk and promotive factors among young children in US military families. *American Journal of Community Psychology, 57*, 190–202. doi:10.1002/ajcp.12025.

Warner, C. H., Breitbach, J. E., Appenzeller, G. N., Yates, V., Grieger, T., & Webster, W. G. (2007). Division mental health in the new brigade combat team structure: Part I. Predeployment and deployment. *Military Medicine, 172*, 907–911.

White, C., de Burgh, H. T., Fear, N. T., & Iverson, A. C. (2011). The impact of deployment to Iraq or Afghanistan on military children: A review of the literature. *International Review of Psychiatry, 23*, 210–217.

Zeff, K. N., Lewis, S. J., & Hirsch, K. A. (1997). Military family adaptation to United Nations operations in Somalia. *Military Medicine, 162*, 384–387.

SECTION III

Personal Crises and Family Separation

10

Children as Providers and Recipients of Support

Redefining Family Among Child-Headed Households in Namibia

MÓNICA RUIZ-CASARES, SHELENE GENTZ, AND JESSE BEATSON ■

Across time and space, families and communities have found ways to care for children when they are orphaned. Over the past quarter of a century, the HIV/AIDS epidemic placed unprecedented pressure on families and communities, particularly in sub-Saharan Africa, and thus challenged customary orphan childcare arrangements. Researchers have found that when their father is deceased, most children remain with their mother, whereas children are often placed with extended family if the mother dies (Richter & Desmond, 2008). Family members from the maternal or paternal side, as dictated by cultural norms, are often preferred over other caregivers (Beard, 2005; Heymann, Earle, Rajaraman, Miller, & Bogen, 2007; Rotheram-Borus et al., 2002). Nonetheless, high rates of orphanhood may force changes in those cultural norms and customary foster care arrangements (Drah, 2014) and result in the emergence of child-headed households (CHH; Van Rensburg, Human, & Moleki, 2013). While CHHs do not necessarily emerge following parental death, many do, particularly in contexts hard hit by severe epidemics.

The process of CHH formation is rather complex. Some studies have found that the proportion of households with no adults has not increased in the past couple of decades despite growth in the number of orphans and that children living in CHHs do not necessarily have more unmet basic needs than children in adult-headed households (Ciganda, Gagnon, & Tenkorang, 2012; Meintjes, Hall, Marera, & Boulle, 2010; Richter & Desmond, 2008). At the same time, and despite their low prevalence, children living in CHHs confront specific challenges

(Donald & Clacherty, 2005; Mturi, 2012). Concerns over the quality of care and access to necessary resources have resulted in a growing body of literature examining this phenomenon. Over the past two decades, scholars have been documenting the fluidity of CHHs and the strategies and outcomes associated with this type of living arrangement. However, attention to caregiving and parenting and their impact on the well-being of those caring for AIDS-orphaned children is limited (Kuo & Operario, 2009; Malinga-Musamba, 2015) and even more so in the context of CHHs. In this chapter, we review and summarize the state of current research on CHHs.

When they are living on their own, children's relationships with relatives and nonrelatives change, as do expectations and means of communication among family members, task distribution, and children's responsibilities, including parenting of their younger siblings (Haley & Bradbury, 2014). Researchers studying CHHs have explored the composition and functioning of social networks and support systems and their contribution to child well-being (Lee, 2012; Ruiz-Casares, 2010). Just as social support networks can enable child agency, receiving and giving support may increase children's self-esteem and help balance relationships over time, thus contributing to social stability and securing aid (Gouldner, 1960). In this context, immediate and deferred reciprocity serve as a measure of the accessibility and strength of relationships and an indicator of children's changing status and family dynamics. Two case studies from Namibia, one of the countries hardest hit by the HIV/AIDS epidemic, are provided to illustrate some of these changes, as well as children's views and experiences caring for their siblings and how their parenting practices compare to those of their deceased parents or reflect their late wishes.

CHILD-HEADED HOUSEHOLDS: OVERVIEW FROM THE LITERATURE

Definition, Prevalence, Causes, and Composition

CHHs refers to families and households where young people care for their siblings and/or other children independently, without a co-resident adult. Whereas some scholars use the term "child-headed" to denote a household with all members under the age of 18 and the term "youth-headed" to refer to a household where the head is 18–25 years old (Foster, Makufa, Drew, & Kralovec, 1997), others use these terms more loosely or refer instead to other terms such as "junior-headed" and "sibling-headed" household (Dalen, 2009; Kuhanen, Shemeikka, Notkola, & Nghixulifwa, 2008). Other scholars argue that factors such as educational and employment status and caring responsibilities may be more relevant than age to children's well-being outcomes (Evans, 2011, 2012*a*).[1]

Also common is the distinction between "unaccompanied" and "accompanied" CHHs, the former referring to households with no co-resident adult and the latter to those in which adult(s) are present but are sick, disabled, elderly, or otherwise unable to play a significant role in running the household. The current terminology is not fine-grained enough, leading Mturi (2012) to argue that CHHs that form through parent death should be distinguished from other types of CHHs, such as those formed on a more temporary basis, such as due to labor migration.

The lack of a common definition and appropriate survey data make estimating the prevalence of CHHs challenging. As a result, the question of whether they are on the rise is contested in many settings. For instance, whereas some describe an increase in CHHs (Richter & Desmond, 2008), others claim the notion that CHHs are on the rise in South Africa is not empirically substantiated (Meintjes et al., 2010). Overall, official estimates are generally low (0.5–13% of all households in several sub-Saharan African countries), yet there is large variation by country and depending on whether "accompanied" households are also included in the count (Phillips, 2011). In most places, the prevalence of this living arrangement has not been monitored systematically over time, thus hindering trend analyses. The fluid nature of CHHs, where children may move in and out of adult-headed households, further complicates the calculation of reliable estimates.

CHHs emerge in contexts where there are high rates of parental and caregiver loss, as in countries and regions hard hit by the HIV epidemic, and particularly where the extended family network is overstretched (Van Rensburg et al., 2013). In fact, many interpret the emergence of CHHs as indicative of an overburdened extended family system (Mturi, 2012). Although some scholars suggest involving the extended family as the best approach to alleviating challenges faced by CHHs (Foster, 2000), others have noted that children themselves are sometimes the most wary of extended family members for fear of maltreatment, losing inheritance, or sibling separation, among other concerns (Evans, 2012*a*; Thurman et al., 2006). In a study we conducted in Namibia, approximately 42% of our respondents reported experiencing property-grabbing by their relatives, and the children wanted to preserve family property. With the presence of sibling relations, many opted to live by themselves (Ruiz-Casares, 2009). Studies across sub-Saharan Africa have shown that households often include an older adolescent (the head) and are composed, on average, of one to three children; nonetheless, larger households, households headed by younger children, and/or those including cousins or unrelated children are commonplace in a number of settings (Phillips, 2011).

Family Life and Caregiving in Child-Headed Households

Several scholars have found that the presence of an adolescent girl can be a determining factor in the establishment of a CHH (Mogotlane, Chauke, Van Rensburg, Human, & Kganakga, 2010; Tsegaye, 2007), although boys head households in other contexts (Ayieko, 1998; Luzze, 2002). In the absence of an adult authority figure, Francis-Chizororo (2010) found new forms of "patriarchal oppression" in CHHs in Zimbabwe, but there is also evidence of resistance. In a study we conducted in Northern Namibia, we found a division of labor in CHHs in which girls often take on a wider range of tasks and, as a result, may be more likely to drop out of school or at least arrive late or leave early (Ruiz-Casares, 2007). Bell and Payne (2009) contradict the picture of CHHs as fully replicating gendered power dynamics in traditional family units: rather, they found CHHs in Zambia and Uganda to be more dynamic entities in which roles and power shift are contested daily.

Yanagisawa, Poudel, and Jimba (2010) developed a framework for categorizing the types of sibling caregiving identified and described in other studies included in their systemic review. In this framework, sibling caregiving comprises four types of care: (1) economic (i.e., income generation, household money management, and paying schooling fees for siblings), (2) physical (i.e., household chores and daily care for younger siblings, including emergency care for illnesses or injuries), (3) psychological (i.e., expression of caring and love that often mimics the role of the parent), and (4) and educational (i.e., training younger siblings to assist in daily burden-sharing as well as taking steps to ensure that they are adequately prepared for eventually being independent). It generally falls on child heads and older children to provide basic needs, advise and supervise younger children, and assign household chores (Lane, Cluver, & Operario, 2015; Mmari, 2011); less attention has been paid to the latter two types of care and their potential impact on the well-being of caregivers and care receivers. Becker (2007) contends that there is a "continuum of caring" for "young carers."[2] The relative amount of time spent and types of tasks performed by child caregivers is often determined by the health status of the care recipient (Evans, 2010). If the person is in critical condition, the child caregiver will tend to engage more heavily in caring tasks related to the chronic and life-threatening illness (Lane, et al., 2015), including "intimate tasks" (e.g., bathing, dressing, giving medication) (Robson, Ansell, Huber, Gould, & van Blerk, 2006).

Relatives, friends, and neighbors provide tangible aid and facilitate access to other resources to children living by themselves (Lee, 2012; Ruiz-Casares, 2010), yet the extent and usefulness of their assistance is unclear (Van Dijk & Van Driel, 2012). Relationships with relatives and friends within social networks can act as a double-edged sword—providing positive support but also acting as a source of most negative interactions (Ruiz-Casares, 2010). Other aspects of social relationships, such as reciprocity, have been rarely studied. The indirect benefit of social support networks to enable agency by enhancing children's sense of control has been highlighted (Lee, 2012).

Impact on Children's Agency and Well-Being

Young people are typically conceptualized as "dependents" and "care recipients" rather than "contributors" or "caregivers" (Evans, 2012*b*). Thus, children in CHHs can be seen as acting counternormatively when they express agency. Moreover, they are sometimes represented in the literature as a risk to themselves and to wider society (Payne, 2012), as members of "deviant" households whose members are more prone to involvement in petty crime or gangs (Mogotlane et al., 2010) and to have early sexual experiences (Foster et al., 1997). "Adultification," a premature exposure of children to adult knowledge, roles, and realities (Burton, 2007) puts a decidedly negative slant on the new responsibilities taken up by children in CHHs.

Living arrangements in CHHs can have physical, psychological, social, and educational impacts on children. Malnutrition and compromised health may affect both the caregiver and the receiver(s) of care (Abebe & Aase, 2007; Boris, Thurman, Snider, Spencer, & Brown, 2006; Mmari, 2011). There is concurrence in the literature that parental death or illness and other related events that fracture the family structure can have a negative impact on these children. Maqoko and Dreyer (2008) even claim that the experience of being in a CHH involves "psychological trauma." Quantitative measures of trauma in CHHs are lacking, but self-reports from child caregivers indicate that experiences such as stress, unhappiness, and grief can have a destabilizing effect (Mandali, 2006).[3] An overwhelming care burden may compound these feelings. In addition to caregiving duties involving younger siblings, there can also be adult dependents such as sick parents or grandparents who require care, although Tamasane and Head (2010) found that grandparents, especially those with pensions, can contribute material resources to lessen the burdens of the child caregiver. As a consequence of being overworked and having to take on multiple challenging roles, often simultaneously, children caregivers can experience "physical, social, economic, and psychological morbidity and vulnerability to HIV infection" (Foster, 2000, p. 55). The social isolation from being prematurely cast into this adult role, often compounded with a loss of friends and peer relationships from a decline in school attendance, challenges the coping resources of child caregivers (Cluver & Gardner, 2007). Finally, several scholars have documented a higher school dropout rate among orphans and child caregivers (Germann, 2006; Landry, Luginaah, Maticka-Tyndale, & Elkins, 2007; Schenk et al., 2008). When confounding variables are controlled, though, school enrollment between orphans and nonorphans is approximately equivalent, even if academic performance can still be negatively affected (Kürzinger et al., 2008). This can have longer term impacts, such as compromising opportunities for employment (Yamba, 2005).

Despite structural constraints, there is evidence that children are able to exercise some autonomy and engage in supportive and interdependent relations (Evans, 2012*b*). There may also be some positive implications for children living in CHHs, such as strengthened sibling ties and reaffirmed caring roles (Evans, 2011), a high degree of emotional sensitivity, and improved interpersonal conflict resolution skills (Donald & Clacherty, 2005). Furthermore, younger siblings may have opportunities to exercise agency in CHH arrangements as well (Mavise, 2011).

Payne (2012) found that children living in CHHs often view their actions as a normal part of their everyday life and argues that a "coping lens" to examining this experience is insufficient. Unfortunately, a lot of the research focusing on the well-being of family members in CHHs represents an adult perspective and neglects the voices of the children themselves (Van Dijk & Van Driel, 2012). When children are asked about their own experiences, a more ambivalent and nuanced picture of well-being tends to emerge. In a study involving heads of 105

CHHs over a 12-month period, for instance, Germann (2006) found surprisingly high self-ratings of quality of life despite adversities. While this may derive from subverting social norms and generational hierarchies and gaining power and autonomy within the family unit, this does not translate for these children into being treated as equals to adults in the community. In fact, children living in CHHs are more likely to be exploited than children living with at least one adult authority figure (Foster, 2000; Mogotlane et al., 2010; Roalkvam, 2005; Ward & Eyber, 2009).

It is possible that negative consequences of being in CHH arrangements are avoidable or could be less dire in cases where caregivers receive adequate support and access to resources (Yanagisawa et al., 2010). How that is done needs to be pondered with care. Interventions can undermine complex new identities that straddle childhood and adulthood (Mavise, 2011). Moreover, concern over the undesirable consequences of nongovernmental organizational (NGO) support to CHHs has been raised, including social stigma and negative reactions from friends and neighbors, including feelings of greed and jealousy (Kipp, Satzinger, Alibhai, & Rubaale, 2010). Alternative approaches such as "mentorship schemes" that install an adult into the CHH on a permanent or temporary basis may violate the family's agency (Payne, 2012) and are not always realistic (Daniel & Mathias, 2012).

THE EMERGENCE OF CHILD-HEADED HOUSEHOLDS IN THE NAMIBIAN CONTEXT

The Republic of Namibia is situated in southern Africa and shares borders with South Africa, Botswana, Zambia, and Angola. The country has a population of 2.1 million, with a large number (37%) still under the age of 15 years (Namibia Statistics Agency [NSA], 2013). Namibia is a diverse country, with 13 recognized languages. Covering a geographical area of 825,616 square kilometers, it is one of the most sparsely populated countries in the world. The large distances between habitations and a sparse population bring challenges for the delivery of health and other services, including child protection, particularly in the rural areas where 57% of the population live (NSA, 2013).

Namibia became an independent democratic republic in 1990 after a period of colonialism and apartheid. As a consequence, the country inherited large inequalities, specifically along racial lines, as well as low economic growth, high unemployment, and a high rate of poverty (National Planning Commision [NPC], 2012). In the more than 25 years since independence, the country has improved its social and economic situation, but many challenges remain (NPC, 2013).

The country's economy is primarily based on mining, manufacturing, tourism, agriculture, and fishing. A human development index (HDI) of 0.628 places it as 126th out of 188 countries (United Nations Development Programme [UNDP], 2015). Namibia has been classified as an upper middle-income country since 2009. However, this classification and the improvements shown in its HDI obscure the large inequalities and widespread poverty that remain. The Gini coefficient (63.9) shows that it is one of the most unequal societies of the world (World Bank, 2013). Furthermore, about one-fourth (24%) of the population live below the international poverty line (less than US$1.25 per day), with 13% of the population in severe poverty, using the multidimensional poverty index (UNDP, 2015). The country also has a high unemployment rate, with 28% of the eligible workforce being unemployed, and, of those in employment, a further 30% are considered as being in vulnerable employment, mostly working as unpaid workers on subsistence or communal farms (NSA, 2015*b*). Children are proportionately more affected by poverty than adults, with about 1 in 3 children qualifying as poor (34% vs. 29% of all ages), in this case defined as consumption poverty (NSA, 2012*a*, 2012*b*).[4]

The responsibility for surviving orphans falls on the paternal and/or maternal relatives—mostly parents' parents and siblings (uncles/aunts), depending on diverse rules or principles of descent. Thus, the Owambo and Kavango communities trace descent to their kin only through their mothers and other females (matrilineal). Other groups in Namibia, such as the Few, were once matrilineal but transitioned to patrilineal, ascribing affiliation through consanguineal relatedness through males; in Zambezi, the Subia display a cognatic pattern (linking relatives of any sex, non-unilineal). Although most San groups are patrilineal/bilateral (i.e., related through relatives of either sex) (Malan, 1995), the Kxoe San are organized around matrilineal clans (Köhler, 1989 reviewed by Guenther, 1991).

Various factors contribute to the emergence of CHHs in Namibia. Among these are the HIV epidemic and the consequent high rates of orphanhood, poverty, and the reconfiguration of the family system. HIV sentinel surveys conducted with pregnant women since 1992 suggest that the HIV epidemic appears to be stabilizing (Ministry of Health and Social Services [MoHSS], 2014); however Namibia remains one of the top 10 affected countries in the world. The first nationally representative HIV prevalence survey conducted—the 2013 Namibia Demographic and Health Survey (NDHS)—reported a national prevalence of 14% in adults between the ages of 15 and 49 (MOHSS & ICF International, 2014). Prevalence varies across regions, with some regions, such as Zambezi in the Northeast, having a prevalence rate as high as 24% (MOHSS & ICF International, 2014). Despite current widespread access to antiretroviral medication, previous high mortality rates resulted in a large number of children left orphaned. The 2011 Namibian census reports that 16% of children in Namibia are orphans, with 3% of these being double orphans (NSA, 2013). The proportion of orphaned children increases with age from 4% in the below 5-year-old age group to 27% in the 15–17 age group. It is not known which proportions of orphans are due to HIV and AIDS, but it is estimated to be almost two-thirds (64%) (United Nations Children's Fund [UNICEF], 2015).

Another factor impacting the emergence of CHHs is the migratory patterns within Namibia, with a large portion of Namibians migrating from rural to urban areas in search of work (International Organization for Migration, 2016). The percentage living in urban areas has increased from 27% in 1991 to 33% in 2001 and to 43% in 2011 (NSA, 2015*a*). In 2011, more than 40% of those residing in the Khomas and Erongo regions, where major urban cities are located, were born outside those regions, which suggests net migration flows into those regions from elsewhere (NSA, 2015*a*). Furthermore, some northern regions, such as Ohangwena, are largely rural and show a large outflow of citizens. In many instances, parents do not take their children with them due to the high cost of care in urban areas and concerns over the loss of cultural values (Ruiz-Casares, 2010). Children are often left with relatives in rural areas. As such, large numbers of children in Namibia do not live with their parents, even when those parents are alive. In fact, according to the NDHS 2013, 28% of children are not living with either parent although both are alive, suggesting that many children in Namibia are still cared for by relatives (MOHSS & ICF International, 2014). Unfortunately, no research has documented how many children in Namibia may find themselves in a temporary CHH situation due to migration for employment (Mturi, 2012).

We have suggested that different factors, including the loss of parents through the HIV epidemic as well as migration of adults for employment, have contributed to the potential for the emergence of CHHs. A further factor has been the general weakening of the extended and kinship care system due to the increasing number of orphans and number of children living without their parents (Foster, 2000; Kuhanen et al., 2008). Previous research in Namibia has highlighted the importance of child fostering by other family members as a mechanism to care for children (Brown, 2011). Children are often moved "within and outside of large extended kin networks" for various reasons including better access to education and access to economic resources (p. 155). In the case of orphans, these arrangements are often made before the death of the mother. However, there is a concern that the burden of the HIV/AIDS epidemic in the country may cause this system of care to fail as a result of increasing numbers of orphans due to parental death (Brown, 2011). Nevertheless the extended family system remains a considerable resource, illustrated by the generally low numbers of CHHs in Africa despite the orphan crisis. The national prevalence of CHHs in Namibia is just under 2%, with the highest prevalence in the northern regions (NSA, 2013) and rural areas (64%). These households tend to be headed by older adolescents (Ruiz-Casares, 2009).

Few data are available on the situation of CHHs in Namibia, with only two qualitative studies reporting on this issue. Both studies were conducted in the northern and predominantly rural areas of Namibia, where CHHs tend to be more common. Kuhanen et al. (2008) interviewed eight child- and junior-headed households as well as key informants in the Oshikoto and Oshana regions. Junior heads of households were older than 18 years but were included because, according to the authors, local communities perceived and referred to them as "children." In the second study, we interviewed 33 child and youth heads of households between 9 and 21 years of age in the Caprivi, Kavango, and Omusati regions (Ruiz-Casares, 2009). We found that the majority of heads were female (64%), and most were double orphans (64%), although 1 in 10 still had both parents living. The majority of households were formed due to unavailability or unwillingness of relatives to provide support (27%), others because they were commanded (20%) or because of the children's own choice (23%). Both studies found that the households were in economically vulnerable conditions and depended on handouts as the main source of income. While Kuhanen et al. (2008) found that households rarely got support from relatives living outside of the household, we found that the majority of participants (73%) received some form of material support from relatives, and the presence of an adult who oversaw things served as a protective factor for households (Ruiz-Casares, 2009). Heads also relied on working for others and farming as a source of income and material support. Households had fewer assets: fewer had electricity, toilet facilities, or a heating system during the winter months (59%) when compared to what was expected for the respective regions, and the majority of households experienced food insecurity, with 80% reporting going to bed hungry (Ruiz-Casares, 2009). Kuhanen et al. (2008) found that many heads had to drop out of school to take care of siblings and that economic hardship could push junior heads to higher risk behavior to obtain an income.

RECIPROCITY AND PARENTING IN CHILD-HEADED HOUSEHOLDS IN NAMIBIA

Numerous studies have documented how children heading household display concern and protect, care, and provide for their younger siblings (Donald & Clacherty, 2005; Yanagisawa et al., 2010). In so doing, these heads seek and receive support from others, and at times they themselves are sought for assistance, too. Reciprocity, a pattern of exchange with consequences for both individual development and social stability, has received little attention from scholars studying CHHs. This reciprocity contributes to (1) developing and maintaining a strong sense of self-esteem and useful coping strategies, particularly threatened in the context of parental separation[5]; (2) promoting well-being, as equality of support has been associated with mental health among youth and adults (Antonucci & Jackson, 1990; Taniguchi & Ura, 2002, 2005); (3) balancing personal relationships and maintaining or increasing availability of support over time[6]; and (4) building children's skills and social responsibility as contributing members of their communities. We propose, then, the use of the degree of reciprocity of exchange as an indicator of balance in power relations and of stability of the child's position in social networks (Hanneman & Riddle, 2005). The following two cases[7] from work we have conducted in Namibia illustrate family dynamics after parental death or separation among CHHs and help advocate for children as reciprocal support resources, to be treated not only as receivers or targets of support, but also as active agents in their own lives and potential supporters of others. We also highlight how practices of parenting in CHHs are influenced by the practices observed and learned when their parents were living with them. We will show how children preserve points of continuity with practices of their parents as well as points of difficulty for CHHs as they navigate their roles and responsibilities.

Mukuve: Redefining Family in the Light of Mutuality

Mukuve, a 16-year-old head of household in the Kavango region, was interviewed as part of a research study by the first author. Mukuve is the second in a family of six children: the eldest sister passed away recently leaving behind a baby who is also living at home. The five siblings and young nephew occupy several huts made of sticks, mud, and cow-dung covered with grass and, in one case, corrugated iron sheets. The bottoms of empty green glass bottles half-buried in the ground colorfully mark the entrance to the compound. There is no running water or electricity; a stream nearby provides water, and, in the absence of any toilet facility, they "go to the bush." They use wood for cooking, blankets to combat the cold (no heating), and candles (when they can afford them) for lighting. The house is neat, clean, quiet, and feels safe despite its darkness and (relative) isolation.

They are living on their own "because they do not have relatives to look after them." With a nervous smile, Mukuve admitted: "No relatives are visiting us, not even when my mother was sick or when she died. I don't know why." At the death of their father 5 years earlier, purportedly due to malaria, the paternal relatives took the cattle away and never visited again. Their mother died several months before the interview, due to "lack of blood." She left some goats and also her bed and the huts the children still occupy. When asked whether they would have liked to be taken in by relatives, he readily answered: "No! Because they don't look after us, they never come to visit us, they don't care for us." Things were different before their mother passed away: "People came here. From nearby villages, they came to ask for food. Now, they don't come anymore. It is a big difference for me because now it's just me going to my friends."

Only four people come to Mukuve for assistance: Mukonda, a male friend of about his age who provides companionship, advice, emotional support, and validation; Shikongo, an older neighbor "who always gives us advice about how we should live" and for whom Mukuve collects *mahangu*[8] from the field for pay (less than 1 US$ per day); and two of his younger brothers, Theophilus and Kamene—"We take care of each other, give advice to each other and, when we are unhappy, we share." Mukuve is the one who looks after and disciplines children—"If the children are quarrelling, I talk to them and separate them." He is also the one to cook meals—"because the others go to school"—fetch wood and water, clean the house, wash clothes, tend animals, and, when they have any money (usually from fishing and selling the catch), he decides how it should be spent and shops for groceries. Life without his siblings would be too difficult, "because on Saturday and Sunday they help to look after the goats."

Aggregate results for all 27 children interviewed as part of this study show a similar portrait. Children heads of household were asked to reflect on the times that others came to them for help. The relevance of mutuality for children was illustrated by significant correlations between reciprocity and the children's primary networks (p = .000), indicating that reciprocity is at the base of close relationships. Findings from this study also revealed that although children's networks were supportive (n = 288, μ = 10.7) (Ruiz-Casares, 2010), symmetry was low (n = 72, μ = 2.67, range = 0–6), and it did not affect children's satisfaction with their network members. While local sharing without an immediate expectation of repayment tells much about the social context of solidarity and skillful stretching of resources among community members in a context of poverty and survival, and one in which family obligations face changing demands and expectations of care, network balancing[9] may not be the most prevalent form of reciprocity surrounding CHHs. This raises an important issue about the concept of reciprocity and its measurement in a culturally valid way. Future research would benefit from surveying providers and recipients and delving into motives and expectations of the different actors involved.

In general, physical proximity seemed to play a more important role than social proximity; nonetheless, limited mobility in rural areas may confound both types. While friends, relatives, and neighbors did ask children for help, no significant association was found between reciprocity and type of relationship (Table 10.1). In contrast, children were more likely to be sought for assistance by people who lived nearby and interacted with them at least weekly (p = .000). In the case of Mukuve, a larger number of young people than adults turned to children for assistance, particularly in search of advice and help with schoolwork; sometimes they lent each other clothes, toiletries, food, or tools, and plaited each other's hair. This reciprocity may be facilitated by (more) equal power relations (Furman & Buhrmester, 1985) as assistance from similars is often considered as less threatening (Fisher, Nadler, & Whitcher-Alagna, 1982).[10] Not surprisingly, adults rarely sought children for advice, but rather looked to them for "piece work" such as childcare, fetching water or firewood, washing clothes or pots, cleaning the yard, looking after the cattle, or, as in Mukuve's case, plowing their fields.[11]

People who provide all kinds of assistance except material aid turned to children for help. The idea that instrumental support is more likely to be asymmetrical than other types of support (Wellman, 1981) makes even more sense when working with children and in contexts of limited material and financial resources. Relations where power or resource differentials are present generally display little or no reciprocity (Gouldner, 1960; Wellman, 1981). Very few teachers (8%), for

Table 10.1 PERCEIVED SOURCES OF RECIPROCITY BY ROLE RELATIONSHIPS AND AGE GROUPS (N = 356)

Role Relationships							**Age Groups**						
Kin (n = 158)			**Non-kin (n = 198)**				**Children (n = 180)**			**Adults (n = 176)**			
n	μ n^a	SD^a	n	μ n^a	SD^a	χ^2	n	μ n^a	SD^a	n	μ n^a	SD^a	χ^2
30	1.11	1.22	42	1.56	1.28	.27	42	1.56	1.67	30	1.11	1.22	2.18

^{a} Results are calculated on aggregated averages for 27 cases; $^*p \le .05$; $^{**}p \le .01$; $^{***}p \le .001$ (two-sided).

instance, turned to children for assistance. Asymmetric ties largely shape the structure of supportive networks by creating and maintaining a stratified social system characterized by substantial differences in access to power and scarce resources (Wellman, 1981). In fact, not only does social stratification put children in a position of subordination, but also inexistent or unequal exchanges of goods and services may engender or sustain exploitative relations. In this line, the presence of nonsupporters who nonetheless seek children's assistance and the number of network members who turn to children for instrumental support raises concerns about potential instances of abuse. A significant association between positive feedback and unspecified service requested from children may corroborate this concern ($p < .05$) and resonates with problematic situations such as the "sugar daddy/mommy"[12] phenomenon documented in Namibia (Cockcroft et al., 2010). In the case of assistance from organizations, asymmetry may reinforce dependency in children and lead adults (mostly relatives) to neglect their obligations toward children. Further explorations of these associations with a broader sample of children are needed.

Reciprocity strengthens relationships while, at the same time, stronger ties do not require concrete returns. Previous research indicates that between intimates, assistance is offered as a form of insurance for the future, out of affection and/or social pressure and family obligation (Cotterell, 1994). The assumption that relationships will eventually balance themselves over time tends to underlie relationships that involve greater trust and obligation.[13] This is often the case of (close friends and) relatives. Whereas "friends must reaffirm their ties continually, (. . .) kin are not necessarily expected to reciprocate directly as long as they remain members in good standing of the kinship network" (Wellman, 1990, p. 218). Are CHHs considered already out of the kinship network, and, if so, how does this shape the relationships of children with their relatives? Family ties are generally univocally interdependent, not expecting immediate or direct reciprocation but rather acting on "obligation and duty with the exchanges often being generalized" (Scanzoni & Marsiglio, 1991, p. 124). A deferred or communal exchange strategy could in part explain the sizeable number of family members who do not turn to children for help, including relationships with siblings. In some cases, exchanges take place immediately following or preceding a supportive act by a network member. In contrast with the immediate exchange of goods and services, reciprocity may take a broader or deferred approach (mostly with kin and close relations).

Indeed, few siblings ($n = 7$) were listed among all network members (Ruiz-Casares, 2010) and even fewer among reciprocal ties. It is possible that children ignored their acts of unsolicited support or considered their contributions as features of naturally occurring domestic exchanges, thus failing to recognize the specific assistance that they provide to their brothers and sisters. It is also possible that some children understated the support they provide to others, conveying an image of greater need and isolation that may procure them assistance. In contrast, Mukuve highlighted the reciprocal nature of his relationship with his younger brothers. This is in line with findings from other studies documenting mutual emotional care and/or the shared contribution to food production, income generation, and other chores among children in CHHs (Evans, 2011; Francis-Chizororo, 2010; Yanagisawa et al., 2010).

Even if the norm of reciprocity is present in most cultures, the patterns of exchange and the systems of mutual obligations that force people to repay vary significantly worldwide (Gouldner, 1960).[14] Low levels of mutuality with children may be a result of cultural norms (i.e., cultural prohibitions regulating specific supportive repayments) or may also be linked with low expectations of support (Nestmann & Niepel, 1994). The subordinate position of children vis-à-vis adults has been documented in Namibia; for example, a common saying among the Aaumbo of Northern Namibia is that "children are not people, they are children" (Brown, 2013). Just as some children interpreted the reduction in visits and assistance by neighbors and relatives following parental death as a result of their inability to reciprocate,[15] it is possible that children underreported the calls for mutuality because they assess their services as worthless or engage in rather concrete, like-kind of exchanges. These analyses thus establish several areas of opportunity for future inquiry.

Willemina: Parenting Like and Unlike Her Own Parents

Willemina, a single orphan aged 14, lives in a small rural community with her sisters Ana, age 12, and Johanna, who is the head of the household since age 18 years.[16] Willemina and Ana attend the primary school, and Johanna attends the high school in their community. The three have been staying alone in a household for the past 2 years because their mother moved to the city when she fell seriously ill. Their father passed away when Willemina was 8 years old. Although they live alone, they have some telephone contact with their mother and sometimes visit her during holidays.

The household receives some help from relatives. For example, an aunt who lives close by assists with material needs such as food when necessary and, at times, also provides the family with advice. There is also a much older stepsister who helps from time to time, but this is hampered by the fact that she lives very far away and is also ill. Willemina describes the household as functioning quite well, with tasks and activities being divided among the household members. She says: "If I am the one to clean today, then she [Johanna] is the one to clean in the afternoon. And then, if we eat, the little sister will wash the dishes." It seems, however, that the head is responsible for most of the running of the household and for caring and supervision: "When we wake up then my big sister wakes first, and then she boils water for us, like now that she is not at school [finished exams]. Then she pours water for the bath. Then we take a bath. Then she makes our coffee and she makes us sandwiches and then we eat our bread." As in other households in the study, the youngest siblings are allowed to do the least work.

According to Willemina, the main chores and household tasks in their household are conducted in accordance with the way that their mother taught them. For example, when asked who taught her to clean the house, cook the food, and the like, she responds "It's my mother; she is the one that taught us." For example, "on a Sunday when she was busy making a salad then she will call us to come and sit and watch how she is doing it." In the same way, Johanna, who does most of the cooking, learned to cook from her mother. Similarly, their mother used to help with the supervision of homework and now so does the head of the household, Johanna. However, here there are also slight differences: "my mother also helped us, but she only helped me with KKG[17] and with maths," whereas Johanna can help her with all the subjects "she helps me with the first one, then we look if there is any other one, then she helps me with the next one, that is how we do it. And when I finish then she tells me that I have to bath. . . . When we sleep, she also looks at our younger sister's bag to make sure that there is no homework."

In other aspects, differences are rather obvious. Whereas their mother scolded them, Johanna does not like scolding. Their mother never physically hit her, yet Willemina recounts one situation recently where Johanna hit her when she misbehaved—"my sister told me to wash the dishes so I told her 'no' . . . then she hit me. Then I cried and then I washed the dishes"; however, later "she [Johanna] came and asked for forgiveness." The way that Johanna handles the children when emotional problems arise also seems to differ from the way their mother did it. When Ana, the youngest sister, becomes sad and cries because of missing their mother: "We try to calm her. And if there is some money then we buy her something to eat. Johanna will go to her if she is crying and tell her to go and lie down in the room, then she cooks something for her, something nice, and takes it to her. Then she calms down." In contrast, when they got sad, their mother "just scolded." Willemina also mentions the influence of other family members, namely the aunt and the stepdaughter, who may model different caring and supervision behaviors. For instance, she says about her aunt: "She does help us. But she does not scold us. She just tells us what is the way to do it right."

In their comparison of children living in CHHs and other children living in adult-headed households in similar conditions of poverty in South Africa, Donald and Clatcherty (2005) found the former to have greater capacity for emotional support than their peers from the latter group. Children from CHHs also at all times shared food among all the children, no matter how little was available. Thus, despite significant emotional difficulties for children in CHHs, they also tended to display a caring attitude toward their siblings and demonstrated the ability to meet emotional needs and deal with interpersonal conflict. The case of Willemina illustrates this by the way the head provides the younger children with supervision and the way the household tasks are shared and distributed among the different members of the household. Assisting with homework is a theme across other cases in our study. Maria (age 16, the head), who lives alone with her sister Ella (age 15), helps her sister with her schoolwork: "Sometimes, if she did not write her summaries then I write the summaries for her" (see also the case of Jonas, discussed later). However, equal sharing of domestic tasks and chores is not always the case in all CHHs. In Maria's, case she describes how "I clean the house, I do the cooking, I do everything for her. She just waters the garden." Interestingly, when asked about how tasks were distributed when they had lived with their parents and who did the household chores, Maria responds: "It was me . . . and my mother." [So Ella never helped?] "No, she did not. . . ." [And did your mother ever ask your sister to do some of the housework?] "No, never."

In her study of CHHs in rural Zimbabwe, Francis-Chizororo (2010) found that the sharing of household chores, wherein younger siblings help older ones, was a practice usually instilled before the parents died. Age is an important variable in determining who occupies the role of the head, but, at times, the position may be fluid and negotiated between the siblings (Francis-Chizororo, 2010). In the case of Maria and her younger sister, there is only a small age difference of 1 year. This may in part explain the difficulties they had; nonetheless, their challenges may also have been related to the way the household functioned with their parents and how they were repeating the parents practices in their CHH.

The age of the head of the household may also play a role in the parenting practices, particularly when younger children misbehave. Younger heads may rely more on adults for guidance, particularly if the parents are still alive. For example, Jonas, a 13-year-old head who cares for his two sisters (aged 11 and 9) and brother (aged 8) because his mother is sick and unable to live with them, explained that when he tries to help his younger siblings with their homework they do not listen to him. "I just go to my neighbor so that I can phone my mother. Then my mother speaks to them. Like then they listen for the first 2 weeks and then the third week they start again." [Then what do you do?] "I just look at them, but it seems they don't always listen to me." Interestingly, he adds: "they did not misbehave when my mom was here." Indeed, other studies have reported that dealing with younger children's misbehavior is an area of particular difficulty for CHHs (Van Dijk & Van Driel, 2012). When discussing situations where the younger children may contest the authority of the older children, Mavise (2011) comments that "younger children seemed to be aware that the head was only a child despite her [*sic*] seniority, and were able to challenge her [*sic*] authority in ways that could not have been possible if an adult was in charge" (p. 325). In so doing, younger children proved that "they, too, were not simply passive subjects of experiences but also active agents able to influence events and outcomes" (p. 327). It is not clear, though, the extent to which the age gap or age of the head is an issue in how and whether this occurs. Mavise (2011) also reports some cases where having an adult to consult on important decisions may help legitimize the authority of the head, as in the case of Jonas; in other cases, it may limit the power in the households, depending on whether the household perceived the adult as having a full understanding of the situation.

Several of the households in our study shared that the amount of time spent doing household tasks had changed drastically when they started living on their own. In some cases, the chores are shared while in others the responsibility falls only on the head. As Jonas reports: "My mother did everything. She cleaned the house. She cleaned the yard. Only sometimes she asked me and my brother to clean the yard." Similarly, Willemina comments: "When my mother used to stay with us we did not have so much housework. Like after school my mother cooked the food for us, and now Johanna does that." In Tanzania and Uganda, Evans (2012*b*) also reflects on the increase of household tasks taken on often by the head of the household and the older children. Gender roles may also be challenged because the tasks and chores were previously performed by female heads of households, in most cases by the mother. These increased responsibilities experienced by CHHs may contribute to their vulnerability to school dropout and subsequent incomplete education and to lower access to institutional support (Donald & Clacherty, 2005; Kuhanen et al., 2008), particularly for the heads.

Initial findings from our study suggest that the heads of CHHs often adopt parenting practices similar to those of their parents'. However, proximity in age as well as the age of the head may impact the extent of authority between younger and older children and may cause severe distress to the head. More research is needed about parenting practices within CHHs and how these may differ (or not) from the deceased/absent parents'. This can be particularly valuable in the light of the new Child Care and Protection Act (May 29, 2015) in Namibia, which contemplates allowing CHHs "to remain intact, under appropriate adult supervision, if this would be in the best interests of all the children concerned" (Section 225). Any decisions taken by the designated adult or orphan must incorporate consultation with the child head and any children capable of being consulted. Although research has shown that support from members outside of the home is very important (Yanagisawa et al., 2010), other research has shown that such support from, for example, relatives and extended family may also interfere with the agency of the household (Van Dijk & Van Driel, 2012). It is important for the appointed adults to bear in mind the traditions of the family and the practices that the children may have learned from their own parents. For some CHHs, these practices may be a source of pride and help maintain an important connection to their parents and previous adult caregivers. Incorporating the practices learned from their parents may be valuable for young people to feel that they are fulfilling the wishes of their absent parents (Evans, 2011). Simon (age 13), who lives in a CHH with his brother Jakob (the head since age 16), tells us with pride what he learned from his previous caregiver "I learnt something from my grandfather." [Tell me about that?] "He always said that I should use my hands to work. Like I can do needlework, I can wash clothes, I can iron . . . I know how to make and fix fences. And to make those ropes that you use to ride the donkeys, you know. I can do that. I can fix a donkey cart [smiles]."

CONCLUSION

CHHs are a fluid living arrangement that emerge often following parental death. Mostly studied since the 1990s in sub-Saharan African countries ravaged by the HIV/AIDS epidemic, CHHs continue to challenge common understandings of childhood as either a protected time of play and education (Global North) or as subject to adults' decision-making (Global South). They also challenge the common perception that children are left to fend for themselves, completely alone. In contrast, our own research in Namibia (Ruiz-Casares, 2010) as well as studies in other settings have shown that children do maintain and develop supportive relationships with relatives and nonrelatives (including the broader community) and that roles and responsibilities of household members change when children live without adult supervision. Research on intrahousehold relations, as well as relations with extended family, have revealed shifts in family interactions and expectations following parental death or separation.

The sense of obligation that at least partly drives relationships with kin may also be shaken when children live by themselves. In this chapter, we have advanced the use of reciprocity as an indicator of child well-being and social integration. Immediate and deferred reciprocity can serve as a measure of the accessibility and strength of relationships and an indicator of the changing status of children and family dynamics. In turn, lack of reciprocity in individual relationships serves to maintain substantial differences in access to power and resources, to put children in positions of subordination, and to potentially engender or sustain exploitative relations. We continue to challenge the adult-centered perspective on support that places adults as providers and children as receivers exclusively, and we suggest shared coping instead. Providing opportunities to give and receive support in daily matters, and to participate responsibly in relationships and in societal functioning, may not only increase children's self-esteem and help-seeking and -accepting behaviors (Antonucci & Jackson, 1990; Cochran, Larner, Riley, Gunnarsson, & Henderson, 1990; Greenberg & Shaphiro, 1971) but also help balance relationships over time, thus contributing to social stability and securing aid (Gouldner, 1960). Attention must be paid to ensuring that this mutuality of exchange is developmentally appropriate, culturally sensitive, and gives priority to the best interest of the child, creating opportunities for children to feel capable and to develop a sense of independence and responsibility while avoiding behaviors that can put them at risk.

Whereas previous literature in Namibia has shown that family structures are fluid, with children often being cared for by people other than their biological parents (Brown, 2011), the HIV epidemic in particular has introduced specific challenges to these existing modes. In the process of forming a CHH, the family unit is redefined by the absence of adult caregivers. This chapter has reflected on the ways children choose to maintain the practices used by absent parents and caregivers in regards to care and supervision, discipline, and distribution of tasks. This may be an important coping mechanism for household members as they deal with the loss and negotiate the reconfiguration of the family and the multiple challenges they now face by providing a sense of security and continuity with the past. Further attention to children's views and experiences caring for their siblings and how their parenting practices compare to those of their deceased parents or reflect their late wishes would be a valuable addition to the literature.

Many questions remain. To what extent are asymmetrical ties weaker, and what are the implications in the Namibian context? Are children considered resources by themselves, rather than just targets of support until adulthood, or is group membership a prerequisite to reciprocity? More research is warranted to further assess the strength of family ties—the extent to which children are still considered members of the extended family group in spite of living by themselves and whether they are bound by the same rules, privileges, and obligations as their parents were. Only longitudinal, culturally tailored studies will clarify the meaning and significance of reciprocity on child development in a particular cultural context and show whether sustained mutuality in support relationships has any impact on permanent availability of satisfactory support within and beyond family structures (Nestmann & Niepel, 1994). It would be ideal to include full network studies that incorporate perspectives from both recipients and providers of support.

NOTES

1. There are reasons to believe that the age distinction has some utility because while "youths" (>18 years) may not be recognized as social adults, they still may experience advantages owing to a different legal status that enables them to access a broader range of services and make more substantial claims to inheritances. Youths in this sense occupy a particularly liminal category in that they have a legal foothold in adulthood but are not always socially authorized as adults.
2. This term is not specific to children living in CHHs but includes them as they take on a significantly greater set of adultlike responsibilities and are much more involved in care provision activities.
3. Despite the intense feelings that such a situation would provoke, Wood, Chase, and Aggleton (2006) shows how child caregivers are often in the position of having to bracket off their own grieving process in order to focus on comforting younger siblings. An illustrative case provided by Withell (2009) is of an older sibling temporarily hiding the news of their mother's death from younger siblings and fabricating a story about the mother being gone for a trip.
4. The Namibia Household Income and Expenditure Survey (NHIES 2009/10) translates all consumed items by each household into monetary values; if the total consumption of a household is below a certain threshold, they are considered poor. The poverty line for children is a percentage of the adult poverty line and varies by age (i.e., 50% of the adult poverty line for children under 5 years and 75% for children aged 5–16 years).
5. Several authors have emphasized the importance for people of all ages of the need to contribute, to feel that they are useful to others and that they play a significant role in the networks of others (Gottlieb, 1991; Rook, 1987; Wentowski, 1981). There is also evidence that reciprocity helps children develop useful coping strategies and helping experience, making them more resilient to the stresses of separation and developmental transitions (Gottlieb, 1991; Nestmann & Niepel, 1994). This may be because a "preoccupation with the care of others" diverts attention from their own stress or because the children can experience self-esteem, self-efficacy, and control over their caring in an otherwise uncontrollable situation of parental separation and other major life events (Nestmann & Niepel, 1994, p. 325).

6. Individuals engaged in relationships of mutuality benefit not only from the specific exchange of goods, services, and affection, but also from the satisfaction of providing support to others, the maintenance of lasting relationships, and the knowledge that support will be available if needed in the future (Antonucci, Fuhrer, & Jackson, 1990; Wentowski, 1981). Research has shown that not only are reciprocal relationships generally most positively related to life satisfaction (Antonucci et al., 1990; Rook, 1987), but also "the maintenance of reciprocity in support relationships is essential for the permanent availability of satisfactory support" (Nestmann & Niepel, 1994, p. 326).
7. All names have been changed to preserve confidentiality.
8. Local name of pearl millet, the staple food in northern Namibia.
9. Wellman and his colleagues (Wellman, Carrington, & Hall, 1988) distinguish between repayment in the same (*specific exchange*) or different (*generalized reciprocity*) sort of aid that was received, and a more flexible form in which aid is given to a network member within the social circle, not necessarily the original provider of support or the same kind of assistance (*network balancing*). In contrast with the first two types of direct (or restricted) exchange, the latter is a form of generalized or indirect exchange, a mechanism characterized by unilateral resource giving to enhance social solidarity (Takahashi, 2000). Network balancing could be said to occur within kin groups; the assistance that their parents and other relatives previously gave to others may be paying off to some extent now for children, at the same time that it gets them increasingly involved in a domestic circle of obligations. Balanced reciprocity can take place in an immediate or deferred period of time, depending on the intentions and closeness of the people involved (Wentowski, 1981).
10. While equity theorists consider reciprocity as a response to threatening feelings of inequity, the threat to self-esteem model (Fisher et al., 1982) contends that reciprocity may derive from any aid that threatens or supports the recipient feelings of self-worth. From their perspective, people seek less aid when they assess dependency as self-threatening than supportive of their self-esteem. Consequently, not only does type of assistance make a difference, but some authors maintain that adults seem to be more threatened by children than by other adults and thus seek less help from them.
11. In some cases, exchanges take place immediately following or preceding a supportive act by a network member. For instance, children shared how sometimes getting food from neighbors was contingent on their fetching water or cleaning the yard for them first.
12. "Sugar daddy/mommy" refers to an older man/woman who provides reward or support in exchange for sexual relations.
13. Hence, some authors have advocated for a life-long assessment of social exchange (Antonucci & Jackson, 1990; Kahn & Antonucci, 1980). Longitudinal approaches to assess social interactions over time, such as Antonucci and Jackson's (1990) Support Bank system, have the potential to better capture the communal patterns of interaction in Namibia. A view of social support as a resource to be reciprocated over the long term would also enable individuals to continue to be positive about relationships even when they are consistently overbenefitted (Antonucci et al., 1990, p. 521).

14. Since it is the perception of reciprocity that affects well-being, support exchanges need to be assessed within the context of the differing roles, resources, and expectations of reciprocity prevailing in the participating regions.
15. An illustration of this is an old Hambukushu proverb—"the spoon follows the food," which indicates that people with a lot to give have many friends, yet friends disappear when they have nothing to offer (Van Tonder, 1966).
16. Cases reported in this section are part of a study initiated in 2015 in the Khomas region of Namibia. Semi-structured interviews with children in child-only households documented (1) household composition and trajectory, (2) views and experiences with different aspects of parenting, (3) similarities/differences in educating and caring for siblings in comparison with how their parents did it with them, and (4) services that can help children in similar situations. Ethical approval for the study was obtained from Centre de santé et de services sociaux de la Montagne in Canada and the Ministry of Gender Equality and Child Welfare in Namibia.
17. Khoekhoegowab (KKG) is a language spoken by the Damara and Nama people of Namibia.

REFERENCES

Abebe, T., & Aase, A. (2007). Children, AIDS and the politics of orphan care in Ethiopia: The extended family revisited. *Social Science & Medicine, 64*(10), 2058–2069.

Antonucci, T. C., Fuhrer, R., & Jackson, J. S. (1990). Social support and reciprocity: A cross-ethnic and cross-national perspective. *Journal of Social and Personal Relationships, 7*, 519–530.

Antonucci, T. C., & Jackson, J. S. (1990). The role of reciprocity in social support. In B. R. Sarason, I. G. Sarason, & G. R. Pierce (Eds.), *Social support: An interactional view* (pp. 173–198). New York: John Wiley & Sons.

Ayieko, M. A. (1998). *From single parents to child-headed households: The case of children orphaned by AIDS in Kisumu and Siaya Districts.* Geneva, Switzerland: United Nations Development Programme.

Beard, B. J. (2005). Orphan care in Malawi: Current practices. *Journal of Community Health Nursing, 22*(2), 105–115. doi:10.1207/s15327655jchn2202_4

Becker, S. (2007). Global perspectives on children's unpaid caregiving in the family research and policy on "young carers" in the UK, Australia, the USA and Sub-Saharan Africa. *Global Social Policy, 7*(1), 23–50.

Bell, S., & Payne, R. (2009). Young people as agents in development processes: Reconsidering perspectives for development geography. *Third World Quarterly, 30*(5), 1027–1044.

Boris, N. W., Thurman, T. R., Snider, L., Spencer, E., & Brown, L. (2006). Infants and young children living in youth-headed households in Rwanda: Implications of emerging data. *Infant Mental Health Journal, 27*(6), 584–602. doi:10.1002/imhj.20116.

Brown, J. (2011). Child fostering chains among Ovambo families in Namibia, Southern Africa. *Journal of Southern African Studies, 37*(1), 155–176.

Brown, J. (2013). Morals and maladies: Life histories of socially distributed care among Aaumbo women in Namibia, Southern Africa. *Journal of Critical Southern Studies, 1*(1), 60–79.

Burton, L. (2007). Childhood adultification in economically disadvantaged families: A conceptual model. *Family Relations*, *56*(4), 329–345.

Child Care and Protection Act of 2015, No. 3, Republic of Namibia. http://www.lac.org.na/laws/2015/5744.pdf

Ciganda, D., Gagnon, A., & Tenkorang, E. Y. (2012). Child and young adult-headed households in the context of the AIDS epidemic in Zimbabwe, 1988–2006. *AIDS Care*, *24*(10), 1211–1218. doi:10.1080/09540121.2012.661839

Cluver, L., & Gardner, F. (2007). Risk and protective factors for psychological well-being of children orphaned by AIDS in Cape Town: A qualitative study of children and caregivers' perspectives. *AIDS Care*, *19*(3), 318–325.

Cochran, M., Larner, M., Riley, D., Gunnarsson, L., & Henderson, C. R. (1990). *Extending families: The social networks of parents and their children*. Cambridge: Cambridge University Press.

Cockcroft, A., Kunda, J. L., Kgakole, L., Masisi, M., Laetsang, D., Ho-Foster, A., . . . & Andersson, N. (2010). Community views of inter-generational sex: Findings from focus groups in Botswana, Namibia and Swaziland. *Psychology, Health & Medicine*, *15*(5), 507–514. doi:10.1080/13548506.2010.487314.

Cotterell, J. L. (1994). Analyzing the strength of supportive ties in adolescent social supports. In F. Nestmann & K. Hurrelmann (Eds.), *Social networks and social support in childhood and adolescence* (vol. 227, pp. 257–267). New York: Walter de Gruyter.

Dalen, N. (2009). Challenges for orphans in sibling headed households. Assessment of interventions to reduce stigmamin Rakai District, Uganda. *Michael*, *6*, 191–209.

Daniel, M., & Mathias, A. (2012). Challenges and coping strategies of orphaned children in Tanzania who are not adequately cared for by adults. *African Journal of AIDS Research*, *11*(3), 191–201.

Donald, D., & Clacherty, G. (2005). Developmental vulnerabilities and strengths of children living in child-headed households: A comparison with children in adult-headed households in equivalent impoverished communities. *African Journal of AIDS Research*, *4*(1), 21–28.

Drah, B. (2014). "Older women," customary obligations and orphan foster caregiving: The case of queen mothers in Manya Klo, Ghana. *Journal of Cross-Cultural Gerontology*, *29*(2), 211–229. doi:10.1007/s10823-014-9232-y.

Evans, R. (2010). Children's caring roles and responsibilities within the family in Africa. *Geography Compass*, *4*(10), 1477–1496.

Evans, R. (2011). "We are managing our own lives. . . ": Life transitions and care in sibling-headed households affected by AIDS in Tanzania and Uganda. *Area*, *43*(4), 384–396.

Evans, R. (2012*a*). Safeguarding inheritance and enhancing the resilience of orphaned young people living in child-and youth-headed households in Tanzania and Uganda. *African Journal of AIDS Research*, *11*(3), 177–189.

Evans, R. (2012*b*). Sibling caringscapes: Time–space practices of caring within youth-headed households in Tanzania and Uganda. *Geoforum*, *43*(4), 824–835.

Fisher, J. D., Nadler, A., & Whitcher-Alagna, S. (1982). Recipient reactions to aid. *Psychological Bulletin*, *91*(1), 27–54.

Foster, G. (2000). The capacity of the extended family safety net for orphans in Africa. *Psychology, Health & Medicine*, *5*(1), 55–62.

Foster, G., Makufa, C., Drew, R., & Kralovec, E. (1997). Factors leading to the establishment of childheaded households: The case of Zimbabwe. *Health Transition Review*, *7*(2), 155–168.

Francis-Chizororo, M. (2010). Growing up without parents: Socialisation and gender relations in orphaned-child-headed households in rural Zimbabwe. *Journal of Southern African Studies*, *36*(3), 711–727.

Furman, W., & Buhrmester, D. (1985). Children's perceptions of the personal relationships in their social networks. *Developmental Psychology*, *21*(6), 1016–1024.

Germann, S. E. (2006). An exploratory study of quality of life and coping strategies of orphans living in child-headed households in an urban high HIV-prevalent community in Zimbabwe, Southern Africa. *Vulnerable Children and Youth Studies*, *1*(2), 149–158.

Gottlieb, B. H. (1991). Social support in adolescence. In M. E. Colten & S. Gore (Eds.), *Adolescent stress: Causes and consequences* (pp. 281–306). New York: Gruyter.

Gouldner, A. W. (1960). The norm of reciprocity: A preliminary statement. *American Sociological Review*, *25*(2), 161–178.

Greenberg, M. S., & Shaphiro, S. P. (1971). Indebtedness: An adverse aspect of asking for and receiving help. *Sociometry*, *34*(2), 290–301.

Guenther, M. (1991). The world of the Kxoe Bushmen: A review article. *Anthropos*, *86*, 213–219.

Haley, J. F., & Bradbury, J. (2014). Child-headed households under watchful adult eyes: Support or surveillance? *Childhood*, *22*(3), 394–408. doi:10.1177/0907568214548282

Hanneman, R. A., & Riddle, M. (2005). Introduction to social network methods. Retrieved from http://faculty.ucr.edu/~hanneman/.

Heymann, J., Earle, A., Rajaraman, D., Miller, C., & Bogen, K. (2007). Extended family caring for children orphaned by AIDS: Balancing essential work and caregiving in a high HIV prevalence nations. *AIDS Care*, *19*(3), 337–345. doi:10.1080/09540120600763225

International Organization for Migration. 2016. Migration in Namibia: A country profile 2015. Retrieved from https://publications.iom.int/system/files/pdf/mp_namibia_for_web_14june2016.pdf

Kahn, R. L., & Antonucci, T. C. (1980). Convoys over the life course: Attachment, roles, and social support. In P. B. Baltes & O. Brim (Eds.), *Life span development and behavior* (vol. 3, pp. 253–286). New York: Academic Press.

Kipp, W. E., Satzinger, F., Alibhai, A., & Rubaale, T. (2010). Needs and support for Ugandan child-headed households: Results from a qualitative study. *Vulnerable Children and Youth Studies*, *5*(4), 297–309.

Köhler, O. (1989). *Die Welt der Kxoé-Buschleute im südlichen Afrika. Eine Selbstdarstellung in ihrer eigenen Sprache; Bd.1: Die Kxoé Buschleute und ihre ethnische Umgebung.* Berlin: Dietrich Reimer Verlag.

Kuhanen, J., Shemeikka, R., Notkola, V., & Nghixulifwa, M. (2008). Junior-headed households as a possible strategy for coping with the growing orphan crisis in northern Namibia. *African Journal of AIDS Research*, *7*(1), 123–132.

Kuo, C., & Operario, D. (2009). Caring for AIDS-orphaned children: A systematic review of studies on caregivers. *Vulnerable Children and Youth Studies*, *4*(1), 1–12. doi:10.1080/17450120802270418.

Kürzinger, M., Pagnier, J., Kahn, J. G., Hampshire, R., Wakabi, T., & Dye, T. (2008). Education status among orphans and non-orphans in communities affected by AIDS in Tanzania and Burkina Faso. *AIDS Care, 20*(6), 726–732.

Landry, T., Luginaah, I., Maticka-Tyndale, E., & Elkins, D. (2007). Orphans in Nyanza, Kenya: Coping with the struggles of everyday life in the context of the HIV/AIDS pandemic. *Journal of HIV/AIDS Prevention in Children & Youth, 8*(1), 75–98.

Lane, T., Cluver, L., & Operario, D. (2015). Young carers in South Africa: Tasks undertaken by children in households affected by HIV infection and other illness. *Vulnerable Children and Youth Studies, 10*(1), 55–66.

Lee, L. M. (2012). Youths navigating social networks and social support systems in settings of chronic crisis: The case of youth-headed households in Rwanda. *African Journal of AIDS Research, 11*(3), 165–175.

Luzze, F. (2002). *Survival in child-headed households: A study on the impact of world vision support on coping strategies in child-headed households in Kakuuto County, Rakai District, Uganda.* Master's thesis. University of Leeds.

Malan, J. S. (1995). *Peoples of Namibia.* Wingate Park: Rhino Publishers.

Malinga-Musamba, T. (2015). The nature of relationships between orphans and their kinship carers in Botswana. *Child & Family Social Work, 20*(3), 257–266. doi:10.1111/cfs.12121.

Mandali, V. M. (2006). *A situational analysis of child-headed households and community foster care in Tamil Nadu and Andhra Pradesh States, India.* India HIV/AIDS Alliance.

Maqoko, Z., & Dreyer, Y. (2008). Child-headed households because of the trauma surrounding HIV/AIDS. *HTS Teologiese Studies/Theological Studies, 63*(2), 717–731.

Mavise, A. (2011). Child-headed households as contested spaces: Challenges and opportunities in children's decision-making. *Vulnerable Children and Youth Studies, 6*(4), 321–329.

Meintjes, H., Hall, K., Marera, D.-H., & Boulle, A. (2010). Orphans of the AIDS epidemic? The extent, nature and circumstances of child-headed households in South Africa. *AIDS Care, 22*(1), 40–49. doi:10.1080/09540120903033029

Mmari, K. (2011). Exploring the relationship between caregiving and health: Perceptions among orphaned and non-orphaned adolescents in Tanzania. *Journal of Adolescence, 34*(2), 301–309. doi:http://dx.doi.org/10.1016/j.adolescence.2010.05.001.

Mogotlane, S., Chauke, M., Van Rensburg, G., Human, S., & Kganakga, C. (2010). A situational analysis of child-headed households in South Africa. *Curationis, 33*(3), 24–32.

Ministry of Health and Social Services. (2014). *Surveillance report of the 2014 national HIV sentinel survey.* Retrieved from http://www.mhss.gov.na/files/downloads/12f_2014%20National%20HIV%20Sentinel%20Survey.pdf.

Ministry of Health and Social Services & ICF International. (2014). *Namibia demographic and health survey 2013.* Retrieved from https://dhsprogram.com/pubs/pdf/FR298/FR298.pdf.

Mturi, A. J. (2012). Child-headed households in South Africa: What we know and what we don't. *Development Southern Africa, 29*(3), 506–516.

Nestmann, F., & Niepel, G. (1994). Social support in single-parent families: Children as sources of support. In F. Nestmann & K. Hurrelmann (Eds.), *Social networks and social support in chidhood and adolescence* (vol. 227, pp. 323–345). New York: Walter de Gruyter.

National Planning Commision. (2012). *Namibia's Fourth national development plan (NDP4)*. Retrieved from https://www.npc.gov.na/?wpfb_dl=37.

National Planning Commision. (2013). Namibia 2013: *Millenium development goals: Interum progress report no. 4*. Retrieved from http://www.na.undp.org/content/dam/namibia/docs/MDGsReports/undp_na_MDGs Report 24Sept13.pdf.

Namibia Statistics Agency (2012*a*). Child poverty in Namibia: A child-centred analysis of the NHIES 2009/2010. Retrieved from https://www.unicef.org/socialpolicy/files/Namibia_Child_Poverty_Report.pdf

Namibia Statistics Agency. (2012*b*). *Poverty dynamics in Namibia: A comparative analysis using the 1993/94, 2003/04 and the 2009/10 NHIES Surveys*. Retrieved from http://cms.my.na/assets/documents/p19dnar71kanl1vfo14gu5rpbkq1.pdf.

Namibia Statistics Agency. (2013). *Namibia 2011. Population and housing census. Main report*. Retrieved from https://cms.my.na/assets/documents/p19dmn58guram30ttun89rdrp1.pdf

Namibia Statistics Agency. (2015*a*). *Namibia 2011 Census: Migration Report*. Retrieved from https://cms.my.na/assets/documents/Migration_Report.pdf

Namibia Statistics Agency. (2015*b*). *Namibia Labour Force Survey 2014 Report*. Retrieved from http://www.ilo.org/wcmsp5/groups/public/---africa/---ro-addis_ababa/---ilo-pretoria/documents/publication/wcms_368595.pdf.

Payne, R. (2012). "Extraordinary survivors" or "ordinary lives"? Embracing "everyday agency" in social interventions with child-headed households in Zambia. *Children's Geographies, 10*(4), 399–411.

Phillips, C. (2011). Child-headed households: A feasible way forward, or an infringement of children's right to alternative care? Amsterdam: Charlotte Phillips.

Richter, L. M., & Desmond, C. (2008). Targeting AIDS orphans and child-headed households? A perspective from national surveys in South Africa, 1995–2005. *AIDS Care, 20*(9), 1019–1028.

Roalkvam, S. (2005). The children left to stand alone. *African Journal of AIDS Research, 4*(3), 211–218.

Robson, E., Ansell, N., Huber, U., Gould, W., & van Blerk, L. (2006). Young caregivers in the context of the HIV/AIDS pandemic in sub-Saharan Africa. *Population, Space and Place, 12*(2), 93–111.

Rook, K. S. (1987). Reciprocity of social exchange and social satisfaction among older women. *Journal of Personality and Social Psychology, 52*(1), 145–154.

Rotheram-Borus, M. J., Leonard, N. R., Lightfoot, M., Franzke, L. H., Tottenham, N., & Lee, S.-J. (2002). Picking up the pieces: Caregivers of adolescents bereaved by parental AIDS. *Clinical Child Psychology and Psychiatry, 7*(1), 115–124. doi:10.1177/1359104502007001009.

Ruiz-Casares, M. (2007). How did I become the parent? Gendered Responses to New Responsibilities Among Namibian Child Headed-Households. In Dianne Hubbard and Suzanne LaFont (Eds.), *Unraveling Taboos: Gender and Sexuality in Namibia* (pp. 18–166). Windhoek, Namibia: Legal Assistance Centre.

Ruiz-Casares, M. (2009). Between adversity and agency: Child and youth-headed households in Namibia. *Vulnerable Children and Youth Studies, 4*(3), 238–248. doi:10.1080/17450120902730188.

Ruiz-Casares, M. (2010). Kin and youths in the social networks of youth-headed households in Namibia. *Journal of Marriage and Family, 72*(5), 1408–1425.

Scanzoni, J., & Marsiglio, W. (1991). Wider families as primary relationships. In T. D. Marciano and M. B. Sussman (Eds.), *Wider families: New traditional family forms* (pp. 117–133). Binghamton, NY: The Haworth Press.

Schenk, K., Ndhlovu, L., Tembo, S., Nsune, A., Nkhata, C., Walusiku, B., & Watts, C. (2008). Supporting orphans and vulnerable children affected by AIDS: Using community-generated definitions to explore patterns of children's vulnerability in Zambia. *AIDS Care, 20*(8), 894–903.

Takahashi, N. (2000). The emergence of generalized exchange. *The American Journal of Sociology, 105*(4), 1105–1134.

Tamasane, T., & Head, J. (2010). The quality of material care provided by grandparents for their orphaned grandchildren in the context of HIV/AIDS and poverty: A study of Kopanong municipality, Free State. *SAHARA J (Journal of Social Aspects of HIV/AIDS Research Alliance), 7*(2), 76–84.

Taniguchi, H., & Ura, M. (2002). Support reciprocity and depression among elementary school and high school students. *Japanese Psychological Research, 44*(4), 247–253.

Taniguchi, H., & Ura, M. (2005). Support reciprocity and depression among children. *Advances in Psychology Research, 33*, 219–229.

Thurman, T. R., Snider, L., Boris, N., Kalisa, E., Nkunda Mugarira, E., Ntaganira, J., & Brown, L. (2006). Psychosocial support and marginalization of youth-headed households in Rwanda. *AIDS Care, 18*(3), 220–229.

Tsegaye, S. (2007). *HIV/AIDS and the emerging challenge of children heading households.* Addis Abeba, Ethiopia: The African Child Policy Forum.

United Nations Children's Fund. (2015). *State of the world's children 2015: Reimagine the future.* New York: Author.

United Nations Development Programme. (2015). Human development report 2014: Work for human development. Retrieved from http://hdr.undp.org/sites/all/themes/hdr_theme/country-notes/NAM.pdf

Van Dijk, D., & Van Driel, F. (2012). Questioning the use-value of social relationships: Care and support of youths affected by HIV in child-headed households in Port Elizabeth, South Africa. *African Journal of AIDS Research, 11*(3), 283–293.

Van Rensburg, G., Human, S., & Moleki, M. (2013). Psycho-social needs of children in child-headed households in South Africa. *Commonwealth Youth and Development, 11*(1), 56–69.

Van Tonder, L. L. (1966). *The Hambukushu of Okavangoland. An anthropological study of South-Western Bantu people in Africa.* Port Elizabeth: Express Litho Services.

Ward, L. M., & Eyber, C. (2009). Resiliency of children in child-headed households in Rwanda: Implications for community based psychosocial interventions. *Intervention, 7*(1), 17–33.

Wellman, B. (1981). Applying network analysis to the study of support. In B. H. Gottlieb (Ed.), *Social Networks and Social Support* (1st ed., pp. 171–200). London: Sage.

Wellman, B. (1990). The place of kinfolk in personal community networks. In D. G. Unger & M. B. Sussman (Eds.), *Families in community settings: Interdisciplinary perspectives* (pp. 195–228). Binghamton, NY: Haworth.

Wellman, B., Carrington, P. J., & Hall, A. (1988). Networks as personal communities. In B. Wellman & S. D. Berkowitz (Eds.), *Social structures: A network approach* (1st ed., pp. 130–184). Cambridge: Cambridge University Press.

Wentowski, G. J. (1981). Reciprocity and the coping strategies of older people: Cultural dimensions of network building. *The Gerontologist, 21*(6), 600–609.

Withell, B. (2009). The prebereavement psychological needs of AIDS-affected adolescents in Uganda. *International Journal of Palliative Nursing, 15*(3), 128–133.

Wood, K., Chase, E., & Aggleton, P. (2006). "Telling the truth is the best thing": Teenage orphans' experiences of parental AIDS-related illness and bereavement in Zimbabwe. *Social Science & Medicine, 63*(7), 1923–1933.

World Bank. (2013). *World Bank development indicators.* Retrieved from: http://data.worldbank.org/indicator.

Yamba, C. B. (2005). Loveness and her brothers: Trajectories of life for children orphaned by HIV/AIDS in Zambia. *African Journal of AIDS Research, 4*(3), 205–210.

Yanagisawa, S., Poudel, K. C., & Jimba, M. (2010). Sibling caregiving among children orphaned by AIDS: Synthesis of recent studies for policy implications. *Health Policy, 98*(2), 121–130.

11

Parenting From Prison

The Reality and Experience of Distance

JOYCE A. ARDITTI AND JONATHON J. BECKMEYER

The United States has the highest incarceration rate in the world, with approximately 6.9 million persons under some form of correctional supervision (Glaze & Herberman, 2013). A great number of these incarcerated person are parents confined in local, state, and federal facilities. Parental separation as a result of incarceration is a potentially adverse childhood experience affecting at least 1.7 million children and adolescents representing 2.3% of the US population under 18 years old at any one point in time (Glaze & Maruschak, 2008). More recent estimates indicate that 5 million youth, or 7% of all US children, experience parental incarceration at some point before reaching the age of 18 (Murphey & Cooper, 2015). The growth in the numbers of incarcerated parents reflects the widespread practice of mass imprisonment in the United States, which signifies a rate of incarceration well above the historical and comparative norm and renders carceral confinement ubiquitous for whole social groups based on their race, age, and class (Garland, 2012; King, Mauer, & Young, 2005).

In this chapter, we examine what mass imprisonment means with regard to the experience of parenting. Approximately 52% of state and 63% of federal inmates have children under age 18; the portion of the inmate population that are parents has grown approximately 79% from 1991 to 2007 (Glaze & Maruschak, 2008). This increase has been more pronounced among mothers compared to fathers, as the number of incarcerated mothers has increased by 131% (compared to 77% for fathers) since 1991 (Glaze & Maruschak, 2008). Among incarcerated females, motherhood is most common among women who are younger (25–34 years old) and married; however, white, black, and Hispanic, as well as more and less educated incarcerated women, are equally likely to be mothers (Glaze & Maruschak, 2008). Focusing on the demographics of women who are incarcerated, however, does not take into account the persistent racial and economic disparities in incarceration. For example, black children are three times more likely to have an incarcerated mother than are white children (Wakefield & Wildeman, 2014). Therefore, although motherhood is quite common across incarcerated women, incarceration is most likely among African-American women.

What do these profound shifts mean for a significant number of individuals who might attempt to parent from prison and maintain family ties? As a group, empirical evidence suggests that, even after controlling for other general risk markers (e.g., substance abuse, parental mental health, and environmental risks), parental incarceration predicts behavior problems and poor developmental outcomes for children (Dallaire, Zemen, & Thrash, 2015; Johnson, 2009; Murray, Farrington, & Sekol, 2012; Turney, 2014; Wakefield & Wildeman, 2014). Although the burgeoning literature has begun to address the implications of parental incarceration for children's development, a critical aspect of understanding outcomes involves considering how incarceration alters imprisoned parents' family roles and dynamics. Here, we focus on the processes that bear on parenting from prison. We first consider incarceration as a context for parenting, highlighting key intraindividual and family processes that shape incarcerated persons' parenting experiences. We end our chapter with a brief discussion of policy and practice interventions aimed at incarcerated parents and their families.

INCARCERATION AS A CONTEXT FOR PARENTING

The United States currently incarcerates a greater proportion of its population than at any other point in history and at a much higher rate than other democracies (World Prison Population List, 2013). We may have almost 5% of the world's population, but the United States houses about 25% of the world's inmates (National Association for the Advanced of Colored People [NAACP], 2011), and the American "prison boom" seems to have limited "crime fighting" benefits, particularly as individuals who are incarcerated today are quite different from those who were incarcerated in previous generations. Incarceration used to be reserved for the most serious violent offenders, but today's prisoner is likely to be a person of color, involved in a petty or nonviolent offense, and a parent (Wakefield & Wildeman, 2014). For example, racial and ethnic minorities make up more than 60% of the prison population (The Sentencing Project, n.d.*a*), with blacks, on average, eight times more likely to be in prison than whites (Pettit & Western, 2004). These disproportionate rates reflect that incarceration is concentrated among individuals of color, particularly blacks and Hispanics (Lopez & Light, 2009; Pettit & Western, 2004). Moreover, Mass incarceration also disproportionately affects those of lower sociodemographic status, effectively foreclosing economic mobility for the most marginal in society and creating a viscous and intergenerational cycle of poverty and crime (Western & Pettit, 2004, 2010).

In this manner, mass imprisonment is believed to correspond and contribute to deepening socioeconomic, racial, and ethnic disparities between African-Americans and whites, and, more recently Hispanics, who have been the fastest growing imprisoned subpopulation in the past decade (Lopez & Light, 2009). These disparities extend to youth, with 1 in 4 black children born in 1990 having a father in prison compared to less than 4% of white children (Wildeman, 2009); youth with parents in prison are more likely to go to the prison themselves (Western & Pettit, 2010). In addition to racial and ethnic disparities, incarcerated individuals are also likely to have experienced intense histories of cumulative disadvantage including criminal victimization and perpetration, mental illness, substance use and addiction, and economic and residential instability (Arditti, 2012*a*; Phillips & O'Brien, 2012).

In sum, parental incarceration occurs in a context of cumulative disadvantage and economic, social, and racial inequalities. These inequalities extend into the realm of parenting and family functioning. Notably, For children, parental incarceration is associated with numerous other adverse experiences such as homelessness, health inadequacies, exposure to family and neighborhood violence, and parental substance abuse (Murphey & Cooper, 2015; Wakefield & Wildeman, 2014). Moreover, For parents, carceral confinement places limits on the exercise of reproductive and parenting rights on already marginalized men and women (Genty, 2007). In the next section, we examine two important ways incarceration can change parenting and the implications of these changes for families and children.

HOW INCARCERATION CHANGES PARENTING

Incarceration alters parenting in two important ways. First, it significantly disrupts one's parental identity, changing the way parents see themselves. Second, incarceration precludes the enactment of key family and parenting functions, such as membership and family formation, economic support, education and socialization, and the provision of protective care of family members. Patterson (2002) defines these family functions as relational processes—therefore, for parents who engaged in these processes prior to incarceration, their cessation can profoundly impact parent adjustment, children, and their nonincarcerated family members.

Prisonized Parenting Identities

Incarceration can disrupt parental identities by incapacitating the incarcerated parent via the "pains of imprisonment" (Sykes, 1958). These "pains" involve an array of physical and social strategies designed to punish, coerce, and psychologically intimidate prisoners by withholding liberty, goods and services, heterosexual relationships, autonomy, and security. Rapidly expanding prison populations, prison overcrowding, and the abandonment of rehabilitation as the rationale for imprisonment has made prison more alienating and stigmatizing than ever before (Austin & Irwin, 2001; Haney, 2002; Irwin, 2005). Subsequently, more prisoners have experienced the psychological costs of imprisonment for longer periods of time and under more difficult conditions, threatening greater psychological distress and long-term dysfunction (Haney, 2002).

With regard to offender incapacitation stemming from the deprivations associated with prison life, separation from family is "one of the most difficult features of prison life to endure" (Cochran & Mears, 2013, p. 253; Hairston, 1991). The ways parents adapt to the separation and the constraints associated with prison life extract a high cost that goes beyond individual adjustment and has implications for parent–child relationships. *Prisonization* is the process through which incarcerated persons adapt to carceral confinement—a process that involves acculturation to the punitive penal environment through the incorporation of the norms and values of prison life into one's way of thinking, feeling, and acting (Clemmer, 1940). Penal environments require that inmates abandon self-sufficiency and initiative such that they become increasingly dependent on the institutional structure. Haney (2002) elaborates on this process: "Correctional settings surround inmates so thoroughly with external limits, immerse them so deeply in a network of rules and regulations, and accustom them so completely to such highly visible systems of minoring and restraints that internal controls may atrophy or, in the case of especially young inmates, sometimes fail to develop altogether" (p. 40). This institutionalization renders many without an internal compass when the external structure of prison is taken away. Haney (2002) points out that formerly incarcerated persons may not know how to do things on their own or how to refrain from self-destructive behaviors after release from prison.

Prisonization spills over into the realm of family relationships and parenting because it may equate with prisonized *family* identities that run counter to effective and responsible parenting roles due to feelings of distress, helplessness, and a lack of control (Arditti, Smock, & Parkman, 2005; Dyer, Wardle, & Day, 2004). As a result, a great number of mothers and fathers perceive themselves as "losing their place" with their children (Enos, 1997) and feel forgotten (Arditti, Beckmeyer, & Tripp, 2012; Nurse, 2002). A sense of mattering to one's children (i.e., seeing oneself as significant) is a crucial dimension of parental identity (Marshall & Lambert, 2006). Furthermore, prisonized family identities can continue after release and are manifested by a paradoxical dependence on kin that run counter to the enactment of adult roles (Arditti & Parkman, 2011) and a sense that their social identities have been irreparably "spoiled" due to the stigma of incarceration (Crawley & Sparks, 2005; Jones, 2003). Indeed, many incarcerated persons express concerns and fears about their ability to return to family roles upon release (Nurse, 2002; Schmid & Jones, 1991; Tripp, 2009) and doubt their parenting competence (Houck & Loper, 2002). Ultimately, prisonized parental identities can equate with disengagement from family and children and a withdrawal or repression of parental roles. Fragile parental identities undermine parenting efficacy and the ability to be successful and involved in parenting roles (Goldberg & Smith, 2009; Minton & Pasley, 1997).

Incarceration and Parenting Roles

In addition to changes in the incarcerated parent's identity, confinement precludes the enactment of key parenting functions. Child outcomes stemming from parental incarceration depend in part on how much the parent engaged in these functions prior to incarceration (Hagan & Dinovitzer, 1999). Unfortunately, we know little about relationships between children and their incarcerated parents prior to confinement beyond the fact that parental incarceration signals disadvantage (Wakefield & Wildeman, 2014). For example, the social situation of children prior to a parent's incarceration (and in particular paternal incarceration) is characterized by economic difficulties, lower father engagement, and risky or harmful behaviors on the part of the justice-involved parent—such as substance abuse, domestic violence, and antisocial behavior (Phillips, Erkanli, Keeler, Costello, & Angold, 2006; Wakefield & Wildeman, 2014). Yet, there is great heterogeneity in child effects, and a lack of prior involvement on the part of the incarcerated parent does not necessarily mean that his or her imprisonment will not be harmful to his or her children (Geller, Cooper, Garfinkel, & Mincy, 2010; Wakefield & Wildeman, 2014).

A parent's physical presence in the household prior to confinement has been used as one indicator of their role relative to their children. It appears that many parents were living with their children prior to incarceration, with about 64% of mothers and 44% of fathers in residence at the time of admission to prison (Mumola, 2000). Beyond the issue of whether parents were physically present in the household preincarceration, little is known regarding the nature of their relationships with children. National data on federal and state prisoners suggest that incarcerated mothers were more likely to be responsible for children's day-to-day care than were incarcerated fathers (Glaze & Maruschak, 2008), although studies with less representative samples suggest that incarcerated fathers report spending considerable time with their children (Day, Acock, Arditti, & Bahr, 2001; Lattimore, Steffey, & Visher, 2009).

Involvement metrics of justice-involved parents may simply depend on the data source. Recent interview data from children with an incarcerated parent (mostly fathers) and their caregivers were not indicative of highly involved and vital relationships between children and their imprisoned parents preincarceration. Almost half of the children never lived with their incarcerated parent, and more than half the children in the study with an incarcerated parent ($n = 27$) reported the parent as uninvolved or never seeing him or her prior to the incarceration (Arditti, 2015). Other studies with larger samples have found similar results, demonstrating fairly high levels of parental nonresidence (relative to children) and residential instability on the part of incarcerated parents (Johnston, 2001). Despite heterogeneity in the limited data available regarding how involved parents were prior to incarceration, national data reveal that many incarcerated parents were family providers. About half of the parents in state prison reported being the primary financial provider for their minor children, with 75% of those reporting employment and salary or wages in the month prior to their arrest

(Glaze & Maruschak, 2008). Furthermore, children may lose child support as a result of a parent's incarceration, particularly in the case of fathers' incarceration (Arditti, Lambert-Shute, & Joest, 2003; Geller, Garfinkel, & Western, 2011). It seems likely that the loss of parental financial support as a result of incarceration undermines child well-being and increases economic vulnerability for a substantial number of families (Hagan & Dinovitzer, 1999; Murray & Farrington, 2006; Wildeman, 2010).

HOW INCARCERATION CHANGES FAMILY SYSTEMS

Imprisonment not only changes parenting identities and roles for the incarcerated, but has direct and indirect consequences for their families. Criminal justice policy has not been historically formulated with the needs of families in mind. Therefore, because the consequences of incarceration are unintended, unknown, or not chosen by families (Caplan, 2008), family and child effects stemming from parental imprisonment have often been conceptualized as "collateral" (Hagan & Dinovitzer, 1999). Collateral costs of parental incarceration are believed to harm children as a result of family separation as well as to the diminished social and economic capital of families and communities connected to incarcerated persons (Genty, 2002; Hagan & Dinovitzer, 1999; Mauer & Chesney-Lind, 2002; Ramirez-Barrett et al., 2006). A "collateral consequences" perspective highlights the repercussions to families and children of parental incarceration from a macro perspective; however, it falls short of unpacking how family dynamics are altered as a result of a parent's imprisonment. Here, we take a "family perspective," which situates families and children as central to the discourse on criminal justice policies and practices (Arditti, 2012*a*). From a family perspective, parental incarceration is a proximal and dynamic experience that potentially alters the way families function because it necessitates parenting and communicating from a distance within a set of highly constrained parameters. In the next section, family processes that include the incarcerated parent and contribute to the collateral consequences of parental incarceration are discussed.

Incarcerated Parents' Contact With Family

During incarceration, families maintain their relationships through three tangible forms of contact: letter writing, phone calls, and in-person visits. Letter writing is the most common form of family contact (70% of state inmates and 84% of federal inmates), followed by phone calls (53% of state inmates and 85% of federal inmates) and in-person visitation (42% of state inmates and 55% of federal inmates; Glaze & Maruschak, 2008). Mothers seem to have more contact with their children than do fathers (Bales & Mears, 2008; Glaze & Maruschak, 2008), perhaps due in part to less restrictive contact policies that characterize some women's prisons (Hoffmann, Dickerson, & Dunn, 2007). In-person visits are more common when prisoners have less time to serve, families live closer to correctional institutions, families experience fewer problems during visits, and the incarcerated have less conflictual relationships with children's current caregiver (Arditti, Smock, & Parkman, 2005; Glaze & Maruschak, 2008; Poehlmann, 2005*a*).

Although letters, phone calls, and in-person visits allow parents to remain involved in their families' lives, in-person visitation is believed to have the greatest influence on parental roles and relationships during incarceration (Arditti, 2012*a*; Cochran & Mears, 2013). For example, the frequency and quality of in-person visitation are associated with the nature of parent–child relationships (Beckmeyer & Arditti, 2014; La Vinge, Naser, Brooks, & Castro, 2005), parenting stress and mental health (Beckmeyer & Arditti, 2014; Poehlmann, 2005), incarcerated persons' behavior while incarcerated (Cochran & Mears, 2013), and recidivism (Bales & Mears, 2008).

In-person visitation, however, is not a universally pleasant or beneficial experience. In general, the prison environment is not conducive to high-quality family interactions. Visit rooms are often cramped, loud, and lack privacy (Arditti, 2003; Comfort, 2008). Family members may have to endure long waits at the institution before they are able to see each other (Arditti, 2003). The rules that govern visits are designed to maintain order in the visit environment and thus regulate and limit contact between family members and what families can do during visits (Boudin, Stutz, & Littman, 2013; Shlafer, Loper, & Schillmoeller, 2015). For example, families may be limited to a single short hug at the beginning and end of a visit, but, for the rest of the visit, they have to sit opposite one another (Hairston, 2007). For children in particular, the restrictions on contact and activities during visits can make visitation both a boring experience and emotionally overwhelming, possibly leading to increased stress levels for children and parents (Poehlmann-Tynan et al., 2015). Finally, it is increasingly common for correctional institutions, particularly local jails, to institute *no-contact* visit policies (Arditti, 2003) wherein the incacerated and their families are not allowed to physically touch each other due to being physically separated by a barrier (Boudin et al., 2013; Shlafer et al., 2015).

The potential for in-person visitation to elicit negative experiences has led scholars to label in-person visits as a *developmental paradox* as they can facilitate but also undermine family relationship and role maintenance (Arditti, 2012*b*). For example, researchers have found that the quality rather than the frequency of in-person visitation is associated with parent–child relationship quality (Beckmeyer & Arditti, 2014; Poehlmann, 2005). During visits, parents, children, and other family members may experience emotional distress and pain akin to what they felt when parents were first arrested and incarcerated (Arditti, 2003; Arditti & Savla, 2013; De Masi & Bohn, 2010). To avoid reexperiencing emotional distress and/or experiencing visitation problems, prisoners may discourage family members from visiting (Arditti et al., 2012; Shlafer & Poehlmann, 2010; Tewksbury & DeMichelle, 2005).

Although imprisoned parents have opportunities to interact with children and family members, incarceration significantly impedes their ability to maintain, enact, or strengthen their parenting role. Parent–child relationships are typically maintained and strengthened through shared leisure activities and by providing warmth, support, and guidance during times of distress (Brotherson, Yamamoto, & Acock, 2003; Gray & Steinberg, 1999). Incarcerated parents are prevented from these processes due to restrictions in the time they can spend with children, the activities they can engage in, and the physical affection they can show children. The limited opportunities incarcerated parents have to engage in parenting can increase parenting distress and decrease parental competency (Loper, Carlson, Levitt, & Scheffel, 2009; Tuerk & Loper, 2006). Separation from children is believed to be the most damaging aspect of women's imprisonment in particular (see Bloom, Owen, & Covington, 2003; Costa, 2003), with mothers' loss of contact with their families and children a primary barrier to maintaining family relationships. Compared with male prisoners, the disruption to the parenting and family roles experienced by incarcerated mothers ultimately make reintegration and family reunification more difficult following release (Bloom et al., 2003). Due to the limited opportunities to engage in direct parenting of their children, incarcerated parents, particularly mothers, shift their beliefs regarding what constitutes *good parenting*, choosing to focus on improving their parenting skills and being knowledgeable about what is going on in their children's lives (Faris & Miller, 2010; Richie, 2001). Incarcerated parents may also shift their parenting role into one of primarily co-parenting or "co-cargiving" (discussed in the next section).

Enacting a *prisonized identity* (as discussed earlier) can lead incarcerated parents, particularly fathers, to pull away (e.g., refusing visits or phone calls) from their family roles and relationships to avoid the emotional pain associated with being separated from their children. We refer to the narratives incarcerated parents create surrounding this process as a *discourse of distance*, viewing it as a way for imprisoned parents to manage the conflicting feelings of both wanting to matter for their children, but also desiring to avoid the emotional pain that can accompany seeing their children while still incarcerated (Arditti et al., 2012). For example, researchers have found that fathers may avoid contact with their children in order to simplify the experience of "doing time" and due to their shame about where they were in life and a preference for not wanting their children to see them so "down and out" (Arditti et al., 2005; Edin, Nelson, & Paranal, 2001). Incarcerated mothers are also keenly aware of their failure to live up to cultural prescriptions of good motherhood, along with how their imprisonment has impacted their children, and may find visits distressing (Arditti & Few, 2008; Hairston, 1991). The "push–pull" of in-person visits during confinement illustrates the "visitation paradox" (Arditti, 2012*b*) and the underlying psychological processes that create distance between incarcerated parents and their kin. That is, on the one hand, in-person visits are essential for parents to "be remembered" and stay connected to family. Yet, visits involve the potential for painful emotions and identity confusion for confined parents and their families. Comments from a qualitative analysis of fathers in jail in Florida illustrate this paradox (Arditti et al., 2012; Tripp, 2009). A desire to avoid emotional strain and pain appears to underlie men's decisions to avoid contact or, at the very least, reinforce boundaries that keep fathers' distant enough from children to maintain some level of emotional detachment. For example, Greg, a 32-year-old, single African-American father of six children ranging in age from 14 months to 8 years, described the reason he does not like to talk with his youngest son on the phone:

> It's hurtin', it's been hurtin' bad, I mean, cause I ain't never been away from him for more than 2 days since he's been born. . . . He's been missing me. I talked to him for the first time you know, since I been in here, I didn't really want to talk to him, but I talked to him for just a little bit on the phone.

Another father in the study, Ozzy, also noted how hard visits could be and why he avoided getting too close to family: "I don't get as close to my old lady as I used to, I don't think it'd ever change anything with my daughter, it just depresses me more, the more I see her grow, the more she learns I haven't witnessed (her life)."

Therefore, a significant issue for incarcerated parents is how they construct this "discourse of distance" and how they perceive mattering for their children. As illustrated by Ozzy's comments, incarcerated parents acknowledge that they are limited in what they can do for their children and are likely to miss many important milestones in their children's lives. Parental absence during these times can serve to weaken both parents' and children's commitment to each other, resulting in severed ties (Edin et al., 2001). Incarcerated parents who want to be remembered by their children and kin while incarcerated may make more consistent efforts to have contact with their children (Arditti et al., 2012; Houck & Loper, 2002). Vital and functional family ties can potentially support positive parental identities and allow for the reestablishment of noncriminal relational bonds and roles upon release (Martinez, 2009; Maruna & Roy, 2007).

Co-Parenting

In the context of parental incarceration, coparenting involves contributing to children's care by communicating with their caregivers to learn about children's activities and well-being and discussing parenting issues pertaining to one's children. Researchers have previously found that when incarcerated parents are active co-parents, they have greater contact with their children, children have better behaviors, and incarcerated persons are better able to transition back into their parenting roles following release (Arditti & Few, 2008; Baker, McHale, Strozier, & Cecil, 2010). Incarcerated parents' ability to co-parent, however, is determined by children's caregivers, who can prevent or enhance contact between the incarcerated, their children, and other family members (Arditti, 2012*a*; Roy & Dyson, 2005). Incarcerated mothers may have an easier time being an active co-parent because their children are mostly being cared for by a maternal relative

(Enos, 2001; Hanlon, Carswell, & Rose, 2007) who is more likely to try to keep the parent involved in their children's lives (Cecil, McHale, Strozier, & Pietsch, 2008). Incarcerated fathers' children, on the other hand, are most often cared for by the children's biological mothers, who may or may not have a continued relationship with children's fathers (Nurse, 2002).

Maternal Gatekeeping and Paternal Incarceration

Co-parenting in contexts of parental nonresidence can be challenging in the best of circumstances. Even in family situations that do not entail a parent's imprisonment (e.g., parental divorce), adults may struggle to engage in cooperative co-parenting after separation (Arendell, 1995; Beckmeyer, Coleman, & Ganong, 2014; Sobolewski & King, 2005). In households involving parental nonresidence, tasks central to effective co-parenting involve the need to navigate boundary changes and power shifts in the family along with accepting the loss of control over certain aspects of children's lives (Emery, 1994). This loss of control can be difficult for incarcerated parents to accept, given that imprisonment is by definition involuntary and the incarcerated must completely rely on their children's caregiver for any form of contact—a scenario rife with the possibility of discontent. Men's ties with their children are seen as particularly fragile (Brodsky, 1975; Roy & Dyson, 2005), given that children with incarcerated fathers typically reside with their mothers (who are past or current intimate partners of male inmates) and may be spread across multiple households (Hairston, 2009; Nurse, 2002). The notion that mothers control fathers' access to their children is referred to as "maternal gatekeeping" (Allen & Hawkins, 1999). Since intimate relationships tend to deteriorate as a result of imprisonment, it is no surprise that incarcerated men may feel cut off from their families. Family scientists Kevin Roy and Omar Dyson (2005) characterize maternal gatekeeping in prison contexts as the "babymama drama" reflecting a "risky balance of conflict and support between incarcerated fathers and their former or current partners" (p. 296). Several qualitative studies have revealed that incarcerated fathers believe their children's mothers actively discouraged contact with their children (Arditti et al., 2005; Edin et al., 2001; Nurse, 2002). Therefore, the quality of incarcerated fathers' relationships with their children will largely depend on the quality of their relationships with children's mothers (Tach, Mincy, & Edin, 2010).

Maternal Incarceration and Co-Caregiving

In contrast to residential patterns for children affected by paternal incarceration, children with mothers in prison or jail are relatively unlikely to live with their other parent (i.e., biological fathers). Rather, children experiencing maternal incarceration tend to live with relatives and most frequently maternal kin (Cecil et al., 2008; Glaze & Maruschak, 2008). Loper, Phillips, Nichols, and Dallaire

(2014) refer to the co-parenting relationships between incarcerated mothers and their children's caregivers as "co-caregiving relationships" to reflect the reality of children's corresponding nonparental care arrangements. Co-caregivers who are relatives, as opposed to estranged intimate partners, are believed to do more to keep the incarcerated parent's psychological presence alive for their children and facilitate contact during confinement (Cecil et al., 2008). Positive co-caregiving appears to be particularly likely in instances when incarcerated mothers report warm and accepting relationships with maternal grandmothers and trust the care they are providing for children (Loper & Clarke, 2013).

Yet co-caregiving relationships among incarcerated mothers are not without vulnerability as women in prison often report histories of troubled family relationships that may be difficult to mend (O'Brien, 2001). Fragility in co-caregiving relationships may also stem from caregivers, shame and disappointment in the incarcerated mother (Hungerford, 1996), as well as differing perspectives between caregivers and the mothers with regard to guiding children (Loper et al., 2014; Tuerk, 2007). In sum, co-caregiving relationships can be a source of connection or distress for mothers. A higher sense of alliance with children's caregivers is a protective factor for incarcerated parents, associated with fewer depressive symptoms (Loper et al., 2009) and more frequent mother–child communications (Houck & Loper, 2002).

Kin Support as a Cultural Asset

Up to this point, we have discussed the multiple vulnerabilities that seem to characterize incarcerated parents and their families and the disproportionate and negative impact of parental incarceration on families of color. Whereas research on parental incarceration documents a great deal of risk especially for children, there is an emerging literature that examines family strengths and the resilience of incarcerated parents and their family members. *Resilience* refers to positive adaptation in the context of significant adversity (Masten & Powell, 2003). Kinship ties may be a culturally unique protective mechanism among African-American families (Hall, 2007), although it bears repeating that the experience of parental incarceration can be difficult for even the most resilient families, and the criminal justice research yields a relatively superficial understanding of the implications of race and ethnicity for those involved in the criminal justice system (Haskins & Lee, 2016).

Some insight regarding how culture may be a source of family resilience can be gleaned from the qualitative research, which has identified protective factors within the family that seem to lessen vulnerability and enhances competence under stress. African-American families in particular may possess characteristics that enhance the likelihood of positive developmental trajectories for children under adversity due to resourcefulness, broad and flexible family boundaries, and supportive kin networks (Burton, 1992; Jarrott, 2010; Miller, 2007). Resilient kin networks that characterize many African-American families include a strong sense of familial obligation and robust systems of mutual aid that render children a "collective responsibility" (Moras, Shehan, & Berardo, 2007). The view and practice of sharing responsibility for children is a cultural asset of incarcerated parents and their children, particularly in cases of maternal incarceration in which families typically require a great deal of assistance (Arditti, 2012*a*; Hanlon et al., 2007). For example, nonparental care has been identified as a risk factor for children that can undermine adjustment and well-being, with kin arrangements connected to the best child outcomes and placement stability, particularly for African-American children (McWey & Sevenson Wojciak, 2015; Vandivere, Yrausquin, Allen, Malm, & McKlindon, 2012). Children's close relationships with relative caregivers have been documented among African-American youth with incarcerated mothers, as well as the fact that African-American mothers are more likely to have family members care for their children during their incarceration than are white mothers (Enos, 1997). Other literature has also pointed to the positive benefits for at-risk African-American children of interacting with multiple caregivers in the context of family adversity and parental unavailability (e.g., Brown, Cohon, & Wheeler, 2002; Hall, 2007).

PROGRAMS AND POLICIES SUPPORTING PARENTING WHILE INCARCERATED

Incarceration is a challenging nonresidential context from which to parent from afar. We have noted that incarceration significantly disrupts parental identity and roles, contact between parents and children, and the quality of family relationships. In the face of these challenges, kin support seems to be a particularly important cultural asset among criminal justice–involved families. As we conclude this chapter, we focus on how ongoing reforms to criminal justice policy and correctional institutional policies and practices can help reduce the collateral consequences of parental incarceration.

The experience of parental incarceration may be most impacted by recent efforts to reform criminal justice policy away from the use of mass incarceration, particularly for first-time and/or nonviolent criminal offenders (Travis, 2014). Specifically, states and the federal government have reduced or eliminated mandatory minimums, reduced the sentences of certain types of prisoners, and expanded the use of probation and parole (Porter, 2013). Recent trends show declines in the prison populations of 34 states, and the overall US state prison population has declined by 2.4% since 2009 (The Sentencing Project, n.d.*b*). Yet the downward trend in prison population growth is modest and largely driven by the release of prisoners in California's overcrowded facilities as well as the taxing economy of incarceration on government budgets (Glaze & Herberman, 2013; Minton, 2011). Regardless of the causes, even small departures from mass incarceration policy equate with fewer families experiencing parental incarceration and its significant collateral consequences. However, it is important to note that justice-involved families are likely experiencing other types of disadvantage that may still place them at risk for less than optimal family outcomes (Arditti, 2012*a*; Murphey & Cooper, 2015).

From a family perspective, central challenges involve reducing confinement's disruptions to parental identities and roles, enhancing incarcerated parents' contact with children, and facilitating positive co-caregiving processes. Correctional institutions may attempt to reduce collateral consequences of parental incarceration by offering programs specifically for parents and/or changing visitation policies when children visit their parents (Hoffmann, Byrd, & Kightlinger, 2010). For example, many prisons offer parenting education programs that aim to increase knowledge of child development and effective parenting behaviors and increase parenting self-efficacy (Loper & Tuerk, 2006). Such programs may help imprisoned parents maintain their parental identities and help them continue to feel as if they matter for their children. Researchers have found that incarcerated parents are particularly interested in parenting programs as a way to strengthen and perhaps even rebuild their family relationships (Kazura, 2001). Evaluations of prison-based parent education programs support their effectiveness, finding that they can improve parenting knowledge, attitudes, and competency as well as increase co-parenting with children's current caregivers (Loper & Tuerk, 2011; Sandifer, 2008).

A persistent limitation of parenting programs, however, is that they typically only involve the incarcerated parent (Hoffmann et al., 2010). Thus, these programs often do not provide imprisoned parents with meaningful opportunities with their children to use the skills and knowledge they have learned in the prison classroom. Although in-person visits can provide opportunities for meaningful family and parenting interactions, the typically loud, chaotic, and controlled visiting experience also makes it difficult to act like a family during in-person visits (Arditti, 2003; Kazura, 2001). In order to address the numerous problems associated with traditional in-person visits, some correctional institutions have developed family-friendly visits. Family-friendly visits attempt to address the problems typically associated with in-person visits by creating an environment conducive to normal family interactions by relaxing rules about physical contact and movement (Dunn & Arbuckle, 2002). Family-friendly visits may also provide activities for children so they do not have to sit still for the entire visit. A benefit of these less structured visits is that they can provide incarcerated parents with opportunities to engage in meaningful parenting for practice skills they may be learning in parent education programs (Sandifer, 2008), which may help parents maintain their parental identity. Some correctional institutions provide imprisoned parents and their children opportunities to participate in traditional youth development programs (e.g., Boy Scouts, Girl Scouts, 4-H) inside the institution (e.g., Block & Potthast, 1998; Dunn & Arbuckle, 2002). The nature of these programs requires parents and their children to work together to achieve positive goals, allowing parents and children to build their relationships through the types of shared leisure activities that are common outside of prison.

A final way to support incarcerated parents and their children involves efforts to strengthen family ties, particularly at reentry. In recent years, family-focused reentry support strategies have proliferated. These programs largely aim at encouraging the individual's desistance from crime after release from jail or prison under the logic that leveraging family support will contribute to more successful reentry outcomes (Fontaine, Gilchrist-Scott, Denver, & Rossman, 2012). The most effective programs acknowledge former prisoners' often complicated family networks and the needs of family members' themselves. One of the best known programs is the La Bodega/Family Justice Model, which uses culturally sensitive, supportive inquiry techniques to identify strengths of the formerly incarcerated, family strengths, and naturally occurring sources of support (Meyerson & Otteson, 2009). Female kin seem to be particularly important sources of social support for formerly incarcerated individuals returning to their communities (Fontaine et al., 2012). In general, strengths-based, inclusive family support programs for the formerly incarcerated demonstrate modest effects in terms of promoting successful reintegration, although complexities in engaging family members as well as intergenerational dysfunction can pose a challenge to the success of such programs (Meyerson & Otteson, 2009; Fontaine et al., 2012).

In conclusion, efforts to strengthen relationships between incarcerated parents and their family members can make a difference. Throughout the United States, we are beginning to see the first glimmers of criminal justice reform aimed at less punitive sentencing for nonviolent drug offenses and a growing emphasis on rehabilitation (Adelman, 2014; Travis, 2005). Intervention in the context of meaningful criminal justice policy reform holds promise in promoting more positive outcomes for incarcerated parents and their families.

REFERENCES

Adelman, L. (2014). Criminal justice reform: The present moment. *Wisconsin Law Review*, 2015 (2), 181–202. Retrieved from: wisconsinlawreview.org/wp.../Adelman-Final.pdf.

Allen, S. M., & Hawkins, A. J. (1999). Maternal gatekeeping: Mothers' beliefs and behaviors that inhibit greater father involvement in family work. *Journal of Marriage and Family*, *61*, 199–212.

Arditti, J. A. (2003). Locked doors and glass walls: Family visiting at a local jail. *Journal of Loss and Trauma*, *8*, 115–138. doi:10.1080/15325020390168735.

Arditti, J. A. (2012*a*). *Parental incarceration and the family: Psychological and social effects of imprisonment on children, parents, and care-givers.* New York: New York University Press.

Arditti, J. A. (2012*b*). Child trauma within the context of parental incarceration: A family process perspective. *Journal of Family Theory and Review*, *4*, 181–219. doi:10.1111/j.1756-2589.2012.00128.x

Arditti, J. A. (2015). A stress process model of how parental incarceration impacts youth mental health: The role of stigma, stress, and coping. Unpublished raw data.

Arditti, J. A., Beckmeyer, J. J., & Tripp, B. G. (2012, November). Parenting in prison. In M. A. Curran (Chair), *New approaches to studying American families in a changing society.* Symposium conducted at the annual National Council on Family Relations Conference, Phoenix, AZ.

Arditti, J. A., & Few, A. (2008). Maternal distress and women's reentry into family and community life. *Family Process*, *47*, 303–321. doi:10.1111/j.1545-5300.2008.00255.x.

Arditti, J. A., Lambert-Shute, J., & Joest, K. (2003). Saturday morning at the jail: Implications of incarceration for families and children. *Family Relations*, *52*, 195–204. doi:10.1111/j.1741-3729.2003.00195.x.

Arditti, J. A., & Parkman, T. (2011). Young men's reentry after incarceration: A developmental paradox. *Family Relations*, *60*, 205–220. doi:10.1111/j.1741-3729.2010.00643.x.

Arditti, J. A., & Savla, J. (2013). Parental incarceration and child trauma symptoms in single care-giver homes. *Journal of Child and Family Studies*, *24*, 551–561. doi:10.1007/s10826-013-9867-2.

Arditti, J. A., Smock, S., & Parkman, T. (2005). "It's been hard to be a father": A qualitative exploration of incarcerated fatherhood. *Fathering*, *3*, 267–283.

Arendell, T. (1995). *Fathers & divorce*. Thousand Oaks, CA: Sage.

Austin, J., & Irwin, J. (2001). *It's about time: America's imprisonment binge*. Belmont, CA: Wadsworth.

Baker, J., McHale, J., Strozier, A., & Cecil, D. (2010). Mother-grandmother coparenting relationships in families with incarcerated mothers: A pilot investigation. *Family Process*, *49*, 165–184. doi:10.1111/j.1545-5300.2010.01306.x.

Bales, W. D., & Mears, D. P. (2008). Inmate social ties and the transition to society: Does visitation reduce recidivism? *Journal of Research in Crime and Delinquency*, *45*, 287–321. doi:10.1177/0022427808317574.

Beckmeyer, J. J., & Arditti, J. A. (2014). Implications of the visit experience for incarcerated parents' family relationships and parenting role. *Journal of Offender Rehabilitation*, *53*, 129–151. doi:10.1080/10509674.2013.868390.

Beckmeyer, J. J., Coleman, M., & Ganong, L. H. (2014). Post-divorce coparenting typologies and children's adjustment. *Family Relations*, *63*, 526–537. doi:10.1111/fare.12086.

Block, K. J., & Potthast, M. J. (1998). Girl scouts beyond bars: Facilitating parent-child contact in correctional settings. *Child Welfare*, *77*, 561–578.

Bloom, B., Owen, B., & Covington, S. (2003). *Gender-responsive strategies: Research, practice, and guiding principles for women offenders*. Washington, DC: US Department of Justice, National Institute of Corrections.

Boudin, C., Stutz, T., & Littman, A. (2013). Prison visitation policies: A fifty state survey. *Yale Law & Policy Review*, *32*, 149–190.

Brodsky, S. (1975). *Families and friends of men in prison*. Lexington, MA: Lexington Books.

Brown, S., Cohon, D., & Wheeler, R. (2002). African American extended families and kinship care: How relevant is the foster care model for kinship care? *Children and Youth Service Review*, *24*, 53–77.

Brotherson, S. E., Yamamoto, T., & Acock, A. C. (2003). Connection and communication in father-child relationships and adolescent child well-being. *Fathering*, *1*, 191–214.

Burton, L. M. (1992). Black grandparents rearing children of drug-addicted parents. *The Gerontologist*, *32*, 744–751.

Caplan, B. (2008). Externalities. In D. R. Henderson (Ed.), *Concise encyclopedia of economics* (2nd ed.). Indianapolis, IN: Library of Economics and Liberty. Retrieved from http://www.econlib.org/library/Enc/Externalities.html.

Cecil, D. K., McHale, J., Strozier, A., & Pietsch, J. (2008). Female inmates, family caregivers, and young children's adjustment: A research agenda and implications for correctional programming. *Journal of Criminal Justice*, *36*, 513–521. doi:10.1016/j.lcrimjus.2008.09.002.

Clemmer, D. (1940). *The prison community.* New Braunfels, TX: Christopher Publishing House.

Cochran, J. C., & Mears, D. P. (2013). Social isolation and inmate behavior: A conceptual framework of theorizing prison visitation and guiding and assessing research. *Journal of Criminal Justice, 41*, 252–261. doi:10.1016/j.jcrimjust.2013.05.001.

Comfort, M. (2008). *Doing time together: Love and family in the shadow of prison.* Chicago: University of Chicago Press.

Costa, R. D. (2003). Now I lay me down to sleep: A look at overnight visitation rights available to incarcerated mothers. *New England Journal on Criminal & Civil Confinement, 29*, 67–98.

Crawley, E., & Sparks, R. (2005). Older men in prison: Survival, coping and identity. In A. Liebling & S. Maruna (Eds.), *The effects of imprisonment* (pp. 343–365). Cullompton: Willan.

Dallaire, D. H., Zemen, J., & Thrash, T. (2015). Children's experiences of maternal incarceration-specific risks: Predictions to psychological maladaptation. *Journal of Clinical Child and Adolescent Psychology, 44*, 109–122. doi:10.1080/15374416.2014.913248.

Day, R., Acock, A., Arditti, J., & Bahr, S. (2001). From prison to home: Men's reentry into family and community life. Unpublished raw data.

De Masi, M., & Bohn, C. (2010, September). Children with incarcerated parents: A journey of children, caregivers and parents in New York State. Council on Children and Families. Retrieved from http://ccf.ny.gov/files/2413/7968/3887/childincarceratedparents.pdf.

Dunn, E., & Arbuckle, J. G. (2002). *Children of incarcerated parents and enhanced visitation programs: Impacts of the Living Interactive Family Education (LIFE) program.* Columbia: Family and Community Resource Program of University of Missouri-Columbia Outreach and Extension. Retrieved from http:// http://extension.missouri.edu/4hlife/evaluation/reports/G2_lifereport8-02.pdf.

Dyer, W. J., Wardle, B., & Day, R. D. (2004, April). *Fathers in prison: How identity is affected and what it means for the fathers and their children.* Paper presented at the meeting of the Society for Research in Child Development, Atlanta, GA.

Edin, K., Nelson, T. J., & Paranal, R. (2001). *Fatherhood and incarceration as potential turning points in the criminal careers of unskilled men.* Evanston, IL: Institute for Policy Research, Northwestern University.

Emery, R. (1994). *Renegotiating family relationships: Divorce, child custody, and mediation.* New York: Guilford.

Enos, S. (1997). Managing motherhood in prison: The impact of race and ethnicity on child placements. *Women & Therapy, 20*, 57–73.

Enos, S. (2001). *Mothering from the inside: Parenting in a women's prison.* Albany: SUNY Press.

Faris, J., & Miller, J. (2010). Family matters: Perceptions of fairness among incarcerated women. *The Prison Journal, 90*, 139–160. doi:10.1177/0032885510361824.

Fontaine, J., Gilchrist-Scott, D., Denver, M., & Rossman, S. (2012). *Families and reentry: Understanding how social support matters.* Retrieved from http://www.urban.org/sites/default/files/alfresco/publication-pdfs/1001630-Families-and-Reentry-Unpacking-How-Social-Support-Matters.PDF.

Garland, D. (2012). *Punishment and modern society: A study in social theory.* Chicago: University of Chicago Press.

Geller, A., Cooper, C., Garfinkel, I., & Mincy, R. (2010). Beyond absenteeism: Father incarceration and its effects on children's development. *Fragile Families Working Paper: WP09-20-FF.* Retrieved from http://crcw.princeton.edu/workingpapers/wp09-20-ff.pdf.

Geller, A., Garfinkel, I., & Western, B. (2011). Parental incarceration and support for children in fragile families. *Demography, 48,* 25–47.

Genty, P. (2002). Damage to family relationships as a collateral consequence of parental incarceration. *Fordham Urban Law Journal, 30,* 1670–1684.

Genty, P. M. (2007). Some reflections about three decades of working with incarcerated mothers. *Women's Rights Law Reporter, 29,* 11–14.

Glaze, L. E., & Herberman, E. J. (2013, December). *Correctional populations in the US, 2012* (NCJ 243936). Washington, DC: US Department of Justice, Office of Justice Programs.

Glaze, L. E., & Maruschak, L. M. (2008). *Parents in prison and their minor children.* Bureau of Justice Statistics Special Report NCJ222984 [revised 3/30/10]. Washington, DC: US Department of Justice, Office of Justice Programs. Retrieved from http://www.bjs.gov/content/pub/pdf/pptmc.pdf.

Goldberg, A., & Smith, J. (2009). Perceived parenting skill across the transition to adoptive parenthood among lesbian, gay, & heterosexual couples. *Journal of Family Psychology, 23,* 861–870.

Gray, M. R., & Steinberg, L. (1999). Unpacking authoritative parenting: Reassessing a multidimensional construct. *Journal of Marriage and the Family, 61,* 574–587.

Hagan, J., & Dinovitzer, R. (1999). Collateral consequences of imprisonment for children, communities, and prisoners. *Crime and Justice, 26,* 121–142.

Hairston, C. F. (1991). Family ties during imprisonment: Important to whom and for what? *Journal of Sociology and Social Welfare, 18,* 87–104.

Hairston, C. F. (2007). *Focus on children with incarcerated parents: An overview of the research literature.* Baltimore, MD: The Annie E. Casey Foundation.

Hairston C. F. (2009). *Kinship care when parents are incarcerated: What we know, what we can do.* Baltimore, MD: Annie E. Casey Foundation.

Hall, J. C. (2007). Kinship ties: Attachment relationships that promote resilience in African American adult children of alcoholics. *Advances in Social Work, 8,* 130–140.

Haney, C. (2002, January). *The psychological impact of incarceration: Implications for post-prison adjustment.* Retrieved from http://www.urban.org/CraigHaney.

Hanlon, T., Carswell, S., & Rose, M. (2007). Research on caretaking of children of incarcerated parents: Findings and their service delivery implications. *Children and Youth Services Review, 29,* 348–362.

Haskins, A., & Lee, H. (2016). Reexamining race when studying the consequences of criminal justice contact for families. *Annals of the American Academy of Political and Social Science, 665,* 224–230.

Hoffmann, H. C., Byrd, A. L., & Kightlinger, A. M. (2010). Prison programs and services for incarcerated parents and their underage children: Results from a national survey of correctional facilities. *The Prison Journal, 90,* 397–419. doi:10.1177/0032885510382087.

Hoffmann, H. C., Dickerson, G. E., & Dunn, C. L. (2007). Communication policy changes in state adult correctional facilities from 1971 to 2005. *Criminal Justice Review, 32*, 47–64. doi:10.1177/0734016806297646.

Houck, K. D. F., & Loper, A. B. (2002). The relationship of parenting stress to adjustment among mothers in prison. *American Journal of Orthopsychiatry, 72*, 548–558. doi:10.1037/0002-9432.72.4.548.

Hungerford, C. (1996). Caregivers of children whose mothers are incarcerated: A study of the kinship placement system. *Children Today, 24*, 23–34.

Irwin, J. (2005). *The warehouse prison: Disposal of the new dangerous class*. Los Angeles: Roxbury.

Jarrott, R. L. (2010). *Building strong families and communities: Lessons from the field*. Research presentation at the Children, Youth and Families at Risk Annual Conference, May 5, San Diego, California.

Johnston, D. (2001). *What works for children of prisoners: The "Children of Criminal Offenders in the Community" study*. Paper presented at the Annual Research Conference of the International Community Corrections Association, Philadelphia, PA.

Johnson, R. C. (2009). Ever-increasing levels of parental incarceration and the consequences for children. In S. Raphael & M. Stoll (Eds.), *Do prisons make us safer? The benefits and costs of the prison boom* (pp. 177–206). New York: Russell Sage Foundation.

Jones, R. (2003). Ex-con: Managing a spoiled identity. In J. Ross & S. Richards (Eds.), *Convict Criminology* (pp. 191–208). Belmont CA: Wadsworth: Thomson Learning.

King, R., Mauer, M., & Young, M. (2005). *Incarceration and crime: A complex relationship*. Retrieved from http://www.sentencingproject.org/doc/publications/inc_iandc_complex.pdf.

Kazura, K. (2001). Family programming for incarcerated parents: A needs assessment among inmates. *Journal of Offender Rehabilitation, 32*, 67–83.

King, R., Mauer, M., & Young, M. (2005). *Incarceration and crime: A complex relationship*. Retrieved from http://www.sentencingproject.org/doc/publications/inc_iandc_complex.pdf.

La Vinge, N. G., Naser, R. L., Brooks, L. E., & Castro, J. L. (2005). Examining the effect of incarceration and in-person family contact on prisoners' family relationships. *Journal of Contemporary Criminal Justice, 21*, 314–335. doi:10.1177/1043986205281727.

Lattimore, P. K., Steffey, D. M., & Visher, C. A. (2009). *Prisoner reentry experiences of adult males: Characteristics, service receipt, and outs of participants in the SVOPR multi-site evaluation*. Research Triangle Park, NC: RTI International.

Loper, A. B., Carlson, L. W., Levitt, L., & Scheffel, K. (2009). Parenting stress, alliance, child contact, and adjustment of imprisoned mothers and fathers. *Journal of Offender Rehabilitation, 48*, 483–503. doi:10.1080/10509670903081300.

Loper, A., & Clarke, C. N. (2013). Attachment representations of imprisoned mothers as related to child contact and the caregiving alliance: The moderating effect of children's placement with maternal grandmothers. *Monographs of the Society for Research in Child Development, 78, 41–56*.

Loper, A. B., Phillips, V., Nichols, E. B., & Dallaire, D. H. (2014). Characteristics and effects of the co-parenting alliance between incarcerated parents and child caregivers. *Journal of Child and Family Studies, 23*, 225–241. doi:10.10007/s10826-012-9709-7.

Loper, A. B., & Tuerk, E. H. (2006). Parenting programs for incarcerated parents: Current research and future directions. *Criminal Justice Policy Review, 17*, 407–427. doi:10.1177/0887403406292692.

Loper, A. B., & Tuerk, E. H. (2011). Improving the emotional adjustment and communication patterns of incarcerated mothers: Effectiveness of a prison parenting intervention. *Journal of Child and Family Studies, 20*, 89–101. doi:10.1007/s10826-010-9381-8.

Lopez, M., & Light, M. (2009). *A rising share: Hispanics and federal crime*. Washington DC: Pew Research Center. Retrieved from http://pewhispanic.org.

Marshall, S. K., & Lambert, J. D. (2006). Parental mattering: A qualitative inquiry into the tendency to evaluate the self as significant to one's children. *Journal of Family Issues, 27*, 1561–1582. doi:10.1177/0192513x06290039.

Maruna, S., & Roy, K. (2007). Amputation or reconstruction? Notes on the concept of "knifing off" and desistance from crime. *Journal of Contemporary Criminal Justice, 23*, 104–124.

Martinez, D. J. (2009). *Rekindling family support: Former prisoners and their families, social roles, and informal supports*. Paper presented at the annual meeting of the American Society of Criminology (ASC), Retrieved from http://www.allacademic.com/meta/p127251_index.html.

Masten, A., & Powell, J. (2003). A resilience framework for research, policy, and practice. In S. Luthar (Ed.) *Resilience and vulnerability: Adaptation in the context of childhood adversities* (pp. 1–26). New York: Cambridge University Press.

Mauer, M., & Chesney-Lind, M. (2002). *Invisible punishment: The collateral consequences of mass incarceration*. New York: The New Press.

McWey, L. M., & Stevenson Wojciak, A. (2015). The diverse family contexts of youth in foster care. In J. A. Arditti (Ed.), *Family problems: Stress, risk, and resilience* (pp. 117–131). Malden, MA: John Wiley & Sons.

Meyerson, J., & Otteson, C. (2009). *Strengthening families impacted by incarceration: A review of current research and practice*. St. Paul: Wilder Research. Retrieved from http://www.wilder.org/download.0.html?report=2180.

Miller, K. (2007). Risk and resilience among African American children of incarcerated parents. *Journal of Human Behavior in the Social Environment, 15*, 25–37.

Minton, T. (2011, June). *Jail Inmates at Midyear 2010—Statistical Tables.* Washington, DC: US Department of Justice, Bureau of Justice Statistics.

Minton, C., & Pasley, K. (1997). Fathers' parenting role identity and father involvement. *Journal of Family Issues*, 17, 26–45.

Moras, A., Shehan, C., & Berardo, F. (2007). African American families: Historical and contemporary forces shaping family life and studies. In H. Vera & J. Feagin (Eds.), *Handbook of the sociology of racial and ethnic relations* (pp. 145–160). New York: Springer.

Mumola, C. (2000, August). *Incarcerated parents and their children.* Bureau of Justice Statistics Special Reports (NCJ 182335). Washington, DC: Department of Justice, Office of Justice Programs.

Murphey, D., & Cooper, P. (2015). *Parents behind bars: What happens to their children?* (Publication No. 2015-42). Bethesda, MD: Child Trends, Inc.

Murray, J., & Farrington, D. P. (2006). Evidence-based programs for children of prisoners. *Criminology and Public Policy, 5*, 721–736.

Murray, J., Farrington, D. P., & Sekol, I. (2012). Children's antisocial behavior, mental health, drug use, and educational performance after parental incarceration: A systematic review and meta-analysis. *Psychological Bulletin, 138*, 175–210. doi:10.1037/a0026407.

National Association for the Advanced of Colored People (NAACP). (2011). *Misplaced priorities: Over incarcerate, under educate.* Baltimore, MD: Author. Retrieved from http://naacp.3cdn.net/ecea56adeef3d84a28_azsm639wz.pdf.

Nurse, A. M. (2002). *Fatherhood arrested: Parenting from within the juvenile justice system.* Nashville: Vanderbilt University Press.

O'Brien, P. (2001). Just like baking a cake: Women describe the successful ingredients for successful reentry after incarceration. *Families in Society, 82*, 287–295.

Patterson, J. M. (2002). Integrating family resilience and family stress theory. *Journal of Marriage and Family, 64*, 349–360.

Pettit, B., & Western, B. (2004). Mass imprisonment and the life course: Race and class inequality in US incarceration. *American Sociological Review, 69*, 151–169.

Phillips, S., Erkanli, A., Keeler, G., Costello, J., & Angold, A. (2006). Disentangling the risks: Parent criminal justice involvement and children's exposure to family risks. *Criminology and Public Policy, 5*, 677–702.

Phillips, S., & O'Brien, P. (2012). Learning from the group up: Responding to children affected by parental incarceration. *Social Work in Public Health, 27*, 29–44.

Poehlmann, J. (2005). Incarcerated mothers' contact with children, perceived family relationships, and depressive symptoms. *Journal of Family Psychology, 19*, 350–357. doi:10.1037/0893-3200.19.3.350.

Poehlmann-Tynan, J., Runcion, H., Burnson C., Maleck, S., Weymouth, L., Pettit, K., & Huser, M. (2015). Young children's behavioral and emotional reactions to Plexiglas and video visits with jailed parents. In J. Poehlmann-Tynan (Ed.), *Children's contact with incarcerated parents: Implications for policy and intervention* (pp. 39–58). New York: Springer.

Porter, N. D. (2013). *The state of sentencing 2012: Developments in policy and practice.* Washington DC: The Sentencing Project.

Ramirez-Barrett, J., Ruhland, E., Whitham, H., Sanford, D., Johnson, T., & Dailey, R. (2006). *The collateral effects incarceration on fathers, families, and communities.* Retrieved from http://static.prisonpolicy.org/scans/ccj/CEI%20FINAL%2003312006.pdf.

Richie, B. E. (2001). Challenges incarcerated women face as they return to their communities: Findings from life history interviews. *Crime & Delinquency, 47*, 368–389. doi:10.1177/0011287010470030050.

Roy, K. M., & Dyson, O. L. (2005). Gatekeeping in context: Babymama drama and the involvement of incarcerated fathers. *Fathering, 3*, 289–310.

Sandifer, J. L. (2008). Evaluating the efficacy of a parenting program for incarcerated mothers. *The Prison Journal, 88*, 423–445. doi:10.1177/0032885508322533.

Schmid, T. J., & Jones, R. S. (1991). Suspended identity: Identity transformation in a maximum security prison. *Symbolic Interaction, 14*, 415–432.

Shlafer, R. J., Loper, A. B., & Schillmoeller, L. (2015). Introduction and literature review: Is parent-child contact during parental incarceration beneficial? In J. Poehlmann-Tyann (Ed.), *Children's contact with incarcerated parents: Implications for policy and interventions*. New York: Springer.

Shlafer, R. J., & Poehlmann, J. (2010). Attachment and caregiving relationships in families affected by parental incarceration. *Attachment and Human Development, 12,* 395–415. doi:10.1080/14616730903417052.

Sobolewski, J. M., & King, V. (2005). The importance of the coparental relationship for nonresident fathers' ties to children. *Journal of Marriage and Family, 67,* 1196–1212.

Sykes, G. M. (1958). *The society of captives.* Princeton, NJ: Princeton University.

Tach, L., Mincy, R., & Edin, K. (2010). Parenting as a "package deal": Relationships, fertility, and nonresident father involvement among unmarried parents. *Demography, 47, 181–204.*

Tewksbury, R., & DeMichelle, M. (2005). Going to prison: A prison visitation program. *The Prison Journal, 85,* 292–310.

The Sentencing Project (n.d.*a*). *Racial disparity.* Retrieved from http://www.sentencingproject.org/template/page.cfm?id=122.

The Sentencing Project (n.d.*b*). *US prison population trends: Broad variation among states in recent years.* Retrieved from http://sentencingproject.org/doc/publications/inc_Prison_Population_Trends_fs.pdf.

Travis, J. (2005). *But they all come back: Facing the challenges of prisoner reentry.* Washington, DC: The Urban Institute Press.

Travis, J. (2014). Assessing the state of mass incarceration: Tipping point or the new normal? *Criminology & Public Policy, 13,* 567–577. doi:10.1111/1745-9133.12101.

Tripp, B. (2009). Fathers in jail: Managing dual identities. *Applied Psychology in Criminal Justice, 5,* 26–56.

Tuerk, E. H. (2007). *Parenting from the inside: Assessing a curriculum for incarcerated mothers.* Unpublished dissertation, University of Virginia.

Tuerk, E. H., & Loper, A. B. (2006). Contact between incarcerated mothers and their children: Assessing parenting stress. *Journal of Offender Rehabilitation, 43,* 23–43.

Turney, K. (2014). Stress proliferation across generations? Examining the relationship between parental incarceration and childhood health. *Journal of Health & Social Behavior, 55,* 302–319. doi:10.1177/0022146514544173.

Vandivere, S., Yrausquin, A., Allen, T., Malm, K., & McKlindon, A. (2012). *Children in nonparental care: A review of the literature and analysis of data gaps.* Washington, DC: US Department of Health and Human Services, Office of the Assistant Secretary for Planning and Evaluation.

Wakefield, S., & Wildeman, C. (2014). *Children of the prison boom: Mass incarceration and the future of American inequality.* Oxford: Oxford University Press.

Western, B., & Pettit, B. (2004). Mass imprisonment and the life course: Race and class inequality in US incarceration. *American Sociological Review, 69,* 151–169.

Western, B., & Pettit, B. (2010). Incarceration & social inequality. *Daedalus, 139,* 8–19.

Wildeman, C. (2009). Parental imprisonment, the prison boom, and the concentration of childhood disadvantage. *Demography, 46,* 265–280.

Wildeman, C. (2010). Paternal incarceration and children's physically aggressive behaviors: Evidence from the fragile families and child wellbeing study. *Social Forces, 89,* 285–309.

World Prison Populations List. (2013). 10th Edition. Retrieved from http://images.derstandard.at/2013/11/21/prison-population.pdf.

12

Distance Mothering

The Case of Nonresidential Mothers

MICHELLE BEMILLER ■

Family diversity is the topic of great discussion and debate. The traditional nuclear family is no longer the norm (Coontz, 1992). According to a Pew Research Center analysis of recently released American Community Survey and Decennial Census data, fewer than half of children in the United States (43%) under the age of 18 live in a traditional, nuclear family (i.e., a family with two, married, heterosexual parents). This is a drastic shift when compared to statistics from the 1960s that indicate 73% of children lived in this family form and data from the 1980s that show that 61% of children lived in nuclear families (Livingston, 2014).

The structure of the family in the United States has changed in many important ways. For example, increasing numbers of families consist of dual earners (Boushey, 2011). In addition, ideological shifts have led to more individuals choosing to cohabit rather than marry (Copen, Daniels, & Mosher, 2013; McLanahan, 2004) and to leave marriages that they see as problematic or unsatisfying (Coontz, 2011). As a result of such circumstances, families spend less time together as a unit or are separated geographically from one another, forced to redefine what it means to be a family and the roles and responsibilities of members therein.

There are many configurations and contexts in which families live geographically apart, as illustrated by the various contributions in this volume. This chapter sheds light on distance parenting in the context of divorce or separation, with a specific focus on women who live apart from their dependent children in such circumstances.

Recent Census data suggest that more than 14 million parents were raising 23 million children under the age of 21 on their own while the other parent lived somewhere else (Grall, 2016). In 2014, mothers maintained custody of dependent children in 82.5% of divorced or separated families. In contrast, 17.5% of fathers were awarded sole custody. This figure has not changed significantly since 1994

(Grall, 2016). Earlier data, as far back as the 1880s, illustrate significant shifts in the number of mother-headed families—8% in 1880 to 11% in 1970. From 1970 to 1990, a doubling of this statistic occurred, increasing the number of children in mother-only families to 22% (Kreider & Ellis, 2011). While some of these women were never-married mothers, the numbers still illustrate the more common trend of mothers maintaining the role of primary caregiver and custodian of dependent children.

Since mothers maintain custody of their children in the majority of divorced or separated families, one might ask, why focus on women who do not have custody? The reason is because these families provide a unique opportunity to explore and better understand the complexities of distance parenting through the intersecting lenses of gender and geography. Moreover, because noncustodial mothers do not fit the mothering "norm," these women and their children have a unique familial experience that involves redefining the mother–child relationship and combating cultural stigmas centered on dominant motherhood ideologies. In some cases, mothers and children create families that cope with the distance between them through attempts to accommodate dominant cultural expectations. In other cases, resistance of dominant ideals is the only option (Bemiller, 2010).

This chapter begins with a historical overview of child custody structured to provide important knowledge about potential court outcomes in custody disputes. When mothers lose or give up custody, they fall outside of dominant motherhood expectations. To help the reader situate the noncustodial mothers' experiences with motherhood within dominant cultural ideals, a discussion of what it means to be a mother in Western society is provided. After providing this necessary background, the remainder of the chapter will draw attention to how noncustodial mothers adapt to living apart in a society that expects mothers to be primary caregivers. In other words, the crux of the chapter focuses on how mothers both accept and reject the dominant definition of "mother" and how that impacts how they see themselves as mothers, as well as how they parent their children from a distance—part of which is dependent on their relationship with the custodial parent. The chapter will end with a brief overview of the implications of dominant cultural ideals for women and their children, as well as recommendations for helping women and children in such circumstances.

CHILD CUSTODY AND THE NONCUSTODIAL MOTHER

It is important to note that the majority of research presented in this chapter focuses on women's experiences in Western society. The experiences of families in non-Western societies vary in terms of experiences with motherhood as well as experiences with child custody and family court—some differences are outlined later in this chapter. In Western culture, one of the main reasons that men and women parent their children from a distance is due to separate living arrangements that are the result of divorce, separation, or the breakdown of a more informal intimate relationship (e.g., the couple produced a child or children but never lived together). Historically, in the United States, the collapse of such relationships has occurred within a political climate that has touted two-parent nuclear families as the best environment for children to grow. Debates regarding such arrangements have been waged by scholars. One such notable debate occurred between David Popenoe and Judith Stacey in 2001. Popenoe's (2001) argument claimed the two-parent nuclear family is better for children and that scholars should be concerned with the decline in this family form.

Stacey (2001) argued that scholars must reconceptualize the family and that viewing the family as a positivistic, empirical institution is problematic. Stacey (2001) asserted that the family is not an institution; rather, it is "an ideological, symbolic construct that has a history and a politics" (p. 545). In the United States, this family ideology has typically encompassed heterosexual, married, nuclear, domestic units in which males are the primary breadwinners and females are primarily the homemakers. Research on nonresidential mothers in Western society, as well as on other long-distance parenting arrangements have been criticized for their limited focus on white, middle-class women's experiences with long-distance mothering. As a result, feminists have called for an increase in research on women who fall outside of these parameters. Some of this research is discussed later in this chapter.

The breakdown of the nuclear family has meant an increase in the number of families who are filtered through the family court system. Similar to the culturally specific assumptions associated with families in Western culture, the family court is culturally unique.

Prior to the 19th century, in both divorce and nonmarital cases in the United States, standard practice was to grant custody to mothers (Buehler & Gerard, 1995). This decision was based on gender norms that viewed the mother as the better caretaker of children. Contemporary custody decisions, however, are now based on a determination of the "best interests" of the child statute (King, 2007; Wall & Amadio, 1994). The goal of this doctrine is to ensure that a child is placed in an environment where she or he can thrive physically and emotionally. Many states have gone even further, creating provisions that encourage both parents to be equally involved in their children's lives (Cancian, Myer, Brown, & Cook, 2014).

Such modifications have led to various custody options becoming available to families and the courts. A parent may be awarded *sole custody*—children primarily live with one parent while the other parent has scheduled visitations and occasional overnights with the child. Cancian and colleagues (2014) note that the award of sole custody is often based on a process of bargaining and negotiation. In such cases, the parent who has more power in the relationship (e.g., more financial resources, an attorney during custody proceedings) may be more likely to receive sole parenting (see also Bemiller, 2008).

In contrast, *shared custody*, also known as "shared parenting," is more often awarded when both parents are employed, and it provides an arrangement where dependent children share equal amounts of time with both parents (Cancian et al., 2014; Crosbie-Burnett, 1991). It is also possible for parents to have *split custody*—an arrangement where one child lives with mother and the other child lives with father. Beyond these custody arrangements, it may be the case that children will live with grandparents or other relatives rather than biological parents (Cancian et al., 2014; Seltzer, 1994).

The family court system in the United States is similar to courts in other Western nations (e.g., France, Sweden, England, Wales) in terms of the focus on the best interests of the child, the predominant placement of children with mothers after divorce, and movement toward joint custody arrangements (Fine & Fine, 1994). It is important to note, however, that in non-Western cultures, the process related to both divorce and child custody and visitation is quite different and is often connected to religious belief systems. For example, in some Islamic states, the father is viewed as the guardian of the children; therefore, the best interest of the child is not considered. It would be a violation of religious law for the state to interfere in the father's role as guardian and protector. The courts do, however, emphasize the importance of children maintaining contact with all family members, even those beyond the mother and father (Stark, 2005).

In the United States, mothers are still awarded sole custody more often than are fathers, which makes it all the more significant when mothers do not have custody of their children (Grall, 2016). When mothers are not awarded custody of the child, people often make assumptions that center on personal failings rather than structural impediments of nonresidential mothers, creating a stigma for these women (Babcock, 1997; Bemiller, 2005, 2010).

In reality, women give up or lose custody for a variety of reasons that include personal choice connected to increasing their education or furthering their careers (Bemiller, 2005, 2010; Gustafson, 2005), child choice of residency (Arditti & Madden-Derdich, 1993; Bemiller, 2005, 2010; Fischer & Cardea, 1981), financial difficulties (Bemiller, 2005, 2010; Clumpus, 1996; Fischer & Cardea, 1981; Greif & Pabst, 1988), and mental or physical illness (Bemiller, 2005, 2010; Santora & Hays, 1998; Zuravin & Greif, 1989).

Mothers may voluntarily relinquish custody of their children, or they may be forced to involuntarily relinquish custody. Herrerias (1995) described the voluntary noncustodial mother as someone who has willingly entered into either a formalized legal or informal agreement in which one or more children live with another caretaker, usually their biological father. Women who give up custody voluntarily do so because of work demands, because they are pursuing an education, or because their children wish to live with their fathers (or another guardian).

The involuntary noncustodial mother has been forced to relinquish custody of her children through some form of protective services intervention, criminal confinement, long-term mental or physical health recuperation, child kidnapping, or court custody finding on behalf of someone other than the mother (Bemiller, 2005, 2008; Chesler, 2011; Herrerias, 1995; Kielty, 2006). How custody is relinquished, as well as the custody arrangment, has a significant impact on how women see themselves as mothers (Bemiller, 2005, 2010). Such perceptions align with literature that explores constructions of motherhood in Western cultures.

THE DOMINANT MOTHERHOOD PARADIGM

Mothers who are not awarded custody of their children experience a stigma because they are not living up to the dominant motherhood ideology that permeates Western society (Bemiller, 2005, 2010). Within this ideology, contemporary motherhood is conceptualized through a lens that encourages intensive mothering, comparison, and competition (Chae, 2015). *Intensive mothering* is a form of mothering that requires women to expend massive amounts of energy, time, and money to raise their children (Hays, 1996).

Despite increasing diversity in family forms and configurations, diversity in the definition of motherhood has not been completely embraced. Emphasis is still placed on motherhood as a natural phenomenon, something that should not be questioned (Ahall, 2012). Dominant ideologies of motherhood support self-sacrifice and unconditional love (i.e., intensive mothering). It is an ideology that encourages mothers to cater to their children emotionally and materially. A good mother will worry about her children constantly (Glenn, 1994; Hays, 1996; Johnson, 1997). Such assumptions place a great deal of pressure on women to live up to unrealistic standards. The reality is that motherhood is a political and cultural construction that varies historically and culturally (Gillis, 2002; Gustafson, 2005; Hays, 1996; Hill Collins, 1994; Phoenix, Woollett, & Lloyd 1991). For the most part, the dominant ideology of motherhood has been based on the life experiences of white, middle-class women, thus negating the experiences of all other women (Glenn, 1994; Hays, 1996; Hill Collins, 1994; Phoenix et al., 1991). Assumptions of universal mothering are problematic given the differential access to resources that individuals have based on race, class, gender, sexuality, and, in the case of this chapter, geography/distance.

Because of such differences, not all mothers can (or wish to) participate in the dominant motherhood ideal. There are varying degrees of conformity to the motherhood ideal and competing ideologies of motherhood across socioeconomic lines, cultural community, race, and ethnicity. For instance, Uttal (1996) interviewed 31 working mothers from northern California about the meaning of childcare. The way that mothers defined and internalized the need for childcare demonstrated their contestation of dominant definitions of motherhood. Most notably, Uttal found that the women's discussions of using childcare challenged the assumption that mothers should always be present in their children's lives and that mothers are all-powerful. The women in Uttal's study discussed mothering as transferable and did not feel that it was essential to be in their child's lives 24 hours a day, 7 days a week—a finding that is in stark contrast to the dominant ideology of motherhood.

In her research on working American mothers, Garey (1999) pointed out that working a full-time job forced the mothers to fall outside of the dominant ideology of mothering. While they did practice several strategies to attempt to meet the cultural ideal of motherhood, they ended up resorting to redefinitions of the mothering role that fit better with their lives. To reconcile the contradiction between mothering and working in paid labor, many of Garey's participants began to redefine their mothering role, arguing that "good mothers" provide for their children and, by providing for their children, serve as role models of accomplishment and self-sufficiency. Thus, employment became a dimension of good mothering. This more inclusive definition can also be seen in Hill Collins's (1987, 1994) work on black mothers. Hill Collins (1987) wrote that,

> African-American women have long integrated economic self-reliance with mothering. In contrast to the cult of true womanhood, in which work is defined as being in opposition to and incompatible with motherhood, work for Black women has been an important and valued dimension of Afrocentric definitions of Black motherhood. (p. 124)

Similarly, Aymer (1997) found financial support of family to be an instrumental component of migrant domestic worker's definitions of motherhood. Aymer completed intensive 4-hour qualitative interviews with 26 migrant female domestic workers in Aruba. These women's children lived with relatives while they worked full-time to financially support their family. The women came from relatively poor homes with a non-nuclear structure. They began having children in their mid to late teen years. These demographic characteristics help in better understanding why financial stability plays a role in their definition of motherhood.

Chae (2015) discusses how Korean mothers' experiences of motherhood align with White mainstream definitions. Korean women place a great deal of emphasis on the importance of mothering. Mothers who sacrifice everything for their children are highly valued. In Korea, education is generally highly valued, and the mother's role in helping her child's path toward high levels of education is paramount. Raising a smart child who goes to a prestigious university is very desirable and creates an atmosphere rife with intensive mothering strategies (see also Okizaki & Kim, Chapter 15 in this volume). Such examples illustrate conceptions of motherhood in various contexts, including notions of motherhood through the lens of working mothers as well as migrant mothers. In the case of noncustodial mothers, mothers negotiate not just nontraditional models of parenthood but also the intricacies of parenting from a distance.

NEGOTIATING NONCUSTODIAL MOTHERHOOD

Noncustodial mothers are often marginalized and forced to redefine motherhood because they live apart from their children (Bemiller, 2005, 2010). Given their unique mothering situation, noncustodial mothers offer the opportunity to explore mothering strategies as related to the dominant or ideal construction of motherhood in Western societies. Since she does not live with her children on a full-time basis and is often unable to provide materially for their care, the experiences of the noncustodial mother deviate from the ideology of the "good mother" (see Clumpus, 1996; Fischer & Cardea, 1981; Glenn, 1994; Greif & Pabst, 1988; Gustafson, 2005; Hays, 1996; Snowdon & Kotze, 2012).

Because of this deviation from accepted mothering practices, noncustodial mothers are often labeled as the "other," relative to the norm of two-parent and divorced families in which mothers retain primary custody of children. In other words, the noncustodial mother is measured against the cultural standard of the "good mother," who has her children with her, and the noncustodial father, who is assumed to be continuing in the gender-appropriate role of providing financial support for children while living away from the children. Given her position as "other," the noncustodial mother provides a rich opportunity to better understand the contradictions of motherhood that exist for mothers who do not live with their children on a full-time basis (Bemiller, 2005)—mothers who often parent from a distance.

The byproduct of this contradictory mothering location is often a feeling of stigmatization—sometimes real and at other times perceived. Some mothers are able to point out instances where they have been negatively evaluated because of their custody status, while other mothers do not have explicit examples but discuss the belief that people see them as deviant mothers due to lack of custody (Bemiller, 2005). Similarly, Babcock (1997) conducted in-depth qualitative interviews with 41 noncustodial American mothers who either relinquished physical custody of at least one minor child formally (through the courts) or informally (to another family member). Findings illustrated feelings of stigmatization and its resultant transformation of women's mothering styles. In particular, experiencing stigma resulted in an altering of the mothering role to more closely match social expectations. According to Babcock's analysis, the mothers increased physical visitation and contact by phone and letter, demonstrating their dedication to their children. When these efforts to be more like "traditional" mothers failed, the mothers resisted this dominant ideology and became more like sisters, aunts, or friends to their children. The participants claimed that these relationships were mutually satisfying for themselves and their children.

More than 10 years after the publication of Babcock's study on noncustodial mothers, Bemiller (2010) found that noncustodial mothers were still trying to negotiate motherhood by either accommodating or resisting and redefining dominant definitions of motherhood. Bemiller (2010) completed one-on-one interviews with 16 noncustodial mothers in northeast Ohio. Interviews lasted between 1 and 3 hours. The sample consisted of 12 white women and 4 African-American women, with an average annual income of about $21,000. In this study, some noncustodial mothers attempted to accommodate the ideal definition of motherhood while others resisted and redefined what it meant to be a mother as a result of the geographic divide between themselves and their children. Out of the 16 women interviewed, 7 maintained efforts to accommodate the dominant cultural ideal of motherhood while the remaining 9 moved in the direction of resisting this ideal.

Mothers who accommodated the dominant ideology of motherhood increased their mothering role when they had their children with them for weekends or other special occasions. These mothers never showed signs of resistance to this ideology, which was very difficult to maintain (Glenn, 1994; Hays, 1996). Respondents proudly described the meals they cooked for their children and the toys and clothing that they would buy despite being unable to afford them, as well as how much they helped their children with homework. They also emphasized efforts to maintain communication by phone and letter when they were apart from their children. Their discussions of the mothering role centered on putting their children's needs ahead of their own (Bemiller, 2010).

Mothers who were leaning in the direction of resisting this dominant ideology talked about the restrictive nature of the "ideal mother" definition when children live outside the home. Some women talked about their children as long-distance friends due to the distance between them. The women who were beginning to reject the dominant ideology of motherhood discussed the restrictive nature of this definition when children live outside of the home. They also discussed the importance of pursuing their own happiness through activities like work and enhanced education. Despite such assertions, there were still glimpses of guilt for not being able to maintain intensive mothering standards (Bemiller, 2010).

In a somewhat similar vein, Eicher-Catt (2004) reflects on her experience as a nonresidential mother in a poignant autoethnography. She characterizes herself as a "visiting mother" and "mother yet not mother" (pp. 74–75). Given the "unique temporal and spatial parameters" through which she must mother, Eicher-Catt (2004) discusses her attempts at emulating traditional mothering while struggling with the reality of the distance between herself and her children (p. 81). Such struggles led her to experience an identity crisis as she performs mothering for multiple audiences.

Snowdon and Kotze (2012) note that noncustodial mothers number in the tens of thousands in Aotearoa, New Zealand, and describe the "inside/outside" phenomenon that they experience as they negotiate motherhood (Snowdon & Kotze, 2012, p. 142). These women live "outside," experiencing a marginalized mothering identity, no longer "inside" the normative day-to-day activities of their children. As a result, the women fight to deflect images of themselves as "bad mothers" (Snowdon & Kotze, 2012, p. 145).

Whereas numerous studies point to the stigmatizing effect of nonresidential status, there are certainly examples where women are pleased with their status, which tends to be the case when mothers feel that they are able to actively participate in their children's lives and meet their children's needs. If these women see that their children are happy, they tend to be less stressed about their situation (Babcock, 1997; Greif & Pabst, 1988; Kielty, 2006). For example, in Bemiller's (2010) study described earlier, several respondents accepted their nonresidential positions and were quite content with their lives. Annie is one such mother, who noted,

> I love my life now. I'm young enough still to have the most fun that I've ever had in my adult life. I don't get to see Paul [her son] as much as I would like,

> but the point of being a parent is to raise children to be independent people. (Bemiller, 2010, pp. 178–179)

Relationships With Children and Child Well-Being: Does Distance Matter?

Research on the impact of distance and separation on the mother–child relationship has yielded mixed findings. Several studies indicate either no differences or more positive reports of mothers' general parenting experiences, involvement, and overall satisfaction of noncustodial compared to noncustodial fathers. For example, in some studies, noncustodial mothers report that they remain very involved in their children's lives, both when they have visitation and when their children are with the custodial caregiver (Arditti, 1995; Bemiller, 2005, 2010; Furstenburg, Peterson, Nord, & Zill, 1983; Greif, 1987; Greif & Pabst, 1988; Herrerias, 1984; Maccoby & Mnookin, 1992). Others find that nonresidential mothers' time spent with children varies little from that spent by nonresidential fathers (Greif, 1997; Stewart, 1999*a*, 1999*b*). Furstenburg and colleagues (1983) found that nonresidential mothers were more likely to have higher levels of contact with children than noncustodial fathers. Noncustodial mothers were more likely to visit their children regularly, to have overnight visits, and to write letters and phone the children.

In a mixed-methods study, Herrerias (1984) studied 130 noncustodial mothers and report that roughly 97% maintained an active relationship with their children and that the majority (71%) were happy with their decision to give up custody and with their mother–child relationships. Nearly 77% described their relationships with their children as close and caring. Similarly, Greif and Pabst (1988) found that mothers remained involved with their children after relinquishing custody. Out of 517 noncustodial mothers, roughly 23% of the mothers claimed to be very involved, 33% were somewhat involved, 29% were slightly involved, and 15% were not involved at all.

Maccoby and Mnookin (1992) examined divorced families in California and found that noncustodial mothers were more involved in day-to-day aspects of parenting such as buying clothes, keeping track of doctor appointments, and supervising homework than were noncustodial fathers. Noncustodial fathers also reported more problems monitoring their children's activities during visitation than did noncustodial mothers. Similarly, Arditti (1995) argued that clear distinctions exist between noncustodial mothers and fathers, especially with regard to involvement with children. Mothers were much more likely to feel a connection with their children despite their living arrangements, and mothers were more likely to try to maintain an active relationship with their children through visitation, phoning, and letters.

In a more recent analysis, mothers in Bemiller's (2010) research reported physical visitation and caregiving activities that emulated the ideal construction of motherhood (e.g., cooking for children, helping with homework, shopping for clothing). One specific example from this study comes from a statement made by a woman named Wendy:

> I cook for them. They eat better over here than at their dad's. I pick them up Friday and take them back Sunday night so they eat more here . . . he does a lot of drive-in instant food so that drives me crazy. So here we don't eat out hardly ever. Everything I make so they get home-cooked food and that makes things better. (p. 175)

In contrast, several other studies have found that mothers are just as likely as fathers to have reduced involvement in their children's lives once custody is relinquished. Based on reports from 1,136 custodial fathers, Greif (1987) found that ex-wives were somewhat involved in the lives of their children. Seventy-three percent of the ex-husbands polled indicated that their ex-wives were somewhat or slightly involved in face-to-face visitations with their children, while only 7% of the men indicated that their ex-wives were very involved. Greif (1987) found that mothers tended to be more involved with their children when (1) the father shared responsibility for the break-up with the ex-wife, (2) custody was gained through mutual agreement, (3) the father was earning the higher income, (4) the father was raising one or two children (rather than three or more), and (5) the mother lived nearby.

According to Greif (1997), parents may pay child support and visit their children regularly, but this is not indicative of involvement in their children's daily lives. For example, noncustodial fathers have been dubbed "Disneyland Dads" because they do not actively participate in their children's day-to-day routine (e.g., helping with homework), but instead engage in social and recreational activities (Hetherington, 1993). Stewart has argued a similar phenomenon with nonresidential mothers, pointing out their tendency to participate in just as many leisure activities as nonresidential fathers (Stewart, 1999*a*).

More specifically, Stewart (1999*a*) points out that structural impediments (e.g., living far away, lack of finances) make long-distance parenting difficult for both nonresidential mothers and fathers. Parents who lived farther away from their children were less likely to see their children and, when they did so, were more likely to participate in leisure activities rather than school or organized activities. Parents with low levels of education were more likely to focus on leisure activities when they were with their children. Level of earnings had no impact on the choice to participate in leisure versus school activities. Overall, Stewart's findings revealed that both noncustodial mothers and fathers have similar types of visitation patterns, leading to the conclusion that emotional issues and practical barriers make day-to-day contact with children difficult to maintain regardless of parents' gender (Stewart, 1999*a*).

In a similar analysis using the same dataset, Stewart (1999*b*) found that nonresident mothers were slightly more likely to maintain contact via phone and mail than were fathers. About 30% of nonresident mothers talked to their children several times a week, compared to 20% of fathers. Stewart found no difference between how many times mothers and fathers saw their children during the year. Yet, overall, children spent significantly more weeks visiting nonresident mothers than nonresident fathers. More than two-thirds of nonresident fathers reported never having had their children come to stay with them compared to half of mothers. More than one-third of nonresident mothers reported that their child stayed with them for longer than 1 month in the past year, compared with only 14% of fathers.

All in all, women who maintain contact with their children do so during face-to-face visitations, speaking to children by phone, and sending letters. Such contact has been shown to positively affect children's well-being. Using data from 294 adolescents from the National Longitudinal Study of Adolescent Health who resided with their fathers and stepmothers, King (2007) found that adolescents who were closer to their nonresidential mothers experienced fewer adjustment problems than comparable adolescents. One of the more interesting findings from this research was that black adolescents reported feeling significantly closer to their nonresidential mothers than did whites. King states that this would be a fruitful area for future inquiry but does not speculate as to why this finding exists. We can, however, look to Hill Collins's (1992) scholarship on black mothers for a possible reason. Hill Collins discusses the importance of all family (kinship networks) in raising children in the black community. As such, children in African-American families may be encouraged to maintain stronger ties to nonresidential mothers than are children in white families due to the important cultural emphasis placed on familial ties.

In a study of 1,503 children with nonresident mothers from the National Survey of America's Families (NSAF), Stewart (n.d.), found that regular visitation (at least once a week) with nonresident mothers was related to greater school engagement and less behavioral and emotional problems in both younger (6–11) and older (12–17) children. In addition, financial support from nonresidential mothers led to greater school engagement. Her findings suggest that social and financial involvement in children's lives contributes to child well-being in the case of both nonresidential mothers and fathers.

Relationships with Custodial Caregivers: The Gatekeepers

It is clear that having a relationship with nonresidential parents is beneficial for children's psychosocial development. This has been documented for both nonresidential mothers and fathers (King, 2007; Stewart, n.d.). Research has demonstrated the importance of having positive relationships with custodial caregivers in order to facilitate visitation. When relationships are positive, women are able to see their children more often, and they are better able to make decisions regarding their children's lives (Bemiller, 2005; Kielty, 2006).

In her qualitative analysis of noncustodial mothers, Bemiller (2005) found that loss of power and control to gatekeepers—individuals who have physical custody of the children and control the children's lives—resulted in dissatisfaction with mothering and motherhood. For the mothers in Bemiller's study, there was a connection between the amount of contact that the women had with their children and the level of power and control that the mothers felt that they had over their children's lives. Even though most custody arrangements were mandated in family court, these arrangements were rarely followed by the mothers and custodial guardians. Some women saw their children more than the original plan stipulated, while others were denied access to their children on a regular basis. Thus, the ability to maintain contact and control depended on the relationships that the women had with the guardians of their children. If the women had good relationships, they saw their children more often and had more decision-making power than women in adversarial relations—with one exception. If women were required to have supervised visitation through the family court, they could only have contact with their children when and where the court stipulated. In essence, both custodial caregivers and state supervisors became gatekeepers who were able to deny the women access to and control over their children on a regular basis.

Rachel serves as an example of a case where there was animosity between her and her ex-husband, and she felt that she had no decision-making power in matters related to the upbringing and care of their daughter. All decisions were made by her ex-husband and his new wife:

> They don't tell me of any school functions. If there's something going on the only way I hear of it is from Jessie if she happens to mention it. They don't invite me to anything. Never. She graduated from fifth grade and she's going to a new school. They never once mentioned it. They never once invited me.

This lack of involvement made Rachel feel disconnected from her daughter's life. Her ex-husband regularly told her: "You're not part of her everyday life. We don't even mention your name." Similarly, because of her ex-husband's new wife, another mother, Grace, claimed not being able to speak to her ex-husband and was often prevented from phoning her son. The experiences of both Rachel and Grace emphasize the role that stepmothers may play in the visitation process. Several studies have found the presence of a stepparent to be associated with fewer visitations from the nonresident parent (Aquilino, 1994; McKenry, McKelvey, Leigh, & Wark, 1996; Spruijt & Iedema, 1998). Counter to these findings, Buchanan, Maccoby, and Dornbusch (1996) found that when fathers were happily remarried, they were more amenable to allowing the nonresidential mother to visit the children. Nonetheless, such examples point to how visitation can sometimes be used as a weapon against noncustodial mothers, with custodial parents acting as "gatekeepers" to the children (Bemiller, 2005; Chesler, 2011; Kruk, 2010). Such instances affect women's ability to participate in distance parenting as well as the relationship that the child has with their residential caregiver.

Physical and Emotional Abuse

In addition to denial of visitation, nonresidential mothers have reported abuses that occur in their relationships to their children's other parents prior to divorce or separation, as well as continued abuse during visitation negotiations. In her qualitative analysis of nonresidential mothers, Bemiller (2008) found that all 16 of her respondents had experienced some form of partner abuse during their intimate relationships (e.g., physical, emotional, or sexual abuse). Thirteen of these women cited abuse as the reason for the termination of their relationships. Five of the sixteen women reported charges of intimate partner violence to the police and also brought these charges up during the custody litigation. Unfortunately, the charges were all but ignored by the family court system. This issue of abuse is a concern that has been discussed in other studies as well (see Ford, 2005; Neustein & Lesher, 2005).

After custody was awarded to the fathers, many of the women (n = 12) were further subjected to abuse by their ex-partners, as were their children. This abuse manifested itself in both physical and nonphysical forms, including stalking, threats of physical violence, emotional abuse, and manipulation of their relationship with and access to children. Such violence against women and children has been documented in similar research completed by Neustein and Lesher (2005) and Ford (2005). In both Ford and Neustein and Lesher's research, relationship abuse and abuse of children were discussed at length. Despite such abuses, primary custody of children was still awarded to the abusive father.

Discussion and Implications

Noncustodial mothers parent children in a web of interconnected institutions that include the legal system, the family, and the broader cultural context in which they negotiate through societal interpretations and expectations with regard to motherhood (and consequently, being a mother without one's children). The intersection of the legal system in Western society and meanings attached to gender and family can be seen as women navigate child custody disputes that are difficult for parents and children alike.

The experience of being a nonresidential mother is unique and rife with challenges. Due to gendered expectations that mothers automatically receive custody of their children after divorce or separation, and because of the inextricable nature of the status of women and motherhood in societal views, losing children (or giving children up) to fathers in such disputes leads to the assumption that nonresidential mothers are bad or unfit mothers or that they must have done something unthinkable to not receive full custody. Although not necessarily the case, nonetheless, nonresidential mothers experience a stigma that can have important implications for their well-being. In addition, nonresidential mothers must negotiate visitation with ex-husbands within the confines of an often contentious relationship. They must also accept that they will not see their children as much as they used to when they were custodial caregivers.

For nonresidential mothers, distance parenting is constantly being defined and negotiated within a Westernized social construction of motherhood—one that emphasizes intensive mothering strategies. Definitions developed within this construction are limited and difficult to maintain for any mother, but are especially hard for women who do not live with their children. Noncustodial mothers recognize that they are no longer mothers in the traditional sense of the word. As a result, they either attempt to maintain ties to the dominant motherhood ideology—participating in intensive mothering strategies and traditional mother roles when they visit their children—or they move toward rejecting this paradigm. Rejection of the paradigm means redefining their role as a mother in light of their spatial circumstances. Such definitions incorporate new roles and obligations. Women begin to view themselves as long-distance "sisters" or "friends" to their children rather than mothers. Mothers who accept modifications to their mothering role tend to be better adjusted and happier as mothers than do those who insist on conforming to traditional mothering expectations.

Whether mothers accommodate or resist dominant mothering strategies, children tend to fare best when they see both of their parents on a regular basis. Recent research points to the importance of shared parenting strategies when possible. One of the participants in Bemiller's (2005) study discussed her interest in pursuing joint custody rather than her current situation of seeing her children every other weekend. Her reason for this was that joint custody would allow her to see her children more and, in her mind, was less stigmatizing.

These arrangements, however, must be mandated with caution, especially in cases where abuse has been an issue in the relationship. In such cases, the court must be sensitive to the fact that shared parenting may open the door for continued abuse, even after dissolution of the marriage. Mothers should not, however, be penalized in terms of access to their children because of their spouses' abusive behaviors. Courts must find ways to encourage equal visitation in such cases. One option might be to provide a court official who takes the child from one home to the next or to mandate that exchanges of children must happen at a public location such as a local law enforcement agency.

Since traditional mothering definitions tend to have a negative impact on nonresidential mothers (as well as other mothers who parent from a distance), we must begin to have open conversations about how mothering comes in many forms. Such dialogue would benefit noncustodial mothers who fight against stigmas and work to better themselves at work and school—a reason given by some nonresidential parents for the decision to give custody of children to fathers or other family members—as well as children, fathers, and other individuals involved in the raising of children in this type of family configuration.

Chapters in the current volume each challenge us to broaden our definitions of family and parenting. Other mechanisms (e.g., traditional media and social media platforms such as Facebook, with open and closed groups in which nonresidential parents can connect) can also further break down stereotypes and help society acknowledge how parents in various situations participate in their children's lives in many alternative forms. Outlets that allow men and women to talk freely about their lived experiences and allow them to embrace varied parenting situations and reach out to each other knowing that they are not alone in noncustodial parenting can be helpful in supporting these parents and their families. Some such media sources, especially when open access, may allow the general public a glimpse into the lives of such families, demonstrating that these are individuals with real emotions and important experiences. As the numbers of nonresidential mothers increase, it is critical to shed light on and understand different parenting styles and family forms. Open dialogue and discussion can only benefit individual families and society at large as children feel accepted and valued within their families and communities, regardless of the nature of their family structure.

REFERENCES

Ahall, L. (2012). Motherhood, myth and gendered agency in political violence. *International Feminist Journal of Politics*, *14*, 103–120.

Aquilino, W. (1994). Impact of childhood family disruption on young adults' relationships with parents. *Journal of Marriage & the Family*, *56*, 295–313.

Arditti, J.A. & Madden-Derdich, D. (1993). Noncustodial mothers: Developing strategies of support. *Family Relations*, *42*, 305–314.

Arditti, J. A. (1995). Noncustodial Parents: Emergent Issues of Diversity and Process. *Marriage and Family Review*, *20*, 283–304.

Aymer, P. (1997). *Uprooted women: Migrant domestics in the Caribbean*. Westport: Praeger.

Babcock, G. M. (1997). Stigma, identity dissonance, and the nonresidential mother. *Journal of Divorce & Remarriage*, *28*, 139–156.

Bemiller, M. (2005). *Mothering on the margins: The experience of noncustodial mothers* (Unpublished doctoral dissertation). University of Akron, Akron, OH.

Bemiller, M. (2008). When battered mothers lose custody: A qualitative study of abuse at home and in the courts. *The Journal of Child Custody*, *5*(3-4), 228–255.

Bemiller, M. (2010). Mothering from a distance. *Journal of Divorce and Remarriage*, *51*(3), 169–184.

Boushey, H. (2011). Not working: Unemployment among married couples. Retrieved from: https://www.americanprogress.org/issues/labor/report/2011/05/06/9620/not-working-unemployment-among-married-couples/

Buchanan, C. M., Maccoby, E. E., & Dornbusch, S. M. (1996). *Adolescents after divorce*. Cambridge: Harvard University Press.

Buehler, C., & Gerard, J. M. (1995). Divorce law in the United States: A focus on child custody. *Family Relations*, *44*, 439–458.

Cancian, M., Myer, D. R., Brown, P. R., & Cook, S. T. (2014). Who gets custody now? Dramatic changes in children's living arrangements after divorce. *Demography*, *51*, 1381–1396.

Chae, J. (2015). "Am I a better mother than you?" Media and 21st-century motherhood in the context of the social comparison theory. *Communication Research*, *42*, 503–525.

Chesler, P. (2011). *Mothers on trial*. Chicago: Lawrence Hill Books.

Clumpus, L. (1996). The feminism & psychology undergraduate prize 1995: Prizewinning entry no-woman's land: The story of noncustodial mothers. *Feminism & Psychology*, *6*, 237–244.

Coontz, S. (1992). *The way we never were: American families and the nostalgia trap*. New York: Basic Books.

Coontz, S. (2011). *A strange stirring: The Feminine Mystique and American women at the Dawn of the 1960s*. New York: Basic Books.

Copen, C. E., Daniels, K., & Mosher, W. D. (2013). First premarital cohabitation in the United States: 2006–2010 national survey of family growth. Retrieved from: http://www.cdc.gov/nchs/data/nhsr/nhsr064.pdf–2010 National Survey of Family Growth [PDF - 227 KB]</a>.

Crosbie-Burnett, M. (1991). Impact of joint versus sole custody and quality of the co-parental relationship on adjustment of adolescents in remarried families. *Behavioral Sciences and the Law, 9*, 439–449.

Eicher-Catt, D. (2004). Noncustodial mothering: A cultural paradox of competent performance–performative competence. *Journal of Contemporary Ethnography, 33*(1), 72–108.

Fine, M. A. & Fine, D. R. (1994). An examination and evaluation of recent changes in divorce laws in five Western countries: The critical role of values. *Journal of Marriage and the Family, 56*, 249–263.

Fischer, J. L. & Cardea, J. M. (1981). Mothers living apart from their children: A study in stress and coping. *Alternative Lifestyles, 4*, 218–227.

Ford, C.B. (2005). *The women of Courtwatch*. Austin: University of Texas Press.

Furstenburg, F., Peterson, J. L., Nord, C. W., & Zill, N. (1983). The life course of children of divorce: Marital disruption and parental contact. *American Sociological Review, 48*, 656–678.

Garey, A. (1999). *Weaving work and motherhood*. Philadelphia: Temple University Press.

Gillis, J. R. (2002). Mothers giving birth to motherhood. In N. P. McKee & L. Stone. (Eds.), *Readings in gender and culture in America* (pp. 112–134). Upper Saddle River, NJ: Pearson Publishing.

Glenn, E. (1994). Social constructions of mothering: A thematic overview. In E. N. Glenn, G. Change, & L. R. Forcey (Eds.), *Mothering: Ideology, experience, and agency* (pp. 1–32). New York: Routledge.

Grall, T. (2016). Custodial mothers and fathers and their child support: 2013. Retrieved from: https://www.census.gov/content/dam/Census/library/publications/2016/demo/P60–255.pdf.

Greif, G. (1987). Single fathers and noncustodial mothers: The social worker's helping role. *Journal of Independent Social Work, 1*, 59–69.

Greif, G. (1997). *Out of touch: When parents and children lose contact after divorce*. New York: Oxford University Press.

Greif, G. & Pabst, M. S. (1988). *Mothers without custody*. Lexington, MA: DC Heath.

Gustafson, D. L. (2005). *Unbecoming mothers: The social production of maternal absence*. Routledge: Haworth Clinical Practice Press.

Hays, S. (1996). *The cultural contradictions of motherhood*. New Haven: Yale University Press.

Herrerias, C. (1984). *Noncustodial mothers: A study of self-concept and social interactions* (Unpublished doctoral dissertation). University of Texas at Austin.

Herrerias, C. (1995). Noncustodial mothers following divorce. *Marriage & Family Review, 20*, 233–255.

Hetherington, E. M. (1993). An overview of the Virginia longitudinal study of divorce and remarriage with a focus on early adolescence. *Journal of Family Psychology, 7*, 39–56.

Hill Collins, P. (1987). The meaning of motherhood in Black culture and Black mother/daughter relationships. *Sage, 4*, 3–10.

Hill Collins, P. (1992). Black women and motherhood. In B. Thorne & M. Yalom (Eds.), *Rethinking the Family: Some Feminist Questions* (pp. 215–245). Boston: Northeastern University Press.

Hill Collins, P. (1994). Shifting the center: Race, class, and Feminist theorizing about motherhood. In E. Glenn, G. Chang, & L.R. Forcey (Eds.), *Mothering: Ideology, experience and agency* (pp. 45–66). New York: Routledge.

Johnson, A. (1997). *The gender knot: Unraveling our patriarchal legacy.* Philadelphia: Temple University Press.

Kielty, S. (2006). Similarities and differences in the experiences of non-resident mothers and non-resident fathers. *International Journal of Law, Policy and the Family 20*, 74–94.

King, B. (2007). When children have two mothers: Relationships with nonresident mothers, stepmothers, and fathers. *Journal of Marriage and the Family, 69*, 1178–1193.

Kreider, R.M. & Ellis, R. (2011). Living arrangements of children: 2009. https://www.census.gov/prod/2011pubs/p70-126.pdf. Retrieved July 7, 2016.

Kruk, E. (2010). Collateral damage: The lived experiences of divorced mothers without custody. *Journal of Divorce & Remarriage, 51*, 526–543.

Livingston, G. (2014). Less than half of U.S. kids today live in a "traditional" family. Retrieved from: http://www.pewresearch.org/fact-tank/2014/12/22/less-than-half-of-u-s-kids-today-live-in-a-traditional-family/

Maccoby, E.E. & Mnookin, R. (1992). Dividing the child: Social and legal dilemmas of custody. Cambridge: Harvard University Press.

McKenry, P. C., McKelvey, M. W., Leigh, D., & Wark, L. (1996). Nonresidential father involvement: A comparison of divorced, separated, never married, and remarried fathers. *Journal of Divorce and Remarriage, 25*, 1–13.

McLanahan, S. (2004). Diverging destinies: How children fare under the second demographic transition. *Demography, 41*, 607–627.

Neustein, A. & Lesher, M. (2005). *From madness to mutiny: Why mothers are running from the family courts—and what can be done about it.* Lebanon: Northeastern University Press.

Phoenix, A., Woollett, A. & Lloyd, E. (1991). *Motherhood: Meanings, practices, and ideologies.* Newbury Park, CA: Sage Publications

Popenoe, D. (2001). American family decline, 1960-1990: A review and appraisal. *Journal of Marriage and the Family, 55*, 527–542.

Santora, J. & Hays, P. A. (1998). Coping outside traditional roles: The case of noncustodial mothers and implications for therapy. *Women & Therapy, 21*, 53–66.

Seltzer, J. (1994). Consequences of marital dissolution for children. *Annual Review of Sociology, 20*, 235–266.

Snowdon, J. & Kotze, E. (2012). I'm not a bad mother –stories of mothering-on-the-edge. *Australian and New Zealand Journal of Family Therapy, 33*, 142–156.

Spruijt, E., & Iedema, I. (1998). Well-being of youngsters of divorce without contact with nonresident parents in the Netherlands. *Journal of Comparative Family Studies, 29*, 517–531.

Stacey, J. (2001). Good riddance to "the family": A response to David Popenoe. *Journal of Marriage and the Family, 55*, 545–547.

Stark, B. (2005). International family law. Burlington: Ashgate Publishing Co.

Stewart, S. D. (1999a). Disneyland dads, disneyland moms? How nonresident parents spend time with absent children. *Journal of Family Issues*, *20*, 539–556.

Stewart, S. D. (1999b). Nonresident mothers' and fathers' social contact with children." *Journal of Marriage and the Family*, *61*, 894–907.

Stewart, S. D. (ND). Parental involvement, living arrangements, and wellbeing among children with nonresident mothers. Retrieved from: http://www.soc.iastate.edu/staff/stewart/Stewart_FinalMS_5%2010%2010.pdf.

Uttal, L. (1996). Custodial care, surrogate care, and coordinated care: Employed mothers and the meaning of child care. *Gender & Society*, *10*, 291–311.

Wall, J. C. & Amadio, C. (1994). An integrated approach to child custody evaluation: Utilizing the "best interest" of the child and family systems frameworks. *Journal of Divorce and Remarriage*, *21*, 39–57.

Zuravin, S. & Greif, G. L. (1989). Low-income mothers without custody: Who are they and where are their children? *Journal of Sociology and Social Welfare*, *16*, 163–180.

SECTION IV

Family Separation as a Normative Cultural Practice and in Pursuit of Education

13

"Raising Another's Child"

Gifting, Communicating, and Persevering in Northern Namibia

JILL BROWN

The configuration of family life around the world is vast and depends on factors as varied as climate, inheritance, and modernization. Parenting practices around the world reflect this divergence, but often practices that deviate from traditional nuclear family models are seen as problematic (Nsamenang, 2005). In this chapter, I am presenting a study on how people engage in parenting from a distance within the practice of child fosterage (*okutekula*), or the "raising of another's child." I aim to show how, in northern Namibia, long-distance family life is not just normative in sheer numbers or in cultural explanations but adaptive.

Upon visiting homes in sub-Saharan Africa, one often finds many children of different ages living in one house or homestead. Some are the biological offspring of the mother and father. Some are relatives (e.g., nieces or nephews) of the mother or father. Others are not biologically related to either the mother or father. In many African communities, this family composition is due to the childcare practice of *fosterage*. Fosterage has been defined in several ways. In early work in West Africa, Goody (1973) defined it as "institutional delegation of the nurturance and/or educational elements of the parental role. Fosterage does not affect the status identity of the child, nor the legal rights and obligations this entails. Fosterage concerns the process of rearing" (p. 23). Biological parents still hold legal rights to children they foster, and most continue relationships with the children throughout their time in fostering arrangements with another family. Other definitions exist, with most agreeing that fosterage is the rearing of a child by someone other than the biological parent. Unlike adoption in the Western sense, fostering involves no permanent change in kinship or status and no permanent forfeiting of rights. It is an additive, not a substitutive model of childrearing that allows for biological and social parenting (Bowie, 2004). What makes fosterage unique is the semi-permanent yet adjustable nature of the relationship, one of the most distinct elements of African families.

In the north of Namibia, the Owambo people parent through elaborate and overlapping social networks that share and raise children; this is possible, in large part, because of the ideals of socially distributed child care—a set of loosely interwoven ecological circumstances, beliefs, and practices that coexist and contribute to one another (Weisner, Bradley, & Kilbride, 1997). The core characteristics of socially distributed childcare include, but are not limited to:

- Child caretaking often occurs as a part of indirect chains of support in which one child assists another, who then assists another. Support is not always immediate and not necessarily organized around exclusive relationships between parent and child.
- Children look to other children for support as much or more than they look to adults.
- Care often occurs in the context of other domestic work.
- Aggression, teasing, and dominance coincide with nurturance and support and come from the same people. Dominance increases with age.
- Food and other material goods are used to threaten, control, soothe, and comfort.
- Elaborate verbal exchanges and question-framed discourse rarely accompany support and nurturance for children. Verbal bargaining and negotiations over rights, choices, and privileges between the caretaker and child are infrequent.
- Social and intellectual competence is judged by a child's ability to manage domestic tasks, demonstrate appropriate social behavior, do child care, and nurture and support others.
- Children are socialized within the system through apprenticeship learning of their family roles and responsibilities.
- Mothers provide support and nurturance to children as much by securing that others will support their children as by supporting their children directly. Fostering and other forms of child sharing are common. (Weisner, Bradley & Kilbride, 1997)

My first experience with socially distributed childrearing and child fosterage was in the mid 1990s when I was a Peace Corps volunteer living with a family in rural northern Namibia. Families are intimately connected by fosterage as some children leave and others are brought into homes. Here is a reflection, excerpted from my field notes:

> I have been with the Kolo family for almost 18 months when I am sitting on a mat reading under the tree. On the mat with me are Nduefewa (10), Lina (11) and Timo (6). A woman I have not met is walking in the sand towards the house and Ndeufewa gets up to greet her as we all watch. She runs into the big house and Meme (45) comes out and greets the woman. She reaches

in her pocket and gives Meme some money and a bottle of cooking oil she has with her. She then calls Timo (6) over to her. As he gets up, Lina (11) brushes the dust off his face. I hear Meme then ask Timo to greet the woman. Timo keeps his eyes down at the ground and after a few seconds walks back to our mat. I ask Ndeufewa who the woman is and she says it is Timo's mother.

Fieldnotes, J. Brown, June 1997

I had lived with this family for almost 2 years and had missed a crucial piece of information: Timo was not their biological child. This experience led me to pose several questions that I have attempted to answer in the past 20 years of research: Who are the "real parents" of the children at my house (Brown, 2009)? Why are they leaving and returning (Brown, 2009)? Does it affect their development and attachment (Brown, 2009)? What's in it for the parents (Brown, 2011)? What are the cultural rules of this process (Brown, 2013)? In working toward an understanding of these issues, knowledge of the structure, function, and experience of child fosterage emerged.

CHILD FOSTERAGE (*OKUTEKULA*)

Okutekula is an Oshiwambo word for "raising another's child." Fosterage is not unique to Africa, however. In an extensive study of adoption and fostering in Oceania, Brady (1976) describe a number of ways in which it is possible to foster. One may make regular contributions of food and clothes, feed another, or let another sleep regularly in one's house. In Oceania, a distinction between fosterage and adoption is made by identifying who is involved in the principal negotiation of the arrangement. In a fostering arrangement, initiation may be by the person being fostered, the one who will care for him or her, or an interested third party not involved in the relationship directly. In contrast, the persons wishing to adopt, in Western adoption, typically initiate adoption. In this respect, fosterage represents a fundamentally different practice. In reviewing the literature, I did not find the distinction between adoption and fosterage made in African societies.

The concept of fosterage has been elusive in the literature and appears under several labels. In 1937, Herskovits used the term "quasi-adoption" to describe the practice in Haiti of "giving" peasant children to wealthier families in the capital. "Giving" of the child was seen as an act of friendship, and the child repaid the foster family through housework and chores. Clarke (1957) studied Jamaican families and differentiated between fostering/adoption and "schooling-out." Adoption occurred at an early age while schooling-out occurred later: in both, often children were often sent to strangers of a higher social status or better circumstances, and, in these circumstances, the children were not thought of as equals but rather as servants. Schooling-out was a business deal between parents and adults of the recipient household—a child's maintenance and schooling were exchanged for services. Additional terms used include "child switching" (Goode,

1964), "child loaning" (Gonzalez, 1969), and "child keeping" (Payne-Price, 1981). Carroll (1970) uses the term "adoptive fosterage" to differentiate between adoption in America and adoption practiced in Western Polynesia. This term brings into focus most clearly the problem of trying to derive a single definition to describe a range of practices.

CURRENT RATES OF FOSTERING IN AFRICA

Historically, data on child fostering were often obtained while researchers were in the process of collecting standard data on fertility (Isiugo-Abanihe, 1985). Early demographers found gross inaccuracies in answers to seemingly standard questions like "How many children do you have?" Probes were asked, and the following three questions became the gold standard in census reporting in Africa on number of children: number of children living at home, number dead, and number living away from home. Early work focused on west Africa, but southern Africa, in fact, had the highest rates of fosterage in 2003 (Monasch & Boerma, 2004). According to data from the Demographic and Health Survey (DHS) conducted by US Agency for International Development (USAID), the percentage of children living away from their mothers ranges from as low as 3% in Sudan to as high as 30% in Namibia. In the northernmost regions of Namibia, rates as high as 36% among Owambo communities have been reported (Brown, 2013). In West Africa, Liberia has a 26% nonmaternal residence rate but may be an outlier as other West African countries range between 10% and 15%. In East Africa, Sudan and Kenya have exceptionally low rates of nonmaternal residence, with Uganda having the highest (19%).

The high rates of fostering observed in southern Africa are due in part to relatively high rates of migration for work, nonmarital births, divorce, and death, which were brought about in part by the segregationist policies of apartheid but which persist in the postapartheid era. Black Africans often have to travel to find jobs, migratory labor patterns mean that one or both of a child's parents are often not present for much of the year, and parents often rely on family members other than spouses for support with the household and childrearing (Anderson, 2005).

MOTIVATIONS AND OUTCOMES

Ester Goody (1973) was one of the first to describe the practice of fosterage among the Gonja of Cameroon. In her field notes, she documented the Ganja word *kabitha* "a girl given to someone" and *kaiyeribi* "a boy given to someone." Understanding the nuances of fosterage still proves to be a complex task. The motivations of the recipient family and the donor family are often multifarious (Brown, 2011) and encompass the desire to teach discipline (Bledsoe, 1990), to provide a better education for a child (Isiugo-Abanihe, 1985), gifting and sharing between families (Madhavan, 2004), establishment of social bonds (Bledsoe, 1990), enhancement of fertility (Isiugo-Abanihe, 1985; Pennington, 1991), the need to be childless when entering a new relationship with a man (Pennington, 1991; Vandermeersch, 2002), and times of crisis, like sickness and famine (Madhavan, 2004). Payne-Price (1981) sampled 45 cultures using the Human Resource Area File (HRAF) that reported adoption practices. Of the 45 cultures, 35 reported adoption or fosterage practices. The three primary motives for fostering in a child were the need for a helper, either short or long term; the need for an heir; and tokens of friendship. The need for a helper was identified as the primary motivation. Motivations to foster out a child included illegitimacy, poverty, too many children, death of one parent, and death of both parents. The Namibian fostering system is a recognizable variant of the more general customs that surround fostering throughout Africa (Brown, 2009).

The predictions regarding child fosterage conducted by most researchers trained in Western paradigms of developmental psychology usually question how this practice could not harm "nonbiological children." Disparities do exist between fosterees and biological children. Oni (1995) sampled 1,538 Yoruba households in Nigeria in order to understand the effects of fosterage from both the foster parent's and the child's perspectives. Her findings reveal differential treatment of foster and nonfostered children. The mother was the first person to notice a child's illness 89% of the time if it was her biological child but only 42% of the time for foster children. Foster children reportedly complained in 29% of cases, compared to 4% for biological children, before an illness was noticed. The mean duration of time between awareness of illness and treatment also favored biological children. In follow-up case studies, adults who were fostered out as children overwhelmingly describe the experience as one filled with pain and favoritism (Oni, 1995).

Similarly, Bledsoe and Brandon (1992) found that children fostered were at greater risk for death and fell sick more than their biologically related counterparts. The authors conclude that this may be due to discrimination and deprivation in times of food shortages. Anderson (2005) utilized a demographic survey to examine whether the coefficient of relatedness predicts greater household expenditures on food and education for 11,211 black South African children. Controlling for characteristics that might vary between households, he found that the more closely related a child is to the household, the less likely he or she is to be behind in school. Similarly, being more related to the household is a positive predictor of expenditures on food, healthcare, and clothing. In rural samples, however, increased relatedness was associated with reduced expenditures on food and healthcare. The cultural script of "all children are treated equally" is found throughout parental accounts of fostering in Africa (Brown, 2011). The nature of the relationship between families plays a role in the treatment of children (Brown, 2011; Verhoff & Morelli, 2007).

The current study adds to what is known about child fosterage by exploring this practice in a southern African context among the Owambo of northern Namibia, specifically addressing how Owambos' "parent from afar." Through ethnographic research, the study helps paint a portrait of Namibian parents and children and attempts to capture the complexities of how economic, moral, and social motivations to foster children away from the natal home and to accept a child into a home play out in the organization and texture of family life.

METHOD

The Owambo Context

The Owambo people live primarily in two regions in Namibia. Their traditional homeland is located in the north of the country and is home to the majority of the more than 400,000 Owambo speakers in Namibia. Traditionally, the Owambos are agro-pastoralists having both subsistence plots of millet (*omahango*) and herds of cattle (*eengobe*) and goats (*eekombo*). A large number of Owambos have migrated to Windhoek, the capital, in search of work and education, and live primarily in Katatura, the settlement created on the outskirts of Windhoek during the apartheid era. Seven of the participants in the study were residing in Windhoek. English is the official language, with several other indigenous languages spoken. Owambo-speaking people represent the largest portion of Namibia's population, nearly 50% (CIA Factbook 2017).

Owambo societies during the precolonial and colonial periods were predominantly matrilineal agro-pastoralist societies demarcated from each other by large areas of forest and savanna in the north of the country (Salokowski, 1998). Until 1840, these areas had remained almost totally free from European influence. When the first Finnish missionaries arrived in 1870, the majority of Owambo societies were headed by "kings." In 1948, the Afrikaner-led National Party gained power in South Africa. Namibia exchanged one colonial experience for another. During the apartheid era, blacks were relegated into traditional homelands. For the Owambos, this was the north of the country, where the majority still live today. Owambos not living within the boundaries of the newly created "Owamboland" were relocated and required to carry a workpass when leaving Owamboland. Namibia gained its independence in 1990 after more than a century of colonial rule, first by Germany and then by South Africa. Much of the struggle for independence between 1966 and 1988 was carried out in Owamboland. Nine of the participants of the study still resided in the northern homeland

Kinship is an organizing principle in Namibia holding more importance than class and playing a critical role in decisions regarding socially distributed childrearing (Hayes, 1998). What class does in advanced capitalistic societies like the United States, kinship does in Namibia—shaping peer relationships, choices about marriage, and with whom one could be raised. Matrilineal descent systems are found among Owambo speakers (Hayes, 1998). Children traditionally belong to their mother's family, and men do not pass on their matrilineal membership to children. The mother's brother often plays a pivotal role in the care of the children, including providing care through fosterage. Even within this system, however, there is significant variation and complexity.

Participants

Data for this study were collected within a broader ethnographic study of child fosterage. In November–December 2014, 15 interviews were conducted with Owambo-speaking people in Namibia. All participants were involved in child fosterage in different ways. Twelve of the participants were fostered themselves as children. Eight were parents who had or are currently fostering their biological children. Participants were recruited through a purposeful, snowball sampling technique. This technique's advantage is that one informant refers the researcher to another so that the researcher has a good introduction for the next interview. A disadvantage is that the variation in the sample may be limited because it consists of informants who belong to the networks of the index cases. This was the case in my sample, so three cases were chosen through maximum variation sampling to increase the variation of experiences of fosterage. Interviews were semi-structured in nature and lasted between 1 and 3 hours. Twelve interviews were conducted in English and three were conducted in Oshiwambo with a translator. All interviews were transcribed.

Data Analysis

A multiple case study technique was used to analyze the data. A case study is a type of ethnographic design (Stake, 1995) and is an exploration of a "bounded system" or a case over time through detailed, in-depth data collection involving multiple sources of information and rich in context (Merriam, 1998). In this study, the multiple cases will serve the purpose of "illuminating a particular issue" (Creswell, 2003): namely, how do families parent from a distance within the child fosterage system? Analysis of the case study followed Stake's (1995) technique and occurred in three phases. The author and a research assistant performed initial coding and thematic analysis. First, a detailed description of each participant was created from the field notes, observations, and other information gathered in the interviews. All interviews and field notes were typed for analysis. Second, thematic analysis was performed on two levels: within each case and across the cases (Stake, 1995). Thematic analysis of the interview data was done by (1) initially reading the data for overall understanding and writing preliminary notes, (2) partitioning segments of text and labeling them with codes, (3) aggregating similar codes together to develop themes (4), connecting and interrelating the themes, and (5) constructing a narrative. The interconnected themes were of particular interest to the study as the relationships that exist between families are the central questions of the study. The final phase of analysis is to integrate the cases and themes and report on the "lessons learned" or assertions put forth from the study (Stake, 1995).

The cases reveal the complexity of the practice of child fosterage and the complexity in the way parents view parenting from a distance. For each theme, a "case" will be used to help elucidate the intricacy of the practice.

Children as Gifts

Tate Hambo is 73 at the time of my interview. He was the principal at the village elementary school for many years and is now retired. He has seven biological children of his own. He recounts that he did not want to foster any of his children, but his wife "gave one away" to her grannie. The child only stayed away 2 years, then he called for her to be returned. To call for a child to return is not a common practice among Owambos as fosterage arrangements are usually honored for the duration of childhood. There are many children around the yard this morning, and several approach Tate Hambo with a tenderness not usually seen between children and men in Owamboland. I learn that all these children have been fostered in because Tate Hambo's biological children are grown. As I ask about each child, he explains that most were "gifted" to him—some as a way to repay a debt, some for being a good teacher, others to help with the house. We sit in his yard for this interview, and chickens and goat provide a backdrop of rural life. Tate Hambo was fostered as a child after his father died when he was 9 year old. He was the youngest in the family and the only sibling to not remain at his natal home. He was fostered to his "godfather," a friend of his father's, not a relative, and moved 15 kilometers away and remained there until age 15. Tate's experience with his father's friend was one of work and loneliness with little memory of affection. After 2 years at the house, he decided to run away in the middle of the night and return to his natal home. The road was very dark and long, and he slept sometimes under the trees. When he arrived, his mother was sitting together with some of his siblings and she looked at him and said "go back, just go back . . . even right now, just turn around and go back." He remembers crying.

Tate Hambo's account of being given children as "gifts" prevails in many narratives. Girls are named *Ndapewa* or "the gift," and many children are renamed or nicknamed this after being fostered in as "a gift" to another family. Tate Hambo says there are three *Ndapewas* currently living with him. I have known more than 10 *Ndapewas* in my time doing work in Namibia.

Child fosterage has been defined as a social welfare system in places without institutionalized welfare. Families in and out of crisis move children in culturally normative ways. Nonetheless, I argue that it is in the theater of acquiring surplus social capital, not a handout, that this practice has evolved. The definition of welfare is the provision of a minimal level of well-being and social support for citizens without current means to support basic needs. One cannot consider the practice of fosterage without considering the economics of the practice, specifically, the value of a child as a "gift." Pierre Bourdieu's (1986) theoretical project of understanding the "general science of the economy of practices" (p. 252) helps when examining the economy of fosterage. There are many reasons and motivations to foster, and within the system several may be utilized at one time in one fostering arrangement. Some are more economic, as children are moved for education or because mothers need to relocate for employment. But fosterage is an informal system of support, only formalized in the social capital transactions it creates. The debt that a gift creates becomes the social capital to rely on later. Bourdieu defines social capital as the actual or potential resources which are linked to possession of a durable network of relationships of mutual acquaintance and recognition. Thus, social capital includes obligation and trust.

Gifts play a large role in the creation of obligation and trust. Owambos often speak of gifting when they explain *olutekula.* Ndapewa recalls that "she was given to the Hawanga's as a wedding present." But what is a gift? The fundamental feature of a gift is not found in the motivations of the givers, nor in the binding gift-debt on the receivers, nor in the distinctiveness of the relations between the parties; rather, it is constituted through the need to conform to the demands of the gift as a social form with its own etiquette. For the gift of a child, the social rules and etiquette are the actual parenting practices of fosterage. For a gift to succeed as a gift, it must follow the social forms that usually prescribe that it be an unconditional offer of a present in which explicit recognition of instrumental goals is excluded from the performance. Mauss (1954) says that gifts are "voluntary, disinterested and spontaneous." Bourdieu (1986) refers to this denial of the content of the gift exchange as the *misrecognition.* It is not because people are not smart enough to understand, but is essential to the gift itself. There is a necessity of misrecognition in gift exchange in that the partners do not have to be unaware of the instrumental goals involved, but these goals cannot be made explicit, and, where incompetent performance does make the goals explicit, loss of gratitude and devaluation of the obligation may result. The power of the social capital is mystified.

Several goals or parental ethnotheories of fosterage exist. Even if both donor and recipient know that the goal is, for example, to teach perseverance and moral fortitude, these goals are not made explicit, but instantiated in practice. This helps explain why, when adults are asked the reason that they were fostered as children, many do not know and have never asked their natal parents. When the foster arrangement was not a crisis, like a death or sicknesss, or explicit, like moving closer to a good school, children and parents often reported disparate reasons for fostering. A misrecognition of the reason and the real value of the arrangement is present. In the fostering arrangements, one sees the misrecognition reflected in the explanations told by parents to children, the lack of explicit communication among adults, and the existence of a parenting goal that is reflected in the cultural narratives of childhood.

Explicit Communication: Children, Adults, and Gifts

Communication between children and biological parents varied in frequency, means of communication, and the message conveyed. It is this rupture in the normal communication patterns that families navigate differently. At times, the communication was explicit, and both parents and children discussed the goals of the communication, as in the case of Kano.

Kano is 23 years old and lives in the capital city of Windhoek, where she works in management at a large bank. She describes herself as introverted but never wants to be home on a Saturday night. She is originally from northern Namibia.

I have known Kano since she was 4 years old. She is the last-born biological child of her parents. At age 7, she was fostered to her maternal uncle, a very common practice among the matrilineal Owambo people. Kano believes that parents have the idea that "if we send out children to Windhoek to get an education, it will be better. So they sent me right after preschool."

Education fostering makes up a large proportion of the cultural practice, and many rural children are fostered to more urban areas for more educational choices (Brown, 2009). Kano remembers the experience when she was young as "the saddest parts of my life" and does not attribute it to being away from home but to her foster aunt's differential treatment between the biological children of the house and herself. She noted, "I can see that I am not being treated the same and that is the part that I really hated most. I always wanted to go home and see my mom." When she would visit her birth home for holidays, Kano at times would tell her mom about the treatment and how she felt, but her mother usually responded with the cultural narrative of "you should just get used to it. You are in somebody's house, and we are not here to tell them how to raise you." Kano would try to call her mother on the house phone, but this only happened once per week until she was in secondary school and could buy a cell phone.

Children often expressed a deep wish to reconnect to biological parents through more frequent explicit communication; however, this communication with the children varied by the age of the child. Agnes (44) would work odd jobs to get airtime to call her son who was fostered to a maternal aunt. She remembers,

> I just want him to know me. When I come there, he doesn't really know me but he just says, "that is my mom." I want him to say more than that, to see me and want to come by my side.

Children were creative in their ability to gather resources to contact biological parents. Many wrote letters or worked odd jobs to pay for phone time.

The texture of the communication was often fraught with longing from the children but a stoic disinterest from parents when children complained about their treatment at the new house. Fundamental to the practice of fosterage is that biological parents do not intervene in the matters and rules of the foster family. Kano remembers hours on the phone with her biological mother, telling her "I miss you and I want to be home and why can't I go to a school close to you," but that she would get no explanation. This is reflected in Helvi's account:

> After I grew up, I asked my parents, "why would you leave me here?" But not as a child. I used to tell them I love them but not about any bad treatment I was receiving. There is no way even to tell them. It is not about what they would say because I cannot even think of how I could tell them. It is unspeakable.

Communication was absent for some. Kolele recalls not once having his biological father initiate contact. He would only contact his father via telephone to tell him that he was going to be visiting on school holiday. Time also dissipated contact as several women discussed that they would try to initiate communication frequently in the time immediately after the arrangement, but this contact would lessen over time.

Buying gifts played an important role for some families separated by fosterage. Biological parents communicated love and good intentions to their biological children through gifting. Gifting was often the fondest memory of the biological relationship after the fosterage arrangement. When asked how she felt love as a child, Aune responded, "I felt it when my parents would bring me gifts. It was the time I felt a unique love."

Parents who foster out children do not leave instructions or communicate about the children because this would show mistrust. When the children are in the new house, the rules of the new house are final. Inherent in a gift is its disinterested nature. This is seen explicitly in the cultural practice that privileges the rules of the recipient family. Donor parents do not tell recipient parents how to parent or give even the slightest parenting advice unless elicited from the recipient parent. When communication did happen between donor and recipient parents, it was primarily regarding money. Money passed between these houses often, but not always with positive feelings. Lina, who fostered her daughter to paternal grandparents explains,

> You don't even have to communicate with the adults. They call me when there is a problem. Only a problem. If they need something then I must send it. Even when they could afford something themselves, they call me for small amounts. It is just our arrangement.

This, and similar experiences, were remembered by participants who were fostered as children as well as those who are in the midst of a fosterage arrangement. For adults, the exchange of money is complex. At times, participants reported gifting and giving money as a way to repay the debt of caring for their child. It passed freely and with positive feelings from the donor to the recipient. For others, like Lina, it was a burden. If the practice of child fosterage is shrouded in the veil of gifting but meant to increase the available network and, ultimately, the social capital of families, then Bourdieu's idea of the trust and obligation necessary to increase social capital is reflected in the lack of involvement of the donor parent in the parenting process.

Even though there is a lack of explicit communication about parenting during the arrangement, past work reveals that the relationships that are built through fostering are lasting and often continue well after the children leave. For example, Paulus still brings presents, even though he describes his treatment as bad. Kano still brings gifts to her aunt's house at holiday, even in the absence of feelings of love.

Implicit Communication: Teaching Perseverance and Boundaries

Suffering was closely linked to moral development and a sense that suffering made you stronger. Fosterage has a direct relationship to suffering. Many women reported that children suffer when not living with their biological parents but that this suffering was needed to grow into a healthy adult who would be ready for a hard life if need be.

Helvi is my age exactly, shy 4 months. At the time of this interview, she was 41. I have known her since 1996. At that time, she was 23 and the mother of a 5-year-old girl named Lollie who stayed with her at her childhood home. Helvi's home has always struck me as exceptional in some way. The family displayed an openness to others, including many children who were fostered in. The family also had the ability to survive with very little because not much money was coming into the home when as many as 15 people resided there. Nineteen years later, Helvi had her second child, named after her mother; little Victoria is now 3 years old. Little Victoria is fostered to Helvi's mother. She is fostered out of necessity. Helvi is working but not married at age 41 and does not feel she has a proper home. The dynamics of big and little Victoria are not one of teaching only perseverance through suffering. Helvi says,

> Yes, they love her too much and they are old. To be honest the love for her is not like I felt from them. My parents consider her their own. I don't even have the right to give her to someone else. I want to give her to Naita [Helvi's sister], she doesn't have a child. At first my mom said yes, it is ok but later she said no 'cause Naita has too many friends and little Victoria would be alone. Even the father's family wants her but I cannot decide. My mom and dad will not allow it.

When Helvi was 9, she was fostered to her maternal aunt, who lived in the same village and worked in the hospital. She remembers being fostered for moral teaching of perseverance. She recounted,

> My father used to tell me, he wants me to be strong. I was told that the reason they are doing this is if you grow up with your parents you won't be disciplined because it isn't easy to stay with others. He was strict. It doesn't mean he didn't love me, but he wanted me to have a brighter future and for him it was to be apart from the people you love most.

Although Helvie understands that her parent's motivation for fostering her was to communicate the lesson of perseverance and strength, she also knows that her daughter is not receiving the same lesson. Women hoped for their children to learn the lessons that fostering teaches, but it was an implicit lesson, one that had to be lived. In past research using life history interviews with women who were fostered, many reported this connection (Brown, 2011). One woman remembered,

> My mother died earlier so I got that love but not too much; let me say that if you are staying longer with your mother then you have to learn more, how to

> suffer, how to survive. That is what I used to tell my kids "don't think you will always stay with your parents."

Fosterage affords parents a culturally appropriate outlet to prepare children for the death of a parent or to acquire the emotional survival skills they will need to face loss. The reality of parental death is present for children. Namibia has a life expectancy of 65 years and an HIV rate of around 15–17% (UNAIDS, 2015). Levine et al. (1994) points out that the role of child survival should be looked at when studying parenting styles and practices. What parents want for their children can be thought of in terms of a universal hierarchy of goals, ranging from providing basic survival to fostering economic capabilities to acquiring cultural values. In societies like Namibia and many in sub-Saharan Africa, infant mortality is high and parents' caregiving is organized around the most basic of the goals: survival. As education and industrialization increase, even within a society, one can see different goals emerge, like the acquisition of skills and cultural values. Helvie also holds this belief when asked to reflect on her own parenting:

> I think it is good to not treat kids like more special because if you pass away they will suffer, always thinking "if only my mother was around." You can give them food as they wish, but they have to work and they have to learn how to live in peace.

Others agreed that people foster children out "because they want to teach children to survive." While fostering to teach a moral lesson is repeated in many of the stories and narratives of Namibians, little is known about how the lesson is instantiated in practice. Helvie also reflects,

> You know the rules of your mother's house and no matter if you do something wrong, she will say "oh it's my child, it's ok," but at the other house the parents keep their own children close and you feel left out. It's not the same.

When asked about the moral lessons that were learned, there was agreement. Tate Hambo learned through the hard work of herding animals and the emotional work of being separated from his birth parents; he was prepared for anything in the future. Preparing for the harsh environment that might await them in adulthood was understood by everyone as the lesson of fosterage: "If I die, they will know how to do things."

Boundaries

Paulus is a 53-year-old man and a respected member of his community. I have known Paulus for more than 20 years. He was a soldier in the liberation and is the person both financially and emotionally responsible for his very large extended family. He is also thought of as one of the smartest people in his village.

Paulus has three biological children. The oldest child (now 23), was 2 years old when I first met Paulus and his wife, Longo. Paulus was fostered to his maternal aunt as a 4-year-old boy. He clearly remembers not being informed that he was moving households; instead, he was told that his aunt had "sweets" and when he was there he could eat them. He stayed with his maternal aunt and uncle until he was 12 years old and would visit his natal home a few times a year. He would see his birth parents and siblings on Sundays at church. He describes his communication with his parents:

> It was totally broken down, and it only happened when I would see them at church. We would meet at church and perhaps I would show off and my auntie would dress me nice so I could show off to my parents. I couldn't even imagine writing a letter at that time, there was completely nothing, no communication.

Paulus speculates that he was fostered because he was eight of nine children, and his aunt had little children that he could help care for. Paulus has consciously avoided fostering his own children and accounts many strategies to avoid the cultural obligations implicit in the practice of fosterage. Paulus has fostered-in many children in his home, and when asked about it says, "what else can I do, if they have nowhere to go?"

Fosterage creates boundaries that parents believe are impossible to achieve in the natal home. Paulus recalls that if he wanted to go to his birth mother's room, he just went, but, at his foster mother's house he could not go until he was invited: "There are boundaries and there are many things you cannot just go and get on your own. You have to wait until you are allowed." The shifting boundaries begin to emerge in both the foster and the natal home. Paulus describes his natal home as always being home, but Helvi describes her childhood as being one of a "continuous visitor." Like the majority of fostered children, she went back to her natal home for school holidays, but her status had changed, at least existentially for her. She could not ask for things as her siblings did who had not left. She no longer jumped on her mother's lap. She was only visiting. She recalls "even if I needed something when I was home at my mom and dad's, I didn't know how to ask. My other siblings would just ask, but not me. I waited." Paulus recalls that as a child, "when I would get beaten or hurt by someone, I always go and run to my mother for comfort but with my aunt [foster mother], I sit still and wait until she calls me to come and asks me what is wrong. With my mom I go straight and direct, but with my auntie I stand a bit until I am called."

CONCLUSION AND IMPLICATION

In this chapter, I discussed a culturally normative way of parenting at a distance: child fosterage. The practice challenges Western research on parenting that treats the nuclear, traditional family as the norm. Children are parented within the child fosterage system through explicit communication with the biological family, with gifts representing love and love lost. Implicit messages of moral teachings of survival and perseverance are taught as boundaries between biological and foster parents are shifted and reinvented. The findings challenge the belief that parenting from a distance is only born out of crisis. On the contrary, families are making conscious decisions to teach values through child fosterage.

The meaning of a "gift" as understood by Mauss (1954) can be seen in the practice of fosterage because the explicit reason for fosterage is often shrouded from the knowledge of children. For a gift to succeed as a gift, it must follow the social forms that usually prescribe that it be an unconditional offer in which explicit recognition of the goals is excluded from the practice. Parents appear to be the active agents in the performance of child fosterage as many children do not know the reasons that they are fostered. Families are bound together by these gifts, creating adaptive circuits and connections within which resources are shared.

Fosterage is a culturally born system sensitive to the ecocultural context. Like any sensitive system, it is also evolving with the context in Namibia. For example, following Levine's (1994) predictions of how parenting practices follow from universal goals of parenting, as education increased and people moved to more urbanized cities, they were more inclined to try to deny the fostering of their own children. For example, Paulus explained that he would purposefully not be at home when he knew someone who wanted to be gifted one of his children would be visiting. Others, like Tate Hambo, were fostered as a child and did not want their children to be taught the lesson of suffering that is part and parcel of fosterage. The denial of fostering with increased urbanization and education makes one wonder what cultural values will replace teaching moral development through perseverance and suffering, and how these values are culturally informed. As social capital is needed less and real monetary capital is increasing, how will fosterage evolve?

This study attempts to question the logic of Western ideas of childrearing and attachment as universally appropriate and attempts to broaden our understanding of how parents parent from a far. John Bowlby (1971) and other scholars of early childhood theorized that it is the quality of our relationships and the attachments we form that predict later psychological health. We know that children in child fosterage are taken from their primary attachments and placed in the home of another caregiver. Primary attachments are often broken, and new attachments are hopefully formed. The experience of foster children has elucidated that sibling relationships, not just maternal relationships, are often those that remain consistent and crucial to their psychological well-being while living away from their biological parents. Remembering siblings in the practice of fosterage is an important piece to the puzzle to how African families are maintaining care for more than 10 million orphans through this system of fosterage (Sewpaul, 2001), but also imagining that the breaking of that primary attachment may be a preferred cultural practice that evolved in ecocultural contexts like southern Africa. By understanding how fosterage is experienced by Owambos and how it fits into the ecological niche of raising children to survive and thrive in Africa, one truly extends hegemonic Western views of development and adds parenting from a distance into the realm of possibility.Conscious choices that parents make to raise anothers' child become imaginable in the toolbox of good parenting.

The implications of understanding how families configure and reconfigure themselves in and out of crisis is needed now more than ever because the HIV/AIDS epidemic is far from over. The insights gained through better understanding child fosterage can be used in caring for the most vulnerable children. One possibility suggested by this study is that moving children to foster families through culturally established and normative practices before the death of a parent may better help with a child's later adjustment and grief. Most HIV/AIDS orphans in my research were fostered before the death of their parent. To continue to do this may preserve the continuity of the practice through the "misrecognition" of the gift and the absence of the explicit recognition of the goals of the arrangement (namely, HIV/AIDS). Thus, children are embedded in a normative situation in the midst of a non-normative one (parental death). Through knowing more about the practice of fosterage, social services and nongovernmental organizations may be able to cast a wider net to potential caregivers even earlier in the process of securing care.

REFERENCES

Anderson, K. (2005). Relatedness and investment in children in South Africa. *Human Nature, 16*(1), 1–31.

Bledsoe, C. (1990). The Politics of Children: Fosterage and Social Management of Fertility among the Mende of Sierra Leone. In W. P. Handwerker (Ed.), *Births and Power: Social Change and the Politics of Reproduction* (pp. 81–100). Boulder Co: Westview Press.

Bledsoe, C., & Brandon, A. (1992). Child fosterage and child morality in sub-Saharan Africa: Some preliminary questions and answers. In E. Vande Walle, G. Pison, & M. Sala-Diankanda (Eds.), *Mortality and society in sub-Saharan Africa* (pp. 279–302). Oxford: Claredon Press.

Bourdieu, P. (1986). The Forms of Capital. In J Richardsons (Ed.), *Handbook of Theory and Research for the Sociology of Education* (pp. 241–258). New York: Greenwood press.

Bowie, F. (2004). *Cross-cultural approaches to adoption*. London: Routledge.

Brady, I. (1976). Adaptive engineering: An overview of adoption in Oceania. In Ivan Brady (Ed.), *Transactions in Kinship: Adoption and Fosterage in Oceania,* Honolulu: University Press of Hawaii.

Brown, J. (2013). Morals and maladies: Life histories of socially distributed care among Aaumbo women in Namibia, Southern Africa. *Journal of Critical Southern Studies, 1*(1), 60–79.

Brown, J. (2011). Child fostering chains among Owambo families in Namibia. *Journal of Southern African Studies, 31*(1), 155–176.

Brown, J. (2009). Child fosterage and the developmental markers of Ovambo children in Namibia: A look at gender and kinship. *Childhood in Africa: An interdisciplinary journal, 1*, 4–10.

Carroll, V. (1970). What does adoption mean? *Adoption in Eastern Oceania.* Honolulu: Univeristy of Hawaii Press.

CIA Factbook (2017) Namibia: The world factbook. Retrieved: May 15, 2017, https://www.cia.gov/library/publications/the-world-factbook/geos/wa.html

Clarke, E. (1957). *The mother who fathered me.* London: G. Allen and Unwin.

Creswell, J.W. (2003). *Research design: qualitative, quantitative and mixed method research.* Thousand Oaks, CA: Sage.

Gonzalez, N. (1969). *Black Carib household structure.* Seattle: University of Washington Press.

Goode, W. (1964). *The family.* New Jersey: Prentice-Hall, Inc.

Goody, E. (1973) *Contexts of kinship: An essay in the family sociology of the Gonja of northern Ghana.* London: Cambridge University Press.

Hayes, P. (1998). *Namibia under South African rule: mobility and containment 1915-1946.* Athens, OH: Ohio University Press.

Herskovits, M. (1937). *Life in a Haitian valley.* New York, NY: A.A. Knoff.

Isiugo-Abanihe, U. C. (1985). Child fosterage in West Africa. *Population and Development Review, 11*(1), 53–73.

LeVine, R. A., Dixon, S., LeVine, S., Richman, A., Leiderman, P.H., Keefer, C.H., & Brazelton, T. B. (1994). *Child care and culture: Lessons from Africa.* New York: Cambridge Univeristy Press.

Madhavan, S. (2004). "Fosterage Patterns in the Age of AIDS: Continuity and Change." *Social Science & Medicine, 58*, 443–454.

Mauss, M. (1954). *The Gift.* Glencoe: Free Press.

Merriam, S. (1998). *Qualitative research and case study applications in education.* San Fransisco: Jossey-Bass.

Monasch, R., & Boerma, J. T. (2004). Orphanhood and childcare patterns in sub-Saharan Africa: an analysis of national surveys from 40 countries. *AIDS, 18*(2), S55–S65.

Nsamenang, A. B. (2005). African Culture, Human Ontogenesis.In Fisher, C., & Lerner, R. (Eds.), *Encyclopedia of Applied Developmental Science.* Thousand Oaks, CA: Sage.

Oni, J. (1995). "Fostered children perception of their health care and illness treatment in Ekiti Yoruba households, Nigeria." *Health Transitions Review, 5*(1), 21–34.

Payne-Price, A. (1981). Etic variations on fosterage and adoption. *Anthropological Quarterly, 54*(3), 134–145.

Pennington, R. (1991). Child fostering as a reproductive strategy among southern African pastoralist. *Ethology and Sociobiology, 12*(2), 83–104.

Salokowski, M. (1998). "An analysis of the Big-Bird Ritual and its relation to the consolidation of kingship during the mid-1800s in the Aaumbo societies of northern Namibia." Working paper.

Sewpaul V. (2001). Models of intervention for children in difficult circumstances in South Africa. *Child Welfare,* (5), 571–586.

Stake, R.E. (1995). *The art of case study research.* Thousand Oaks, CA: Sage

Vandermeersch, C. (2002). Child fostering under six in Senegal in 1992-1993. *Population, 57*(4/5), 659–685.

Verhoff, H. & Morelli, G. (2007). "A child is a child": Fostering experiences in Northwestern Cameroon. *Ethos, 35*(2), 33–64.

Weisner, T, Bradley, C., and Kilbride, P. (eds) (1997). *African families and the crisis of social change.* Westport, CT: Bergin and Garvey.

14

Satellite Babies

Costs and Benefits of Culturally Driven Parent–Infant Separations in North American Immigrant Families

YVONNE BOHR, CINDY H. LIU, STEPHEN H. CHEN, AND LESLIE K. WANG ■

Every year, in North American immigrant communities, thousands of infants experience lengthy separations from their parents when they are left or sent to live with extended family overseas. The practice of transnational, temporary boarding of these "satellite babies" is widespread and poorly understood (Bohr & Tse, 2009). Versions of this practice have been documented in North American Chinese, South Asian, Caribbean, and Filipino communities (Aulakh, 2008; de Guzman, 2014; Glasgow & Ghouse-Sheese, 1995; Kwong, Chung, Sun, Chou, & Taylor-Shih, 2009). Such family separations have provoked worry among child developmentalists and community clinicians regarding potentially harmful consequences to children and parents (Liu, Li, & Ge, 2009; Miranda, Siddique, Der-Martirosian, & Belin, 2005; Suarez-Orozco, 2001). In recent years, media reports and several documentaries have contributed to the unease generated by parent–infant separations (e.g., Bernstein, 2009; Duncan & Garcia, 2016; Keung, 2009; Schweitzer, 2016; Wang, 2016). However, research in this area has been scant, and there exists some concern that transnational separations may be misunderstood and prone to unnecessary stigma based on a lack of cultural understanding.

In this chapter, we briefly review extant research that fuels the unease surrounding parent–infant separations. We examine motives for and repercussions of separating parents and infants for extensive periods of time. We then contextualize our analysis within a framework of parental ethnotheory as it applies to *family stress management during the process of settlement and acculturation.* Parental ethnotheories are the cultural belief systems, or schemas, that inform the everyday parenting practices of parents (Harkness & Super, 1996). Cultural schemas are organized sets of beliefs and interpretations that are shared between members of a culture and that become implicit in the way that parents make sense of the children's and their own behaviors and thoughts (Harkness & Super, 2006). Ethnotheories may play a protective role during migration, for example, by providing stability in family life or by offering strategies for dealing with challenging circumstances during resettlement. Parental ethnotheories play a significant role in supporting the practice of transnational parent–child separation and may result in clashes between belief systems that exist within the sending and the receiving cultures. Here, we consider the protective benefits of applicable cultural values and practices in addition to the risks, as they apply to deconstructing the phenomenon of satellite babies. Last, we review unanswered questions that would benefit from expanded research.

We focus primarily on the Chinese immigrant community as an exemplar for the proposed framework and draw on new data that provide a more complete picture of this practice than has thus far been available to the scientific and clinical communities.

PREVALENCE OF PARENT–INFANT SEPARATIONS IN NORTH AMERICAN CHINESE IMMIGRANT FAMILIES

Globally, more than 200 million migrants relocate each year (Koser & Laczko, 2010). About half a million arrive in the United States every year (Papademetriou & Newland, 2014) and another quarter million in Canada (Statistics Canada, 2016). Many of these migrants are members of families who have adopted transnational lifestyles after settling in their new country, often doing so after their children are born. Indeed, it is believed that every year among large urban centers in the United States and Canada a significant number of infants and toddlers experience separations from their parents as they are sent to live with extended family in the family's country of origin, a tradition that is often culturally sanctioned.

Until recently, there was little formal evidence available on the prevalence of the custom of parent–infant separation in North America, but many community clinicians believed that this practice might be increasing in some communities. Indeed, in 1999, *The New York Times* reported that up to 20% of approximately 1,500 babies born at the New York Chinatown Health Center were sent back to China (Sengupta, 1999). By 2009, a survey of 219 New York immigrant mothers from Fujian Province in China found that 57% of mothers intended to separate from their infants because of a need to return to work and lack of access to childcare (Kwong et al., 2009). Reports from a study of undocumented Chinese immigrants from New York City 2 years later indicated that more than 70% of participants may have sent infants back home (Yoshikawa, 2011). Anecdotal evidence gathered from social service workers in culture-specific Toronto community centers also suggests a high incidence of separation in the Chinese community of Canada's largest metropolitan area (Bohr & Tse, 2009). Community workers in programs designed to help families cope with transnationalism and deal with the challenges of reunification have expressed concern that "[the practice] has become a serious issue among families in the Chinese community" as it is estimated that "over half of Chinese women in perinatal programs across Toronto face this heartbreaking decision" (St. Stephen's Community House, 2008). More recently, the second, third, and fourth authors have conducted an ongoing study on examining stress and well-being among Chinese immigrant families in Boston Chinatown. Although not a population-based design, of approximately 150 parents with children between the ages of 0 and 10 who were surveyed, nearly 20% of respondents reported separating transnationally from their children for at least 5 months.

WHY SHOULD WE BE CONCERNED ABOUT TRANSNATIONAL PARENT–INFANT SEPARATION?

The child development literature points to many potential dangers of separating children and their parents. Classic attachment theory, for example, suggests that repeated disrupted attachments in childhood, such as those experienced by satellite children in transnational situations, could potentially result in mental health crises for some immigrant communities. Attachment theory stipulates that healthy socioemotional development in humans results from secure attachments to one or more primary caregivers who are consistently available to respond sensitively to the infant (Ainsworth & Bowlby, 1991). Furthermore, numerous attachment theorists have provided compelling evidence for the negative repercussions of separating infants from their primary caregivers in various contexts (Bowlby, 1958; Sroufe, 1988; Van van IJzendoorn & Bakermans Kranenburg, 1996). Repeated separation and disrupted attachments in early childhood have been associated with poorer developmental outcomes (Cassidy, 2008; Karen, 1994; Kobak & Madsen, 2008).

However, not surprisingly, questions have been raised of late about the cultural appropriateness of these stipulations based on the fact that, in many areas of the world, infants are raised by multiple caregivers in often fluid extended family networks (Seymour, 2013). Such networks do not neatly fit the conditions that presumably beget secure attachment, yet there is little evidence to suggest that fewer securely attached children emerge from such arrangements. Furthermore, previous research has shown that children may form productive attachment relationships with different caregivers for months or years at a time at different points in their development (Keller, 2012; Leinaweaver, 2014). In the case of satellite babies, disruptions to their attachment system occur at multiple levels and across multiple contexts. Indeed, these infants' attachment relationships with their first caregivers—their biological parents—are disrupted when they are sent away to form new relationships with the surrogate family abroad. The quality of the new relationship may be more or less secure, only to then be disturbed at the time when the infant is returned to the family of origin; this creates multiple ruptures in attachment relationships, which is qualitatively different from the case of children who enjoy multiple simultaneous bonds with caregivers. Whether the formation and rupturing of multiple serial attachment bonds is traumatic and damaging or does in fact create resilience through repeated experience with forming new relationships is likely multidetermined and dependent on numerous temperamental and environmental factors (e.g., the sensitivity and supportiveness of the child's successive caregivers, preparation of the child for the separation and reunion, and the child's understanding of the circumstances that warranted the separation). Clearly, the long-term benefits and costs of such serial arrangements for specific families and children need to be more fully studied.

Until recently, practitioners in the field of child development had to rely largely on theoretical discussions of disruptions of attachment and childhood loss when it came to understanding the potential sequelae of transnational parent–child separations. However, while the developmental pathways of infants who have experienced early separation remain to be examined more systematically, a growing number of mostly small and qualitative surveys of young adults' retrospective perceptions and feelings about earlier separations from their parents now offer some insight into the long-time consequences of family separations (e.g., Artico, 2001; Glasgow & Ghouse-Sheese, 1995; Hicks, Lalonde, & Pepler, 1993; Smith, Lalonde, & Johnson, 2004). Several researchers found evidence that immigrant children who have been separated from their parents are more prone to depression, low self-esteem, and behavioral problems (Brown, Harris, & Bifulco, 1986; Smith et al., 2004; Suarez-Orozco & Suarez-Orozco, 2001). Two studies of the impact of parent–child separation in adolescents from the Caribbean whose mothers had migrated to the United States are helpful in elucidating the often unintended consequences of domestic workers' relocation without their children. Youth from these studies who had joined their parent after several years of separation were at greater risk for internalizing disorders due to the loss of relationships back home, loneliness, and disappointed expectations upon arrival in the United States (Fletcher Anthony, 2006; Lemy, 2000).

The impact of parent–child separation and reunification has also been explored, on a small scale, in South Asian families. Srinivasan and Raman (1988) found that children in India who had experienced a separation of more than 3 months from fathers or both parents, or who had experienced multiple separations, were at increased risk for psychopathology in late adolescence. Messent, Saleh, and Solomon (2005), in a study of Bangladeshi immigrants in Great Britain, showed that separated families exhibited communication difficulties following reunification. In addition, a recent small-scale qualitative study (Whitfield, 2014) queried parents from three immigrant communities about child-focused concerns, parent-focused concerns, and parent–child relational concerns in the context of their separation from and reunification with their child. Interviews consistently revealed a host of parent concerns about child behavior, parenting struggles, and parent–child relationship challenges, beginning during periods of parent–child separation and generally persisting and/or worsening post-reunification. To date, the most serious potential outcomes for youth were reported by Morgan et al. (2007), who concluded that early separations from parents may account for a significant increase in the rate of psychotic disorders in a UK Caribbean community. Last, the intuitively salient notion that parent–child separations may also adversely affect the *parents* should not be discounted. Several studies have highlighted the cost to mothers of prolonged separation from their offspring (Black, 2006; Lam, Chan, & Tsoi, 2005; Miranda et al., 2005). It would seem that the emotional challenge of missing one's infant can only add to the known trials for the entire family system of acculturation and settlement in a new environment (Bohr, 2010; Duncan & Garcia, 2016; Wang, 2016).

PERSONAL AND SOCIAL ENVIRONMENTAL FACTORS THAT DRIVE PARENTS TO CONSIDER A SEPARATION

In light of the many potential pitfalls of separating infants from their parents, a Canadian pilot study (Bohr, Hynie, Whitfield, Shih, & Zafar, 2011) sought to explore several variations of the custom of temporarily boarding young children with relatives overseas through focus groups and interviews in three Toronto immigrant communities. Thirty-four parents of children 6–12 years old, all of whom had children who had returned to Canada after a separation period of at least 1 year and had lived in another country with extended family, friends, or other alternate caregivers, were interviewed in small groups or individually. Families were referred by community support workers as well as recruited through advertisements in local, language-specific media and announcements in community centers. It should be noted that many participants took part on the condition that they would not have to share personal information other than their impressions about their families' transnational experiences and associated hardships. This concern was undoubtedly linked to worries about stigma, fears about the possibility that child welfare agencies would become involved when reporting voluntary separations from infants, and/or struggles with challenging child behavior upon return of their offspring. This study was designed to address the factors that drive family separation, the negative consequences reported by affected families, and cultural features that support separation, as well as common sequelae experienced by families. The authors used a cross-disciplinary, community-based participatory approach and combined community leaders', service providers', and parents' perspectives to identify some of the unmet needs of transnational families, with the goal of proposing interventions and implications for policy. In this study, parents in the Chinese community emphasized the pressures of immigration and resettlement as the factors that drove them to separate from their children, in particular the financial strain of establishing themselves in Canada. The cost of living, in particular the cost of accommodation, was cited. Trying to find a good job and retraining was made all the more difficult in light of the lack of social support and scarce, expensive childcare resources:

> Our income was not so stable. If the child was here [in Canada], with our rent for housing and others, our cost for living would increase. Because if you have your children around, we will have to rent a whole place. If we didn't have our child around, with our finances, we would consider probably

> renting a smaller place or I would choose to live in the basement. (Mother from Toronto Chinese community focus group)

Many participants related being completely exhausted by the rigors of adapting to their life in a new country. Relying on relatives back in China for childcare was deemed necessary for the sake of maximizing resources for the betterment of the family; another mother noted, "With work and study at hand, I could not handle it. After sending my children away, I slept for 48 hours straight. . . . [My reason] was simple. I didn't have enough energy."

An ongoing investigation by the second, third, and fourth authors examines transnational separation experiences among Chinese immigrant families in Boston Chinatown. In the process of conducting a larger study of stress and well-being among Chinese immigrant families, the investigators' community partners highlighted transnational separations as a unique, salient, and underresearched source of stress among families in the community. As such, qualitative semi-structured interviews were conducted with 30 parents who experienced transnational separations from their children. Each parent was interviewed individually in either Mandarin or Cantonese for between 60 and 90 minutes. Interview questions assessed various aspects of the separation experience, including factors influencing the decision to separate, challenges of separation and reunion, and the impact of the separation on family relationships. Interviews were audio-recorded, transcribed, and translated into English by bilingual research assistants.

Preliminary analyses of interview transcripts have identified a number of key factors motivating the transnational separation process. For example, some interviews have underscored the impact of the financial challenges that would result from keeping the child in the United States:

> You'd be burdened. You'll be extremely pressured. If one parent goes to work while the other stays home, the one who stays home won't be able to do a good job with the kids because of how much pressure they're under. This would negatively influence the child's temper as well. It's bad for their growth. But if your financial situation isn't so bad, it's better for you to look after your own kid. (Mother from Boston study)

Parents recognized both benefits and costs of the decision to allow extended family in China to provide childcare. As one mother notes:

> Even though I missed him all the time, there's just no way you can get everything you want, right? You want to make money but you also want to take care of your kid, there's no way so we had to give something up. We felt like it'd be safer and better for our family to be the ones looking after him instead of sending him off to someone else's home. (Mother from Boston study)

Among the Chinese-Canadian parents studied by Bohr and her colleagues in this and prior studies (2009, 2011), cultural factors have always featured prominently and consistently in families' decisions to board infants with relatives. For example, the traditional role of grandparents was greatly valued, as was the importance of children spending time with their grandparents. Elders were seen as crucial for providing instrumental and emotional support to the young family. In addition, given that many of the grandparents had themselves previously separated from their own children, boarding them with parents or extended family, spending time with the current grandchildren was seen as a way of compensating the grandparents for the loss of time with their own offspring, an expectation and perhaps a "right" of sorts:

> When we left the country, it was painful for our elders, they missed us a lot. So actually, having our child to stay with them is a great way to comfort them. They were really happy in those years although it made them really busy . . . for seniors . . . you actually bring many happiness into their lives. (Mother from Toronto Chinese community focus group)

Parents highlighted additional cultural benefits. To have one's child exposed to Chinese culture and language while back in China, for example, was seen as one of the definitive advantages of sending one's offspring to China. One father from the Toronto Chinese focus group reports, "[We don't want them to] forget that we are all still Chinese, no matter where he or she is born or what kind of nationality." Reflecting similar sentiments, one mother reasons, "We think, here [in Canada], once children go to daycare, it is possible that she or he will only speak English and will be reluctant to speak Chinese."

In addition to language exposure, respondents deemed the Chinese educational system more positively with regard to preparing young learners for success:

> Here [in Canada], children only play every day. And this is what bothers me. . . . My daughter in China, she only took a year of kindergarten. Within that year, she learned 100 Chinese words. (Father from Toronto Chinese community focus group)

PARENTS' EXPECTATIONS ABOUT THE SEPARATION AND ITS OUTCOMES

Parents from Boston Chinatown noted certain benefits to separation, particularly in regards to increased flexibility in their schedules that allowed them to devote themselves to work and/or study full time. At the same time, some parents acknowledged that the decision was "risky" in terms of its long-term impact on children. This may have been due to information they received about possible risks for sending their children to China:

> They write in the papers about how the child can't adapt to new environments, schools, doesn't want to go to school, doesn't have a great relationship

with his parents. The parent–child relationship is damaged from the experience. After reading all of that, I feel so relieved that we brought him back a lot earlier than planned. (Mother from Boston study)

Inferences were also made regarding their children's understanding of and emotional response and adjustment to the separation. Some parents considered children's young ages and lack of understanding as potential protective factors that could buffer possible adverse effects of the separation.

She probably didn't understand. We went to the airport with my cousin. She knew my cousin . . . didn't understand she was going to go somewhere very far. But at the airport, she went in, and cried a little . . . then my cousin played with her, and she became less sad, then she got on the plane and went back. (Mother from Boston study)

When asked directly about the appropriate age for bringing a child back, parents expressed that the child's level of understanding and his or her own temperament were important considerations. One mother from the Boston study noted,

I think anything before 3 years old is good. 5 years old is too much. He's already starting to understand things at the age of 3, so 5 is a lot older and that might affect your relationship with your child.

Reporting similar sentiments about younger children being less affected, another mother opined,

It's better for the child and for the parents in terms of communication. When they're young, around 1 year [old], and they still don't really know how to walk and they don't really understand anything, it's easier. When they're 4 years old, it's different. It's also better for kids who are extroverted, they adapt better. (Mother from Boston study)

Participants were asked about their child's adjustment in regards to both the initial separation from parents and with the eventual separation from the caregiver in China. Most felt that their children adjusted within a few months.

There were lots of fun stuff for her in China . . . and she got used to them eventually, and she didn't ask to come back to mom. . . . When she first came out [to the United States], she was very sad. She was sad about leaving her grandma. (Mother from Boston study)

Several parents in Bohr's (2009, 2011) studies were keenly aware of the many potential consequences of their separation from the children, including, among other things, their own sense of alienation from their offspring over time and a feeling of not knowing the child, as reflected in statements they made such as, "I feel that currently, I don't really know him" (mother from Toronto study). Another parent elaborated on her experience of growing distance from her daughter as a result of separation:

> Like my daughter. . . . She was in China. In the beginning, we call each other every day. Also, when we talk on the phone, she has a lot to say. As time passed by, she slowly stopped wanting to talk to me. One reason being maybe because she has grown up now, our connection naturally becomes not as close as before. (Mother from Toronto study)

A mother in the Boston Chinatown sample provided a similar reflection on the impact of separations on family relationships:

> When he first came back he was so unfamiliar with me that he didn't even want me anymore. I was thinking about how having other people raise your child turns the child into someone who doesn't even belong to you anymore. (Mother from Boston study)

HOW PARENTS MANAGED THEIR RELATIONSHIPS DURING THE FAMILY SEPARATION

In both the Toronto and Boston Chinatown samples, parents recalled speaking and interacting periodically with their children over video chat. While the advancements of technology allowed this interaction to take place, the range of communication and engagement with their children or the temporary caregivers varied, especially as caregivers at times attempted activities such as Skyping with children as young as 6 months of age (Bohr & Tse, 2009). One parent from the Boston study reported, "We were busy working, sometimes didn't have time [to talk to him] . . . but when seeing [talking to] him, just talked about food and things, and didn't mind him much." Another respondent noted the challenges of the child's caregiver, "Because my parents didn't know how to use computers, they had to go to the neighbor, and you can't go to the neighbor's every day, so about twice a month . . . we talked on the phone every 2 or 3 days" (mother from Boston study).

In contrast, other parents found long-distance mediated communication more accessible. As one mother from the Boston study described their ease in communication:

> Sometimes every 2 or 3 days, some times whenever we're free, some times every 1 or 2 days. Since it's so easy for us to communicate nowadays, they contact us whenever something comes up and we ask them about his situation whenever we're free.

Although no direct reports were obtained from the temporary caregivers in these studies or, to our knowledge, have appeared in any other study, parents did report that the caregivers were often satisfied with the arrangement. In light of an age-old tradition of grandparents caring for children in China, boosted by the now-defunct one-child policy, the decision to entrust their child to eager grandparents seemed fitting for many of the families. Indeed, this traditional type of arrangement served the dual purpose of helping to maintain family ties and meeting practical childcare needs. Such perceived benefits are reflected in one mother's description of her parents' feelings about caring for her child, "[The grandparents] were quite happy . . . because it was just the two of them at home. Now with a child to take care of, they like it a lot" (Boston study).

On the other hand, some parents were not fully satisfied with the childcare provided by these family members, citing concerns about their lack of knowledge about nutrition or lack of discipline:

> Some grandparents who are educated will understand the importance of balanced nutrition for the children. But some grandparents who live in rural areas or are not educated, they won't understand how to make powdered milk properly, the importance of balanced nutrition and personal hygiene. (Mother from Boston study)
>
> Some grandparents are fine but other pamper their grandchildren a lot so the kids think that they're little kings and princes. (Mother from Boston study)

Aside from socioemotional outcomes, multiple parents and providers have also identified health outcomes, most notably poor dental health, after the child returned to the United States. According to one parent:

> I remember when she first came back to US, she would throw trash everywhere . . . and teeth, very bad teeth. Because grandparents only brushed her teeth in the mornings, not evenings, so she had many cavities. (Mother from Boston study)

In Bohr and colleagues' (2011) study, all parents reported feelings of sadness and guilt when it came to their separations from their children, and many felt that parents should ideally not want to separate:

> Still now I feel hurt, you know, so that's why I don't leave my girl [second child] with my parents, because you don't have that kind of feeling and it's hard to make up, very hard to make up. (Mother from Toronto study)

Parents in the Boston Chinatown study also recalled feelings of sadness during the separation. As one parent reported, "I felt even worse when I saw children of about the same age that reminded me of my own children."

Some parents expressed concerns that the children were distant in their interactions after being reunited with their nuclear family, that they might have been confused about the nature of the relationship with their parents and might be resentful about having been sent away. One parent expressed her challenge during reunification, "When I go back, she didn't even know me, didn't recognize me, as if I never gave birth to her" (mother from Toronto study).

One Toronto mother found a very poignant way of verbalizing what many others attempted to express when describing the inevitable estrangement that was the consequence of months and sometimes years of the infant's separation from her biological parents: "Though she knew us as her mom and dad from her words, she did not have the concept down in her heart."

HOW SHOULD THE PRACTICE OF TRANSNATIONAL PARENT–INFANT SEPARATION BE CONCEPTUALIZED

There are several insights to be taken by policy-makers and clinicians alike from the emerging findings discussed in this chapter. First and foremost, the satellite baby phenomenon is but one illustration of the many forms of coping that new immigrants may resort to everywhere in the world in order to adapt to their new contexts. Indeed, the optimism that immigrants typically associate with opportunities in a new country is often short-lived as they begin to face the numerous challenges that confront them upon arrival. Many immigrants face stressors such as the dismissal of their educational credentials, the inability to work in their prior profession, and a failure to find work that provides sufficient compensation. Combined with the dearth of affordable options for childcare in the United States and Canada, these circumstances can be overwhelming. Among the participants in the studies discussed here, many families resorted to the familiar strategy of temporary family separation in order to cope. Unfortunately, this strategy often yielded further adversity in the form of emotional hardship resulting from parent–child separations in early development. Concerns reported by both parents and adult children in these studies and others include the disruption of the parent–child emotional bond, the emotional turmoil experienced by both parties during separation, and, in some cases, distress post-reunification (Bohr & Tse, 2009). Although parents reported feeling that they had few alternatives, the majority also stated that they would not want to go through the separation process again. Participants from all studies agreed that there is a pressing need for better resources to support new immigrant families in similar situations.

In our studies, Chinese-Canadian and Chinese-American families often described a *push–pull* dynamic, where economic concerns *pushed* parents to send their children elsewhere, while cultural (i.e., grandparental and educational) expectations *pulled* the children back to the home country, resulting in an overwhelming impetus to take advantage of overseas boarding for their young children. The concept of *push–pull factors* has long been used in the area of migration research to describe the dual forces at work in influencing individuals' and families' decision to emigrate: push factors compel one to leave one's home (e.g., economic, environmental, conflict), while pull factors represent those incentives for emigrating to a new context (e.g., availability of work, quality of life, peace, education) (see Settles, 2001; Sussman & Settles, 1993). We use it here to support the notion of parents' dual motivation when it comes to separating from their children in the context of migration: solving what may seem like an intractable problem of lack of resources for caring for their infants in their receiving country *(push),* by giving in to the *pull* of tradition/expectation of kin care. This powerful dual force, perhaps an integral part of a comforting ethnotheory, may explain why some parents ultimately tolerate the sorrow of separating from their very young children.

Given the economic and social adversity and risks faced by immigrants, it is important to consider their resilience, which is often based in the "pull" of cultural practice. Resilience is evident in participants' reports of using culturally embedded and sanctioned customs for coping with unexpected adversity, their tireless work to repair the relationships damaged by family separations, and their overall positivity regarding the outcomes of their immigration journey (e.g., Bohr et al., 2011). Indeed, cultural identity has been identified as a protective factor in Chinese communities as well as in other contexts (e.g., McCubbin & McCubbin, 2005; Shek, 2004).

Family separation in the context of immigration should perhaps be conceptualized as an ethnotheoretical approach similar to the strategies discussed in existing theories and models of coping (e.g., Kuo, 2014; Wong et al., 1993; 2006). In his *Resource-Congruence Model of Effective Coping,* Wong advanced the notion that culturally based expectations influence what is appraised as stressful. More importantly perhaps, this model posits that cultural knowledge also determines what coping behavior is appropriate for any given stressful situation, supporting the "persistent efforts at coping with multiple and often chronic stressors encountered within the new environment" as described by Castro and Murray (2010, p. 376, as cited in Kuo, 2014). An appreciation of culture should clearly factor into any discussions of adaptive versus maladaptive coping processes, acknowledging that individuals and families of diverse cultural backgrounds cope with specific stressors in ways that are congruous with their culture's expectations and accepted practices.

Though boarding infants with kin may be a familiar, culturally embedded practice, the strategy of separating parents and children in transnational situations may ultimately increase the stress load for families, perhaps even contributing to the health problems common to postmigration immigrants (the "immigrant paradox," Escobar, 1998), and may challenge parents' otherwise adaptive ethnotheories. It may be important to recognize that the coping strategy of using grandparents as child minders, although effective in its original form and cultural context, results in greatly decreased efficacy and adverse consequences not because it was faulty to begin with, but rather because it was transplanted to a new context, which, in addition to introducing significant geographic distance, also lacks in necessary social and economic supports. Still, in spite of the documented adverse repercussions, family separation might be usefully conceptualized as an integral feature of a specific parental ethnotheory and thus perhaps a culturally based health-seeking strategy that demonstrates and promotes resilience.

To prevent new immigrants from resorting to health-seeking strategies that might ultimately prove to be counterproductive, societies should aim to eliminate the stressful circumstances that create the need to cope. This can best be achieved through progressive social and immigration policies. However, while these policies may not yet exist across countries, culturally sensitive community resources should be mobilized both to support families that are compelled to separate and to assist with the reintegration process.

It is important for community mental health systems to acknowledge that the social and economic hardships faced by immigrant families in North America are, in many cases, the product of inadequate policies at several levels of government (Bohr et al., 2011). For example, the same degrees and qualifications that bolster immigration applications are, paradoxically, rarely recognized upon arrival in North America, leading to chronic underemployment in immigrant communities. This issue is exacerbated by insufficient access to language training. In addition, housing options in the large urban centers where most newcomers first settle are generally either inadequate or unaffordable. The same is true for the lack of affordable childcare, a problem compounded by difficulties and delays in obtaining immigration permits for longer term stays of extended family members who could be enlisted to help where local social networks are lacking.

Without good policies to address such challenges, immigrant families are often left with no other option than those coping strategies that cause stress and negative health outcomes, ultimately raising the cost of settlement. Current policies that contribute to this dilemma thus must be examined and optimized at federal, provincial/state, and municipal levels, with the goal of streamlining the adaptation, health, and economic success of young immigrant families with children. The areas that should be prioritized are as follows: immigration policy regarding labor qualifications and retraining opportunities; expediency of the immigration process; immigrant settlement and integration, language training programs, and substantive job search assistance; family immigration policies, with particular attention paid to reunification; childcare policy; adaptation and creation of mental health models and interventions that meet immigrant families' needs; and specialized community mental health resources, including family resource centers and parent education.

In addressing the need for community mental health resources, it is crucial to emphasize the importance of cultural competency. Existing service providers may only be competent in Western-oriented psychological models of parenting and family–child functioning and may require retraining in providing resources and approaches that are better suited for immigrant families dealing with separation as well as for those who choose to forego separation. It is important that excellent resources be provided to families that have separated and/or are in the process of reintegrating after reunification. It is also crucial that the often still prevalent use of traditional, Eurocentric family mental health approaches be adjusted or replaced with methods that are more strengths-oriented and culturally sensitive and acknowledge the concrete implications of diverse parental ethnotheories. Such a shift will assist clinicians in understanding culturally grounded coping mechanisms when assessing and intervening, reconceptualizing them as health-seeking strategies and learning to support and optimize them while acknowledging the risks these culturally transplanted strategies may pose to families.

What it means to be a child who has suffered multiple separations and geographical as well as cultural relocations remains to be fully described. There is a great need for systematic, large-scale longitudinal studies of children and parents in diverse immigrant communities that engage in transnational family separations. Such studies will need to find strategies to overcome biases and fears associated with providing what is often perceived to be potentially incriminating information about one's family life. Until we have the opportunity to complete such studies, it may be useful to keep in mind that, regardless of the specific nature of developmental outcomes, ultimately, providing a more welcoming and supportive environment to immigrant families during resettlement will surely help to optimize the health, quality of life, and productivity of a new generation of North American citizens.

REFERENCES

Ainsworth, M. D. S., & Bowlby, J. (1991). An ethological approach to personality development. *American Psychologist, 46*, 331–341.

Artico, C. I. (2001). *Perceptions and memories of Latino adolescents separated in childhood due to piecemeal patterns of immigration*. Dissertation Abstracts International Section A: Humanities and Social Sciences, 61, 9A. (UMI No. 9985096).

Aulakh, R. (2008). The trauma of raising kids an ocean away. *The Toronto Star*. Retrieved from http://www.thestar.com/article/537552.

Bernstein, N. (2009). Chinese-American children sent to live with kin abroad face a tough return. *The New York Times*. Retrieved from http://www.nytimes.com/2009/07/24/nyregion/24chinese.html?_r=0

Black, A. E. (2006). *The separation and reunification of recently immigrated Mexican families*. Dissertation Abstracts International: Section B: The Sciences and Engineering, 66, 11B. (UMI No. 3196552)

Bohr, Y. (2010). Transnational infancy: A new context for attachment and the need for better models. *Child Development Perspectives*, *4*(3), 189–196.

Bohr, Y., Hynie, M., Whitfield, N., Shih, C., & Zafar, S. (2011). *Parent-infant separation in trans-national families: Risk, resilience, and the needs of young immigrant parents*. Report to the Centre of Excellence for Research on Immigration and Settlement, Toronto, ON.

Bohr, Y. & Tse, C. (2009). Satellite Babies in transnational families: a study of parents' decision to separate from their infants. *Infant Mental Health Journal*, *30*(3), 265–286.

Bowlby, J. (1958). *Can I leave my baby?*. London: National Association for Mental Health.

Brown, G. W., Harris, T. O., & Bifulco, A. (1986). The long-term effects of early loss of parent. In M. Rutter, C.E. Izard, & P.B. Read (Eds.), *Depression in young people* (pp.251–296). New York: Guilford Press.

Cassidy, J. (2008). The nature of the child's ties. In: J. Cassidy & P.R. Shaver (Eds.), *Handbook of attachment: theory, research and clinical applications* (2nd ed.) (pp 3–22). Guilford Press, New York.

Castro F. G., & Murray K. E. (2010). Cultural adaptation and resilience: Controversies, issues, and emerging models. In: J. W. Reich, A. J. Zautra, J. S. Hall (Eds.). *Handbook of adult resilience* (pp. 375–403). New York, NY: The Guildford Press.

de Guzman, M. R. T. (2014). Yaya: Philippine domestic care workers, the children they care for, and the children they leave behind. *International Perspectives in Psychology: Research, Practice, Consultation*, *3*(3), 197.

Duncan, J. & Garcia, L. (2016). Helping satellite babies thrive in the US. *CBS News*. Retrieved from http://www.cbsnews.com/news/helping-satellite-babies-china-us-families/

Escobar, J. I. (1998). Immigration and mental health: Why are immigrants better off? *Archives of General Psychiatry*, *55*(9), 781–782.

Fletcher Anthony, W. (2006). *The lived experience of West Indian youth reunified with immigrant parents in the host country: a phenomenological study*. (Unpublished doctoral dissertation). Retrieved from http://wwwlib.umi.com/dissertations/fullcit/3215985.

Glasgow, G.F., & Ghouse-Sheese, J. (1995). Themes of rejection and abandonment in group work with Caribbean adolescents. *Social Work with Groups*, *17*, 3–27.

Harkness, S., & Super, C. M. (1996). *Parents' cultural belief systems: Their origins, expressions, and consequences*. New York: Guilford.

Harkness, S., & Super, C. M. (2006). Themes and variations: Parental ethnotheories in Western cultures. *Parenting beliefs, behaviors, and parent-child relations: A cross-cultural perspective*, 61–79.

Hicks, R., Lalonde, R. N., & Pepler, D. (1993). Psychosocial considerations in the mental health of immigrant and refugee children. *Canadian Journal of Community Mental Health*, *12*, 71–87.

Karen, R. (1994). *Becoming Attached: Unfolding the Mystery of the infant–mother Bond and its Impact on Later Life*. New York: Warner Books.

Keung, N. (2009). The Painful Choice of "Satellite Babies." *Health and Wellness, The Toronto Star*. Retrieved from https://www.thestar.com/life/health_wellness/2009/05/11/the_painful_choice_of_satellite_babies.html

Keller, H. (2012). Attachment and culture. *Journal of Cross-Cultural Psychology*. Published online before print. doi: 10.1177/0022022112472253

Kobak, R., & Madsen, S. (2008). Disruptions in attachment bonds: Implications for theory, research, and clinical intervention. In J. Cassidy, & P. R. Shaver (Eds), *Handbook of attachment: Theory, research, and clinical applications*, (2nd ed) (pp. 23–47). New York, NY, US: Guilford Press.

Koser, K., & Laczko, F. (2010). World migration report 2010. The future of migration: Building capacities for change. *Geneva, Switzerland: International Organization for Migration*.

Kuo, B. C. H. (2014). Coping, acculturation, and psychological adaptation among migrants: A theoretical and empirical review and synthesis of the literature. *Health Psychology and Behavioral Medicine*, *2*(1), 16–33. http://doi.org/10.1080/21642850.2013.843459

Kwong, K., Chung, H., Sun, L., Chou, J.C. & Taylor-Shih, A.(2009). Factors Associated with Reverse-Migration Separation Among a Cohort of Low-Income Chinese Immigrant Families in New York City. *Social Work in Health Care*, *48*(3), 348–359.

Lam, A. M., Chan, T. S., & Tsoi, K. W. (2005). Meaning of family reunification as interpreted by young Chinese immigrants. *International Journal of Adolescent Medical Health*, *17*(2), 105–122.

Lemy, M. E. (2000). The Effect of Early Separation on Parent-Child Attachment among Haitian Immigrants Families. (Unpublished doctoral dissertation). Retrieved from: http://scholarship.shu.edu/dissertations/1547.

Leinaweaver, J. (2014). Informal kinship-based fostering around the world: Anthropological findings. *Child Development Perspectives*, *8*(3), 131–136.

Liu, Z., Li, X., & Ge, X. (2009). Left too early: The effects of age at separation from parents on Chinese rural children's symptoms of anxiety and depression. *American Journal of Public Health*, *99*(11), 2049–2054. http://doi.org/10.2105/AJPH.2008.150474

McCubbin, L. D., & McCubbin, H. I. (2005). Culture and ethnic identity in family resilience. *Handbook for working with children and youth: Pathways to resilience across cultures and contexts*, 27–44.

Messent, P., Saleh, H., & Solomon, X. (2005). Asian families "back home": An unexplored resource. *Contemporary family therapy*, *27*(3), 329–344.

Miranda, J., Siddique, J., Der-Martirosian, C., & Belin, T. R. (2005). Depression among Latina immigrant mothers separated from their children. *Psychiatric Services*, *56*, 717–720.

Morgan, C., Kirkbride, J., Leff, J., Craig, T., Hutchinson, G., McKenzie, K., . . . & Murray, R. (2007). Parental separation, loss and psychosis in different ethnic groups: a case-control study. *Psychological medicine*, *37*(04), 495–503.

Papademetriou, D.G. & Newland, K. (2014). How migration can advance development goals. Migration Policy Institute: Washingtopn, DC.

Schweitzer, J. (2016, July 20). The confusing lives of Chinese_American "satellite babies." *The Atlantic*. Retrieved from http://www.theatlantic.com/video/index/491843/the-confusing-lives-of-chinese-american-satellite-babies/

Sengupta, S. (1999). Women keep garment jobs by sending babies to China. *The New York Times*. Retrieved 3/3/2005, from http://www.huaren.org/diaspora/n_america/usa/news/091499-01.html

Settles, B. H. (2001). Being at home in a global society: A model for families' mobility and immigration decisions. *Journal of Comparative Family Studies*, *32*(4), 627–645.

Seymour, S. C. (2013). "It takes a village to raise a child": Attachment theory and multiple child care in Alor, Indonesia, and in North India. In N. Quinn, & J.M. Mageo (Eds.), *Attachment reconsidered* (pp. 115–139). U.S.: Palgrave Macmillan.

Shek, D. T. (2004). Chinese cultural beliefs about adversity its relationship to psychological well-being, school adjustment and problem behaviour in Hong Kong adolescents with and without economic disadvantage. *Childhood*, *11*(1), 63–80.

Smith, A., Lalonde, R. N., & Johnson, S. (2004). Serial migration and its implications for the parent-child relationship: A retrospective analysis of the experiences of the children of Caribbean immigrants. *Cultural Diversity & Ethnic Minority Psychology*, *10*(2), 107–122.

Srinivasan, T. N., & Raman, K. J. (1988). Early child parent separation and risk for childhood psychopathology. *Indian Journal of Psychiatry*, *30*(3), 283–289.

Sroufe, L. A. (1988). The role of infant-caregiver attachment in development. In J. Belsky & T. Nezworski (Eds.), Clinical implications of attachment (pp. 18–38). New Jersey: Lawrence Erlbaum Associates, Inc.

Statistics Canada. (2016). Permanent resident admissions. Statistics Canada dataset. Retrieved from http://www.statcan.gc.ca/pub/12-591-x/2009001/02-step-etape/ex/ex-census-recensement-eng.htm

Suarez-Orozco, C., & Suarez-Orozco, M. M. (2001). *Children of immigration*. Cambridge, MA, US: Harvard University Press.

St. Stephen's Community House. (2008). A heartbreaking decision. Documentary film. Toronto, ON.

Sussman, M. B., & Settles, B. H. (1993). Policy and research issues regarding family mobility and immigration. *Marriage & Family Review, 19*(3-4), 209–232.

van IJzendoorn, M. H., & Bakermans-Kranenburg, M. J. (1996). Attachment representations in mothers, fathers, adolescents, and clinical groups: A meta-analytic search for normative data. *Journal of Consulting and Clinical Psychology, 64*(1), 8.

Wang, H.L. (2016, October 13). Born in the U.S., raised in China: "Satellite babies have a hard time coming home. *National Public Radio*. Retrieved from http://www.npr.org/sections/ed/2016/10/13/492860463/born-in-the-u-s-raised-in-china-satellite-babies-have-a-hard-time-coming-home

Whitfield, N. (2014). *The return of satellite babies: Two studies exploring and responding to the needs of reunited immigrant families*. (Unpublished doctoral dissertation). York University, Toronto, ON.

Wong, P. T. (1993). Effective management of life stress: The resource–congruence model. *Stress Medicine*, 9(1), 51–60.

Wong, P. T. P., Reker, G. T. & Peacock, E. (2006). The resource-congruence model of coping and the development of the coping schemas inventory. In Wong, P. T. P., & Wong, L. C. J. (Eds.), *Handbook of Multicultural perspectives on stress and coping* (pp. 223–283). New York, NY: Springer.

Yoshikawa, H. (2011). *Immigrants raising citizens: Undocumented parents and their children*. Russell Sage Foundation.

15

Going the Distance

Transnational Educational Migrant Families in Korea

SUMIE OKAZAKI AND JEEHUN KIM

Historically, global migration has involved search for work or asylum. However, in the past few decades, educational migration—particularly from Asian to English-speaking nations—has expanded exponentially. Fueling this growth is the rapid expansion of opportunities for Asian students and families of diverse economic means to study abroad in more varied destinations and at different stages of education. Study abroad and educational migration—previously the exclusive province of children of wealthy families and elite students pursuing postgraduate studies—have diversified considerably in the past few decades (Ihm & Choi, 2015). In addition to a large number of international students from China, Korea, and India at US colleges and universities, a sizable contingent of young students from China and Korea are now enrolled in primary and secondary schools in various destinations around the globe (Waters, 2015*a*).

In this chapter, we focus our review of the scholarly literature on transnational educational migrant families from South Korea, often called *kirogi* (wild geese) families in Korea because of the long distances they travel for seasonal visits to reunite with separated family members, often with the children and their mothers living in English-speaking countries while the fathers stay behind in Korea to work. The "geese family" arrangement represents one common form of "early study abroad" (translated from *chogi yuhak* in Korean), a flexible, short-term educational strategy employed by families in which children studied abroad for short-term education before college. South Korean early study abroad (ESA hereafter) makes for an illustrative case because of extensive scholarship surrounding the rapid expansion, diversification, and gradual waning of the practice within the past two decades. Observations and analyses of the South Korean case, against the backdrop of educational migration from Hong Kong and Taiwan preceding it, may auger what is to come for students and families from other Asian nations such as mainland China and India who have been increasing their participation in transnational educational migration.

An in-depth look at the South Korean ESA also provides a fertile ground for understanding the cosmopolitan desires and the mobilization of social capital that motivate educational migration as a family strategy (Abelmann, Newendorp, & Lee-Chung, 2014; Lo, Abelmann, Kwon, & Okazaki, 2015; Waters, 2012). Arranging a pre-college study abroad requires considerable and coordinated efforts among the adults responsible for the child during the overseas stay, whether they are parents, acquaintances, or local guardians. The *kirogi* family arrangement, which often involves long periods of maintaining transnational split households, may strain not only the family's financial resources but also individual and family wellness and relationships (Waters, 2015*b*). However, despite ESA's well-publicized economic and psychological challenges (Kang & Abelmann, 2011), the practice continued to appeal to and draw in a wider range of Korean families to participate (Kim & Okazaki, 2017). The study of pre-college study abroad provides opportunities for scholars from various disciplines to understand why and how families are willing to engage in this particular form of "parenting from afar" for the purpose of their children's education and mobility.

KEY CHARACTERISTICS OF KOREAN EARLY STUDY ABROAD

Trends Over Time

Over the past two decades or so, thousands of Korean primary and secondary school students have left Korea each year to study abroad in English-speaking countries, either alone or accompanied by one parent. The prime characteristic of the *kirogi* family is that the nuclear family members live far apart for extended periods of time. This parallels similar transnational split family arrangements that first drew public and scholarly attention in the 1990s to families from Hong Kong and Taiwan who sent their children for extended periods to attend high schools in the US or Canada alone as "parachute kids" (Orellana, Thorne, Chee, & Lam, 2001; Zhou, 1998). The terms "satellite children" and "astronaut families" were coined to describe those East Asian families in which children were accompanied by one parent for educational migration (Abelmann et al., 2014). These East Asian practices of voluntary family separation for an extended period in pursuit of English language education challenges the contemporary family form of conjugal co-residence. Indeed, East Asian ESA has drawn both scholarly and popular attention partly because of the way that nuclear family form is disrupted, reorganized, and negotiated and partly because of its participants, who may be considered as an elite equivalent of transnational migrant workers who similarly make sacrifices of motherhood and fatherhood to support their family members in the home countries (Sun, 2013). Initially only conceived of as an (upper) middle-class practice for secondary students, *kirogi* migration has become a much more common educational strategy across Korean families of all classes and ages of children (Kim, 2010; Kim & Okazaki, 2017).

Figure 15.1 shows the official statistics published by the Korean Ministry of Education and the Korean Educational Development Institute of the number of primary and secondary students who withdrew from Korean public schools to attend schools overseas between 1995 and 2014. Notably, the number of Korean ESA accelerated quickly after 2000, with a 10-fold increase between 1995 and 2007 in the number of primary and secondary school students who withdrew from Korean schools to study abroad, and a 40-fold increase in primary school–aged children going abroad for education (Kim, 2010). On the whole, the exponential growth of ESA was driven by increased participation of families with younger children going overseas. It should be kept in mind that the official statistics available from the Korean Ministry of Education likely reflect the overall trend over time but likely underestimate the extent of pre-college Korean students abroad because children who accompany their parents who are working or studying overseas are not included in these figures. Figure 15.1 also shows the number of ESA students peaked in 2006 and declined every year since. Among the reasons for the decline of ESA, scholars have pointed to an increased attention to the challenges of ESA, especially the difficulties faced by returning students (Kang & Abelmann, 2011), as well as the economic downturn in Korea that made ESA an especially costly option for gaining English competency.

Because the Korean ESA phenomenon was driven in large part by the younger age of students who were going abroad, many families arranged for one parent (typically the mother) to accompany the child to an English-speaking country

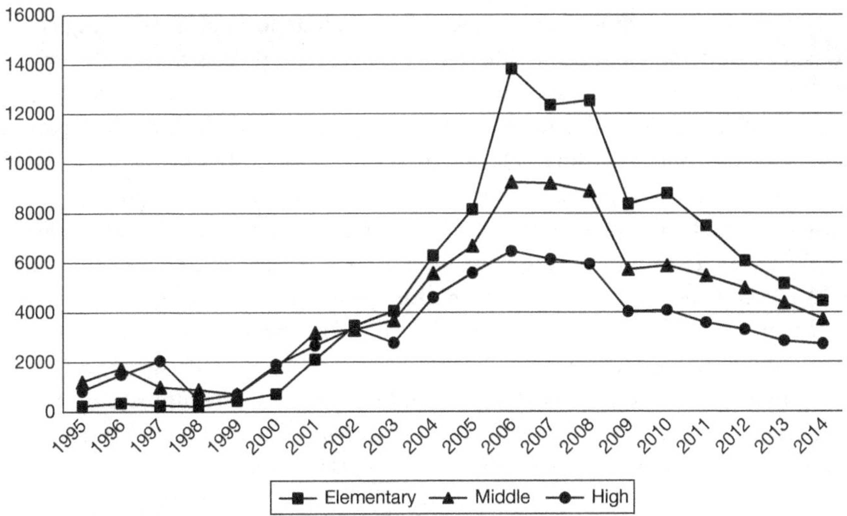

Figure 15.1. Number of students, by school level, who withdrew from schools to study abroad, 1995–2014.
SOURCE: Korean Ministry of Education and Korean Educational Development Institute: Korean Education Statistics Service www.kess.kedi.re.kr

while the other parent (typically the father) continued to live and work in Korea. These *kirŏgi* families maintain two households for a prolonged period of time, and while the children have daily contact with one parent, they may only see the other parent on infrequent visits. Because of visa restrictions, the mothers who accompany their children abroad are often restricted from earning wages in the host countries, further straining the family finances.

Whereas the *kirogi* family arrangement is most common among middle-class Korean families of primary school–aged students, some South Korean primary and secondary students go abroad unaccompanied by parents. Planning for such unaccompanied ESA is frequently conducted in consultation with professional study abroad placement agencies both in South Korea and in the host country, other parents, or relatives who have lived in or are currently living in a foreign country (Park & Bae, 2015). Unaccompanied children are often placed at private boarding schools or with host families.

It is also important to acknowledge that the boundaries are blurry when deciding which South Korean student who studies abroad counts as an ESA student. Although children who accompany their parents on overseas work assignments or those who emigrate for long-term periods are not counted in the official Korean Ministry of Education statistics on ESA, many of these family moves are often motivated, at least in part, by the same kinds of desires and aspirations that motivate ESA. Whereas children who emigrate together with their parents as intact families may suffer less disruption within the family, other stresses of immigration, such as downward economic mobility, challenges of cultural adjustment for parents and children, and the financial instability associated with parents' starting anew as workers in a new country, invariably impact family life (Suárez-Orozco, Suárez-Orozco, & Todorova, 2009).

In fact, some South Korean families who emigrate to English-speaking countries may undergo all of these different family configurations over the course of their journeys—relocating an entire family, splitting the family so that one parent accompanies a child, or having a child live overseas unaccompanied by a parent. Some of these changes in different configurations are likely dependent on children's ages, so that secondary school–aged children are more likely to go abroad (or remain abroad) unaccompanied than are primary school–aged children. Some families plan a series of ESAs for their children, starting from a shorter duration ESA accompanied by a parent to an English-speaking locale closer to South Korea and then transitioning to unaccompanied ESA for the adolescent in a different destination, perhaps farther away from home (Park & Lo, 2012). Changes in ESA plans may occur in response to family members' personal aspirations and changes in socioeconomic context, as has been documented in the case of Hong Kong Chinese transnational families in New Zealand (Ho, 2002).

Factors That Motivate Korean ESA

Given the enormous effort involved in arranging for a young child to study abroad, what has motivated so many Korean families to pursue this form of transnational education? And what factors have influenced their choices of various English-speaking nations? Many scholars view the eager embrace of educational migration in the form of ESA to English-speaking nations as best understood in contexts of economic policies and social and political conditions in South Korea in the past half-century (Lee & Johnstone, 2013). Fueled by aggressive state-sponsored industrial expansion under military rule following the Korean War, South Korean economy grew exponentially from the 1960s to 1990s due to rapid industrialization, technological advances, and an education boom. Under Kim Yongsam's regime (1992–1997), the government embraced a globalization policy (*Segyehwa*) and liberalization of overseas travel, with English language skills becoming increasingly valued as important social capital for Korean competitiveness in the global market. Although English had been held as symbolic capital in South Korea since the late 19th century and played a critical role in its modern nation-building, the Korean government's drive for globalization starting in the 1980s and the introduction of early English education in public schools in 1997 contributed to the privileging of English mastery among its citizens—especially students (Shim & Park, 2008).

By 1996, the Korean economy had achieved a global status, and Korea was recognized as the 29th member of the Organization for Economic Cooperation and Development (OECD). Soon after this achievement, the Korean economy was badly damaged by the Asian financial crisis in 1997. Following an International Monetary Fund (IMF) bailout, the government embraced a more neoliberal economic policy, shifting the economy away from a state-planned, government-investment model to a more market-oriented model. With increased emphasis on individual human capital, decreased confidence in Korean public schools, and rising economic anxiety among the citizens sparked by growing social inequality and the IMF crisis in the 1990s and into the 2000s, South Korean families increasingly sought private, after-school, supplemental education for their children to increase their competitive advantage (Kang & Abelmann, 2011). In particular, the urgency for a South Korean child to gain English language fluency has been dubbed "English fever" (Park, 2009), with English language instruction taking the largest slice of the private after-school market (Park & Abelmann, 2004). The high cost of private after-school English instruction—which was increasingly regarded as necessary for children's future economic opportunities—was a large driver of South Korean ESA. That is, for some families, ESA represented a realistic alternative to expensive domestic after-school private education (Park & Abelmann, 2004).

Another factor fueling the growth of ESA among South Koreans in the 1990s and 2000s was the sheer competition to gain admission to South Korea's top universities (Abelmann, Park, & Kim, 2009). Families viewed ESA as an investment that would increase children's chances of gaining admission to selective foreign-language high schools in Korea and, ultimately, to top universities in Seoul. Scholars (e.g., Park & Abelmann, 2004; Shim & Park, 2008) have argued that English language mastery became valued among Korean families not only as linguistic capital but as a mark of distinction. As ESA gained popularity, families began to also report seeking ESA in order to provide their children a respite from stressful and competitive educational environments in Korea as well as a means to "broaden their horizons" (Kang, 2012; Kim, 2015). Contributing to the exponential rise in ESA was the widely shared sentiment that South Korean public education was broken and ill-equipped to prepare its citizens for global competition (Abelmann et al., 2014).

Diversification of ESA Families and Destinations

Korean ESA in Western destinations such as the United States, Canada, and Australia became popularized in the 1990s through the early 2000s as means for Korean secondary students to learn English and develop a sense of cosmopolitan belonging (Abelmann et al., 2014). Prior to the liberalization of pre-college study abroad by the South Korean government in 2000, ESA was largely limited to a small number of elite South Korean families who could afford to send their children overseas to boarding schools and families who temporarily relocated because of parent's overseas work assignment with a Korean corporation. According to Ihm and Choi (2015), the United States and Canada ranked as Korean parents' top choices for ESA in 2007.

However, as primary school–aged students and less affluent middle-class families from Korea joined the transnational educational migration in increasing numbers (Abelmann et al., 2014), countries in Southeast Asia where the medium of instruction is English in their public schools or in international schools (such as Singapore, the Philippines, and Malaysia) have become increasingly common ESA destinations (Kim, 2010) due to the substantially lower cost of living and geographic proximity to Korea. Figure 15.2 shows the proportion of Korean students who went overseas to different ESA destinations in 2005 (the earliest

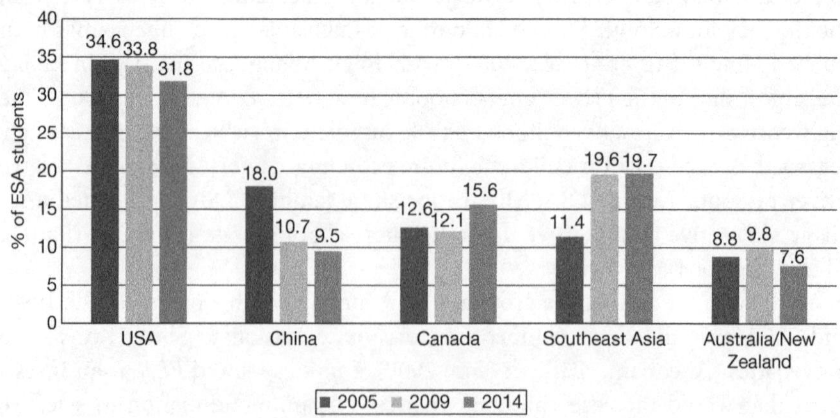

Figure 15.2. Proportion of Korean early study abroad (ESA) cohort in 2005, 2009, and 2014 by destinations.
SOURCE: Korean Ministry of Education and Korean Educational Development Institute: Korean Education Statistics Service www.kess.kedi.re.kr

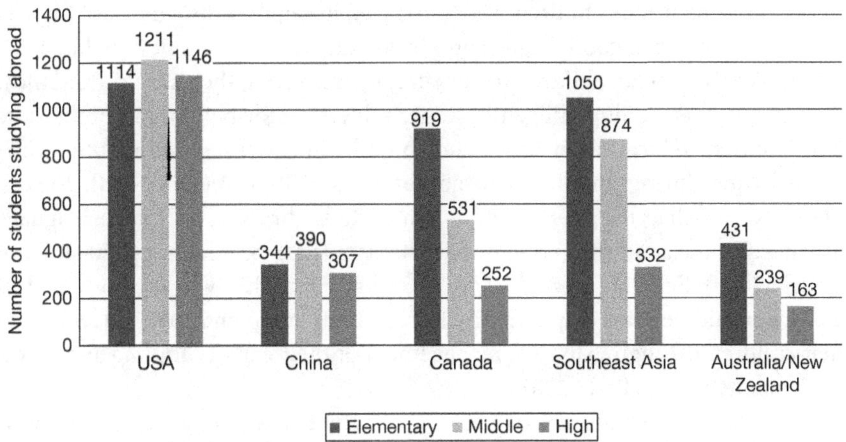

Figure 15.3. Number of Korean students, by school level, studying abroad in 2014.
SOURCE: Korean Ministry of Education and Korean Educational Development Institute: Korean Education Statistics Service www.kess.kedi.re.kr

year that such statistics are available), 2009, and 2014. Although the United States and Canada remain the most popular ESA destinations, the proportion of families choosing Southeast Asia increased by almost twofold in a decade. Kim (2015) argued that ESA in more conventional Western English-speaking destinations may be a part of a long-term endeavor that is sometimes combined with permanent immigration (Ong, 1999; Waters, 2005). In contrast, particularly for those with limited resources, ESA in Southeast Asia can take on a short-term strategy that focuses on spending 1 or 2 years abroad for primary school or the early stage of secondary education and then returning to Korea (Kim & Okazaki, 2017).

The breakdown of ESA destinations by age group supports this notion that Southeast Asian countries are considered the destinations of choice for young Korean children's short-term study abroad. Figure 15.3 shows the 2014 statistics of Korean primary and secondary school students studying abroad in the top five destinations. Although the United States is the most popular destination for Korean ESA students at all grade levels (as well as China, although chosen by much fewer students), Southeast Asia is the second most popular destination for elementary school-aged children's ESA, followed by Canada. In a later section, we review recent research on the appeal, as well as the downsides, for Korean families who choose Southeast Asian destinations for their children's ESA.

FAMILIAL CHALLENGES OF ESA

As increasing numbers of Korean families began to participate in ESA, the considerable amount of economic and cultural capital needed to "succeed" at ESA also became more widely known (Kang & Abelmann, 2011). In fact, modal parents of successful Korean ESA children were portrayed in popular discourse as "[house] wives who can speak good English and husbands who have money" (Cho, 2004, p. 159). For the Korean children to benefit fully from ESA, the parents—and most often the mothers—must diligently gather relevant information and orchestrate their children's education in Korea and abroad with careful consideration of the optimal time during childhood to go abroad and then reenter South Korean schooling, as well as the appropriate length of study abroad to maximize language learning and the acquisition of cosmopolitanism (Park & Abelmann, 2004; Shim & Park, 2008). Scholars saw successful ESA as yet another way for middle-class and upper middle-class stay-at-home Korean mothers to enact their devotion to their children through extensive management of their early schooling and extra-curricular activities (Park, 2007).

In this section, we discuss two sets of literature that pointed to the tensions and challenges that accompanied Korean ESA and that became particularly apparent with the increased participation of a wider range of families in educational migration.

Difficulties of Transnational Split Households

The difficulties of "lone" parenting for mothers who accompany their children abroad or of "long-distance" parenting for children sent abroad alone have been a key theme across various disciplines of scholarship on Korean ESA. Long-distance parenthood and the experience of being apart as a husband or wife has been the key theme in family studies, whereas other disciplines focused more on why the parents make such decisions and how they deal with the challenges they face during temporary separation and/or the experiences of children's overseas schooling.

A number of qualitative studies have focused on the challenges faced by Korean mothers who accompanied their children overseas. Interestingly, the Korean ESA mothers sometimes received a cold reception from local Korean-American communities at their ESA destinations. For example, Ahn (2015) conducted an ethnographic study of 30 Korean transnational split-household mothers in four cities in upstate New York, the majority of whom were active in local Korean churches. Ahn observed that the term *kirogi* mother was used reluctantly and hesitantly in the Korean congregations because of the stigma associated with the phenomenon. Many of the ESA mothers had belonged to a church in Korea and sought out a local Korean church in the United States to seek solace from the acculturative stress they experienced as they navigated living in a foreign country with limited knowledge of local practices and the local language. However, Ahn found that Korean-American churches tended to privilege family-centric participation in their spiritual activities, with expectations that adults participate as husband–wife pairs in the congregational activities. The ESA mothers, especially those who were not visiting scholar visa holders (and thus their visa status was solely for the purpose of accompanying their children in ESA), were critiqued as engaging in a destructive family lifestyle that involved prolonged separation between husbands and wives.

Overall, the portrait of Korean *kirogi* mothers that emerges through existing literature centers around their enactment of gendered and cultural expectation of mothers who are compelled to manage their children's acquisition of a desired cultural and linguistic capital often at a great psychological and emotional cost to themselves. Although there is some research that points to the mothers' sense of empowerment, freedom, and independence (Ahn, 2015; Kim, Agic, & McKenzie, 2014), by and large, the challenges predominate.

ESA Among the Less Affluent in Southeast Asia

Early scholarship on transnational educational migration focused on upper middle-class Korean families. For some of the well-to-do families, an ESA strategy reflected their desires to reproduce their position in society by providing their children who are not succeeding in the South Korean education system with an alternative route to success through the acquisition of valuable forms of cultural capital (Kim, 2015). In fact, the existing body of literature on these transnational educational migrant families has viewed this phenomenon as largely an aspect of the more affluent middle-class families' endeavors to reproduce their advantageous position in society for their children by providing them a more cosmopolitan environment than those available in Korea or with a "second chance" at education (Ahn, 1996; Cho, 2002). For example, Cho (2002) argued that the core ESA participants are upper- to middle-class families who share an "orientation towards prioritizing their children." Until recently, little was known about the transnational schooling experience of the less-affluent Korean families who also began to participate in ESA in sizable numbers in the mid-2000s (Kim, 2010). However, Orellana et al.'s (2001) research on how such students feel "caught between two nations, education systems and ways of growing up" and Huang and Yeoh's (2005) study of mothers from the People's Republic of China living in Singapore are exceptions.

As shown earlier, countries such as Singapore, the Philippines, India, and South Africa—all of which have English as (at least) one of their official languages—have become increasingly popular destinations for Koreans, although many still choose to go to the United States, Canada, or Australia like their Chinese counterparts from Hong Kong and Taiwan (Kim, 2010). These non-Western destinations gained popularity particularly among lower middle-class parents, suggesting that factors other than "learning English" may play a crucial part in the less affluent parents' decision-making process. There are several unique aspects of Korean ESA in Singapore that serve as an illustrative case of the pitfalls of educational migration as a family mobility strategy.

Kim's (2010) study of 12 lower middle-class *kirogi* families in Singapore found that dissatisfaction with the schooling in Korea, the Korean state's emphasis on globalization and international competitiveness, and parental desire to support their children's future social mobility via opportunities to acquire foreign languages were shared by almost all the informants. Many interviewees echoed the sentiment that schooling and after-school learning in Korea is so competitive and so expensive that it requires a "war-like" mentality (Seth, 2003). The participants also echoed the Korean neoliberal education mantra of English and other foreign language skills as valuable assets. The Korean families in Singapore seemed to support the cultural script in which educational migration is considered a viable option, not only for the middle class but also for the lower middle class, especially when they can opt to go to lower cost destinations in Southeast Asia. Kim (2010) observed that *kirogi* migration had become similar to private tutoring in Korea, which has become a norm rather than an option open only to the affluent. Because of its relative geographic and cultural proximity, Singapore is seen as a "family-friendly" destination. It is a 6-hour flight from South Korea, and there is only a 1-hour time difference, making real-time communication via both phone and internet convenient. ESA in Singapore also reduces the sacrifices that family members have to make, making visits less expensive and more feasible. This geographic factor plays a crucial part in parents' decision-making processes. The fact that Singapore was an "affordable option" that offered an added opportunity for the children to learn Chinese as well as English was often named as another reason the families chose Singapore as their children's ESA destination. Malaysia, as an ESA destination, is viewed similarly to Singapore. Although ethnic Chinese are a minority in Malaysia, Chinese is spoken among ethnic Chinese in their everyday life, and there are many private and international schools that offer both English and Chinese language education. These strategic choices can be understood as a Korean version of the social mobility project for families (Heath, Rothon, & Kilpi, 2008; Van Zanten, 1997; Zeroulou, 1988). Notably, Singapore has attracted Mainland Chinese "study mothers," for whom being able to operate in the Chinese language context while accompanying their children overseas for English language study was a matter of convenience (Huang & Yeoh, 2005).

Park and Bae (2015) had described continuities between South Korean and Singaporean schooling in terms of shared cultures of achievement and test-based college admission as one of the primary reasons many Korean families chose Singapore as their children's ESA destination. More affluent families strategically use Singapore's pricey international schools as a springboard for their children's later study abroad in the West. However, whereas Singapore may appear to be an attractive ESA destination for lower middle-class families, Kim (2010, 2015) argued that less-affluent Korean families often find themselves "stuck," unable to leave Singapore, either to return to South Korea or to move to another destination. The primary reason for this class divergence involves elements of incompatibilities between Singaporean and South Korean public schooling.

For one, unlike Korea, Singaporean public schools at primary and secondary levels are hierarchically ranked based on the academic performance of their students. Within a school, students are also divided into different classes based on their academic performance. In addition to the clear ranking of schools, Singapore also has a tracking system for students in the secondary schools, dividing them into "Special," "Express," "Normal (academic)," and "Normal (technical)" streams. Singapore public education is comprised of 6 years of primary school, 4 years of secondary school, plus 2 additional years for those wishing to attend university (for a total of 12 years on the college track). Special and Express streams are 4-year secondary school curricula that prepare students to take an exam that eventually leads to university entrance, whereas the Normal (academic) stream is a 4-year secondary school curriculum that typically leads to a vocational or technical school. Tracking based on academic ability begins in the US equivalent of fourth grade. The Primary School Leaving Examination (PSLE), taken at the end of primary school education, is a high-stakes exam that determines students' tracks in their education. In 2005, among the 47,168 12-year-old students enrolling in Singapore's public schools, only 4,218 were in the Special stream, 25,221 were in the Express stream, 11,796 were in the Normal (academic) stream, and 5,922 were in the Normal (technical) stream (Singapore Ministry of Education, 2006, p. 9). Once an educational track is set for a student, it is very difficult to transfer to a different stream, particularly for those in both academic and technical Normal streams. In 2008 and in 2010, the Singapore government reformed the system to reduce the barrier for students in Normal streams to cross over into college preparatory tracks so as to increase university enrollment (Goh & Tran, 2008; Singapore Ministry of Education [MOE], 2012; Sidhu, 2009). However, at the time of Kim's (2010, 2015) study, it was perceived as nearly impossible for students in Normal tracks to enter a university in Singapore.

The tracking system in Singapore's public schools may have its own merits for Singapore nationals, but it can be a particularly heavy burden for foreign students who are just starting their studies without sufficient fluency in English or in one of the official languages that students must study. Unlike international schools in Singapore or public schools in other English-speaking countries, English as Second Language (ESL) classes, designed to help foreign students' transition smoothly to the core classes, are not available in public schools. Also, students who want to transfer to public school are required to sit for transfer exams in English. Given how early the academic tracking begins in Singapore public schools, international transfer students who may not be English-fluent and academically on par with Singapore peers are likely to experience a difficult entry and transition into Singapore public schools.

Critically, many less-affluent Korean ESA families had failed to realize how the public education system in Singapore often works against the interests of educational migrant families. For example, it is not uncommon in Singapore public school to "downgrade" or "demote" a student, either by placing a non–English-speaking student in a lower grade with younger children upon entrance into the system or by requiring a poorly performing student to repeat a grade. More-affluent Korean ESA families who had access to social capital in South Korea and were forewarned were able to circumvent these limitations of Singapore's public school system by accessing private schooling, international schools, and the private supplementary education market in both Singapore and South Korea.

School demotion (referred to as "downed" among Korean mothers) was a widely shared experience among the working class and lower middle-class Korean ESA families in Singapore. For example, in Kim's (2010) study, only 1 of 12 sampled families and only 1 of 18 children attending public schools had not been affected by demotion of one to three grades from where the children had been in Korean schools because of their performance on the transfer exam (taken entirely in English). The interviews with the Korean ESA families revealed that few had expected this downgrading and tracking system before moving to Singapore, nor had they understood the potentially devastating impact on their children's educational trajectories. First, demotion in Singaporean public schools is permanent unless students can transfer to a private or international school. There is no opportunity to retest into a higher grade or to skip a grade. Thus, children, even after their English has improved, are often stuck relearning material with much younger students. In addition, it is not uncommon for students in Singapore to have to repeat a grade for poor academic performance. This puts transfer students even further behind their original classmates. Because of this system of demotion, as well as academic tracking, the Singaporean public school system seems to be particularly punishing toward less-affluent students who pursue educational migration because of weak school performance in South Korea. While parents believe that educational migration will offer their children a second chance, their academically underachieving children were either "downed" or placed in a vocational track that gave them few opportunities to enter university either in Singapore or in South Korea.

Kim (2010, 2015) also found that less-affluent Korean parents' wish to raise trilingual children through ESA in public schools in Singapore was also met with harsh realities once their children began their ESA stay. The expectation that time would resolve the initial difficulties in adjusting to the new educational system was often not satisfied. In fact, many of the Korean ESA children in Singaporean public schools were asked to drop their Chinese language classes. This was not because the Korean students spent less time and effort but because their late entry into Singaporean public schools as English language learners meant that they were far behind their Singaporean classmates. Because of this structural difficulty, there was only one case (out of 12) interviewed by Kim (2010) in which the child had successfully caught up with the Chinese language in a public school. Some public school attendees attempted to compensate for the absence of Chinese language instruction in their regular schooling through private Chinese language tutorials. However, many of the less-affluent Korean ESA families had limited means to access resources that would improve their children's mastery of English and Chinese languages.

The few working-class Korean ESA families who had been aware of the Singaporean public school system prior to the move had underestimated the importance of such differences and their implications for their children's future. Most interviewees expressed concerns about their children's demotion but were puzzled as to what to do about this matter. Given the dissatisfaction that many Korean ESA families expressed with their experiences in Singapore, what plans did they make for returning home? Kim's (2015) study revealed how these families, "stuck" for the time being in Singapore, were envisioning their future and how such decisions were shaped by their children's ages, family resources, and the context of reception for returnee children in South Korea. On the whole, most *kirŏgi* families seemed not to want to take any further risks with their children's schooling. Although some families with children in the lower primary grades may elect to return to Korea, the families of students who stay in Singapore past the critical period for reentering Korean public school (i.e., prior to middle school) anticipated that readjustment to South Korea would be difficult, based on their experiences of adaptation in Singapore and their difficult schooling experiences in South Korea that had led them to leave in the first place. The parents were concerned that their children would be bullied or ostracized at school for being different. The parents also surmised that their children would be far behind Korean classmates in their schoolwork if they were to return. They therefore made careful calculations about the opportunities available in both countries in their decisions on whether to stay longer in Singapore or when and where to go next.

Many of the families lacked the financial and social capital to move to a third country that might be more hospitable to their children's academic circumstances and concluded that they must stay in Singapore for the duration of their children's schooling. They felt "stuck" in Singapore regardless of the children's abilities; in fact, the Korean children interviewed by Kim (2010) were hard-working, and their parents were making valiant efforts to provide for their children within a tighter budget. In this way, the less-affluent Korean families in Singapore who had followed their more affluent counterparts for ESA appeared to be suffering from unintended negative consequences of transnational educational migration, finding themselves in a situation in which the children were "caught between two nations, educational systems and ways of growing up, which conveys one of the risks of transnational childhoods—feeling marginal in both places" (Orellana et al., 2001, p. 583).

The class differences among Korean families made for very different ESA experiences for the children, a fact that was all too apparent to the less-affluent parents interviewed by Kim (2010). For example, Youngjin's mother described the different experiences of those attending public and international schools from the perspective of parents of public school students. She shared:

> Mothers whose children attend international schools are smiling. . . . Mothers of the local [public school children] are filled with concerns. . . . We can tell from the face of the mothers whether their children go to an international school or to a local school. . . . [Q: Why is that so?] Children [at international schools] do not have [regular and frequent] exams and their classes are fun. Therefore, the pressure is less [for children and mothers]. . . . [Singapore's public schools] are the same as schools in Korea, memorizing and testing. There is so much memorization and so many tests that the children are getting so much stress. (pp. 289–290)

Mothers of both public and international school students echoed similar and clearly notable differences between the experiences of Korean ESA students in public versus international schools.

CONCLUSION AND FUTURE DIRECTIONS

In this chapter, we have argued that scholarship on Korean transnational split families (or *kirogi* families) has led to deepened understandings about the impact of rapid globalization, neoliberal education policy reform, and the accompanying "English fever" and desires for cosmopolitanism among Koreans on the day-to-day lives of Korean families. Although Korean ESA families share many common features with other East Asian educational migrant families, there are also uniquely Korean contexts that motivate families to have their young children study abroad in English-speaking nations, such as a particular type of cosmopolitan desire as well as anxieties created by globalization and neoliberal education reform in Korea. The number of primary and secondary school-aged Korean children going abroad saw an exponential growth in the early 2000s, peaking in 2006 and declining fairly rapidly in the subsequent decade. Accompanying this rise and fall of Korean ESA was the diversification in destinations as well as in the types of families who participate in ESA. Drawing on scholarly literature on *kirogi* families mainly in sociology, anthropology, and family studies mostly published in English, we reviewed two areas of recent scholarship that pointed to the challenges and tensions experienced by Korean ESA families as parents and children navigated unfamiliar cultures, languages, and school contexts, as well as transnational split family arrangements.

Future research on Korean educational migrant families, like other research on immigrants that explores the intersection of family, education, and class issues, will need to address the gaps in existing literature that result from studies that have only provided snapshots of this phenomenon and family-level experiences. Also, we should note that the local sociopolitical contexts vis-à-vis economy and education in Korea have shifted considerably in recent years. For example, neoliberal "reform" on international schools in Korea has opened doors for Korean nationals with the required years of overseas experience to enter into expensive international schools. Also, partly to address the educational exodus and partly to keep up with globalization, some public "international" schools, which in fact enroll only Korean nationals, were opened since the late 2000s. These new schools were intended largely to accommodate Korean students who had completed overseas studies during their earlier stages of primary and/or secondary schooling while accompanying parents who were dispatched abroad for work. However, we should also note that the very wealthy who can afford to send their children to these privileged Korean schools with their "international" curricula no longer need to engage in transnational split family arrangement in order for their children to acquire the desired cosmopolitan and linguistic capital. A crucial reason why the number of ESA students has declined steadily since the late 2000s may be at least partly because of the availability of new schooling options within Korea. Furthermore, although the perceived need to go abroad for English language mastery may have diminished in Korea, the status of English as the marker of distinction within the Korean elite continues. For example, selective Korean universities and colleges recently began to mandate English as the sole medium of instruction in some or all of their curricula (Kang, 2012). Future studies may address the linkages between changing local educational contexts of both Korean and destination countries with the shifts among Korean families' strategies for acquiring or maintaining their families' social and cultural capital.

Another fruitful direction in future research concerns the experiences of educational migrant families across borders and across socioeconomic classes. Despite the fact that research on *kirogi* families has accumulated and developed, studies have rarely taken up a comparative approach across two or countries/regions (Abelmann et al., 2014; Lo et al., 2015). However, whereas earlier studies focused on the domestic- or individual-level factors of educational "exodus," such as the competitive educational environment in Korean society and aspirations for providing global human capital or second chances for children, recent studies have begun to take a much broader interdisciplinary/transnational and comparative perspective (e.g., Lo et al., 2015). Emerging research is seeking to understand Korean *kirogi* families in relation not only to other East Asian educational migrant families but also in relation to other middle-class migrant families, such as professional migrants and married graduate student families (Kim, 2012; Song, 2012).

Finally, another limitation in the existing literature is that studies tend to involve qualitative analyses of small numbers of families at one time point in their educational migration history. Future research may include longitudinal studies to follow the families over the course of their children's education, especially in the context of changing "educational" environments in Korea and abroad. To date, almost no study has been conducted to examine this issue by following original samples over the years. Of course, this type of research would involve methodological and practical challenges, as educational migrants, especially those headed to countries outside North America, seem to have more fluid geographic mobility than others. Like transnational migrant workers who often seek remigration or circular migration instead of staying in one destination country for a fixed amount of time, many Korean educational migrant families are also in constant search of optimal destination countries where their cosmopolitan aspirations can be achieved in a better setting for both the focal children and their parents. Scholars of educational migrant families may benefit from the conceptual and methodological lessons learned from scholars of other types of migrant families.

REFERENCES

Abelmann, N., Park, S. J., & Kim, H. (2009). College rank and neo-liberal subjectivity in South Korea: The burden of self-development. *Inter-Asia Cultural Studies, 10*(2), 229–247.

Abelmann, N., Newendorp, N., & Lee-Chung, S. (2014). East Asia's astronaut and geese families: Hong Kong and South Korean cosmopolitanisms. *Critical Asian Studies, 46*(2), 259–286. doi:10.1080/14672715.2014.898454.

Ahn, B. C. (1996). Study abroad at early age among Koreans: Issues and Problems [North California]. *People and Society, 4,* 423–468.

Ahn, K. (2015). The legal and religious citizenship of Korean transnational mothers. In A. Lo, N. Abelmann, S. A. Kwon, & S. Okazaki (Eds.), *South Korea's education exodus: The life and times of study abroad* (pp. 191–208). Seattle: University of Washington Press.

Cho, M.-D. (2002). The causes of increasing young Korean students who go abroad to study. *The Korean Journal of Humanities and the Social Sciences, 26*(4), 135–152.

Cho, U. (2004). Korean families on the forefront of globalization. *Economy and Society, 64,* 148–171.

Goh, C. B., & Tan, L. W. H. (2008). The development of university education in Singapore. In S. K. Lee, C. B. Goh, B. Fredriksen, & J. P. Tan (Eds.). *Toward a better future: Education and training for economic development in Singapore since 1965* (pp. 12–38). Washington. DC: World Bank.

Heath, A. F., Rothon, C., & Kilpi, E. (2008). The second generation in Western Europe: Education, unemployment, and occupational attainment. *Annual Review of Sociology, 34,* 211–235.

Ho, E. S. (2002). Multi-local residence, transnational networks: Chinese "astronaut" families in New Zealand. *Asian and Pacific Migration Journal, 11*(1), 145–164.

Huang, S., & Yeoh, B. S. A. (2005). Transnational families and their children's education: China's "study mothers" in Singapore. *Global Networks, 5*(4), 379–400.

Ihm, C. S., & Choi, H. J. (2015). Early study abroad: A survey and demographic portrait. In A. Lo, N. Abelmann, S. A. Kwon, & S. Okazaki (Eds.), *South Korea's education exodus: The life and times of study abroad* (pp. 25–39). Seattle: University of Washington Press.

Kang, J., & Abelmann, N. (2011). The domestication of South Korean pre-college study abroad in the first decade of the millennium. *Journal of Korean Studies, 16*(1), 89–118.

Kang, H. S. (2012). English-only instruction at Korean universities: Help or hindrance to higher learning? *English Today, 28*(01), 29–34.

Kim, J. (2010). "Downed" and stuck in Singapore: Lower/middle class South Korean wild geese (*kirogi*) children in Singapore. *Research in Sociology of Education, 17,* 271–311.

Kim, J. (2012). Remitting "filial cohabitation": "Actual" and "virtual" coresidence between Korean professional migrant adult children couples in Singapore and their elderly parents. *Ageing and Society, 32,* 1337–1359.

Kim, J. (2015). The "other half" goes abroad: The perils of public schooling in Singapore. In A. Lo, N. Abelmann, S. A. Kwon, & S. Okazaki (Eds.), *South Korea's education exodus: The life and times of early study abroad* (pp. 103–122). Seattle: University of Washington Press.

Kim, J., Agic, B., & McKenzie, K. (2014). The mental health of Korean transnational mothers: A scoping review. *International Journal of Social Psychiatry, 60*(8), 783–794.

Kim, J., & Okazaki, S. (2017). Short-term "intensive mothering" on a budget: Mothers of Korean children studying abroad in Southeast Asia. *Asian Women, 33*(3), 111–139.

Kim, J., & Okazaki, S. (in progress). *Early study abroad (ESA) students' transnational mobility: Korean ESA families in Singapore through a follow-up study after 5 years of the original study.*

Korean Ministry of Education. (2013). *Statistical Yearbook of Education*. Seoul: Ministry of Education.

Korean Ministry of Education. (various years). Statistics on departing and returning students in primary, middle and high schools.

Lee, E., & Johnstone, M. (2013). Global inequities: A gender-based analysis of the live-in caregiver program and the *kirogi* phenomenon in Canada. *Affilia: Journal of Women and Social Work*, *28*, 401–414.

Lo, A., Abelmann, N., Kwon, S. A., & Okazaki, S. (Eds.). (2015). *South Korea's education exodus: The life and times of study abroad*. Seattle: University of Washington Press.

Ong, A. (1999). *Flexible citizenship: The cultural logics of transnationality*. Durham, NC: Duke University Press.

Orellana, M. F., Thorne, B., Chee, A., & Lam, W. S. E. (2001). Transnational childhoods: The participation of children in processes of family migration. *Social Problems*, *48*(4), 572–591.

Park, J. K. (2009). "English fever" in South Korea: Its history and symptoms. *English Today*, *25*(1), 50–57.

Park, J. S.-Y., & Bae, S. (2015). School choice in the global schoolhouse: How Korean educational migrants calibrate "success" in Singapore. In A. Lo, N. Abelmann, S. A. Kwon, & S. Okazaki (Eds.), *South Korea's education exodus: The life and times of early study abroad* (pp. 85–102). Seattle: University of Washington Press.

Park, J. S.-Y., & Lo, A. (2012). Transnational South Korea as a site for a sociolinguistics of globalization: Markets, timescales, neoliberalism. *Journal of Sociolinguistics*, 16, 147–164.

Park, S. J. (2007). Educational manager mothers: South Korea's neoliberal transformation. *Korea Journal*, *47*(3), 186–213.

Park, S. J., & Abelmann, N. (2004). Class and cosmopolitan striving: Mothers' management of English education in South Korea. *Anthropological Quarterly*, *77*(4), 645–672.

Seth, M. J. (2003). *Education fever: Society, politics, and the pursuit of schooling in South Korea*. Honolulu: University of Hawaii Press.

Shim, D., & Park, J. S.-Y. (2008). The language politics of "English fever" in South Korea. *Korea Journal*, *48*(2), 136–159.

Sidhu, R. (2009). Running to stay still in the knowledge economy. *Journal of Educational Policy*, *24*(3), 237–253.

Singapore Ministry of Education. (2006). *Education statistics digest 2006*. Singapore: Singapore Ministry of Education.

Singapore Ministry of Education. (2012). *Report of the Committee on University Education Pathways Beyond 2015 (CUEP): Final report*. Singapore: Author.

Song, J. (2012). Imagined communities and language socialization practices in transnational space: A case study of two Korean "study abroad" families in the United States. *The Modern Language Journal*, *96*(4), 507–524.

Suárez-Orozco, C., Suárez-Orozco, M. M., & Todorova, I. (2009). *Learning a new land: Immigrant students in American society*. Cambridge, MA: Harvard University Press.

Sun, K. C. (2013). Rethinking migrant families from a transnational perspective: Experiences of parents and their children. *Sociology Compass*, *7*, 445–458.

Van Zanten, A. (1997). Schooling immigrants in France in the 1990s: Success or failure of the Republican model of integration? *Anthropology and Education Quarterly*, *28*(3), 351–374.

Waters, J. L. (2005). Transnational family strategies and education in the contemporary Chinese diaspora. *Global Networks*, *5*(4), 359–377.

Waters, J. L. (2012). Geographies of international education: Mobilities and the reproduction of social (dis)advantage. *Geography Compass*, *6*(3), 123–136.

Waters, J. L. (2015*a*). Educational imperatives and the compulsion for credentials: Family migration and children's education in East Asia. *Children's Geographies*, *13*(3), 280–293.

Waters, J. L. (2015*b*). Dysfunctional mobilities: International education and the chaos of movement. In J. Wyn & H. Cahill (Eds.), *Handbook of children and youth studies* (pp. 679–688). Singapore: Springer.

Zeroulou, Z. (1988). The academic achievement of immigrants' children: A mobilization approach. *Revue Francaise de Sociologie*, *29*(3), 447–470.

Zhou, M. (1998). "Parachute kids" in Southern California: The educational experience of Chinese children in transnational families. *Educational Policy*, *12*, 682–704.

16

Where Should My Child Go to School?

Parent and Child Considerations in Binational Families

EDMUND T. HAMANN, VÍCTOR ZÚÑIGA,
AND JUAN SÁNCHEZ GARCÍA ■

Many chapters in this volume are dedicated to inquiry about the extant reality that many parents around the world now parent their minor (i.e., under age 18) children from afar, but the tack of this chapter is a little different. We ask whether parents *should* parent from afar. We don't pose that as a question about ideals—what would be best if parents had economic security and unambiguous legal residential status—but rather as a more pragmatic one. Given some parents' and children's limited agency in real-world circumstances, what is their best path forward?

Answers to this kind of question vary by context—different children and different parents negotiate different hazards and opportunity horizons—and there is not a "one size fits all" best answer. Furthermore, many parenting decisions are necessarily speculative: "I am doing this now because I hope or anticipate that it will help my child in the future, but I can't know for sure that it will," or "We are selecting to do this because of a prospective hazard that may or may not ever come to pass but that we need to be ready for." So "best answers," even if they are sometimes clear in hindsight, cannot be fully determined in situ. Parenting decisions happen in a messy real world with intriguing possibilities and harrowing pitfalls and dangers.

The three examples presented here come from an ongoing, multiyear, mixed-method study of students in Mexican schools with prior experience in US schools. We have written extensively about that inquiry elsewhere in both English and Spanish (e.g., Hamann, 2001; Hamann & Zúñiga, 2011; Hamann, Zúñiga, & Sánchez García, 2006; 2017; Sánchez García & Hamann, 2016; Zúñiga & Hamann,

2009; Zúñiga, Hamann, & Sánchez García, 2008), but the focus here is a bit different from our other work. Here, we look at the decisions faced by parents (who were not the primary focus of the larger inquiry) rather than children's and teachers' school experiences.

For the larger study, we visited 805 Mexican schools from a stratified sample in four Mexican states, with the stratification being to assure that we had sufficient representation of the range of participation, *municipio* by *municipio* (county by county), in international migration. (Among other things, this strategy showed that schools in areas with higher migration participation in turn enrolled more students with prior experience in the United States.) In those 805 schools, all visited between 2004 and 2011, we surveyed just over 56,000 students and from those surveys identified 1,322 with prior experience in the United States. More recently, in an ongoing inquiry, a fifth Mexican state (Morelos) used our survey to conduct a census of all its *primarias* (elementary schools) and *secundarias* (grades 7–9) to identify students with prior experience in the United States. In both phases of this study, we sometimes followed-up our surveys with return, in-person visits to the surveyed schools. During these visits, we interviewed students, teachers, administrators, and, less frequently, parents.

Our long-term inquiry has yielded a number of significant findings and illuminated some changing patterns over its nearly two-decade span. Several of these are important to keep in mind. It is worth emphasizing that the migration between Mexico and the United States, the largest between any two countries in the world (United Nations, 2016), includes children (Súarez-Orozco & Suárez-Orozco, 2002). This was not always the case (at least not in large number) as the Bracero program, for example, which ran from 1942 to 1964, primarily recruited male workers to come temporarily to the United States to engage in agricultural work but then return to Mexico (Cohen, 2011). But more recently, with the Immigration Reform and Control Act (IRCA) passed during the Reagan Administration allowing more than 2 million Mexican-born migrants to seek permanent residency and citizenship and then to petition for citizenship rights for family members, that pattern began to change; families could reassemble in a single location in the United States. While this new pattern was triggered in part by IRCA's amnesty, the new migration to the United States was not only of Mexicans with documentation to stay in the United States. Often families reunited with some members "legal" and others awaiting the regularization of their status. Still others came without an easy prospect for gaining documentation but pushed by economic changes in the Mexican countryside and pulled by the prospect of social connections to someone with residency rights.

We remember the poignant case in the late 1990s of a student in an Atlanta-area adult English as Second Language (ESL) class (where Hamann volunteered) who needed to miss 2 weeks of classes to return to rural Mexico with the tiny body of a stillborn baby. The baby was from an undocumented couple who were from the same village as the ESL student. The ESL student (a married father in his late 40s) could return to Mexico because, having begun his migration to the United States earlier than the couple, he had gained permanent residency through

IRCA and thus could legally cross and recross the border. We recount this story here because it illuminates both how knowing someone with documentation status was a key form of social capital for the sad couple and also how social ties originating in Mexico facilitated the large-scale migration from Mexico to the United States that occurred particularly after Mexico's peso devaluation in 1982, accelerated with IRCA, and then began to stall with the heightened Immigration and Customs Enforcement (ICE) that characterized the second term of President George W. Bush (Hamann & Reeves, 2012), continued under President Obama, and was exacerbated by the onset of the Great Recession in 2008.

From the 1980s through most of the first decade of the new century, the major migration between the United States and Mexico was South to North (from Mexico to the United States), although even at its height it was not exclusively unidirectional, as our discovery of transnationally experienced students in the schools of Nuevo León, Mexico in 2004 and Zacatecas, Mexico in 2005 both illuminated. This migration clearly included many who were headed North to seek work, but it also included children, spouses, and sometimes other extended family whose mobility was better characterized as a product of the desire to reunify families. The militarization of the US–Mexico border that was one ironic response to 9-11 (ironic because none of the terrorists in that attack crossed into the United States from Mexico) further propelled this dynamic of family reunification in the United States because it made unauthorized border crossing more difficult, more dangerous, and more expensive (Heyman & Campbell, 2012). Rather than undocumented fathers (and increasingly mothers—see Dreby, 2010) being able to return to Mexico to see family and maintain familial ties, the greater hazard of border crossing made it preferable to cross once and then try to stay in the United States. This in turn helps explain why the number of Mexican-born living in the United States grew from 9 million to 12 million between 2000 and 2015 (United Nations, 2016), and, more aptly for a volume about family life across distance, explains how mixed-status households (with some having legal residency, some having birthplace US citizenship rights, and some lacking legal documentation) have become increasingly common in the United States in the previous decade.

However, obscured in the UN's figure comparing 2000 to 2015 are the facts that nearly all that growth preceded the Great Recession that began in 2008 and that, starting in 2009, the balance of migration South-to-North versus North-to-South tipped. Gonzalez-Barrera (2015) estimated that, between 2009 and 2014, the number of people leaving the United States for Mexico was just over 1 million, exceeding those who came to the United States from Mexico by a net of 140,000. Based on our continued work in Morelos, Mexico, accounts shared by researchers at the University of California's "The Students We Share/*Los Alumnos Que Compartimos*" international symposium in Mexico City in September 2016, and new explanations from a number of Mexican education administrators whom we have collaborated with at various stages of this longitudinal study, if anything, the migration from the United States to Mexico has only grown since 2014 and may well be accelerating because of the US election of Donald Trump.

But it may not be whole families who are returning to Mexico. The United Nations' (2016) *International Migration Report 2015* reported that almost 1.2 million people lived in Mexico that year who had been born in another country. Their median age was 15. With 98% of Mexican emigration going to the United States, the UN figure is likely capturing the sizable migration of children born in the United States moving to Mexico, perhaps often accompanied by their Mexico-born parents (who would be invisible in Mexican immigration statistics because they were born in Mexico), but clearly not always accompanied, as one of our three cases makes clear.

From our own research, we have estimated that, as of 2010, there were 420,000 children enrolled in *educación básica* (grades 1–9) in Mexican schools who had prior school experience in US schools and an only partially overlapping tally of 330,000 students who had been born in the United States and thus had US citizenship status because of birthplace (Zúñiga & Hamann, 2014).[1]

To reconcile the two numbers, it is worth noting that some children with prior US school experience were born in Mexico, moved to the US, and moved back, while, related to the second figure, some children born in the United States moved with their parents to Mexico (in their parents' case, moved back to Mexico) without ever attending US schools. These figures, however they combine, are smaller than the 2013 estimate by Zong and Batalova (2014) that the Mexican-born under-18 population in the United States was 700,000, but they are not much smaller.

To summarize then, before moving on to the three cases: migration between Mexico and the United States is voluminous, it is increasingly bidirectional, it often involves children (and thus parent decision-making), and it is in flux. A Mexican parent living without documentation in the United States might choose to live unified as a whole mixed-status family unit in the United States. But another parent in the same circumstances might instead decide that dangers in US neighborhoods (Reese, 2002), fear of their own prospective detention by ICE, the chance to gain extended family support in childrearing, and/or the wish to have their children know and love Mexico instead support the child living in Mexico apart from his or her parent or parents. In contrast, Mexican parents living in Mexico with prior experience in the United States (and with experience of sending their children to US schools) might decide that educational and economic opportunities in the United States are better than in Mexico and that it is wiser or more in their child's interest to have their child live in the United States (with extended family) and to parent from afar.

UNDER THE MANGO TREE: AN IDEAL OR A TRAGEDY?

We have previously described the cases of Noelia and Manuel in a chapter (Sánchez García, Hamann, & Zúñiga, 2012) published in *Diaspora, Indigenous, and Minority Education* that focused on the cosmologies of the youngest students we encountered who had previously lived in the United States. We posited there that the reflections of a 7-year-old were almost automatically different from that of an older child because of the particular and sometimes even magical ways that younger children describe their worlds. Manuel was a 7-year-old at the time we met him, enrolled in second grade. His older sister Noelia was a sixth grader when we met her. Perhaps being overly lyrical in our description, in *Diaspora* we wrote, "Manuel later became almost effervescent as he described a favorite mango tree in his new town that he liked to nap beneath" (p. 158).

Idyllic descriptions aside, however, both Noelia and Manuel were US-born children being raised by their grandparents in a small village in Puebla's Sierra Mixteca mountains, southeast of Mexico City. Their village included mango trees and a small river, but was part of a semi-arid region in which a variety of organ cactus and mesquite seemed to be the dominant plant species. Their village had a road, a *primaria* (elementary school), and electricity. The main sources of income, however, were remittances from the United States and subsistence agriculture.

Both Noelia and Manuel had been born in Chicago to hardworking undocumented Mexican parents. At least we assume they were undocumented; Noelia and Manuel are our sources for that information, not their parents. We never met their parents, who were continuing to live in Chicago at the time our study took to us to Noelia and Manuel's village. By staying in Chicago, the parents continued to be able to earn money and send remittances. Dreby (2010), whose research was also in Puebla as well as Oaxaca, has documented how grandparents relied on remittances (sent for them to care for their grandchildren) as an economic survival strategy in the region. That seems to have been the case in Noelia and Manuel's case. Clearly, they were loved and cared for in their village, and, clearly, they remained connected to their parents and the world they had left behind in the United States.

Noelia told us, in English, that she and her brother had come to their community 18 months earlier, which would have been the summer or fall of 2008. At that time, ICE raids on workplaces in the United States were rising in number (Hamann & Reeves, 2012) and the US economy was beginning to falter. Noelia explained that her parents thought it would be safer for her and her brother to be in Mexico. We inferred that this related to her parents' calculation/fear regarding what might happen to the children if they (the parents) were detained. At the same time that the United States was declaring many parts of Mexico unsafe because of the Drug War (as various cartels viciously competed for territory), Noelia and Manuel's parents were deciding that their US-born, US citizen children were safer in Mexico.

That decision may well have been specifically accurate (we have no idea whether Noelia and Manuel's parents were ever detained or deported after our 2010 interview), but it had some near-term consequences. While Noelia, who had attended 5 years of public school in Illinois, was happy to chat with us in English, her younger brother, who had only attended kindergarten in the States admitted, in Spanish, that his English was slipping. Noelia explained that she and Manuel tried to continue practicing English with some cousins—apparently these cousins also had some US experience—and clearly her proficiency was intact.

Manuel told us in wide-eyed fashion how well-resourced his Illinois school had been, with a library and lots of computers. Although we cannot vouch that Noelia and Manuel's school in Mexico had no computers (perhaps there were some in the director's office), clearly, in Mexico, they attended a materially more spartan school. Indeed, the siblings described to us how they had a series of English-language textbooks that their aunt had sent them. Apparently, the aunt was a janitor at an elementary school in the United States and had rescued the books from the trash.

Of course, parenting is about much more than where your children go to school (although our interview skewed in that direction, given the primary focus of our multiyear study), but there were schooling consequences of Noelia and Manuel's parents' decision to parent from afar and have extended family (particularly Noelia and Manuel's grandparents) become primary caregivers. Noelia and Manuel had access to less-well-resourced schools in Mexico. They were living in a part of the rural countryside that had limited continued education infrastructure. In Mexico in 2010, *secundaria* (grades 7–9) was obligatory, and it was probable that Noelia moved to a *telesecundaria* in the academic year after we met her. *Telesecundarias* are relatively common in rural Mexico and mainly date from the 1992 change in educational law that extended Mexico's constitutional promise of primary education to include grades 7 to 9. Because Mexico did not have an adequate supply of trained content specialists willing to work in rural communities for the available wage, *telesecundarias* were set up literally to have centralized content instruction from a television (with VHS tapes or sometimes now DVDs and the internet,) with the onsite teachers acting more as facilitators. It is fair to say that it is difficult to receive a high-quality education at a *telesecundaria*.

In 2014 (assuming she had successfully progressed through *telesecundaria*), Noelia would have become eligible for *preparatoria*, or high school (grades 10–12). There was a *preparatoria* about 30 kilometers away from her community, but it is unclear whether she would have been eligible to attend or had a means to regularly get there. If she did attend, her parents' remittances were likely crucial for buying books, school uniforms, and covering the other costs associated with going to school in Mexico.

Presumably, the educational pathways available to Noelia would also be available to Manuel, 4 years behind her. During our interview, perhaps because it often code-switched over to English and surely because she was older, Noelia often spoke for Manuel, and it appeared that Noelia played an important role in Manuel's successful adjustment to his new community. We can speculate about whether the fact that the siblings could advocate for each other played any role in their parents' decision to send them to Mexico, but likely the presence of someone familiar with the starkly different contexts of Chicago and rural Mexico meant they were a comfort to each other. It may have also meant that Noelia played an occasional loosely parentlike, or at least more advocatelike than peerlike, role in supporting her brother. We will return to consideration of Noelia and Manuel's parents in the conclusion.

FAMILY UNITY VERSUS EDUCATIONAL OPPORTUNITY

In December 2013, at a *vespertino secundaria* about 45 minutes from the capital of Morelos, Cuernavaca, we met Javier. (*Vespertino* refers to afternoon school; often two schools share the same educational plant, with one school meeting in the morning—the *matutino* shift—and the other in the *vespertino*.) The visit was one of the least comfortable that we have made at any point in the 20 years of work in the United States and Mexico. Javier told us that a thing he liked about US schools was the lack of drugs and a thing he disliked about school in Mexico was the presence of drugs (which was not a dynamic we were told about in interviews at any other school). He said to us in English that he had learned at this new school that "I have to stand up for myself." He told us that he was subject to negative teacher and peer attention, and one of the school leaders told our visit coordinator that Javier had been disciplined related to drugs (presumably something minor like talking about them or bragging about them, as he was still attending the school).

It was Javier's first year at this *secundaria*, but it was his fourth year in school back in Mexico. Javier had been born in Indiana and had attended school in Hammond (a city of 80,000 on the state line with Illinois that forms part of the tri-state Chicago metropolitan area). When he was in fourth grade, his father was detained at his workplace and then deported for lacking documentation to live and work in the United States. His mother decided that, for family unity, she and Javier would move back to Mexico to reconnect with his father. However, Javier had a 19-year-old brother who was out of school and working in Indiana. The brother stayed in the United States. Javier was clearly interested in leaving Mexico to go live with his brother, an option he claimed he had discussed with his parents and that they were open to. (With Javier, our only data source on the topic, we have no take as to whether the brother was interested in hosting Javier or whether this idea was in any way viable.)

Attending to the theme of parenting from afar, we know that, faced with that prospect, Javier's mother had opted not to have Javier grow up away from his father. When his father's deportation took away the option of living together in the United States, she opted to return to Mexico. In other words, Javier's parents decided not to parent him from afar, at least not initially, when Javier was only 9 or 10 at the time of his father's deportation. Whether this is the decision they *should* have made or should continue to make projecting forward is less clear. (As noted in the introduction, we use the term "should" polemically—we clearly do not know enough about Javier or his family to make a defensible recommendation about what was best for him, but we do know enough about his case to use it to raise various topics that parents negotiating the Mexico–US binational migration domain have to take on.)

Javier was clearly unhappy in Morelos and struggling in school. He struck us as particularly bright—he was particularly inquisitive about the nature of our study and asked for ideas regarding which of Mexico's various *secundaria* formats might work best for him—but his academic future on his current trajectory did not seem promising. He told us he was interested in becoming an engineer, but also reported that his math grades in Mexico were weak (inhibiting the likelihood of his being able to enter that field). In turn, the talk about drugs was concerning. Whether Javier was a (prospective) dealer of drugs, consumer of drugs, or just a big talker about drugs, each of those was highly dangerous in contemporary Mexico, where more than 160,000 civilians were killed between 2007 and 2014 as part of the drug wars there (Breslow, 2015).

Because of his US birthplace (and the 14th Amendment's promise of citizenship to anyone born in the United States), Javier could aspire to a US adulthood. He had protections in the United States that his father (and perhaps his mother, too) lacked. Yet for him to convert these rights into opportunities would require either greater success in school in Mexico than he was currently experiencing (and then later transferring his Mexico-learned skills back to a US context) or the prospect of living with an economically independent older brother, whose rights to stay in the United States were not clear and whose skills as a surrogate parent were equally unclear.

Having lived in both the United States and Mexico, Javier clearly felt that he had been more successful in one (the United States) than the other, but it is unclear how much of that preference came from comparing American elementary school (where one has the same teacher all day long and there is not the peer posturing of early adolescence) to Mexican *secundaria*. Nor is it clear whether his father's deportation was the key disorienting variable. An event like that clearly is traumatic, and it is possible that, had Javier and his mother stayed in Indiana (with Javier's father in Mexico)—the path untaken and untested—Javier's academic trajectory would have suffered there, too. Although writing about the disorientation of parent unemployment rather than deportation, Tapia (1998) did find that the trauma of parent unemployment had a negative effect on Latino children's academic achievement. It stands to reason that a deportation-related household breakup would be even more consequential. At the time we met him, Javier's parents' decisions as to whether he should stay in Mexico or return to the United States were intertwined with issues of where he would be safest, where he would be academically most successful, and how adequate the infrastructure was to surround him with love and nurturance in either country.

A VEXING QUESTION

Also in Morelos, but as part of a much more pleasant 2013 visit, we met John and Daisy, plus their mother, at a rural *primaria* relatively near Cuernavaca. Like Noelia, Manuel, and Javier, John and Daisy had also been born in the United States near Chicago and so, like them, had US citizenship rights by birthplace. However, unlike these first three, John and Daisy were back in Mexico (as third and fourth graders respectively) because their mother felt it was important for them to know Mexico and learn Spanish. They intended to return to the United States at the end of the year to reconnect with their father (who continued to work there) and re-enroll at the elementary school they had attended prior to coming to Mexico. The year we met them their father was parenting them from afar, but they were living with their mother who was clearly involved in their schooling (as her presence at the school when we came for interviews illuminated—our inclusion of her in the interview was serendipitous, not planned).

Both John and Daisy told us that they liked school in the United States better. Fondly remembering Ms. Potter, his second-grade teacher, John told us that he liked "*los dulces cuando se portaban bien* [the candy rewards for good behavior]." He also liked the "*ojas de dibujar* [the sheets to draw on]." Daisy also referred to behaviorist conditioning with rewards for good behavior—"*premios para buen compartamiento*"—and then code-switched to English, describing her former third-grade teacher, Ms. Martinez, as "funny." When asked, both John and Daisy said they had never been given candy or other little prizes for good behavior or good grades in Mexico. It seemed like none of their Mexican classmates received awards like that either; that was not the way of Mexican schooling.

John and Daisy were clearly happy, loved, and academically successful kids, so their mother's question at the end caught us off guard. She asked whether we felt the US or the Mexican education system was better. She reasoned that we knew a lot about schooling in both countries, and, in essence, she wanted to know where she should parent. While clearly US schools were generally better resourced, we did not offer a specific answer, pointing out that the question was contingent. Where were John and Daisy going to live as adults (they had citizenship rights in both countries)? Where did economic responsibilities and opportunities aid or impede how much she or her husband could engage in direct parenting? What orientations, language skills, and affinities did she hope John and Daisy would develop? In the near term, she faced the question of raising John and Daisy near their father (in the United States) or their grandparents (in Mexico), or in some hybrid of the two. Which mattered most?

CHOOSING TO PARENT FROM AFAR

The parents we occasionally met, or more often heard of from the students and teachers we interviewed, faced complicated and vexing issues as they considered where to parent as they and their families negotiated the changing dynamics of US–Mexico relations, politics, and economic conditions. Among the core considerations was whether to parent sharing a household with their children or whether to parent from afar, whether that meant continuing to live and work in the United States while children came of age in Mexico, or, vice versa, whether to stay in Mexico as children connected with older siblings or extended family members to live in the United States. Although little illuminated here (because our dataset did not shed much light on it), clearly the decision to parent from afar was intertwined with calculations about how loving and supportive the "near" adults in their children's lives would or could be. Noelia and Manuel's parents would not have sent them to "safer" Mexico if they did not have a sense that grandparent caretakers could offer security and support.

Attending to safety was clearly a priority, but what constituted safety was not singularly definable. Noelia and Manuel's parents wanted them safe from the trauma and vulnerability that would arise if they (the parents) were detained in an ICE action. By that calculation, rural Puebla, at least in 2010, was safer. Yet, in Morelos, in 2013, at a *secundaria*, Javier was possibly in more jeopardy than had he stayed in the United States, even as his father was safer in Mexico. That may not have been a concern of John and Daisy's parents, who gave no indication that (absence of) legal status was a factor in their decision-making about where they or their children should be. John and Daisy's safety was more psychological, safeguarding their right to a sense of where they were *of* or *from*, although the goal was possibly not being as realized as intended, given both children's articulation that they preferred the United States.

Yet, as with Maslow's hierarchy of needs, children's safety was only one of the factors considered in the "where to parent (from)" decision. Describing John and Daisy's mother's (and likely their father's) goal for them to know Mexico and to be familiar with that identity component of who they were was perhaps primarily not an issue of safety. In their calculation, perhaps this was citizenship work larger than either country's school system could support unilaterally. In this sense, it was OK for John and Daisy to spend a year (at least) apart from their father living in Mexico to attend to this goal. Maybe knowing Mexico was also a factor for Noelia and Manuel's parents and Javier's mother, although not likely the dominant one.

Javier's case reminds us that the decision to parent from afar (or not) is not just made once and then put to rest. His mother had decided that his parenting (and/or her marriage) would be hampered by living apart from his deported father, but that calculation, made when Javier was 9, was not necessarily unalterable. As challenges, dangers, and frustrations loomed in Javier's Mexican school experience (and perhaps in other domains of his life in Mexico), the calculation about whether he should remain there (and whether it still made sense *not* to parent him from afar) was perhaps shifting.

Ultimately, parenting from afar is one of the contingencies available in the childrearing of the early 21st century. As other chapters in this volume indicate, it is likely more frequent in circumstances of international migration and extended family displacement in two or more countries, but a key assertion here is that it would be simplistic to assert that it is intrinsically good or bad or circumstantially avoidable. Defensible parenting strategies can include parenting from afar, although even then that strategy is not without consequences, linguistic, cultural, legal, and, most importantly and obviously, familial.

NOTE

1. In 2012, Mexico decided to expand the number of years of obligatory education. So, by 2022, *preparatoria* (grades 10–12) will also be included in *educación básica*,

but those more advanced grades were not required in the year of our estimate, and our sample did not include any students more advanced than ninth grade.

REFERENCES

Breslow, J. (2015). The staggering death toll of Mexico's drug war. *Frontline*. Retrieved from http://www.pbs.org/wgbh/frontline/article/the-staggering-death-toll-of-mexicos-drug-war/

Cohen, D. (2011). *Braceros: Migrant citizens and transnational subjects in the postwar United States and Mexico.* Chapel Hill, NC: University of North Carolina Press.

Dreby, J. (2010). *Divided by borders. Mexican migrants and their children.* Berkeley, CA: University of California Press.

Gonzalez-Barrera, A. (2015). More Mexicans leaving than coming to the US *Pew Research Center Hispanic Trends.* Retrieved from http://www.pewhispanic.org/2015/11/19/more-mexicans-leaving-than-coming-to-the-u-s/

Hamann, E. T., (2001). Theorizing the sojourner student (with a sketch of appropriate school responsiveness). In M. Hopkins & N. Wellmeier (Eds.), *Negotiating transnationalism: Selected papers on refugees and immigrants* (Vol. 1, pp. 32–71). Arlington, VA: American Anthropology Association.

Hamann, E. T., & Reeves, J. (2012). ICE raids, children, media and making sense of Latino newcomers in flyover country. *Anthropology & Education Quarterly, 43*(1), 24–40

Hamann, E. T. & Zúñiga, V. (2011). Schooling and the everyday ruptures transnational children encounter in the United States and Mexico. In C. Coe, R. Reynolds, D. Boehm, J.M. Hess, & H. Rae-Espinoza (Eds.), *Everyday ruptures: Children and migration in global perspective* (pp. 141–160). Nashville, TN: Vanderbilt University Press.

Hamann, E. T., Zúñiga, V., & Sánchez García, J. (2006). Pensando en Cynthia y su hermana: Educational implications of US/Mexico transnationalism for children. *Journal of Latinos and Education, 5*(4), 253–274.

Hamann, E. T., Zúñiga, V., & Sánchez García, J. (2017). Identifying the anthropological in a mixed methods study of transnational student in Mexican schools. *Current Anthropology, 58*(1).

Heyman, J., & Campbell, H. (2012). The militarization of the United States-Mexico border region, *Revista de Estudos Universitários, 38*(1), 75–94.

Reese, L. (2002). Parental strategies in contrasting cultural settings: Families in México and "El Norte." *Anthropology & Education Quartlerly, 33*(1), 30–59.

Sánchez García, J., Hamann, E.T., & Zúñiga, V. (2012). What the youngest transnational students have to say about their transition from US schools to Mexican ones. *Diaspora, Indigenous, and Minority Education, 6*(3), 157–171.

Sánchez García, J., & Hamann, E. T. (2016). Educator responses to migrant children in Mexican Schools. *Mexican Studies/Estudios Mexicanos, 32*(2), 199–225.

Suárez-Orozco, C., & Suárez-Orozco, M., (2002). *Children of immigration.* Cambridge, MA: Harvard University Press.

Tapia, J. (1998). The schooling of Puerto Ricans: Philadelphia's most impoverished community. *Anthropology and Education Quarterly, 29*(3), 297–323.

United Nations (2016). *International migration report, 2015.* New York: United Nations, Department of Economic and Social Affairs.

Zong, J., & Batalova, J., (2014). *Mexican immigrants in the United States*. Washington, DC: Migration Policy Institute. Retrieved from http://www.migrationpolicy.org/article/mexican-immigrants-united-states-4

Zúñiga, V. & Hamann, E.T. (2014). Going to a home you have never been to: The return migration of Mexican and American-Mexican children. *Children's geographies, 13*(6) 1–13.

Zúñiga, V. & Hamann, E.T. (2009). Sojourners in Mexico with US school experience: A new taxonomy for transnational students. *Comparative Education Review, 53*(3), 329–353.

Zúñiga, V., Hamann, E. T., & Sánchez García, J. (2008). *Alumnos transnacionales: Las escuelas mexicanas frente a la globalización*. Mexico, DF: Secretaria de Educación Pública.

INDEX

Note: Page numbers followed by *f* refer to figures.